The New York Times

Season-by-Season Guide to Home Maintenance

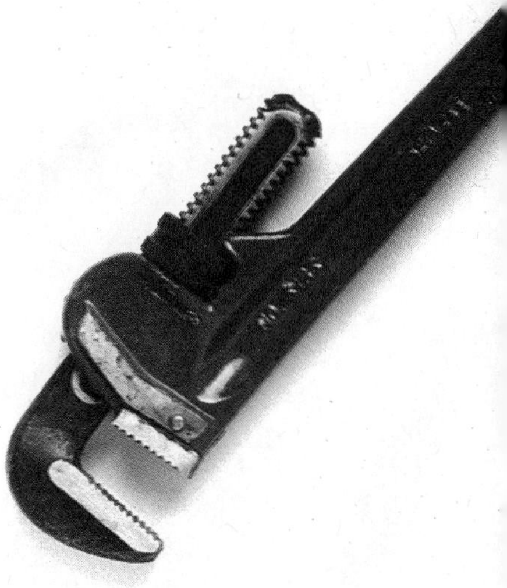

The New York Times

Season-by-Season Guide to Home Maintenance

JOHN WARDE

Illustrations by Ed Lipinski

TIMES BOOKS

RANDOM HOUSE

 Published in the United States by Times Books, a division of Random House, Inc., New York, and simultaneously in Canada by Random House of Canada Limited, Toronto.

Portions of this work were originally published in *The New York Times.*

Library of Congress Cataloging-in-Publication Data
Warde, John.
The New York Times season-by-season guide to home maintenance/ by John Warde.
p. cm.
Consists of Warde's columns for the New York Times.
Includes index.
ISBN 0-8129-1882-7
1. Dwellings—Maintenance and repair. I. Title.
TH4817.W353 1991
643′.7—dc20 90-46388

ART DIRECTION: NAOMI OSNOS
BOOK DESIGN: WARREN INFIELD
PHOTOGRAPHS: GRAHAM HABER
ILLUSTRATIONS: ED LIPINSKI

Manufactured in the United States of America
9 8 7 6 5 4 3 2
First Edition

Acknowledgments

No book of this sort is possible without the help of many people. Accordingly, much thanks is hereby given to the myriad technical consultants, industries' and manufacturers' representatives, trade association spokespersons, government information officers, service personnel, tradespeople, and other home improvement professionals to whom I turned in the course of writing the weekly newspaper columns that are its basis. These people provided me with invaluable information, instruction, and advice. I also thank the staff of *The New York Times*—particularly Jane Traulsen, former editor of the Home section; its current editor Stephen Drucker; and the able, indefatigable copy editors of the Style desk—for receiving my work so graciously and for helping me, often with painstaking effort, to achieve the *Times*'s high standards of quality, clarity, accuracy, and completeness.

To Ed Lipinski, friend and colleague for nearly a decade and a half, I owe special gratitude: for introducing me to Bernard Gladstone, originator of the *Times*'s home improvement columns; for creating the hundreds of clear, capable illustrations that have enhanced the columns over the years; and for supplying the illustrations that appear in this book, all of which have been redrawn from the originals published with the columns and in many cases thoughtfully revised. I am also indebted to my agent, Bob Tabian, and editor, Ruth Fecych, for helping transform this book from a concept into a reality. Above all, I indebted to my wife, Kathy, whose support and patience have been and continue to be my constant source of inspiration.

Contents

The New York Times

Season-by-Season Guide to Home Maintenance

PART 1:

A Home Maintenance Almanac

For most homeowners, household maintenance and improvement are perpetual activities, as there always seems to be something that needs doing.

Fortunately, for all things there also seems to be a season. On the following pages is an almanac of common home maintenance projects that can help you to organize a year-round repair and improvement schedule. Of course, you needn't feel that you've got your marching orders: The monthly entries can also serve as a guide for putting off at least until tomorrow tasks you otherwise might feel tempted to perform today!

January, and all midwinter months, is best for performing indoor tasks. Work off holiday overindulgence and get into the spirit of the new year by doing heavy indoor cleaning chores—walls, carpeting, kitchen appliances—and patching plaster and wallboard. Because humidity levels are usually lower than during other seasons, wooden items inside homes have shrunk their maximum amount and any cracks or gaps in them are at their widest. Consequently, this is a good time for repairing squeaky floors and stairs, and for planing wooden doors that rub against their frames.

February is short, so consider it a month for puttering. Straighten the workshop, sharpen tools and kitchenware, repair furniture (avoid refinishing projects unless adequate ventilation can be provided), lubricate hinges and the moving parts of cabinets and appliances.

Also inspect home security and fire-safety systems (smoke detectors). If you use a woodstove or fireplace regularly, make a midseason check of the stovepipe or chimney to reduce chances of a fire caused by accumulated soot. If midwinter blues set in, now is a good time to brighten your home and your mood by applying new wallpaper or floor coverings.

March rains and thawing snow, ice, and frozen ground keep many homeowners busy with basement leaks this month and next. Outdoor activity is still several weeks away, so why not take this opportunity for performing indoor plumbing and electrical repairs.

Of course, March is also a good time for starting major indoor remodeling tasks. With spring about to arrive, you won't feel trapped in a house full of rubble, and windows can be opened occasionally for ventilation.

April is the month to tour your home's exterior. Make spot repairs to the roof and siding, if necessary, and clean the chimney or stovepipe (or have the job done by a professional) after the last fire of the season. If you wait until fall, soot deposits will harden, making removal more difficult and increasing the risk of fire.

Prepare window and door screens; if spring comes early you can install them. On a warm, sunny day, wash venetian blinds and shades outdoors.

May marks the unofficial beginning of the outdoor maintenance season. As early as possible, check and repair roof gutters and downspouts, and begin planning major projects such as painting, re-siding, roof work, masonry repairs, and additional construction. While you are at it, prepare outdoor furniture for use.

June is the time for starting serious outdoor home repair and remodeling projects (the ones you planned in May). If several projects must be coordinated, begin with those that could cause trouble if not finished by fall. Days are long this month and next, so much work can be done.

July should see the continuation of major outdoor maintenance. With the weather fine and dog days still a month away, heed the farmers' adage and "make hay while the sun shines."

Now is also a good time to perform window repairs, and to take on indoor home improvements that require thorough ventilation, such as painting and floor refinishing.

August is vacation time for many people. Finish those large-scale summer projects, resurface the driveway (best done during prolonged hot weather), then take a well-deserved break.

Before you relax completely, make plans to have the heating system checked. Seeing to this necessary chore now will put you ahead of the rush, and your home will be prepared in case of an early cold snap.

September often brings cool nights and sometimes even frost. However, the warm days and lingering evenings provide ample time for installing insulation, weatherstripping, and caulking compound to seal out the coming winter weather.

September is particularly appropriate for winterizing: moderating temperatures make working in attics bearable; opening doors and windows to attach weatherstripping causes no discomfort; and caulking compound, which stiffens and bonds poorly in cold weather, is easy to apply.

October days are shorter. Daylight saving time ends. This month store summer items, including the air conditioner. Clean and sharpen garden tools before putting them away; also apply rustproofing paint to metal items that will remain outdoors. Clean the garage and lubricate and adjust the door.

Before lighting the first indoor fire in the fireplace or woodstove, check the chimney or stovepipe for debris deposited by storms or pests.

November ushers in the holidays and winter. Clean the gutters after the leaves have fallen. To prevent any outdoor pipes from freezing, shut off indoor valves supplying them with water.

If your home is equipped with steam or hot-water radiators, these may need bleeding (releasing trapped air) when they're first turned on.

December is usually filled with so much social activity that there is little time for home repair. Satisfy an urge to tinker by touching up damaged household surfaces before the holidays commence. Wax the floors and polish furniture and metal.

But take it easy: January is just around the corner!

PART 2:

Necessary Tools and Skills

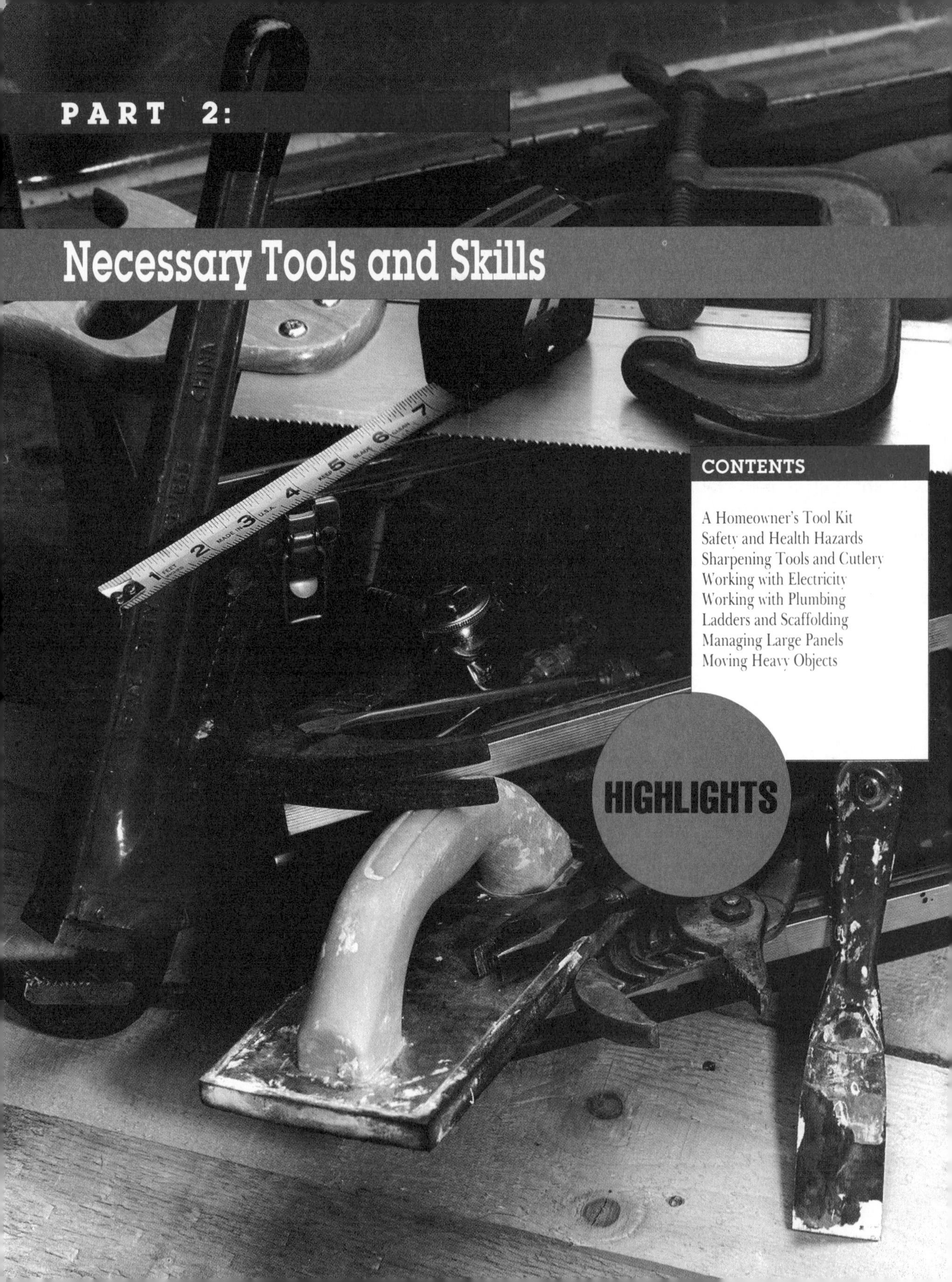

CONTENTS

HIGHLIGHTS

A Homeowner's Tool Kit

Anyone, amateur or professional, who is familiar with home repairs doubtless would agree that happiness is having the right tool for the job. But although this might imply the need for many tools, the truth is that most home maintenance can be accomplished with only a relatively small assortment, easily obtained and for the most part inexpensive.

Aside from putting together a basic set of tools to have on hand, an overall strategy for acquiring tools is not to buy any until you need them and are sure your present tools cannot act as substitutes. When you do decide to buy, choose only from among tools made by established manufacturers; others may function poorly, wear out quickly, and carry no warranty against defects or breakage.

Also, check prices at different types of stores before purchasing. Prices for the same tool can vary widely among sources such as hardware stores, building supply stores catering to professionals, and mail-order retailers.

A Basic Tool Kit

An essential set of tools for home repair should include a 10- or 12-foot flexible steel tape measure. The ¾-inch-wide size is standard, but the 1-inch-wide variety can be extended farther without bending. For a bonus, select one with useful carpentry information—nail and screw sizes, for example—printed on the back.

You will also need a claw hammer. Choose one with a 13-ounce head if you are unpracticed or will need it primarily for light work, such as driving nails for picture hanging. Otherwise, select the 16-ounce size.

Purchase at least two medium-size screwdrivers—one with a flat-sided blade, the other with a Phillips blade for screws with cross-slotted heads. One Phillips model is usually sufficient, but you will find it helpful to purchase two more flat-bladed screwdrivers: small and large. Often, you can find all three as a set.

An adjustable wrench, rather than pliers, is preferred for holding and turning nuts and bolts. It is a crucial tool to own. The 6-inch-long size fits into tight spaces yet affords enough leverage for general use. If you supplement it with a 10-inch model, you will be equipped for heavy tasks and will be able to hold a recalcitrant bolt with one wrench and turn the nut with the other.

As for pliers, you probably won't need the familiar slip-joint variety nearly so much as the long-nose type, which are enormously useful for forming wire loops and gripping tiny objects. Buy a 6-inch-long pair with straight jaws and a sharp slot for trimming wire. Be sure the ends of the jaws fit together precisely.

Channel-type pliers, also called water pump pliers, are useful. The large size, which is recommended, is rather expensive, but these pliers ease plumbing chores considerably and make short work of tight lids.

Select a moderately priced, ⅜-inch variable-speed electric drill. As a rule, drills requiring cords are more powerful than cordless models; however, for general home repairs and especially for spur-of-the-moment jobs like hanging pictures, a cordless drill with a motor that requires at least 7.2 volts is a better choice because of its versatility.

Equip the drill with a packaged assortment of general-purpose high-speed bits and a screwdriver bit. For drilling screw holes in furniture, purchase individual profile bits the same size as the screws you are using. For holes larger than ⅜ inch in diameter, purchase individual spade bits. With the right attachments, you can also use an electric drill to sand, strip paint, polish metal, and even buff furniture and shoes. If you plan to install wallboard with screws, obtain a clutch attachment that automatically stops power to the bit when the screw reaches the correct depth.

Complete your collection of essentials with a plumber's plunger. Although some people might not consider this a tool, it is probably the one item you will need the most for plumbing maintenance. Certainly it's the one to have in case of emergency.

TIP:

Handsaws for wood will stay sharp longer if stored in the cardboard sleeves they come in or in saw cases available from tool supply stores. To store a hacksaw, remove the blade from the frame after each use, turn it upside down, and refasten it so that the teeth face upward. The saw can then survive unprotected in a toolbox.

ATTENTION

Purchase the funnel-cup type, which is designed for toilets. For sinks, the cup folds inward.

Supplementary Tools

• Acquire a handsaw for general-purpose work. Most carpenters use a medium-priced, eight-point (the number of teeth per inch) crosscut saw with a 26-inch-long blade. For easier handling purchase a 22-inch saw instead, and for a smoother finished edge select a ten-point blade.

• For cutting curves, get either a coping saw, which is a hand tool, or a variable-speed electric saber saw. Both can be fitted with blades for sawing wood, metal, and plastic.

• A back saw and a saw guide called a miter box are useful for cutting molding. A back saw has a rectangular blade stiffened by a metal bar across the top. The smoothest cuts are made by blades with at least fifteen teeth per inch. Choose an adjustable miter box made of metal or hard plastic.

• For cutting pipes and solid metal, get a hacksaw. To cut sheet metal, purchase a pair of straight-cutting aviation shears. Those with offset handles are more comfortable to use than shears whose blades and handles form a straight line. Aviation shears are also useful for cutting screen, chicken wire, vinyl, and carpeting.

• To measure and mark guidelines for sawing, purchase a combination square. You can also use this tool for general layout work and for checking right- and 45-degree angles. Get the 12-inch size, equipped with a level and small scriber in the handle. Buy a larger level—at least 24 inches long—for installing shelves and cabinets and to double as a straightedge. Another useful item for installing shelves and cabinets is an electronic stud sensor. This device finds studs and other structural members in walls and ceilings, eliminating the need for drilling test holes.

• Moderately priced wood chisels with impact-resistant handles are helpful in door, stair, and floor repairs and miscellaneous paring jobs. Three useful sizes—½-, ¾-, and 1-inch wide—are commonly available as a set.

• For more extensive paring jobs, invest in a good-quality block plane (buy a "low-angle" model), and if you have the money, add a 9-inch or longer bench plane. Buy a double-sided sharpening stone to maintain all edge tools.

• To smooth and shape wood, buy an 8-inch long shoe rasp (also called a four-in-hand rasp), which is a combination rasp and file with flat and half-round sides.

TIP:

Allowing chisels to bump other tools is the quickest way to dull them. Besides storing them in compartments or tool rolls as described on pages 10–12, inexpensive plastic chisel guards can be purchased. These are simply protective caps that fit over the sharpened ends of the blades.

ATTENTION

TIP:

When using a pipe wrench, be sure the pressure produced by turning the wrench is directed toward the fixed jaw, not the adjustable one. The wrench will grip the nut better and the adjustable jaw—which is vulnerable to breakage—will encounter less strain.

ATTENTION

• For smoothing metal and sharpening light tools like paint scrapers, purchase an 8-inch mill bastard file with a handle. A file brush will keep both tools clean for effective cutting.

• You can never own too many clamps to assist you during shaping or fastening. Start with a pair of C-clamps with a 4-inch jaw capacity, and expect to add to your collection as necessary.

• For widening cracks in masonry or plaster to repair them, and for cutting thick metal items like nails or bolts that cannot be reached with a hacksaw, obtain one or two steel cold chisels (½-inch wide or ¾-inch wide). For striking them, you will need a 16- to 24-ounce ball peen hammer. (Using a claw hammer to strike hardened steel is dangerous because the head may shatter.)

• A flexible putty knife 1¼ inches wide and a wall scraper (stiff-bladed putty knife) 3 inches wide are essential for filling cracks in wood and wallboard, and for removing old paint. Compile a specialized tool kit for these and related patching purposes by adding a retractable-blade utility knife equipped with replaceable razor blades, a wire brush, assorted sheets of sandpaper, and several grades of steel wool. Purchase either a wallboard saw or a coarse-toothed keyhole saw for cutting openings in wallboard.

• For prying away molding, removing nails, and for heavy work like taking down walls, buy a flat pry bar at least 12 inches long. For sinking nails below the surface of molding or wood floors, buy a nail set; it can be struck with a claw hammer.

• For electrical work, supplement your screwdrivers and long-nose pliers with a pair of 7-inch-long lineman's pliers, a set of nut drivers for reaching small nuts in cramped areas, a combination wire stripper and cutting tool, and a flashlight. For testing whether household wiring is safe to work on, an inexpensive circuit tester (a small bulb with two wires attached) is invaluable.

• For plumbing, acquire a 10-inch pipe wrench and a pair of locking pliers with semicircular jaws for holding 1¾-inch pipes. A basin wrench for gripping nuts and bolts in hard-to-reach places like the area beneath a sink is also useful.

• Finally, be sure to have polycarbonate safety goggles that meet the standards of the American National Standards Institute (ANSI); a box of disposable dust masks approved by the National Institute for Occupational Safety and Health (NIOSH) to protect against damaging dusts and mists, including home insulation and asbestos; and a replaceable-filter mask, also approved by NIOSH, to protect against paint vapors and other fumes.

Basic Power Tools

Portable power tools have become as much a part of homeowners' tool kits as hammers and nails. Most modern power tools are surprisingly light and easy to handle, thanks to new technologies and to tool manufacturers' strong interest in satisfying the needs of amateurs. Electric drills are by far the most popular portable power tools manufactured; they are described earlier as part of a basic tool kit. Running a close second however are portable power saws.

For making straight-line cuts, particularly in lumber and plywood, choose a circular saw, which has a disk-shaped blade rimmed with teeth that cut as the blade revolves at high speed. Circular saws come in many sizes and price ranges, but bigger is not always better, especially if you are not likely to use the saw often enough to acquire the skill and strength of a professional.

Although the most common size for circular saws accommodates a blade 7¼ inches in diameter, most homeowners would do well to consider a recently introduced model designed for 6-inch-diameter blades instead. It is lighter and easier to handle, but no less powerful or versatile for an amateur than larger sizes.

For cutting curves, you need a saber saw, often called a portable jigsaw. It has a thin, straight blade that cuts by moving up and down like a handsaw. Saber saws are very versatile, and are easier to use and quieter than circular saws. But because they will not cut through thick materials like two-by-four lumber, saber saws cannot substitute for circular saws.

A saber saw's chief use is to cut sheet materials of all kinds, especially plywood and paneling. With special blades a saber saw can cut sheet metal, pipes, carpeting, resilient flooring, cardboard, Styrofoam, and leather. It can also make extremely intricate scroll cuts in wood.

Buy the most powerful saber saw you can afford, and look for one that blows sawdust away from the blade during operation to prevent the path of the cut from becoming obscured.

An electric sander is worth acquiring if you refinish furniture or other woodwork, or assemble furniture from kits. The principle advantage of a sander is that it saves enormous amounts of time and physical energy.

There are two types: pad sanders, which accept flat sheets of sandpaper, and belt sanders, which accept a continuous loop of sandpaper made for the purpose.

For furniture finishing buy a pad sander, preferably one with both orbital (circular) and straight-line (back-and-forth) motion. A tool with both motions will produce results almost as good as hand sanding.

Palm-size pad sanders are highly maneuverable but useful only for finishing tasks like sanding between coats of paint or varnish. A larger pad sander, with handles for two-hand opera-

TIP:

A newly introduced third type of sander is a random-orbit type, which accepts sandpaper disks. Random-orbit sanders are as effective as belt sanders for all but the heaviest jobs, yet are as easy to use and unlikely to leave marks as pad sanders do.

ATTENTION

TIP:

To help keep extension cords from becoming tangled, wind them in opposite directions—clockwise one day, counterclockwise the next—each time they are coiled for storage.

ATTENTION

tion, can quickly sand broad areas like tabletops and shelf boards, and can also do light refinishing projects.

But for sanding old finishes down to bare wood, or for smoothing worn, warped, or rough-hewn wood, choose a belt sander. This is much faster and more powerful than the pad type, and it takes some practice to learn to use skillfully. But belt sanders make short work of many time-consuming, muscle-tiring chores, from smoothing irregularities in floors to shaping wooden furniture parts. A good belt sander is expensive. Look for the one with the most powerful motor among models in the same price range. Other desirable features are an easy mechanism for changing belts and a vacuum attachment to trap dust during operation.

Something to remember: Since the cords attached to the tools are frequently quite short, most power tools require extension cords. Buying the proper extension cord is important. Be sure the extension cord suits the amperage of the tool or tools you will be using, and that its receptacle end matches the plug on the tool. Never use an ordinary light-duty household extension cord, even if the tool has only a two-prong plug.

Keeping Tools Handy

Storing tools where they are both handy and safe is important. Misplaced or inaccessibly stored tools can complicate even simple household repair chores, and tools that are stored haphazardly can injure someone sorting through them or damage the tools themselves.

Whether you own many tools or few, keep them in one place if possible. Searching for them can add time and frustration to tasks that might ordinarily require only a few minutes' work. Disorganization also leads to using tools that are at hand rather than tools that are appropriate.

For accessibility, and to prevent tools from damaging each other, storage compartments are best. In a workshop or utility room where security needs are minimal, compartmentalized storage can be achieved with wall racks, which also permit tools to be seen and selected easily.

Least expensive and often most practical are homemade racks made of perforated hardboard, available at lumberyards, home centers, and hardware and department stores. The perforations allow you to attach special hardware designed for this type of paneling: hooks, spring clips and small shelves, and small bins and cabinets.

Perforated hardboard is easy to install. The usual procedure is to use screws inserted through perforations at the corners and along the sides at intervals of about a foot. Install a flat metal washer on each fastener on the outside of the panel to distribute the pressure of the screw heads.

Install one or two thick rubber or synthetic spacing washers, often included in hardware kits for perforated hardboard, on the shaft of each fastener between the panel and the wall. The spacing washers hold the panel about a quarter of an inch away from the wall, creating the space necessary for attaching the hardware.

Also available for storing tools are wood, metal, and plastic racks with magnetic strips or conventional hooks and clips. These fasten with screws directly to any flat surface. A rack with clips that hold tools tightly can be mounted on the back of a closet or cabinet door.

Where there are children or when security is a concern, install wall-mounted cabinets with locks instead of open racks. Cabinet doors, which can be fitted with tool racks, should swing open—not slide back and forth—to expose all the tools inside. Cabinets may be fitted with shelves or made with perforated hardboard backs.

If wall space is unavailable or if portability is essential, store tools in compartmentalized boxes made for the purpose. Almost all of them keep tools more accessible and in better condition than unpartitioned toolboxes.

For general use, consider a tool caddy or carryall. Usually made of high-impact plastic, they combine trays and slots for tools and other essentials, like an oilcan or tape measure, with sliding drawers for fasteners and other small items. Some tool caddies double as footstools.

Compartmentalized cloth bags with handles or drawstrings are also good for tools. Marine supply stores are a good source for them, since some styles are designed to hold sailors' tools.

Chisels, screwdrivers, wrenches, and other long, narrow tools can be kept in canvas tool rolls, available from hardware and automotive stores and from woodworking supply stores. A tool roll is a large piece of cloth stitched to create rows of slim pockets into which individual tools slide. The entire arrangement folds into a cylindrical package that is tied with string.

A variation is a roll-up storage system made of plastic containers instead of pockets, bound side by side with nylon straps. This is a relatively new product, available in some hardware stores.

Professional carpenters have long favored a simple, homemade, compartmentalized tray made of lumber ¾ inch thick. Its wooden construction protects tools with sharp edges.

Typical trays are rectangular and measure about 30 inches

long—the length of most handsaws—and 12 inches wide. The sides rise 6 or 8 inches, and the ends normally rise 12 inches. A hole near the top of each end accommodates a broomstick or dowel spanning the length of the tray to form a handle.

Of course, conventional metal tool chests are still worthwhile for storing tools that are infrequently used and that will not suffer if thrown together. Even so, it is best to separate the contents. Choose a model with a tray for small tools, and keep groups of similar tools together in tool rolls or other containers.

Metal tool chests with locks are secure and sturdy. To further deter tampering or theft, you can fasten the chest with a chain through the handle and around the chest to a post in the garage or to the interior of an automobile trunk.

Safety and Health Hazards

No home repair is worth personal injury or exposure to substances that may threaten health. Safety—yours and that of others working with you or living in the house—must always be your first thought when using tools or performing any home repair activity.

Throughout this book, safe practices and potential hazards are described within the context of situations where they are most relevant. For example, specific advice about working safely with electricity is found in chapters covering electrical skills and repairs. This chapter covers general safety considerations: proper dress and work habits, the safe handling of tools and building materials, and coping with potentially dangerous substances like dust and chemicals.

Preventing accidents is largely a matter of using common sense. The best overall strategy is to limit risks.

Dress and Work Habits

Wear safety glasses or goggles whenever your work may endanger your eyes; wear hearing protectors (the kind that muffle sound but do not block it completely) whenever noise levels are high. Also wear an appropriately rated dust mask or respirator whenever airborne particles or chemical fumes may be present. Keep extras of these items on hand for onlookers and assistants (although for safety, visitors while you are working should be kept to a minimum).

Clothing should suit prevailing circumstances but should always be close-fitting so that it cannot catch on protruding items or on moving equipment. Wear sturdy shoes with thick, nonslip soles for protection and sure footing. If you have long hair, tie it back and wear a hat. Remove neckties and jewelry, especially rings, necklaces, and bracelets. When operating power tools, remove even your wristwatch.

Never carry sharp tools in your pocket unless they have protective covers. Instead, carry tools like chisels, knives, and screwdrivers in a toolbox or tray. Also, never carry anything in your mouth; wear a nailer's apron (available at most hardware and building supply stores) or a tool belt with pockets for carrying fasteners, pencils, and other small items.

Heavy work gloves and chemical-resistant rubber gloves offer protection from injury, irritation, and chemical burns. But gloves should not be worn when using power tools or when performing delicate work like electrical wiring.

Above all, be alert when you are working. Make sure there is plenty of light and ventilation. Avoid distractions, and postpone activities if you are not feeling well or are unable to concentrate. Keep a first-aid kit and eye-washing solution handy, and also the telephone numbers of the fire department and poison-control center. Always work where your shouts would bring immediate assistance.

Using Tools Safely

With hand tools, probably the most important safety rule is to always keep your body—especially your hands—behind the tools' cutting edges. If other people are nearby or holding pieces you are working on, see that they are out of harm's way, too.

Like all equipment, hand tools should be kept in good condition: Cutting tools should be sharp so they cannot slip; hammers should have handles that are firmly attached and not cracked.

Safety with power tools requires knowledge of their operation and also some practice, because most power tools operate at high speeds and can cause serious injury instantly.

When buying power tools, look for those with as many built-in safety features as possible. One of the most important is double electrical insulation, which will protect you from electrical shock even if the household wiring is faulty. To determine whether a power tool is double-insulated, look for an identifying label and a two-prong plug. (A three-prong plug provides safe grounding only if the household wiring is sound.)

Double insulation may not fully protect against electrical shock due to moisture. For this, the electrical outlet into which the tool is plugged must be protected by a device called a ground-fault circuit interrupter, or GFCI for short. A plug-in GFCI that requires no electrical skill to install is available at some hardware and electrical supply stores. But even with both types of protection, it is not safe to use power tools under damp conditions or to allow their cords to rest on damp surfaces.

Before using a new power tool or one with which you are unfamiliar, study the literature that came with it, or a book or magazine article about it. If possible, watch someone who is experienced use the tool. Then practice with the tool on scrap material before using it on an actual project.

When using a power tool, make sure your footing is secure, that the path for the tool is clear, and that the cord will not get stuck or be in the way. Use clamps to hold work pieces wherever possible, and always keep your eyes focused on the part of the tool entering the material.

Never set a power tool down until it stops moving completely, and develop the habit of unplugging tools each time you set them down. Never make adjustments involving the moving parts of any power tool until the tool is unplugged.

Handling Materials

Long or heavy items are most safely carried by two people. Use safe lifting techniques to prevent injuries (lift by bending your knees, not your back) and be careful of your footing when carrying materials across frozen, wet, or slippery surfaces.

Stack materials neatly and keep work areas clean. Not only will this help eliminate bumping into items accidentally, it will help keep building materials from getting dirty, damaged, or lost. Nails protruding from lumber should be removed or hammered flat the moment they are spotted.

Harmful Substances

Increasingly, substances in building materials are being found potentially hazardous to health and safety. Knowledge is your best ally when working with dangerous materials or under possibly harmful conditions.

Before using chemicals like finishes, solvents, and cleaners, read and understand the manufacturer's instructions printed on the label—and always follow them completely. Keep informed of new findings about substances that require special handling, like paint that may contain lead or mercury, and building materials that may contain asbestos or chemicals that release fumes.

Sources of specific information about these items are governmental agencies like state and local health departments and regional offices of the Occupational Safety and Health Administration (OSHA). These are listed in the telephone book. Home improvement articles in newspapers and magazines, and programs about home improvement on television, are other sources.

Naturally, flammable items must be handled with caution. Use them only in well-ventilated areas where there is no open flame. Dispose of oily rags, scraps of combustible materials, wood shavings, volatile chemicals, and the like by removing them promptly from the house. Flammable and poisonous chemicals should be purchased only in small quantities; if you must keep leftover amounts, store them in locked, ventilated, fireproof cabinets, preferably in a shed or other building not attached to the house.

Wear a protective mask when working in dust or fumes. Be sure the mask is approved by an authority like OSHA or the National Institute for Occupational Safety and Health (NIOSH) for protection against the substances it must withstand. Do not allow other people to enter the area unless they are similarly protected, and take precautions to prevent the spread of harmful substances to other parts of the house. In the case of dust and larger particles, vacuum the area thoroughly to clean it after repairs are finished.

> **TIP:**
>
> Among woodworking enthusiasts, Japanese water stones have become more popular than traditional oilstones. These stones are less messy to use (they are saturated with water instead of oil), sharpen tools faster, and in some cases produce a keener edge than oilstones. Drawbacks to using them are that they must be stored in water (if a stone is allowed to dry out repeatedly, salts left by evaporation eventually clog its pores, sometimes ruining it) and, because they are softer material than oilstones, skill is needed to keep them from wearing unevenly.

ATTENTION

Sharpening Tools and Cutlery

Keeping cutting tools sharp is important. Dull tools, in-cluding kitchen knives and scissors, are ineffective; they are also dangerous because they require more effort to use than sharp tools and so are more difficult to control.

The process of sharpening is really only that of grinding away metal at an angle from a thick, dull edge to make it thinner and thus sharper. But because tool designs vary, sharpening techniques differ from tool to tool. Chisels, planes, and knives are relatively easy to sharpen. Tools like saws, scissors, and drill bits are more difficult and should be sharpened professionally. Sharpening services are listed in the telephone book; many hardware stores also offer them.

Chisels and Planes

Sharpening a chisel or plane is done by removing metal from the sloping or beveled edge of the blade. This is accomplished by scraping the blade against a harder surface such as a sharpening stone.

For amateurs, the simplest sharpening stone to use and the least expensive is a man-made combination oilstone. Called a coarse/fine India stone, it is made of aluminum oxide abrasives bonded to form a rectangular block. One side of the stone consists of coarse particles that remove metal quickly. The other side consists of finer particles that hone the sharpened surface to a cutting edge.

TIP:

Instead of using a honing guide, experienced sharpeners often make a template against which to check the blade's bevel during freehand sharpening. Fold a piece of paper to form a right triangle whose longest side slopes at the same angle as specified for the bevel. Temporarily place the template on its base between the underside of the blade and the stone to find the angle at which the blade must be held. As sharpening proceeds, hold the template against the side of the blade to gauge progress.

ATTENTION

Before and during use, the stone must be saturated with lightweight cutting oil or mineral oil. The lubricant captures the metal particles that are scraped from the blade and prevents them from ruining the stone by clogging its pores.

Most hardware stores carry combination oilstones. A 2-inch-wide stone measuring 6 to 8 inches long is usually sufficient. However, if you own hand planes with blades 2 inches wide or wider, consider a more expensive 2½-inch-wide stone. The extra width makes sharpening plane blades easier. In both cases obtain as long a stone as possible. Store and use an oilstone in a sturdy, close-fitting wooden box sold for the purpose.

The most important part of sharpening, and the skill most difficult to acquire, is maintaining the angle formed between the beveled edge and the underside of the blade. This angle is crucial to the cutting ability of the blade and is easily altered by careless or unskilled sharpening strokes.

To prevent altering the angle, buy a honing guide. This is a device with a clamp that holds the blade at a constant angle to the stone. Several styles are available. All incorporate a roller that glides along the surface of the stone or along the work surface on which the stone rests. The former style is the easiest to use and the most accurate.

To sharpen a damaged or very dull blade, begin by sharpening with a coarse stone. Its purpose is not to produce a cutting edge but to scrape away enough metal to establish a fresh surface. Make sure the stone is saturated with oil beforehand. When you are ready to begin sharpening, spread a thin film of fresh oil on the surface.

Clamp the honing guide to the blade so that the beveled edge forms a 25-degree angle with the surface of the stone. The instructions that come with the guide will explain how to do this. Then place the blade and guide on the stone and sharpen the blade by moving the assembly back and forth from one end of the stone to the other.

Apply moderate pressure with your fingers on the tip of the blade or on the guide as the instructions recommend. To prevent wearing a groove into the stone, move the blade and guide in an S-shaped or figure-eight pattern along the stone. After about fifty strokes, reverse the stone end for end if it is necessary to continue sharpening.

As the oil on the stone's surface becomes blackened by particles of metal, wipe it off with a paper towel or a cloth and add fresh oil. Check the beveled surface frequently and adjust the pressure of your fingers if one area of the surface seems to be

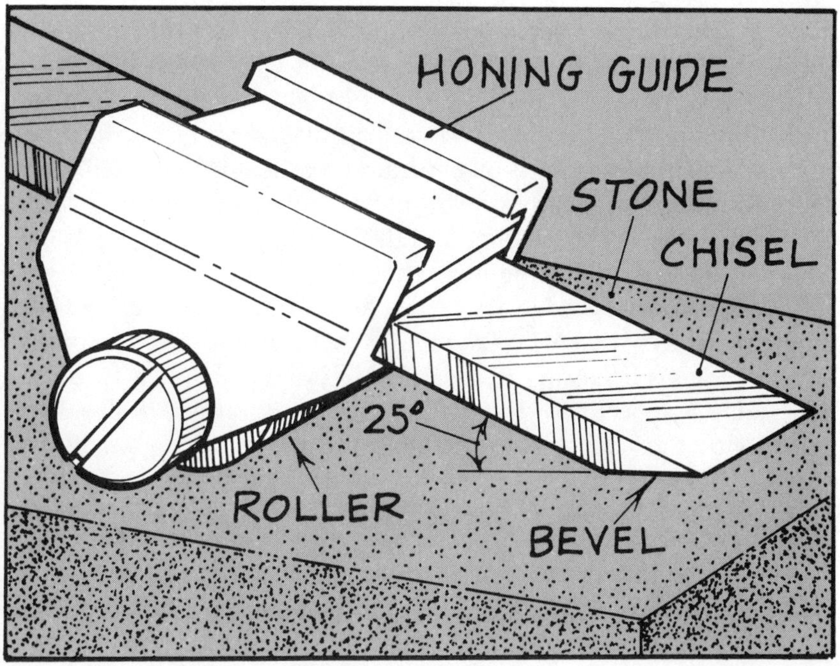

Use a honing guide to maintain the proper blade angle.

wearing more quickly than another. Use a carpenter's square to make certain that the cutting edge of the blade remains precisely at right angles to the sides.

Continue sharpening until the beveled edge is completely shiny and you can feel a lip of rough metal, called a burr, on the underside of the blade along the entire cutting edge.

Now turn the stone over and hone the blade with the smooth side. Begin by applying a film of fresh oil. Then, without removing the guide, lay the underside of the blade flat on the stone and rub it back and forth a few times to grind away the burr. Be sure to keep the blade absolutely flat on the stone at all times.

When the burr cannot be felt, turn the blade over and follow the procedure described for coarse sharpening, but use lighter finger pressure. Continue until a burr is produced.

Very light rubbing of the underside of the blade against the stone will remove the burr and yield a finished edge suitable for general work and carpentry. However for a sharper, longer-lasting edge, perform the following two procedures instead:

First, readjust the honing guide so the blade is held at a 30-degree angle to the stone. Then hone the blade on the smooth side of the stone approximately a dozen strokes. This should produce a very narrow secondary beveled edge of uniform width across the blade's cutting edge.

Second, strop the blade. Do this by alternately stroking the underside and the beveled side of the cutting edge several times against a strip of smooth, oil-saturated leather or dry cardboard. The motion is similar to one you use when house painting with a brush. The object is to stretch and thin the burr until it breaks off. This should leave a cutting edge that is razor sharp.

The secondary edge can be rehoned and stropped several times, provided you do so frequently, before rehoning the entire beveled edge is necessary. Regardless of how the blade is finished, unless damage occurs or the blade becomes extremely dull, sharpening with the coarse side of the stone will never again be required.

Knives

Sharpening a knife on an oilstone is similar in many ways to sharpening a chisel or plane except that the blade is turned over after each stroke. This produces a bevel on each side of the cutting edge.

Start by saturating the coarse side of the stone with oil and applying a thin layer to the surface when you are ready to begin. Anchor the stone firmly to a bench or tabletop.

Hold the handle of the knife in one hand and the tip of the blade with the other. Place the blade at the end of the stone nearest you and tilt the back of the blade upward so that the cutting edge meets the stone at an angle of about 20 degrees (honing guides are available for kitchen and hunting knives, but are too large for use on pocket knives). It does not matter whether the edge faces you or points away; however, detecting a burr will be easier if the cutting edge trails on each stroke, rather than leads.

Make sharpening strokes by pushing the knife away from you until it reaches the end of the stone, then flipping it over (do not reverse it end for end in your hands) and pulling it back. At the same time, slide the knife sideways from the handle to the tip so that the entire blade comes in contact with the stone during each stroke. Go slowly so that you can keep the blade at a uniform angle to the stone. If the angle varies, the blade will not get sharp.

When you can feel a burr along the length of the cutting edge, switch to the finer side of the stone and repeat the process using lighter strokes. Finish by stropping.

Working with Electricity

Most homeowners are intimidated by the thought of performing household electrical repairs, and it is important to respect the potential dangers involved. But many electrical repairs are well within the capabilities of amateurs. This chapter describes how to handle common electrical emergencies—failed circuits and sparking appliances—and the basic techniques for working with household wiring. To supplement your knowledge of these topics and to enhance your understanding of the electrical projects covered in other chapters, study specialized books on household electricity for amateurs, available in libraries and bookstores.

Before undertaking any electrical repair or improvement, consult a local building inspector to find out whether amateurs in your community are allowed to do the work and what regulations must be followed.

APARTMENT OWNERS:

For safety reasons, electrical repairs or improvements may be the responsibility of the maintenance supervisor. Before proceeding, check your ownership agreement or other rules for your building.

HINT

When a Circuit Breaker Trips or a Fuse Blows

When a circuit breaker governing a household electrical circuit trips or a fuse blows, power to the circuit is immediately shut off to reduce the chance of fire and injury from electric shock. Restoring power by resetting the breaker or replacing the fuse is usually simple. But care must be taken to proceed safely, and only after the cause of the circuit's malfunction has been corrected.

When a circuit fails, note how long the items connected to it had been operating. If items and switches had been operating for at least a few moments, the most likely cause of the circuit failure

APARTMENT OWNERS:

If the service panel for your apartment is not located inside the apartment, make sure you know its location in case of emergency. Regardless, find out from the maintenance supervisor or some other authority whether the panel for your apartment is also a service entrance —a point where the municipal power supply enters the building from outside—or only a subpanel controlling a branch of circuits linked to a master service entrance elsewhere in the building.

HINT

was current overload—too many items connected to the circuit and operating at once. If the circuit failed the instant an item was plugged in or a switch was turned on, the problem was probably a short circuit, a fault caused by damaged wiring in the circuit, item, or switch.

Generally, the first step in both cases is to unplug all items connected to the circuit and to turn off all wall switches governing the circuit. But if you notice smoke, fire, or continued sparking, the safest action is to leave the building immediately. Warn the other occupants and call the fire department from a nearby phone.

If sparking at a switch, receptacle, or permanently mounted fixture like a ceiling light occurs at the moment the circuit fails but then stops, turn off the switch or unplug electrical cords; use a thick, dry towel or a heavy work glove, and stand in a dry area. Before restoring power, consult an electrician.

Follow the same procedure to unplug a portable item that has sparked; but there is usually no need to call an electrician unless sparking occurred in the wall receptacle. Instead, have the item professionally serviced before using it again.

Go next to the electrical service panel, the large metal box that houses the circuit breakers or fuses. To avoid a possible shock from faulty electrical components, make sure your hands are dry and that the floor, too, is dry. If necessary, stand on a dry board or rubber mat.

Open the panel door with one hand while keeping the rest of your body away from all other objects. As an added precaution, keep your other hand behind your back or in a pocket, or use it to hold a plastic-enclosed (thus insulated) flashlight.

If the panel is equipped with circuit breakers, the one that has tripped should be easy to spot. Its switch will be out of alignment with the others, and a red dot or other indicator on the breaker will be visible.

To reset most breakers and restore power to the circuit, push the switch first to the position marked "off" or "reset," then in the opposite direction to the position marked "on."

If the panel is equipped with plug fuses—the type that screw into sockets—the blown one can be found by carefully inspecting their windows. look for a fuse with a blackened window or one in which the tiny metal strip, visible inside the window, has melted. Some plug fuses contain tiny springs as well as metal strips. When these are blown, the strip is detached from the base of the fuse and is usually bent upward by spring tension.

High-voltage circuits for electric ranges and other large appliances are almost always controlled by cylindrical cartridge fuses mounted in brackets called fuse blocks. These are easy to distinguish in the service panel. They are made of black plastic and are equipped with wire handles. Cartridge fuses show no signs of being blown; the easiest way to test them is by replacing them.

Before removing a fuse, shut off the main power supply by pulling the fuse block(s) labeled "main" out of the panel. Use only one hand.

Unscrew a blown plug fuse from its socket and replace it with a new one of the same type, labeled with an identical amperage rating. Likewise, cartridge fuses should be replaced with exact duplicates. To remove and install them, use a tool called a fuse puller, available at hardware stores. To restore power, reinstall the main fuse block(s).

Before using the circuit after resetting a breaker or replacing a fuse, correct the cause of the failure.

If the problem seemed to be a current overload, reconnect only a portion of the items that were operating on the circuit when it failed. Install the remaining items in outlets served by different circuits. If the circuit fails a second time, call an electrician before restoring power.

With all short circuits except those occurring completely within an item that plugs in, an electrician should check the wiring and make necessary repairs before the circuit is used.

If the problem seemed to be a short circuit and you saw no sparks or other clues to its location, you can find the faulty area by the following method. First, unplug every item connected to the circuit and turn off all wall switches served. Restore power to the circuit at the service panel.

If the circuit falls immediately, the fault is somewhere in the circuit wiring. If it remains on, operate the wall switches one by one.

If the circuit fails when a switch is operated, the problem is either in the switch, in the wiring linking the switch to a permanently mounted item, or in the item itself.

If none of these steps causes the circuit to fail, the fault is in one of the items previously plugged in. These should be tested individually before reconnecting them, using a continuity tester available at hardware and electronics stores. Follow the instructions that come with the device.

Working with Electric Wire

When working with household electrical wiring, it is of utmost importance to make safe, reliable connections. Be sure the power is turned off before beginning.

Most household wiring is in the form of cable—several separate wires grouped together and enclosed in flexible plastic or metal sheathing. Cable with plastic sheathing is called nonmetallic sheathed cable; Romex is a leading brand. Cable with metal sheathing is called armored cable; BX is a common brand name.

With either type of cable the first step in making connections is to strip away the sheathing to expose the individual wires inside. To strip nonmetallic sheathed cable, use either a sharp utility knife or a cable stripper, an inexpensive tool made from a folded, narrow piece of metal.

When using a utility knife, lay the cable flat on a smooth work surface. Adjust the knife so that only a corner of the blade protrudes from the handle. Hold the knife parallel to the cable, insert it into the sheathing about 8 inches from the end and then slit the sheathing by drawing the knife toward the end of the cable. Keep the knife at a shallow angle to avoid cutting into the wires.

To use a cable stripper, grip it so the folded end is nearest the heel of your hand. Thread the cable through the tubular section and out the other end until about 6 inches of cable emerge. Squeeze the tubular part together so that the point on one side penetrates the sheathing. Then pull the tool back toward the end of the cable to slit it.

After either method, trim off the slit sheathing with a knife or pliers designed for cutting.

To strip sheathing from armored cable you can usually use electrician's diagonal-cutting pliers. Double the cable about 8 inches from the end and squeeze the portions together to form a sharp bend. Snip through one of the armor coils, then straighten the cable and slide the severed armor section off the end.

Or use a hacksaw instead of the pliers. Lay the cable flat on a work surface and saw partway through one of the coils, perpendicular to the seams. Then grasp the cable on each side of the cut and twist it to break the coil.

To protect the wires inside the cable from the sharp edges of the armor, always cap the cut end of armored cable by inserting a plastic or fiber bushing sold for the purpose. If the cable contains a thin metal strip (called a bonding strip), bend this backward over the outside of the armor after installing the bushing. The bonding strip serves the same purpose as the grounding wire in other types of cable.

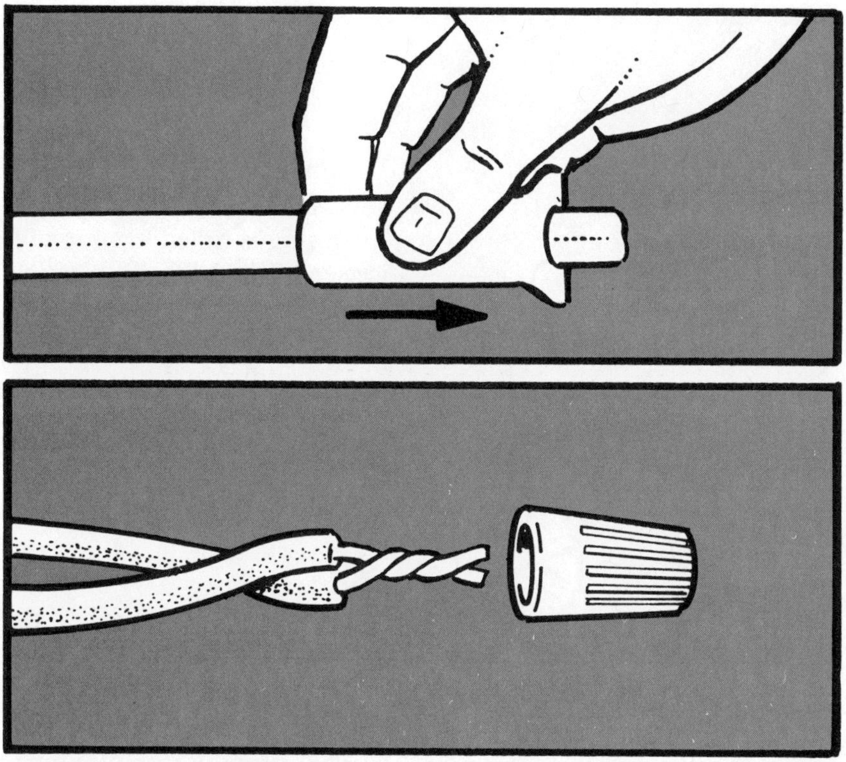

To remove plastic cable sheathing, use a cable stripper. Twist the ends of wires clockwise before joining them with a wire nut.

The next step is to remove the insulation around individual wires. This is best done with a wire stripper, a tool resembling pliers.

Grip the wire about an inch and a half from the end by clamping it between the pair of grooves in the stripper's jaws marked as being the same size as the wire; the wire size is printed on the insulation and on the cable sheathing. Rotate the stripper around the wire once or twice to cut through the insulation. Then pull the wire through the closed jaws to strip it.

You can also strip wire using a sharp knife. Hold the blade at an angle to the insulation and pare gently to avoid nicking the wire. Cut all the way around the insulation, then pull off the severed section.

Plastic connectors, called wire nuts, are usually used to join wires. These resemble small thimbles and come in many sizes. Choose wire nuts made to accommodate the number and size of wires being joined.

TIP:

Unless instructions that come with the wire nuts specify, there is no need to twist solid wires that are so stiff as to require pliers when joining them with wire nuts. Simply place the wires side by side and screw the nut down over them as tightly as possible. Wrapping two or three turns of electrical tape around wire nuts and wires after joining them helps keep moisture and stray wires—two potential sources of dangerous short circuits—from other connections out of the splice. But never use tape to supplement a loose wire nut or weak splice.

ATTENTION

To fasten a wire to a terminal screw, make a hook by first bending the wire to form a right angle, then twisting the end with needle-nose pliers. The hook should extend clockwise, three quarters of the way around the screw.

Prepare the wires by placing them side by side so that the ends of their insulated portions are flush. Trim the bared portions to equal the length of the wire nut. Twist the bared portions of the wires together clockwise, using your fingers or square-jawed lineman's pliers. Then screw the nut over the twisted wires by turning it clockwise until no bare wire is visible. Test the connection by gently pulling the wires.

Use a somewhat different procedure when joining a solid wire with a wire made up of several strands. Strip about twice as much insulation from the wire made of strands, wrap it clockwise around the solid wire with your fingers, then use pliers to fold the end of the solid wire over the wrapped part before installing the wire nut.

To fasten cable wires to the terminal screws of wall switches, receptacles, and similar outlets, a small hook must be carefully made in the end of each wire. Begin by baring only enough wire to go around the screw. Next, use long-nose pliers to bend the entire length of bared wire in a right angle to the left, as viewed when facing the terminal screw. Then grasp the end of the wire near the tip of the pliers and twist the end smoothly to make the hook. Fit the hook around the terminal screw so that tightening it will tend to close the hook. Tighten the screw securely.

The hook should extend between two thirds and three quarters of the way around the screw. If the wire is too short or too long, if the hook is not completely covered by the screw head, or if the insulation is farther than a quarter of an inch from the screw head, take the connection apart and make a new hook.

Wires can be fastened to some switches and receptacles simply by inserting them into clearly marked holes in the backs of these devices. A gauge line stamped on the back, also clearly marked, shows how much insulation to strip. It is important to insert the wires so that no bare parts are exposed.

Aluminum Wiring

Many homes built from the 1960s to the mid-1970s contain aluminum wiring instead of copper. Aluminum wiring resists the flow of electricity through it more than copper; as a result it can get hotter, creating a fire hazard. It also expands and contracts more than copper under changing temperature conditions, and over time this can cause aluminum wiring connections to loosen.

Additionally, when aluminum wire is fastened to the brass terminals on items like receptacles and wall switches, contact between the dissimilar metals causes corrosion. And when aluminum is stripped of insulation, exposing the metal to air, oxidation results. The corrosion and oxidation further increase resistance; this, too, increases the chance of a fire.

When replacing receptacles and switches connected to aluminum wiring, make sure new ones are marked "CO/ALR." This indicates that they are suitable for use with both copper and aluminum wiring. After you strip insulation from aluminum wires to connect them, coat the bare wire with oxide-inhibiting compound, available at electrical supply stores. When fastening aluminum wires to terminals, tighten the connections firmly.

Never fasten aluminum wires to receptacles or other items using the push-in connectors installed on the backs of these devices.

Working with Plumbing

Household plumbing systems can be complicated, especially in an older or remodeled home. Local codes, too, are often confusing. As a result, except for replacing existing fixtures like basins or toilets, or sections of pipe that are easily accessed, most homeowners rightly leave plumbing jobs to professionals.

But understanding your home's plumbing system and developing the skills to make repairs and improvements are not difficult. Household plumbing systems consist of two parts: supply lines that carry water from the municipal source or a well, and drain-waste-vent lines (abbreviated DWV) that carry used water to the sewer or septic system.

Supply lines were once typically made of galvanized steel pipe. Nowadays they are either copper, chlorinated polyvinyl chloride (CPVC) plastic, or polybutylene (PB) plastic. Water pressure in supply lines is usually between 50 and 60 pounds per square inch.

Pipe in DWV systems is commonly polyvinyl chloride (PVC) plastic or an older material, acryaonitrile-butadiene-styrene (ABS) plastic. Before plastic pipe was introduced, DWV pipes were most often of cast iron. Water in DWV pipes is not under pressure; the pipes slope downward so that gravity causes the water to flow. However, in multistory buildings the weight of water inside DWV pipes can apply as much as or more pressure than that in supply lines.

APARTMENT OWNERS:

As a tenant or as a landlord, you may find that codes permit only professional plumbers to repair and install apartment plumbing, especially in cities. To avoid problems, check with a building inspector before beginning any plumbing project.

HINT

Plumbing codes specify the type and size of pipe to be used for every major application. Before starting a plumbing project, consult a local building inspector for particulars. It also helps to study specialized books on plumbing for amateurs, available in libraries and bookstores.

Joining Copper Pipe

Several types of copper pipe are common in plumbing systems, but each is either rigid or flexible (the latter is also called tubing). Rigid pipe is usually joined by soldering, described below. It is a procedure that takes practice to master but is not difficult to learn. Tubing is usually joined either with compression fittings or flare fittings that are screwed together.

To assemble a run of rigid copper pipe or to replace a length of existing pipe, first calculate the amount of pipe you will need by measuring the distance between couplings or other fittings and adding the distance that the ends of the pipe project into the fittings. Use a hacksaw or a tubing cutter (a tool resembling a C-clamp) to cut sections of pipe to size. Then, with a small round file or the triangular blade on a tubing cutter designed for the purpose, smooth away any burrs on the inside of the pipe formed by cutting.

For soldering, you will need a propane torch and spark lighter, safety glasses or goggles, solder wire (lead-free solder is often required by code for supply pipes, and is safest to use in any case), a can of noncorrosive soldering flux with an applicator brush, and a piece of fine-grade emery cloth. All materials and tools are available at hardware stores.

If you are soldering near a wall or other area that might scorch, get a piece of sheet metal to use as a heat shield (an old license plate will do). It is wise also to keep a fire extinguisher handy. Never solder near anything flammable or explosive, like workshop clutter or a fuel oil tank.

Start by shutting off any water flowing to the pipe being soldered. If some water still oozes from the pipe, plug it with a small wad of bread. (This is a plumber's trick. The bread need not be removed later; it will dissolve quickly when the water is turned back on.)

If you are soldering a shutoff valve or similar fitting that contains plastic or rubber parts, disassemble it to avoid melting the parts. Then use emery cloth to polish the outer surface of pipes where they will be covered, and the inner surface of fittings that will cover them, until they shine.

Use a tubing cutter and a basin wrench on plumbing.

With the applicator brush or a cotton swab, apply a thin layer of flux to the polished surfaces. Then slip the parts together and position them for permanent fastening.

If necessary, place the heat shield between the area to be soldered and any nearby combustible surface. Unroll about 6 inches of solder wire from the spool and bend it so that while holding the spool you can easily touch the tip of the wire to the seam where the pipe and the fitting join. Do not cut the wire from the spool.

Put on eye protection and light the torch. Adjust the flame until the inner blue cone is 1 to 1½ inches long. Hold the torch in your less-skilled hand (your left hand if you are right-handed) and train the tip of the inner cone against the part of the fitting that covers the pipe. Try to heat the entire circumference of the fitting evenly.

Hold the spool of solder wire in your skilled hand, out of the way. Observe the fluxed seam closely; as soon as the flux bubbles and turns clear, touch the tip of the wire to the seam and move the torch flame about an inch in the opposite direction, away from the solder.

The heated metal should melt the solder wire instantly and draw it into the joint. If the solder turns mushy instead, remove it and apply more heat to the fitting. If the solder sputters and forms tiny balls, the metal is too hot and must be allowed to cool.

Feed wire into the seam until molten solder begins to drip out. Then remove the wire and turn off the torch.

Inspect the entire joint, using a hand mirror if necessary. Solder should be visible in an unbroken ring around the pipe. If there are gaps, apply a little flux to them, then reheat the joint and add more solder.

When the joint is cool, turn on the water and inspect for leaks. If reheating and adding solder does not fix them, disassemble the joint by heating it and pulling it apart with pliers as soon as the solder melts. Polish the surfaces with emery cloth, then apply more flux and resolder the joint.

If you are soldering more than one fitting onto a pipe, place a wet cloth on the pipe to prevent heat from the joint you are working on from melting joints that have been finished.

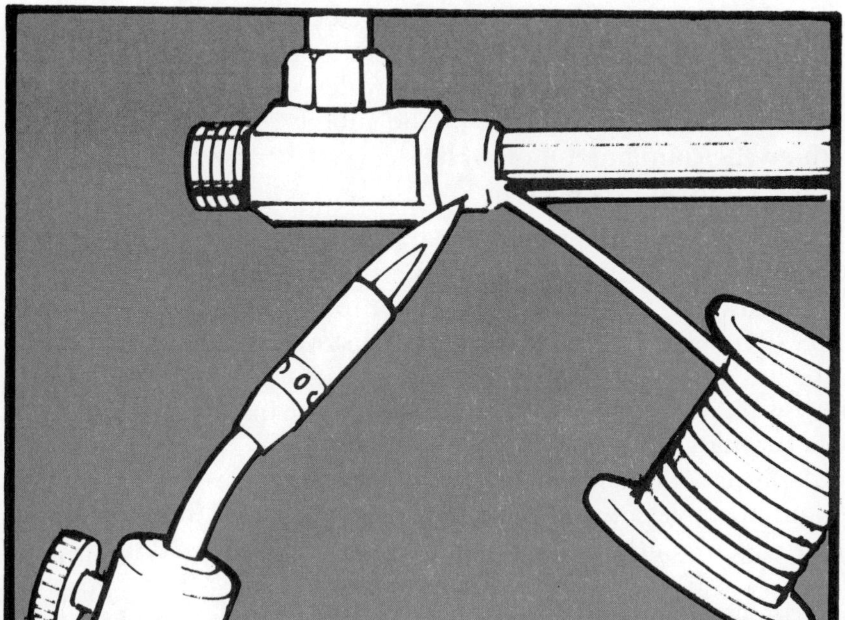

When soldering, apply heat to the fitting. When solder is applied, it should melt and flow instantly into the joint.

To join tubing with compression or flare fittings, calculate the length(s) of tubing necessary as previously described, but allow a small amount extra because, being flexible, tubing cannot be made perfectly straight. Cut the tubing with a hacksaw or tubing cutter; avoid flattening the ends.

Compression fittings generally consist of the fitting, which has a threaded sleeve the same diameter as the outside of the tubing; a soft metal washer called a ferrule that slides over the end of the tubing; and a large nut, called a coupling nut, that also fits over the tubing and compresses the ferrule when threaded onto the fitting.

To install a compression fitting, slide the coupling nut onto the tubing, followed by the ferrule. Place the end of the tubing against the end of the fitting's threaded sleeve (usually the end of the sleeve is slightly tapered to make this easier), then spread the coupling nut onto the sleeve—capturing the ferrule beneath the nut—and tighten it with a wrench.

A flare fitting consists only of the fitting and a coupling nut. However, the sleeve of the fitting, while threaded along part of its length like that of a compression fitting, tapers to a cone at the end. When joining tubing with a flare fitting, a flaring tool (available at hardware stores) is needed to widen the end of the tubing so it will fit over the sleeve's cone-shaped end.

To install a flare fitting, first slide the coupling nut onto the tubing. Next, use the flaring tool to widen the end of the tubing. Finally, fit the widened end of the tubing onto the fitting and tighten the coupling nut onto the sleeve.

Working with Plastic Pipe

Plastic plumbing pipe is ideal for use by amateurs because it is easy to work with and requires no special skills or tools.

It also has many advantages over metal pipe: It is less expensive, lighter in weight, and will not rust or corrode. Also, plastic pipe has insulative qualities that prevent condensation from forming on pipes carrying cold water; these same qualities reduce heat loss through pipes carrying hot water.

Despite its benefits, the use of plastic pipe is limited by the plumbing codes of many communities. If you are in doubt about code requirements in your area, contact the local building inspector.

Rigid plastic pipe is joined with plastic couplings and solvent-based cement. These, as well as separate cleaner and primer fluids necessary for preparing pipe for joining, are available at hardware stores. Be sure to obtain cement, cleaner, and primer specifically designed for the type of pipe you are using.

Calculating lengths for assembling a run of rigid plastic pipe is done the same way as for copper pipe, described earlier. Cut plastic pipe to length using a fine-toothed hacksaw (twenty-four teeth per inch) and a miter box.

Remove the shreds of plastic from the cut ends of the pipe with a penknife. Also bevel the thickness of the pipe walls slightly, inside and out. Beveling on the outside improves the fit of the pipe in the coupling, enhancing the glue joint. Beveling on the inside improves the flow of water through the pipe.

Smooth the outside of the pipe with fine-grit sandpaper, then fit the pieces together. The fit should be snug. Align them exactly as they should be when joined, then draw a line across the end of each fitting onto the pipe to mark its position.

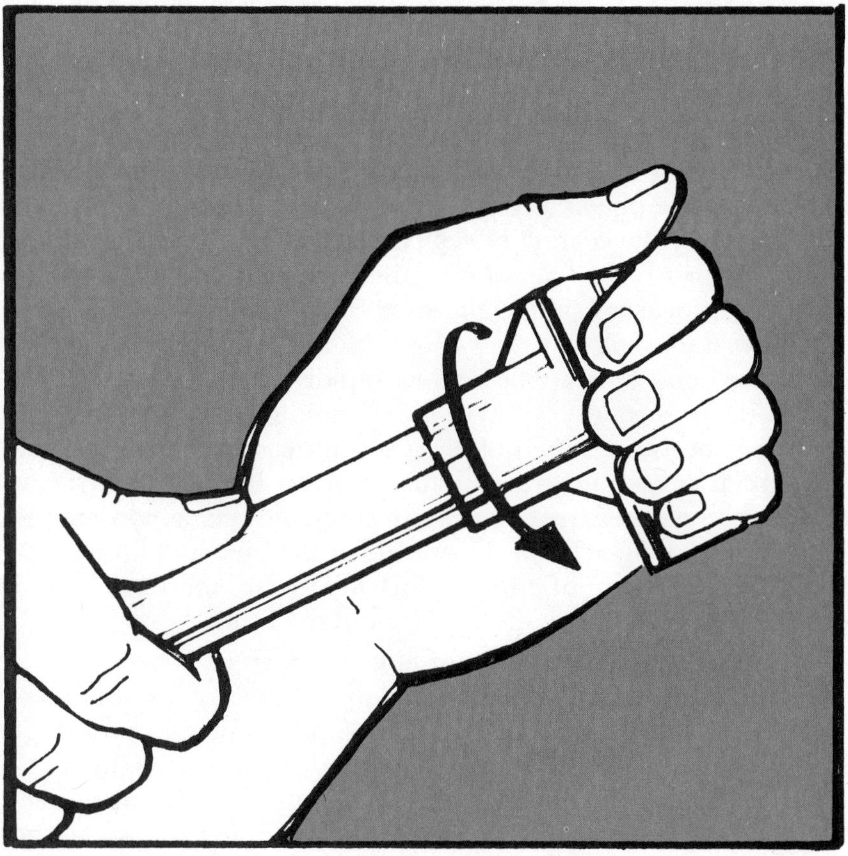

When cementing plastic pipe, press the pieces together and then twist them a quarter turn to align the marks correctly.

Flare fitting for flexible plastic pipe uses a threaded coupling nut for a tight fit.

Disassemble and cement the pieces one at a time. Begin by wiping the end of a pipe and the inside of a fitting with cleaner (omit this if the pipe is already clean). After it dries, apply primer.

Then apply a coating of cement to the end of the pipe, using either the brush that comes with the cement or a natural-bristle artist's paintbrush. Completely cover the portion of the pipe that will enter the fitting.

Once cement is applied, work rapidly. The cement will set within thirty seconds. Apply a liberal amount of cement to the inside of the fitting, then apply a second coat of cement to the pipe; then press the two together. Do this in such a way that twisting the pieces a quarter turn (to spread the cement inside the joint) brings the marks on the outside of the pipe and fitting into alignment. The sign of a satisfactory joint is an unbroken line of squeezed-out cement all the way around the fitting.

Hold the pieces together for at least ten seconds before moving on to the next joint. After completing an entire project, allow the cement to cure fully for at least two hours or the amount of time specified on the cement container. If the new pipes are supply pipes, run water through them at full pressure for thirty seconds to clear them of solvent fumes before using the water the first time.

Flexible pipe is joined with flare fittings made especially for it. Although these resemble the kind used for copper tubing, no flaring tool is needed. To install, cut the pipe to length as for copper tubing. Use a sharp penknife or utility knife. Then, simply slide the coupling nut onto the tubing, force the end of the tubing over the tapered end of the fitting's threaded sleeve, and tighten the coupling nut by hand.

Water supplied by flexible pipes is safe to use immediately after the pipes have been joined. However, it is a good idea to run the water at full pressure for thirty seconds first to clean them.

Ladders and Scaffolding

Ladders are indispensible for many home improvement tasks, indoors and out. For reaching heights less than 10 feet, stepladders are good. These two-piece ladders, hinged at one end, unfold to form an inverted V. When the side braces are locked, they are freestanding and require no support but a flat, firm surface to rest on. They fold flat for storage.

Stepladders range up to 10 feet in height. Because it is dangerous to stand any higher on a stepladder than the second rung from the top—above this height, you and the ladder may tip over—a ladder 5 or 6 feet high is usually the best for reaching most ceilings comfortably.

For outdoor use, where greater heights are encountered, you need an extension ladder. These consist of two straight, sliding sections that hook together to form a single long length.

Extension ladders are commonly available in lengths ranging up to 35 feet when extended. For safety, choose a length that will allow the ladder to extend at least 3 feet higher than that at which you plan to stand, or the surface—such as the edge of a roof—onto which you plan to step.

Whether to obtain a metal, wooden, or fiberglass extension ladder is largely a matter of personal preference. Metal ladders are light and strong, and so are recommended over wood or fiberglass for long lengths. However, many people prefer the extra weight of wooden ladders because they feel more stable underfoot. Fiberglass ladders, which do not conduct electricity, are designed for use where accidental contact with power lines is a hazard. Amateurs should not risk working in these locations.

When selecting any ladder, look for a warranty and a load-rating label that indicates how much weight the ladder will bear. Although most ladders will support several times their rated capacity, the safest course is to obtain the strongest ladder you can afford.

Other features to look for are wide, deeply grooved treads with reinforcing rods or braces underneath, nonskid feet, and on extension ladders, padded ends to prevent the top of the ladder from marring surfaces it rests against. The upper section of an extension ladder should slide easily up and down (the ladder should be equipped with a rope and pulley for this purpose), and the hooks that lock the sections together should function smoothly. Never buy a painted ladder or paint one yourself; the paint can hide dangerous cracks.

Before using a ladder examine it closely for flaws like cracks and loose or damaged hardware. If you find any, don't use the ladder. Also check to make certain there are no obstructions overhead, particularly electric wires. Never raise a ladder in front of a window or door without locking the door, placing a warning sign on the inside of the building, and stationing a helper at the foot of the ladder to warn people away.

APARTMENT OWNERS:

If space for storing an extension ladder is lacking, a combination ladder with hinged sections might be the answer. Although more expensive than an extension ladder of equal height (around 10 feet), this type can be used as both a stepladder and an extension ladder, and can even be folded to support a plank or to rest on uneven surfaces like stairs.

HINT

Handling an Extension Ladder

To raise an extension ladder, lay it flat with its feet resting against the wall of the building. If shrubs or flower beds are in the way, have a helper brace the feet. Make sure the ladder is fully retracted and that the upper section touches the ground. Go to the far end of the ladder, lift the top rung and push upward with both arms until the end of the ladder is overhead.

Walk forward beneath the ladder, pushing it upward by moving your hands from one rung to the next until the ladder swings past vertical and rests against the wall. Then, for stability while raising the upper section, move the base of the ladder a few feet away from the building.

To raise the upper section, pull on the rope. As you do, keep the end of the ladder slightly away from the side of the building to avoid marring the siding. When the top of the ladder is a few inches above the desired height, let the upper section drop downward so that the hooks attached to it slide over the rungs at the top of the lower section and lock securely.

TIP:

For a ladder resting on the ground, extra insurance against the legs slipping can be had by driving long screwdrivers or wooden stakes into the earth in back of the legs. Another effective measure for a ladder resting on pavement or ground is tying one end of a rope to the ladder's bottom rung and the other to a sturdy fixed object directly in front of the ladder, near or attached to the wall against which the ladder rests. (With the latter method, care must be taken that no one trips over the rope.)

ATTENTION

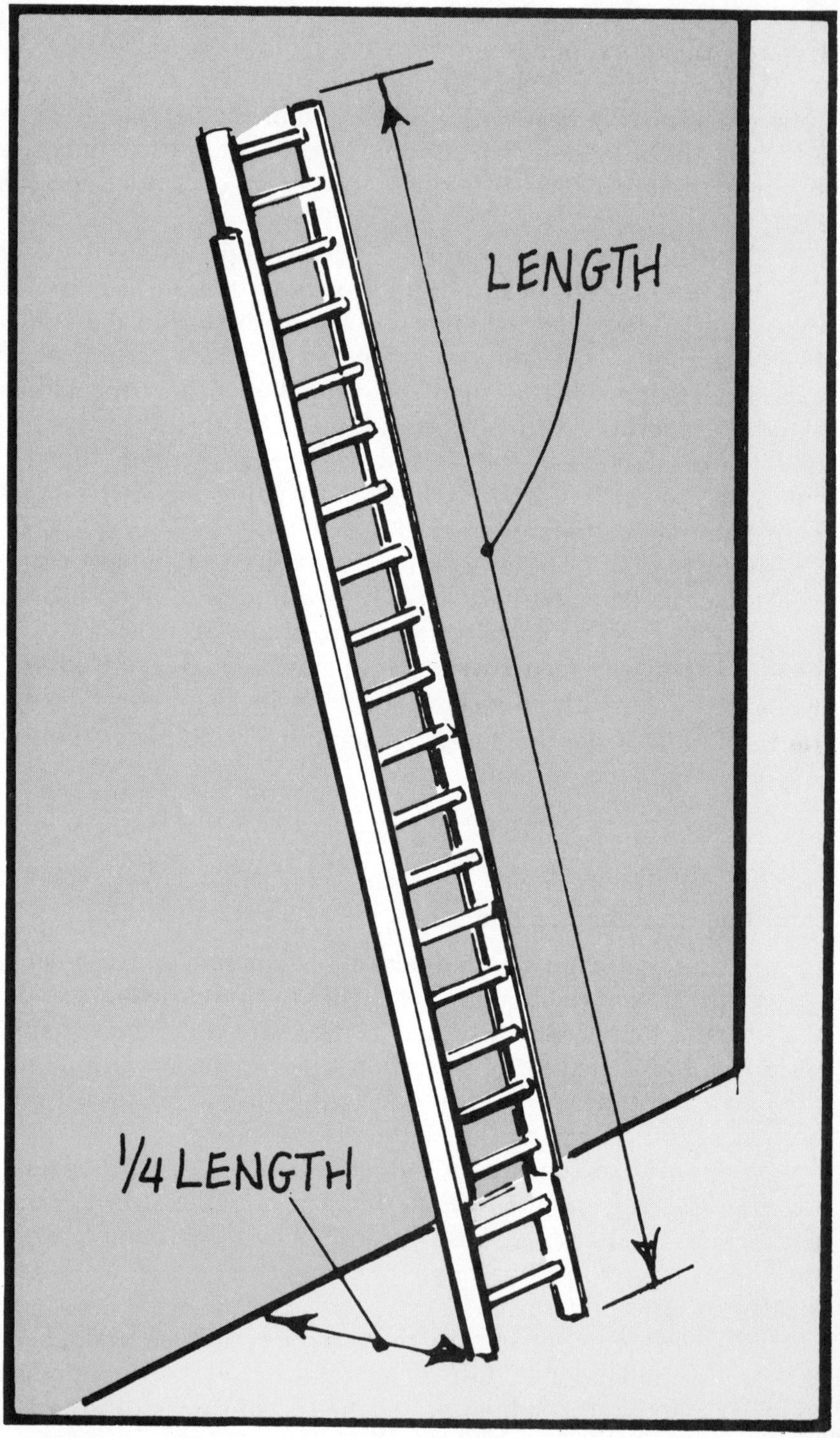

For safety, the distance from the base of an extension ladder to the wall it leans against should equal one quarter of the ladder's length when extended the desired amount.

Adjust the slope of the ladder by pulling the feet away from the building until the distance from them to the base of the wall equals one quarter of the length of the ladder.

If the ground is uneven, place a wide, flat board beneath the feet of the ladder and level it by inserting scraps of plywood beneath the board. To prevent the feet of the ladder from slipping, have a helper brace the ladder at all times while it is in use by pressing against the side rails while standing behind it.

To check the ladder's stability, bounce a few times on the ladder's bottom rung before climbing. When you climb, have both hands free. If you need tools or other equipment when aloft, haul them up in a bucket tied to a rope. Hang the bucket from a rung using an S-shaped metal hook. When working on a ladder, keep your hips and center of gravity between the ladder's side rails. Never reach more than an arm's length in any direction.

If you need to move the ladder, first climb to the ground, bringing all your gear with you. Lift the ladder's feet and reposition them a short distance in the direction you wish to go, then rock the end of the ladder away from the building slightly, and push against the rails until the upper part is vertical.

If you must transport the ladder several feet, position yourself beneath its slope, crouch slightly, and grasp the nearest lower rung with one hand (preferably your strongest) while at the same time grasping the highest rung you can reach with your other hand. Straighten up, then walk carefully to the new location with the ladder held away from the house.

To lower a ladder to the ground, reverse the raising procedure. When the ladder is on the ground, turn it on its side. If you have a partner, both of you can carry the ladder by each taking an end. If you are alone, locate a spot between two rungs near the middle of the ladder where it balances well, then crouch down, slip the shoulder of your stronger arm between the rungs, and stand. Support the ladder on your shoulder and steady it with both arms.

Scaffolding

For large jobs like painting or installing new siding, consider using scaffolding instead of a ladder.

Most rental centers carry scaffolding. It consists of three basic parts—end frames and side braces made of steel tubing, and wooden planks or metal platforms on which to stand. Units are constructed from pairs of end frames linked by the braces and topped by the planks or platforms. Joining units vertically creates a tower; joining them side by side creates a run.

Although scaffolding can be erected by one strong person, having a helper makes the task much easier. Basic assembly instructions and safety guidelines should be available from the rental center. Ask for them if they are not offered.

To assemble scaffolding, first clear debris from the area and check for overhead obstructions. Do not erect scaffolding near power lines.

Where the posts of end frames will stand, place one or two thick boards such as squares of two-by-ten lumber on the ground to support them. Then set one end frame in place and loosely attach a pair of braces to it with the bolts provided. The braces will prevent the frame from toppling. Afterward, attach the other end frame and tighten all the fasteners.

If you are erecting a tower, cover the top of the unit with at least one plank or with a platform section. Place additional blocks or thin pieces of plywood beneath the posts to level the unit if necessary, then construct the next higher unit by lifting additional components into place. Afterward, transfer the plank(s) or platform section to the top of the new unit.

To erect a run, simply attach additional braces and end frames loosely until the run is complete. Then tighten all the fasteners, place planks or platform sections on top, and level the units if necessary.

Managing Large Panels

Large panels like plywood, particleboard, and flakeboard have a major drawback: Their large size makes handling and cutting them difficult.

One way to manage panels is to take advantage of lumberyard services. Most suppliers of panel materials will saw them into pieces for a small charge. Plan your needs by drawing a diagram showing the location in each panel of the pieces of your project. Arrange the pieces so that the panel can be subdivided into smaller, more easily transported sections. Then, when you order the panel, specify that these cuts be made.

To minimize expense, arrange the pieces so that as few cuts as possible are necessary to make the panel manageable. Because extra length in a panel generally makes it more awkward than extra width, plan a layout that calls for crosswise cuts rather than lengthwise ones.

If you must obtain full-size panels, ask about delivery rates. They may be reasonable even for only a few panels, and often you can have items brought right inside or to the backyard. For large projects such as remodeling, ask whether the lumberyard or building supplier offers boom-truck service. If so, you may be able to have panels delivered directly to an upper story of a house or modest apartment building for not much more than the price of having the materials dropped off at ground level.

Of course, once delivered, the problem becomes how to maneuver and cut panels yourself, safely and accurately.

To lift and carry a large panel, stand it vertically on one of its long edges. Raise one end about an inch and slip a block of wood or your toe underneath. Then crouch down and grip the bottom edge of the panel slightly forward of the midpoint with the fingers of one hand.

TIP:

If you expect to lift and carry many panels, for instance when remodeling, invest in a panel-carrying tool, available at many lumberyards and building supply companies. The tool consists of a comfortably shaped metal handle long enough to eliminate stooping and a bracket that fits beneath the edge of panels up to an inch thick. As an alternative, a claw hammer can be used as a hook to carry panels, but it is more difficult to grip and the claw can damage soft materials, especially wallboard.

ATTENTION

Grasp the upper edge of the panel by raising your other arm over your head. Lift the panel by using your thighs to rise to a standing position, then carry it by keeping your back straight and lower arm outstretched. Walk erect, with the panel resting against your shoulder.

For cutting most panels, the best tool is a portable circular saw with a plywood-cutting blade featuring small, uniformly spaced teeth. Carbide-tipped blades are sharper and last longer than ordinary all-steel blades. To prevent splintering the finished side of a panel, place it so that the cutting edges of the saw teeth will exit the panel on the unfinished side. With a circular saw—because the blade rotates counterclockwise—this means placing the panel so the finished side is down. When using a hand saw, place the panel so the finished side is up.

A support for cutting panels safely and comfortably can be made by nailing a pair of 8-foot-long two-by-fours across two sawhorses. Set the sawhorses approximately 6 feet apart (or 2 feet less than the length of the panel) and place the two-by-fours approximately 2 feet apart.

When cutting, adjust the saw's blade depth so that only one or two teeth extend beyond the thickness of the panel. Then position the panel so that the saw will travel over the two-by-fours perpendicular to them. With this method, even though the saw enters the two-by-fours slightly, the panel is supported on both sides of the cut at all times.

Secure the panel with clamps. When a panel must be placed so that a large overhang is created, have an assistant steady the overhanging portion while you cut, even if clamps are used.

If only a few cuts are necessary, the saw can be guided by a straight-edged board clamped to the panel, parallel to the cutting line. Use a wide board such as a one-by-four so that the clamps holding it will not interfere with the saw. To prevent a long guide board from flexing, fasten it to the panel midway along its length with a small finishing nail or brad driven flush with the surface.

Easier to use and often more accurate is a homemade cutting jig. A jig will produce perfect cuts as long as you always use the same saw and blade with which the jig was made, or a replacement blade of equal thickness.

To construct the jig, use a piece of plywood at least ½ inch thick and 22 to 24 inches wide. For cutting panels lengthwise, the piece must be at least 8 feet long. For cutting panels crosswise, the piece must be 4 feet long. In both cases, one of the piece's long edges must be the factory-cut panel edge, which is straight and smooth.

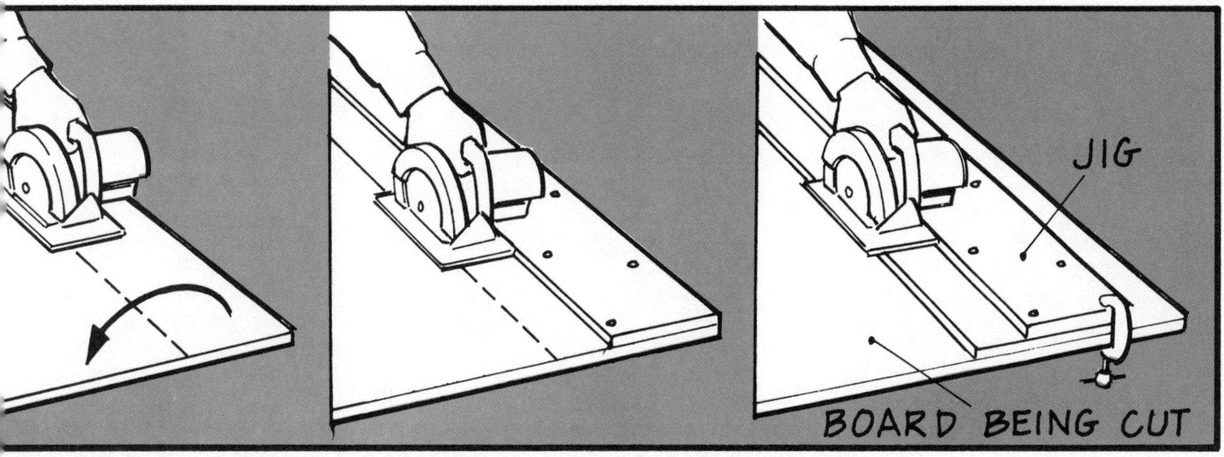

When sawing large panels, make a cutting jig to ensure straight cuts.

First, clamp the piece securely and cut off a lengthwise strip approximately 6 inches wide that includes the factory-cut edge. The strip may be cut freehand, without using a guide board. Flip the strip over and place it on top of the remaining portion of the piece so that the two freshly cut edges are flush. Fasten the strip to the piece with screws sunk below the surface.

Then set the saw on top of the piece, next to the factory-cut edge of the strip. Using the edge as a guide for the saw, complete the jig by making a second cut along the length of the piece. Make this cut carefully, keeping the edge of the saw's base plate pressed against the edge of the strip. Done correctly, the width of the exposed portion of the piece will exactly equal the width of the saw's base plate.

To use the jig, simply clamp or tack it on top of the panel to be cut, so that the edge of the lower piece lies along the cutting line. If you attach the jig over the portion of the panel you wish to keep, set the edge directly on the cutting line. If the jig is attached over the waste portion of the panel, set the edge about an eighth of an inch away from the line so that the outside edge of the saw blade—not the side nearest the jig—touches the cutting line.

Place the saw on the jig with the edge of the saw's base plate against the factory-cut edge of the strip. Make the cut by sliding the saw over the jig, keeping the saw's base plate pressed against the strip.

Moving Heavy Objects

Even an hour of home improvement activities involving lifting can cause a sore back—or possibly an injury—that lasts for days or longer. Back muscles are among the body's weakest, and often they are out of condition from sedentary living.

But avoiding back pain and mishaps when lifting requires more than strength. Techniques must be used that take advantage of the body's strongest features and also incorporate balance, leverage, and other properties of physics.

Generally speaking, to lift and carry loads with the least strain, use the muscles in your thighs and legs. These are the strongest in your body. To prevent the muscles in your back from being stressed, keep your back as straight and vertical as possible.

For example, to lift an object like a large carton from the floor, first stand close to it with your feet about shoulder-width apart. Squat down by bending your knees while keeping your back straight.

Spread your knees so that the carton is between them. Work your fingers underneath the carton at each end—in the middle so that it will balance when lifted—and brace your forearms against the insides of your thighs.

Lift the carton by pulling it upward to your waist. Then stand up, keeping your back straight, using your thigh muscles. Hold the carton close to your body, just above your waist.

When walking with a load, try to keep it slightly above waist height so that it does not interfere with your legs. However, when you are standing with it, reduce the strain on your arms by straightening them. Do this, without causing your back to roll forward, by moving your shoulders back, then dropping them downward while thrusting your chest up and forward. With your shoulders in this position, let your arms straighten.

To set down a load, follow the lifting steps in reverse. Squat while holding the object close to your waist. When you reach the floor, slide the load forward using the insides of your thighs to brace your forearms, then set the load down between your knees. Remove your fingers one hand at a time by tipping the load so that one side touches the floor before the other.

Carrying loads of equal weight like paint cans and toolboxes is easier if you carry one in each hand. Keep your shoulders back and down so that the weight is balanced on each side of your body, not suspended in front of you. With this method you will be able to lift heavier loads and also to walk and stand erect. Your back will not be strained by being pulled to one side.

A helper is also useful. Even professional movers usually work in pairs. For moving very heavy items like refrigerators (or numerous smaller items like cartons of books) do not overlook another tool used by professionals, a hand truck.

Hand trucks come in two basic styles and can be rented. For moving a single large object, use a truck with handles on each side. It has a narrow shelf on which to rest the object and adjustable straps for securing it. Rubber skids attached along the back of the truck make it easier to slide up and down stairs.

Trucks designed exclusively for moving refrigerators usually have handles near the bottom also. These permit safer and more efficient maneuvering on stairs by two people.

To move stacks of smaller items, use a hand truck having a single handle centered at the top. The shelf of this variety is wider, and the single handle enables easier maneuvering of the truck around corners and through narrow doorways.

To load a hand truck, either slide the shelf beneath the load or stack items onto it. When stacking, do not pile items higher than the handle.

Stand behind one loaded truck and place one foot firmly on the axle. Pull backward on the handle(s) to tilt the truck until you feel its weight balance over the wheels. Then gently push the axle with your foot to start the truck rolling.

For rearranging furniture, small, caster-equipped dollies can be helpful. One kind consists of a roughly triangular metal platform with swiveling wheels beneath the corners.

To place an object on these dollies, lift it at each corner and slide a dolly underneath. An object traveling on dollies tends to roll sideways, so having an assistant to help guide it is convenient.

Sometimes a large object like a washing machine can be "walked" from one place to another, provided the floor will not be damaged in the process. To move an object this way, stand behind it and tilt it backward so that it is balanced on its rear edge. Then twist the object so that one side moves forward, pivoting on the corner that remains in place. Repeat the procedure to move the other rear corner in front of the first. Continue this way until you have moved the object to its destination.

To move a heavy item over a smooth, hard floor that might be marred by the methods described, set it on an old throw rug. Then drag the load to its destination.

PART 3:

Spring (March Through May)

HIGHLIGHTS

CONTENTS

A Spring Home Inspection

The first warm weekend in spring is a good time to make an annual inspection of your home's exterior. By performing minor maintenance and repairs promptly you can often prevent the need for major repairs later. And if you find that large-scale repairs are necessary, determining the need for them early allows time for adequate planning and beating the warm-season rush to hire professional help.

Start by examining gutters and downspouts. Check to see if any sections are misaligned or have pulled away from the edge of the roof. Clear debris from the splash blocks—the concrete troughs beneath downspouts—and reposition the blocks if necessary so the water they catch will be channeled safely away from the building's foundation. Improperly placed and missing splash blocks are a primary cause of basement leaks. Splash blocks can be obtained at building supply centers.

Insert a garden hose into the lower opening of each downspout and force it upward to detect blockage. If the hose jams before reaching the top, turn on the water to clear the debris.

If the ground is dry enough to support a ladder safely, climb to the roof and clean the gutters. At the same time, you can realign gutter sections, repair or replace broken brackets, and patch holes that may have developed in the gutter troughs.

If the day is dry and not too windy, walk onto the roof and search for broken or curled shingles, a common cause of leaks. To quickly repair a broken shingle, slide a piece of metal flashing or aluminum siding beneath it and spread asphalt or plastic roofing cement (a black substance resembling tar) liberally between the two.

Splash blocks help prevent basement leaks. Be sure all downspouts have splash blocks and that they are positioned to channel water away from the building.

To straighten a curled shingle, apply roofing cement beneath the corners, then press the shingle flat against the roof. Do this only on a warm day when the shingles are flexible. Stand on the shingle for a few minutes to hold it in place until the cement hardens.

Also inspect the flashing at roof seams and around the chimney, vent stack, and other openings such as skylights. Patch holes and areas of cracked adhesive by covering them with roofing cement, applied in a thick, smooth layer using a flexible putty knife. Avoid creating ridges that can trap water.

To fix wood trim, scrape loose paint from the wood, then test for decay by probing it with a knife blade. If the wood is sound, sand it, apply primer, and then repaint.

Check the chimney for crumbling mortar. Although you may want to wait for warm weather to make repairs (and if damage is widespread you should consult a mason before proceeding), the way to patch crumbling mortar is to chisel it out from between bricks to a depth of about three quarters of an inch, then apply fresh mortar and smooth the joints with a small masonry tool called a brick jointer.

Before leaving the roof, inspect the condition of any additional items such as television antennas and guy wires. Make sure these are in working order and are securely fastened. Apply fresh roofing cement around hardware holding guy wires to the roof.

From the ground, inspect the sides of the house. If you find areas of peeling paint, scrape away the loose material, sand the areas smooth, then brush on a protective coat of primer. The primer can be left exposed if repainting is planned for later in the season. Otherwise, after overnight drying, primer can be covered with exterior housepaint to match surrounding surfaces.

Deeply blistered paint that reveals bare wood when pulled away is a sign of condensation occurring within the walls. Before repainting, you will have to remedy this, otherwise the condition will continue and other damage may result.

Applying vapor barrier material or special paint on the warm (indoor) side of walls helps cure condensation by preventing mois ture generated inside the house from passing into them. Reducing the overall moisture content by adding ventilators and fans and by changing living habits is also important. To ventilate moisture trapped in the walls and that which enters despite preventive measures, install small circular vents designed for the purpose in the exterior side of the walls. Vents and installation tools are available at hardware stores.

Inspect siding. Aluminum and vinyl siding seldom require attention. However, wood siding may crack, warp, or decay.

Fill foundation cracks with caulking compound or patching cement. Big cracks may require excavation.

To repair cracks and opened seams, fill them with caulking compound. Choose a type that accepts paint. Small areas of decay can be restored using epoxy filler sold for the purpose at paint stores and home centers. If damage or rot is severe, the affected siding must be cut out and replaced.

Cracks in concrete and stucco can be filled with caulking compound, patching cement, or with a stucco repair product resembling plaster. However, disguising repairs to concrete and stucco is difficult and hairline cracks can usually be left alone with no ill effect. If the walls are mortared masonry, repair them as described for chimneys.

Examine trim. If paint or caulking has deteriorated between sections, pry it out and apply fresh caulking compound or polyurethane foam sealant (available in pressure cans). Foam sealant must be thoroughly painted when cured to protect it from sunlight.

Scrape away loose paint where it occurs. If decay is present underneath, repair it with epoxy filler or by replacing the damaged section with new wood. Otherwise, sand the area smooth, apply primer, and repaint.

Along with checking trim, inspect the condition of putty around window glass. Moderately cracked putty that does not crumble can be sealed by painting over it. However, if putty can be easily pried loose with a pocketknife or is missing in spots, it should be repaired by scraping away all old material (softening it with a heat gun or hair dryer eases this chore) and applying fresh compound. Allowing glazing compound to deteriorate can permit moisture to enter wooden window sashes, causing decay.

Refasten or replace loose weatherstripping around windows and doors. Weatherstripping is as effective in summer for conserving cool air inside a house as it is in winter for preserving warmth.

Finally, inspect the foundation walls for cracks. Use caulking compound or patching cement to fill any that you find. Monitor cracks every few months to see if they grow. If they do, the foundation may be settling, requiring further repair. Because excavation is usually necessary to repair extensive cracks, schedule major foundation repairs for summer when soil is dry.

Inspecting and Cleaning Chimneys and Fireplaces

Chimneys and fireplaces should be inspected and cleaned at least once a year. This prevents the buildup inside them of creosote and other sooty deposits, which are both a fire hazard and a hindrance to performance. Spring—as soon after the end of the heating season as possible—is the best time for the job, because this enables you to remove deposits before they harden and before they have a chance to cause serious corrosion. In addition, plenty of time is available to perform major repairs, if necessary, before cold weather sets in once again.

A chimney inspection alone can usually be obtained by calling your local fire department. If your chimney and fireplace have not been cleaned within the past twelve months, consider having the job done by a licensed professional chimney sweep who can also inspect the chimney's condition. Chimney sweeps are listed in the telephone directory. Most qualified sweeps are members of either the National Chimney Sweep Guild or the Wood Heating Education and Research Foundation. Once a professional inspection and cleaning has been carried out, you can perform the tasks yearly yourself.

Inspecting

To inspect a chimney, begin by visually examining the exterior for cracks and damaged masonry. These can leak combustion gases indoors, creating a fire hazard, and at the same time admit moisture into the brickwork from outdoors, accelerating deterioration. Small, isolated cracks can be individually repaired with fresh heat-resistant mortar sold especially for chimney repair at heating supply or stove and fireplace stores.

Examine the condition of the chimney cap. If it is cracked but the pieces are still firmly bonded to the chimney, or if only a few areas have crumbled, restore the cap by first filling the cracks and damaged places with heat-resistant mortar and then applying a thin coat of mortar over the entire cap to seal it.

Consider adding a wire mesh spark arrester to the opening of the flue at the chimney top. An arrester not only prevents large embers, which may still be burning, from escaping out of the chimney but also prevents birds and small animals from entering the flue when the fireplace is not in use.

To make a spark arrester, chalk the inside dimensions of the flue opening in the center of a large square of ½-inch mesh hardware cloth. Extend the chalked lines to the edges of the cloth, then use metal-cutting shears to remove the waste areas at the corners, as shown in the diagram.

Fold the sides and ends of the arrester together to form an open box, then push the box upside down into the top of the flue. The fit should be tight so that winds and rising hot air from the chimney do not blow the arrester out of the flue.

All along the chimney, probe suspect mortar joints with an ice pick or nail. If many prove crumbly or loose, have a mason determine whether complete repointing (restoring old mortar) is necessary, and don't use the fireplace until repairs are made.

Also inspect flashing around the base of the chimney. Simple repairs of small holes can be made by covering the damaged portions with asphalt or plastic roofing cement. Torn or badly corroded flashing should be replaced by an experienced roofer.

Inside the fireplace, cracked or crumbling mortar joints between firebricks can be repointed using fireplace mortar, which often comes in a cartridge similar to caulking compound. Chisel out the loose existing mortar, brush away any soot or other debris, then dampen the damaged area using a wet cloth.

Before the surface dries, apply the mortar using a caulking gun, then smooth it flush with the surface of the surrounding firebrick using a flexible putty knife.

Let the mortar cure according to the directions on the label. The first fire you light should darken the new mortar, blending it with the rest of the fireplace interior.

Pay particular attention to the damper, usually positioned at the top of the fireplace where it joins the chimney. If necessary,

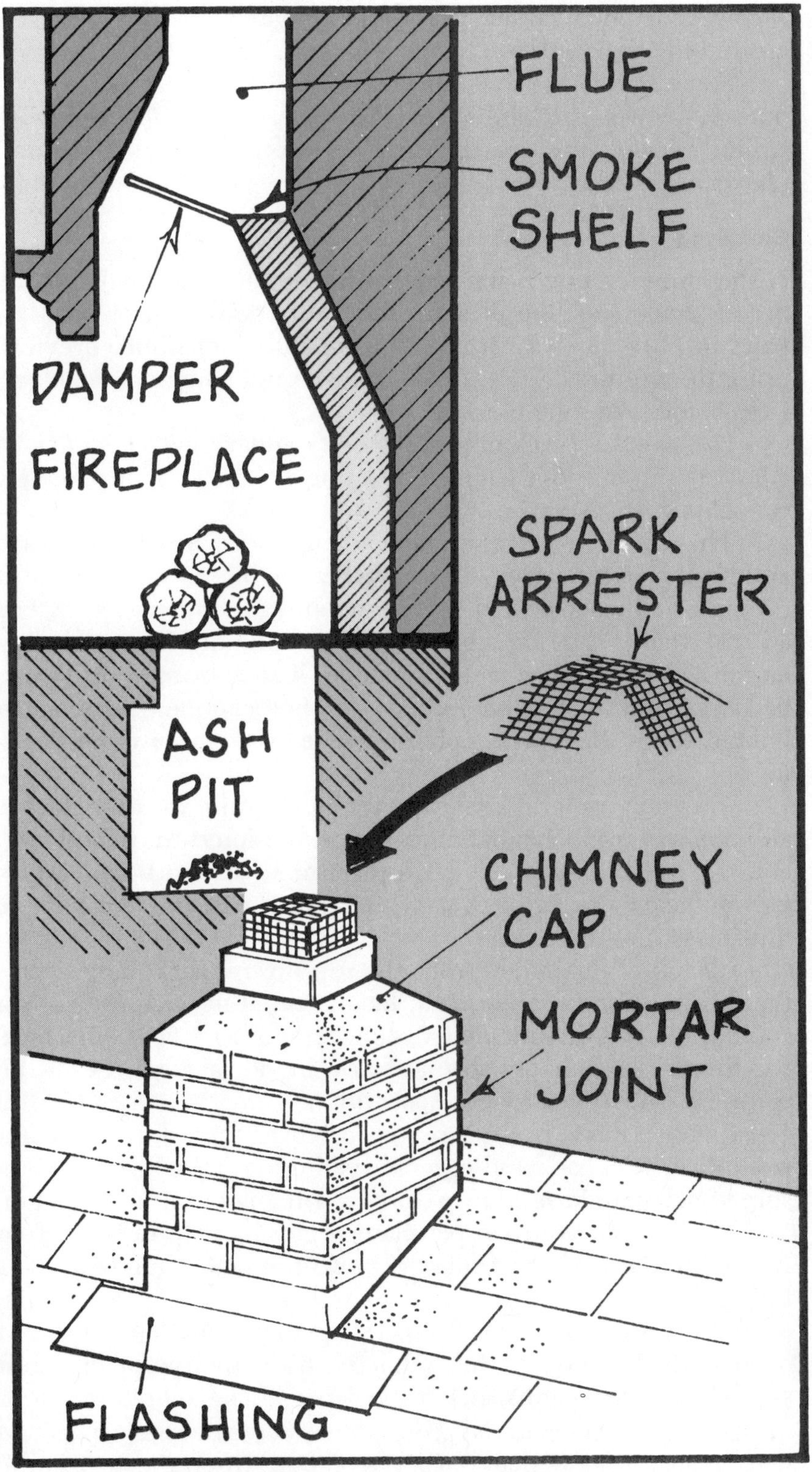

Fireplace areas to check are shown in inset. The spark arrester prevents large cinders from escaping.

replace corroded cotter pins linking parts together and seal around the base with refractory cement.

Some fireplaces have ash pits beneath them, accessible from outside or from the basement. If yours has one, empty the ashes from it, and ensure that the opening leading to it from the fireplace floor is clear.

Cleaning

If the chimney flue is damaged—deteriorated mortar joints between sections of flue tiles are the most common problem—repairs must be made or a replacement flue liner installed before using the fireplace. Obtain bids from several chimney-repair services before ordering the work.

However, if the chimney has been regularly cleaned and is in good condition, do-it-yourself cleaning is a messy but relatively easy chore.

The chief items of equipment you will need are a bristle brush and flexible extension handles called canes. These are available at fireplace and woodstove supply stores and at home centers. Select a brush that is the same diameter as the chimney flue or slightly larger if the exact size is not available. A steel-bristled brush can be used to clean tile-lined chimneys. For chimneys with metal linings, use a brush with polypropylene bristles to avoid scratching.

Also rent an industrial-capacity, heavy-duty vacuum cleaner and obtain a trouble light with a long extension cord. In addition, you will need newspapers, a drop cloth, a wire brush and whisk broom, heavy work gloves, safety goggles, a hat, and a disposable dust mask.

Cleaning a chimney from the top downward is easiest, but the job can also be done from below. In either case, wait for a cool, windless day. Shut all doors and windows in the room where the fireplace is situated so that warm indoor air will rise in the chimney, carrying dislodged soot with it.

Remove items from the room or cover them for protection from dust. Roll back and cover carpeting near the hearth. Then spread newspapers or a drop cloth over the floor of the fireplace.

Next, remove the damper plate, if possible, by working it free from its hinges. If you cannot remove the plate, simply open it fully.

Afterward, cover the fireplace opening completely using a drop cloth. If there is a mantelpiece, drape the top of the cloth over it and use weights such as books or bricks to hold the cloth in place. Tape the material around the sides if there are gaps and leave plenty of loose material at the bottom. Insert the hose of the vacuum beneath the drop cloth and into the fireplace opening, but leave the canister on the outside.

Turn the vacuum cleaner on, then climb to the roof with the brushes, canes, and trouble light. Attach a cane to the brush and insert it into the top of the chimney. Work the brush up and down about a dozen times to clean the upper area of the flue. Use firm pressure, but avoid vigorous brushing that might damage interior mortar joints. Continue to brush, gradually extending the cane as far as you can reach. Then check your work by shining the light into the chimney. If you are satisfied, attach a second cane, repeat the process, then add a third cane and so forth. When the chimney has been cleaned all the way to the bottom, disassemble the brush and return to the ground.

Turn off the vacuum, wait at least an hour for the soot inside the fireplace to settle, then finish the job by cleaning the fireplace.

To clean a chimney from the bottom, attach the brush to a cane and insert it into the chimney before covering the fireplace opening. Afterward, gather a portion of the cover around the cane, then work the brush up and down inside the chimney as you gradually extend the brush toward the top, adding canes when necessary.

If the chimney has a cap on top, be careful not to dislodge it as you reach the final stages of cleaning. When you are finished, withdraw the brush and allow the soot to settle before shining the trouble light upward to inspect the interior.

After cleaning the chimney by either method, operate the vacuum cleaner again for several minutes after the soot has settled. Then remove the cover from the fireplace opening and gather up the newspapers from the fireplace floor. Dispose of these together with the debris inside.

To clean the fireplace, begin by spreading a new layer of newspapers over the floor. Then use the wire brush, whisk broom, and vacuum for cleaning, starting with the smoke shelf at the top. The smoke shelf is the ledge on which the damper rests. Although it is an awkward area, it should be cleaned thoroughly even if you must brush soot from it with a gloved hand. When cleaning the rest of the fireplace, the least messy technique is to hold the vacuum cleaner in one hand and keep it close to the brush held in the other. When brushing, use gentle strokes to avoid producing clouds of soot.

Clean the damper plate. Reinstall it if it has been removed. Set it in the closed position until the fireplace is to be used again. Brush off and vacuum the fireplace back and sides, and then the hearth. After you are finished, dust and vacuum the room. Finally, unroll the carpet and restore the furnishings.

Locating and Repairing Roof Leaks

A **wet spot on the top floor ceiling is usually the first** sign of a leaking roof. Early spring is the season for roof leaks. Most often, the cause is wind-driven rain penetrating roofing that has been weakened or damaged by recent winter weather.

The first step in fixing a leak is to drain the accumulated water that has caused the wet spot. Otherwise, the spot is likely to spread, requiring major repair. To drain the water, drill one or more holes in the spot. Approximately three holes, each ¼ inch in diameter, should be sufficient to drain a 6-inch-diameter spot.

Catch the water in a pan. Later, the holes can be filled with spackling compound and the spot repainted.

Next, try to find the source of the leak from indoors. Unfortunately, this is not always easy. Water can travel in several directions and for some distance over rafters and other roof framing from the point at which it enters the roof to the point at which it is noticed.

If the roof rafters are visible in the attic, inspect them carefully with a flashlight. During or just after a rain, look for wet spots on the rafters or sheathing—the boards or plywood sheets against which the rafters rest. During dry weather, have a helper spray the roof with a garden hose while you watch for spots or drips to appear. During dry weather you may even be able to see sunlight through holes in damaged roofing.

Pay particular attention to areas near the chimney and plumbing vent, and where dormers project or where roof sections join at angles to each other. All of these places normally are protected by metal flashing on the outside of the roof. However, if the flashing has deteriorated or is improperly installed, water may penetrate it or trickle past faulty seams.

When you find a leak, drive a nail or poke a piece of stiff wire through it to mark its position on the outside of the roof. All leaks must be repaired from outside.

If the attic is finished so that the rafters are not visible, or if there is no attic above the ceiling, you will have to find the source of the leak by inspecting the exterior of the roof.

For safety reasons, do this only on a dry day without wind. Be sure the ladder is well braced, and wear soft-soled shoes that provide a sure footing. Climb only onto roofs with low or moderate slope that rises toward the peak at a rate of no more than 4 inches per foot of horizontal distance measured along the gable ends.

Working on more steeply sloped roofs requires special equipment and skills. Roofs covered with wood shingles, shakes, slate, or tile generally are too steep for amateurs to climb. If a leak develops in one of these roofs, call a professional roofing contractor.

To find the source of a leak on the exterior of a roof, first measure indoors from the evidence of the leak to some object that is visible both inside and outside the house, such as the chimney, a dormer, or a window. Then go outside and measure the same distance from the object along the roof.

Begin searching from that point. Because water cannot flow uphill you need not look between the point and the lower edges of the roof. However, hunt above the point as far as the roof line and several feet to each side. Look for curled, torn, or missing shingles; split seams or cracks in flat and roll roofing; and corroded or otherwise deteriorated flashing. Also inspect for open seams in the flashing where it meets the parts of the house it is designed to protect.

Of course, if you have located the leak source from inside, you need only search for the protruding nail or wire inserted through it.

Nearly all leaks can be successfully patched without replacing the damaged roofing material. To patch curled shingles or the edges of flat roofing, or a shingle that will not lie flat, brush away any debris, then liberally apply roofing cement to the underside of the curled or lifted material and to the area beneath it. Press the layers of roofing together and weight them with two or three bricks for an hour or two until the cement hardens. To patch a

TIP:

Professional roofers caution against adding holes to a roof by driving nails from below to mark leaks. An alternative to this method is to estimate the location of the spot by the methods described on page 59.

ATTENTION

blister in flat or roll roofing that has cracked (unbroken blisters are seldom the cause of leaks and can be left alone), obtain asphalt-saturated cotton fabric from a roofing supply company. Slit the blister with a sharp knife, force plastic or asphalt roofing cement beneath the raised material, and press the roofing flat. Spread more roofing cement over the repair and then press the fabric into it, making sure the fabric bonds completely. Finish by troweling a layer of cement over the fabric and several inches beyond it. Smooth the cement so there are no ridges to collect water.

To patch a torn or damaged asphalt shingle, first cut a piece of metal flashing or spare aluminum siding to a rectangle large enough to cover the damaged shingle and extend 3 inches beneath the shingles on each side. Carefully raise the damaged shingle and spread roofing cement liberally underneath. Coat the underside of the metal, slide it into place beneath the raised shingle and beneath the edges of the shingles on both sides, then spread cement on top of the metal and press all of the overlapping shingles, including the damaged one, down on top. Weight the shingles until the cement hardens.

Patch small holes in flashing by covering them with roofing cement. For holes larger than a square inch, coat them with cement, press on a patch made from additional flashing cut 1 inch larger on all sides than the damaged areas, then cover the entire repair with cement.

Repairing Asphalt Roof Shingles

Asphalt shingles normally last fifteen to twenty-five years before needing replacement, but they should be inspected annually for wear and repaired promptly if damaged.

To inspect shingles, choose a dry, windless day (for safety) and climb onto the roof. Make sure the ladder is securely braced and wear soft-soled shoes that provide sure footing.

Climb only onto a roof with a low or moderate slope; it should rise toward the peak at a rate of no more than 4 inches per foot of horizontal distance measured along the gable ends. If the roof is steeper than this, have the shingles inspected—and repaired, if necessary—by a licensed roofing contractor.

On the roof, be careful to maintain your balance—and stay away from the roof's edges. (To examine the edges, stand on a ladder.) For extra protection, tie a rope securely around your waist and toss the end to a helper on the ground on the other side of the roof. The helper should then tie the rope to something solid like a tree or porch railing—but never a vehicle, which may be driven away inadvertently with the rope attached!

Look for shingles that seem dried out, cracked, or worn. If the gritty coating on shingles (designed to protect the asphalt from sunlight) seems thin or is missing, this is a sign that the shingles are wearing out and that reroofing may be necessary.

Shingles that have curled upward or have cracked or torn require immediate repair to prevent roof leaks.

Choose a warm, sunny day for repairing shingles so that they will be pliable. To repair a curled shingle, carefully lift it and

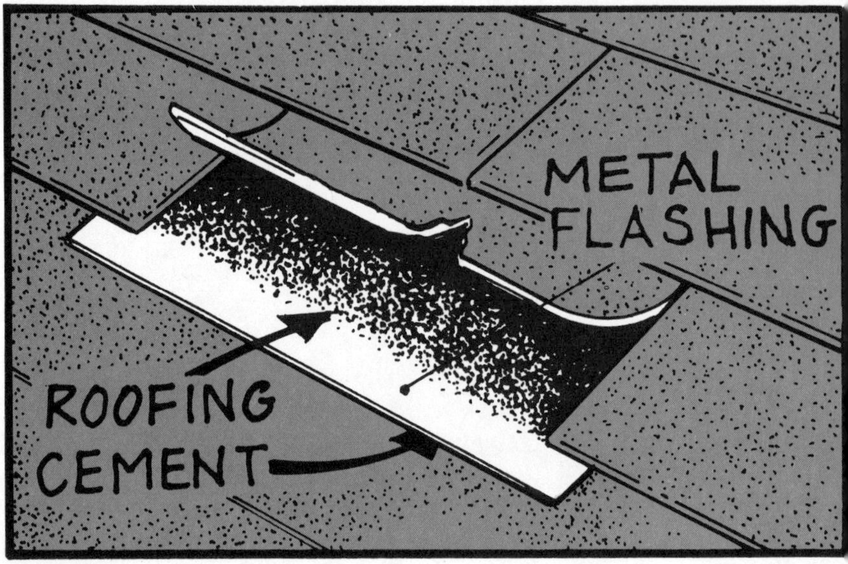

A quick repair for a damaged shingle tab is to cement a sheet of metal flashing beneath it.

sweep away any dirt beneath it with a whisk broom. If the shingle is partly sealed down, gently loosen it with a putty knife.

Also with a putty knife, apply a generous dab of asphalt or plastic roofing cement (available in cans at hardware stores) to the underside of the shingle, about 2 inches from the edge at each corner.

Press the shingle flat by standing on it for a few moments. If the shingle lifts again when you raise your foot, weight it down with a brick or some other heavy object for several hours until the cement hardens.

If a nail has loosened and risen beneath a shingle, first pry it out with a pry bar or claw hammer. Place a scrap of plywood beneath the tool when prying to avoid marring undamaged shingles.

Next, carefully lift the shingle fastened by the nail, prying it up with a putty knife if necessary. Apply roofing cement beneath the shingle to cover the hole, then reseal the shingle by pressing it flat.

Install a new roofing nail into the shingle about an inch to one side of the sealed hole. Then apply roofing cement over the entire area to reseal the shingle above.

To repair a torn shingle from which no pieces are missing, apply roofing cement on the underside to cover the damage and press the shingle flat so that the torn pieces fit together. Then cover the top of the tear with cement, smoothing the surface so that it will not trap water.

If a tear extends beneath a row of shingles, or if pieces of a shingle are missing, proper repair depends on how much of the shingle is damaged. Most asphalt shingles are divided into either two or three sections, called tabs, by slits extending about halfway across the shingle's width. If only one tab is damaged, the shingle can be repaired with a patch. If more than one tab is damaged, the entire shingle should be replaced.

To repair a shingle with a patch, first pry up the nails holding the damaged tab. Fit the pry bar around the nail shaft under the tab and pry upward to lift the nail; then fit the bar around the nail head on top of the tab to pull the nail completely free. Use a scrap block to protect undamaged shingles.

Also remove nails passing through the tab that fasten overlapping shingles. Then lift the overlapping shingles to expose the top of the tab; if you cannot, remove nails from the next higher row of shingles as well.

Cut the damaged tab from the rest of the shingle with tinsnips, using the slots in the shingle as guides. Remove the tab by pulling it out.

Mend damaged building paper beneath the tab by nailing new paper over it and covering the nail heads with roofing cement. If the sheathing beneath the paper has rotted, minor dam-

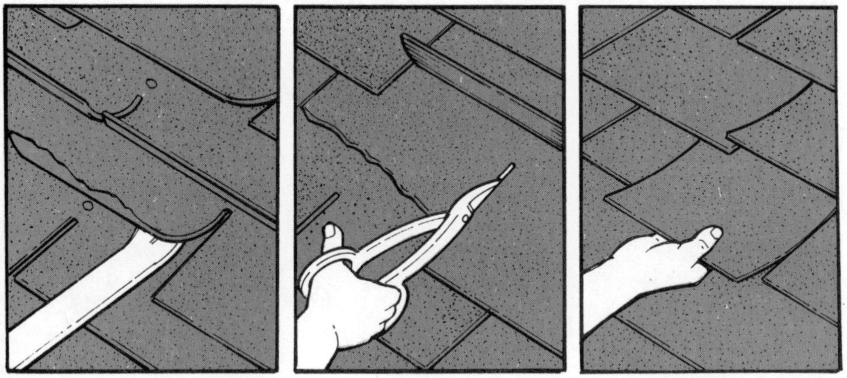

To patch a shingle tab, first remove the damaged tab by prying out the nails and cutting the tab free from the rest of the shingle with tinsnips. Then coat the exposed area with cement and slide the patch into place. Add cement and new nails under the overlapping row of shingles.

age can be repaired with two-part wood hardener available at hardware stores. If decay is extensive, repair the shingle to prevent a leak, but have the roof professionally inspected as soon as possible.

Use the damaged tab as a pattern for cutting a patch from a new shingle. To install the patch, first apply roofing cement to the area it will cover, then slide the patch into place so that its lower edge is even with those of the shingles on each side.

Next, drive two roofing nails through the patch about 1 inch from each side. Place the nails below the adhesive strip that is part of the top of the patch, but make sure they will be covered by the overlapping shingles.

Finally, refasten and reseal the overlapping shingles by following the procedure for repairing a loosened nail.

To replace an entire shingle or an area of shingles, proceed as described above, except that cutting shingles should be unnecessary. When removing a group of shingles, start with the uppermost and work down.

When fastening new shingles, drive nails at the positions marked on each shingle by the manufacturer. If there are no marks, use neighboring shingles as guides.

To replace shingles along a roof peak, professionals generally follow the steps for patching. But an easier method is to cover the damaged shingles with roofing cement and place individual tabs cut from new shingles on top, overlapping them if several are required.

Apply cement between overlapping tabs. Fasten each tab at the corners with roofing nails and cover their heads with cement also.

Repairing Flat Roofs

Flat or nearly flat roofs are usually built up of several layers of roofing felt and either coal tar or asphalt. A layer of gravel or marble chips is often spread over the surface to protect it and to reflect heat.

Other types of flat or near-flat roofs consist of roll roofing—long strips of material the same as that used for asphalt shingles—or metal, usually galvanized steel or aluminum, but sometimes cooper or terne (a copper-bearing steel).

Most metal roofing requires little or no attention. However, built-up and roll roofing should be inspected at least twice a year and repaired promptly if damaged.

When composition roofing—as both built-up and roll roofing are called—develops small cracks due to the hardening and shrinking of the tar or asphalt, or shows other early signs of deterioration, applying liquid roof coating can prolong its life.

Roof coating seals and protects the existing roofing. It is available in 5-gallon containers at hardware stores and home centers either as a black or metallic liquid. The material is thicker than paint but not as thick as tar, and is applied with a long-handled brush resembling a small push broom.

Both types of coating contain asphalt. Black roof coating generally contains more and therefore has greater sealing and waterproofing ability. But the metallic coating contains aluminum and reflects heat that can weaken the roofing material and increase energy bills.

TIP:

The chief reason for using a reflective aluminum coating is to prevent deterioration of the black roofing material over which the coating is applied. A high-quality aluminum coating will add years of life to an asphalt roof besides reducing temperatures under the roof.

ATTENTION

TIP:

Patching material made of asphalt-saturated cotton fabric, which eliminates the need to add new nails when repairing flat roofs, is also available. To use it, slit and patch the blister, then cover the area with roofing cement. Press the fabric into the cement, then trowel on another layer. Allow to harden.

ATTENTION

To apply roof coating, wait for a dry period of warm or hot weather. Wear old clothes and shoes that can be discarded later. Make any spot repairs necessary (these are described further on), then sweep the roof free of loose material. Roof coating can be applied to metal roofs after scouring them with a wire brush to remove rust or corrosion.

Stir the coating thoroughly before use. Dip the brush into the container and begin spreading the material at the point farthest from the ladder so that you can coat the entire roof and still climb down. Spread the coating about an eighth of an inch thick or at the rate specified by the manufacturer.

For maximum waterproofing when applying aluminum roof coating, brush in one direction only and use a minimum of strokes. When you are finished, dispose of the brush rather than attempt to clean it. Tools and hard, smooth surfaces can usually be cleaned with mineral spirits. Unused coating can be stored for up to three years if closed tightly and kept from freezing.

Do not rely on roof coating to stop leaks or repair damaged roofing. If the condition is severe, consult a professional roofer. However, you can repair minor problems like isolated blisters and torn roofing yourself without much trouble.

If you discover a blister in the roofing, first sweep loose material away from the area. Then slit the blister open along its length—one layer at a time if the roof is built up—using either a utility knife or a hook-nosed linoleum-cutting knife.

Examine the interior of the blister. If the layers are dry, the problem usually is not serious. Generally, the cause is poorly adhering felts. To fix, use a putty knife to apply asphalt or plastic roofing cement—a thick black compound resembling tar—into the blister on each side. Then press the area flat.

Spread a ¼-inch-thick layer of roofing cement over the repair and about 3 inches beyond it on all sides. Cut a patch of asphalt-saturated repair fabric (available at supply stores) to fit over the entire area. Press the fabric into the cement, making sure it is completely embedded. Then cover the patch and surrounding area with additional roofing cement, troweled smooth.

Blisters that are wet inside indicate a leak. Squeeze as much moisture as possible from the roofing by standing on the spot, then prop the blister open with a small stick to permit complete drying. Repair the blister as described, but also locate and repair the source of the leak—usually torn roofing or parapet flashing, or cracks around roof openings—to prevent its recurrence.

To repair torn roofing, first sweep away any loose debris. Then, using a straightedge and a utility or a linoleum-cutting knife, cut out a square or rectangle of roofing around the spot. On a built-up roof, cut only as deep as the damaged layer.

Carefully pry out the cut section and use it to trace a patch onto 15-pound or heavier roofing felt thick enough to fill the opening.

Cut the patch. Spread roofing cement over the bottom of the opening and around the edges, then press the patch into place, making sure it adheres completely.

Nail the patch around the perimeter using roofing nails spaced an inch or two apart. Cover the patch with additional cement, then proceed as for repairing a blister. Cover the final layer of cement with gravel, if desired, for appearance.

To patch parapet flashing, first pry up the metal cap protecting the ridge. Apply roofing cement to the damaged area, then cover it with a layer of new flashing material that extends 3 inches beyond the damage on all sides.

Place the upper edge of the new flashing so it will be covered by the metal cap when it is reinstalled. Cement a larger piece of new flashing over the first. Cover it with roofing cement, then reinstall the cap.

To repair cracked seams around vents, chimneys, and other roof openings, apply roofing cement generously to the area.

TIP:

Instead of attaching a second patch with nails, material can be applied as described in the tip on page 66.

ATTENTION

Slit and fill a cracked blister with roofing cement. Press roofing flat and cover with more cement, followed by cotton repair fabric. Finish with a third layer of cement, troweled several inches beyond the patch.

Curing Basement Leaks

Spring rains and thawing temperatures often cause base-ment walls to develop leaks. Unfortunately, while the ground is still frozen or is too muddy to excavate, there is usually little you can do to cure basement leaks the most effective way, by repairing them on the outside of the foundation walls and/or regrading the landscape. But there are several measures you can take that will remedy most problems at least until warmer weather arrives. Sometimes these techniques work so well that no further repairs are necessary.

Of course, the easiest leaks to fix are those that never start. A successful and frequently overlooked strategy is merely keeping water away from the foundation. To do this, regularly inspect gutters and downspouts and clear them if they become clogged with ice and debris. Check that their sections do not separate at the seams or loosen from the building, thus enabling water to spill out.

Be sure that stone or concrete splash blocks are placed under downspouts that do not enter ground-level drainpipes. Splash blocks keep water rushing from the downspouts away from walls and also absorb its impact.

Because of the force with which water falls from rooftop height, any water that misses a splash block can soak deep into the soil along a foundation. And because downspouts deliver so much water to such a small area, the chances of basement leaks nearby are high.

TIP:

After repairing individual leaks, walls can be further waterproofed by applying masonry sealer, a penetrating paint containing cement and sealers like synthetic rubber. It is sold in home centers.

Before applying, prepare the walls by removing all old paint and washing the surface with muriatic-acid solution to remove powdery salt deposits called

(cont. on opposite page)

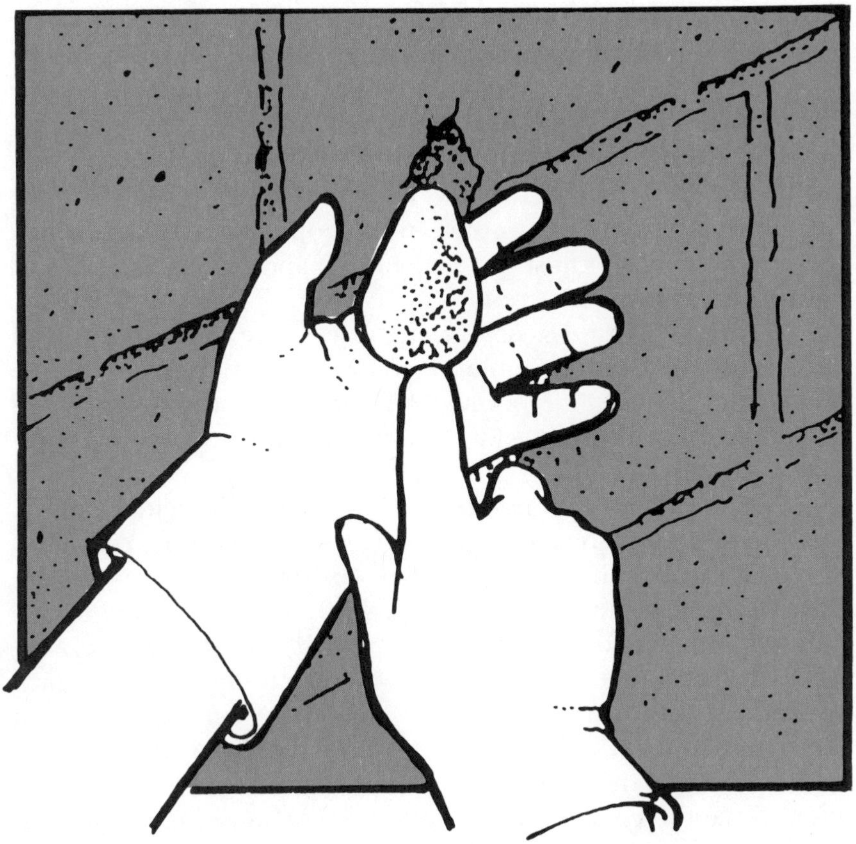

A plug of hydraulic cement will seal a hole even when water is running through it.

TIP (cont.)

efflorescence. Acid solution is sold at home centers; when using it, wear gloves, eye protection, and suitable clothing. Follow all instructions printed on the container.

Apply the sealer with a masonry paintbrush. Adequate ventilation is necessary and the temperature in the basement must be above 50°F. Work the material into the pores of the surface at the coverage rate specified by the manufacturer. Cover the bottom third of the wall and any areas of general seepage first. Wait twenty-four hours for the sealer to dry, then apply a second coat over the entire surface.

ATTENTION

In winter, keep splash blocks free of ice and snow so that water will be deflected in the right direction. Also, avoid piling shoveled snow against the foundation or in areas where melting snow will likely travel toward the building.

Do not let snow accumulate in basement window wells. And keep wells free of leaves, which can block the flow of water into the drain or the layer of gravel at the base of the well.

Where winters are severe, consider installing window well covers. These large, clear plastic bubbles, which are available at home centers, are designed to keep rain and snow out of window wells while letting light enter. They insulate windows by acting as a greenhouse, and can be vented in summer.

If a basement leak does appear, try to find and seal its source. Use caulking compound to close seams around basement windows and door frames, and where sidewalks, steps, or porches meet

TIP:

Chronic basement leaks are usually caused by saturated ground exerting pressure against foundation walls. Besides remedying the problem by trenching around the foundation to install drainpipes and apply waterproofing material or compound to exterior walls, another treatment involves trenching to install drainpipes around the inside of the basement walls instead of the outside. Both methods are the province of professional basement waterproofers; these are listed in the telephone book.

ATTENTION

foundation masonry. Replace and caulk packing that has come loose from openings where plumbing, gas, or electrical supply lines enter the house, and where dryer or other appliance vents penetrate.

If cracks or holes in the masonry itself are the problem, hydraulic cement is usually the answer. This is a type of quick-setting cement that hardens in minutes, even in openings through which water is flowing. Because the cement expands as it sets, it bonds tightly with existing concrete.

To apply hydraulic cement, first use a wire brush to scrub all loose material from the hole or crack. For best results, enlarge breaks slightly using a hammer and cold chisel or masonry chisel to shape the gap so it is wider toward the inside of the masonry than at the surface.

Put on rubber gloves, because the cement is mildly caustic. Mix the cement with cold water in accordance with the container instructions until the mixture is the consistency of soft modeling clay. Do not overmix: Hydraulic cement hardens in three to five minutes and will do so even more rapidly if stirred excessively.

If the opening is a hole with water running through, form the cement with your hands into a cone about 4 inches long with the base about an inch wider than the hole. Wait two or three minutes or until the cone begins to feel warm, a sign of hardening. Then force the cone point-first into the hole and press against it for three to five minutes until it hardens further. Afterward, trim the edges or smooth the surface if desired, using a mason's trowel or putty knife.

To close a leaking crack, apply cement (also at the warm stage) using a trowel or putty knife. Press repeatedly with the tool along the filled seam until the cement hardens.

Fill deep cracks and holes only to within half an inch of their surface. After the cement hardens, apply a second layer to fill them completely. If no water is flowing from a break to be repaired, dampen the area thoroughly with a sponge just before applying the cement.

Water seeping through the seam where basement walls meet the floor presents a different problem. Because the floor often settles slightly, particularly when the soil beneath it becomes saturated in spring, a more elastic filler is necessary. The best is epoxy waterproofing compound made for the purpose and available at home centers.

To apply the compound, mix it according to the manufacturer's instructions. Generally it is a two-part product containing resins plus a hardening agent. Using a wire brush, scrub loose debris away from the seam; then ladle or pour the epoxy into the crack. Smooth the material as it hardens, using a mason's trowel, or for a neater appearance, an old kitchen spoon.

An alternative to waterproofing compound is interior drain channel. This resembles square-edged plastic pipe. Although it does not plug leaks, it collects water seeping from the seam around the basement floor and carries it away, usually to the drain found at the lowest point in the floor of most basements.

If the walls are solid masonry, install the drain channel simply by cementing the sections to the floor and against the wall, using the sealer provided. Water seeping from the seam will flow into the channel from behind it and travel inside to the drain.

If the walls are hollow concrete block, drill small holes into the bottom row of blocks before installing the channel. The holes allow water that collects in the blocks to drain.

Repairing Wallboard

Wallboard, also called drywall or by popular brand names such as Sheetrock, consists of a layer of gypsum sheathed in heavy paper. Although easier to install and more economical than plaster, which it has all but replaced as a building material, it is more easily damaged and sometimes also develops flaws as wooden framing to which it is attached ages or settles.

Happily, most damaged wallboard can be repaired by amateurs, even those with little experience in home repair. Success lies in working patiently and with a light touch. Most important is leveling the repair so that the patched surface will be imperceptible beneath new finish.

Small Repairs

To fix a small dent, such as one made by a doorknob bumping the wall, first roughen the paint covering the damaged area. Use medium- or fine-grit sandpaper. Then fill the depression with spackling compound (a quick-drying paste made especially for repairing minor wallboard damage) or joint compound (an adhesive filler used for joining wallboard panels). Both products are similar in most respects and can be used interchangeably for small repairs. They are available premixed in containers at hardware stores and home centers.

Apply the filler using a flexible-blade putty knife wide enough to cover the damaged area. Usually a 4-inch-wide knife is sufficient. Load approximately half the width of the blade with

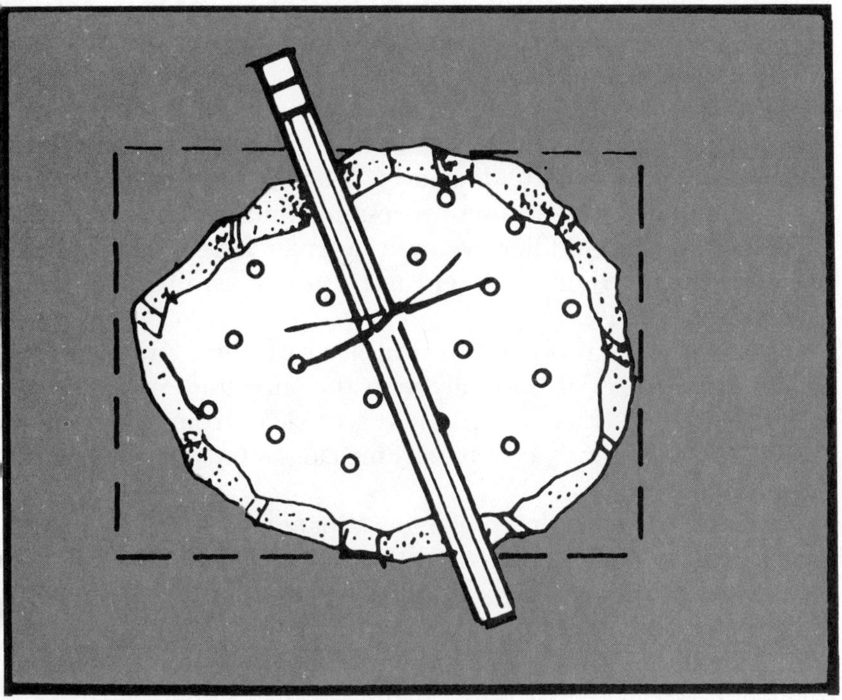

Attach backing against the wall with compound. Clamp with a pencil and wire until dry.

ller. Then, with the knife held almost parallel to the wall, spread ıe material by drawing the knife across the damaged area.

Wipe away excess filler by holding the knife almost perpen-icular to the wall and drawing the blade over the spot again. Best esults are obtained by making this stroke at a right angle to the revious ones.

Fill shallow dents in one application. Dents deeper than half n inch should be filled in two stages, with time allowed between ıem for the first layer of filler to dry. This may take from a few ıinutes to several hours, depending on the type of filler used, the ze of the patch, and the humidity level. Drying times are printed n the container.

After the final layer of filler has dried, sand the area smooth nd level with the surrounding surface. Use fine-grit sandpaper rapped around a flat wooden block or a sanding block sold for ıe purpose. Sanding spackling and joint compounds produces ust that travels readily through the air, clogging nasal passages nd, in large amounts, causing upper respiratory irritation. A amp cloth is best for wiping up sanding dust. If you have more han a few areas to sand, close off the room to prevent a mess and

TIP:

For repairing small holes quickly, self-sticking and iron-on patches with instructions are available at hardware stores, as are patches made of fiberglass mesh that require covering with joint compound. These resist impact well but may not bond to surrounding wallboard as strongly under all conditions as solid patches.

ATTENTION

wear a government-approved dust mask suitable for protection against nontoxic airborne particles. These are inexpensive and available at hardware stores.

If the wallboard is to be covered with wallpaper or textured paint, or if a faint outline of the patched area is acceptable, consider the repair complete. However, for an imperceptible repair, repeat the filling and sanding process again, using an 8-inch-wide putty knife to spread filler over a broader surface. For prominent areas like a living room wall, repeat the process a third time, using an even wider knife.

In each case, apply only a thin layer of filler, and blend the edges of the material smoothly with the surrounding wallboard. Sand gently, and brush the patched area clean from time to time. Do not allow the sandpaper to become clogged with dust, or it can gouge the filler.

Before painting or applying wallpaper over repaired wallboard, always coat the patches with primer. This seals them, further helping to conceal their outlines beneath paint, and prevents wallpaper from adhering to them permanently.

Sometimes nails used to fasten wallboard loosen, producing small bulges called nail pops in the surface. Repairing these is similar to repairing dents but you will need an assistant and either 1¼-inch wallboard screws or 1½-inch ring-shank wallboard nails.

While the assistant presses hard against the wallboard near the protruding nail, drive a new fastener into the wallboard and stud about an inch and a half away from the nail. Sink screws so that the heads lie slightly below the surface but do not tear the panel's paper sheathing.

Drive nails flush with the surface then strike them once more. The extra blow should depress the nail below the surface and create a dimple in the wallboard, but it should not tear the paper.

If an existing nail is so loose that it can be wiggled, remove it with pliers. Then strike the area with a hammer to dimple it. If the nail is not loose, use a nail set to drive it back into the wallboard, then dimple the area. Fill and sand the dimple with spackling or joint compound, as described above.

To repair small holes, first trim away any loose wallboard. Then, if the opening is less than an inch in diameter, pack it to within a quarter of an inch of the surface with cotton or with fiberglass insulation. Fill the remainder of the hole with spackling or joint compound, then finish as described earlier.

For holes up to approximately 4 inches in diameter, begin by drawing a square or rectangle around the damaged area using a pencil or straightedge. Cut away the wallboard within the outline, and make a patch the same size from scrap wallboard. For cutting, use a wallboard saw or a keyhole saw, both inexpensive handsaws with short, pointed blades approximately 6 inches long.

To create a makeshift handle, drive a screw into the center of the wallboard patch, leaving about half an inch exposed. Coat the sides of the patch with spackling or joint compound, then insert it into the opening so that it is approximately an eighth of an inch below the level of the surrounding surface. Scrape away the excess filler while holding the screw, and avoid wiggling the patch. After the filler has dried, remove the screw and fill the depression.

Large Repairs

Repairing holes larger than 4 inches across requires modest carpentry skills and sometimes ingenuity. Patches for large holes must be braced from behind to create a surface to which the patch can be fastened.

To repair holes up to 6 or 8 inches square, use perforated hardboard (commonly called pegboard) as backing.

Begin by using a sharp utility knife to trim away all loose wallboard from the edges of the hole. Then measure the hole and draw on the pegboard a square or rectangle whose sides will extend about an inch beyond the hole all the way around. Cut out the piece, using a saw.

Thread a length of thin wire, such as picture wire, down through a hole near the center of the piece and up again through a hole nearby. Twist the ends together to form a strong loop about 2 inches long.

Spread a layer of joint compound about a quarter of an inch thick around the perimeter of the piece. Then fit the piece through the hole so that when it is positioned parallel to the wall its compound-coated side will be against the inside of the wallboard. You may have to notch the edges of the trimmed hole with the knife to fit the backing piece through it.

When the piece has been inserted, grip the loop and pull the piece firmly against the inside of the wall, spreading the joint compound. Slip a pencil or a length of dowel longer than the width of the hole into the loop and twist it like a propeller to pull the piece tight. Leave the pencil in place as a clamp until the compound dries, which usually takes eight to twelve hours.

When the compound is dry, remove the loop. Fill the hole to within a quarter of an inch of the surface by applying joint compound to the backing piece using a flexible-blade putty knife.

After this compound dries, add another layer about an eighth of an inch thick to fill any cracks that have developed. After it

TIP:

Dried spackling or joint compound that requires only light sanding can be smoothed by rubbing it gently with a damp sponge instead of sandpaper. This method creates no dust; however, some practice is required. Rinse the sponge frequently; after smoothing, allow dampened filler to dry completely before applying finish.

ATTENTION

dries, apply a final layer to bring the repair level with or approximately a sixteenth of an inch higher than the surface.

Spread the compound in the final layer an inch or so beyond the edges of the hole. Use a putty knife or wallboard-finishing knife wider than the repair to create a smooth surface. When the compound is dry, wrap fine-grit sandpaper around a block of wood (or use a wallboard-sanding sponge, available at hardware stores) and sand the compound level with the surrounding area.

For the smoothest repair, apply another thin layer of compound after this, spreading it even farther beyond the perimeter of the hole. Sand the compound after it dries. With both methods, brush a coat of primer over the final sanded surface before repainting it or applying wallpaper.

To repair holes larger than 8 inches square, it is usually easiest to cut away the wallboard surrounding the damage all the way to the nearest wall stud or ceiling joist on each side.

Begin by making a pair of parallel saw cuts, one above and one below the damaged area, between the studs or joists. Then saw straight lines to join the ends of the cuts, using the inside edges of the studs or joists as guides.

After removing the damaged wallboard, build a frame to support the replacement patch. First, cut two strips of one-by-three lumber (this size actually measures $\frac{3}{4}$-inch thick and $2\frac{1}{2}$ inches wide), each 2 inches longer than the sides of the trimmed opening that lie along the studs or joists.

Insert the strips parallel to these framing pieces and fasten them against their sides with nails or drywall screws. The object is to create a lip three quarters of an inch wide (the thickness of a strip) on two sides of the opening. Be sure that the front edges of the strips are flush with those of the studs or joists.

For the next step you will need an electric drywall screwdriver or an electric drill with a screwdriving bit. Cut two strips of the same lumber equal in length to the distance between the strips attached to the studs or joists. Insert them at the top and bottom of the opening, perpendicular to the strips already attached, so that their wide surfaces rest against the inside of the wallboard.

Adjust the strips so that each creates a lip about an inch wide. Then, while holding them in place, fasten them by installing drywall screws through the wallboard above and below the opening. Sink the heads of the screws slightly below the surface of the wall, but avoid tearing the wallboard's paper facing.

Cut a patch of replacement wallboard equal to the dimensions of the opening. Fit it into place, then fasten it with drywall screws to all four sides of the frame.

If you cannot obtain a tool for installing drywall pipes, substitute 4-inch-wide (or wider) strips of wallboard for the second pair of wooden strips. Cement these with joint compound to the inside of the wallboard above and below the opening to create a lip about 1½ inches wide.

After the compound dries, spread additional compound onto the exposed portions of the strips. Then cut a patch of replacement wallboard, fit it into the opening, and fasten it to the wooden strips with nails. Gently press the two remaining sides against the compound-covered strips.

To hide the patch regardless of how it is fastened, cover all the seams with joint compound and wallboard-finishing tape. After the compound dries, add another layer of compound. Sand this layer when it dries and repeat the process one or two more times if desired. Brush on a coat of primer before applying paint or wallpaper.

Repairing Plaster

Most older homes and apartments, but some newer buildings as well, have plaster walls and ceilings. Although plaster has a harder surface and resists wear better than wallboard, cracking and the loosening of plaster from walls or ceilings is common. Poor mixing or improper application can cause plaster to deteriorate, but most often problems are caused by settling of the structure or by moisture. If you find that moisture is at fault, remedy the condition first before repairing the plaster. Damage can also be caused when furniture hits the wall or when fasteners are improperly installed.

Plaster wall finishes usually consist of three layers: two that form a base coat of coarse gypsum with sand or animal hair mixed in, and a third, a finish coat, of fine gypsum mixed with lime. In older buildings, plaster is applied directly to masonry or to wood lath—thin horizontal strips. In newer buildings plaster is usually attached to metal mesh lath or to lath consisting of special wallboard (gypsum) panels.

Minor Repairs

Hairline cracks are common in old plaster. They are usually caused by minute shrinking and swelling of the building materials inside the walls and by shrinking of the lime in the finish coat. As long as the plaster surrounding the cracks has not deteriorated, the condition does not signal trouble. But all cracks must be filled before repainting, otherwise they will show through the new paint.

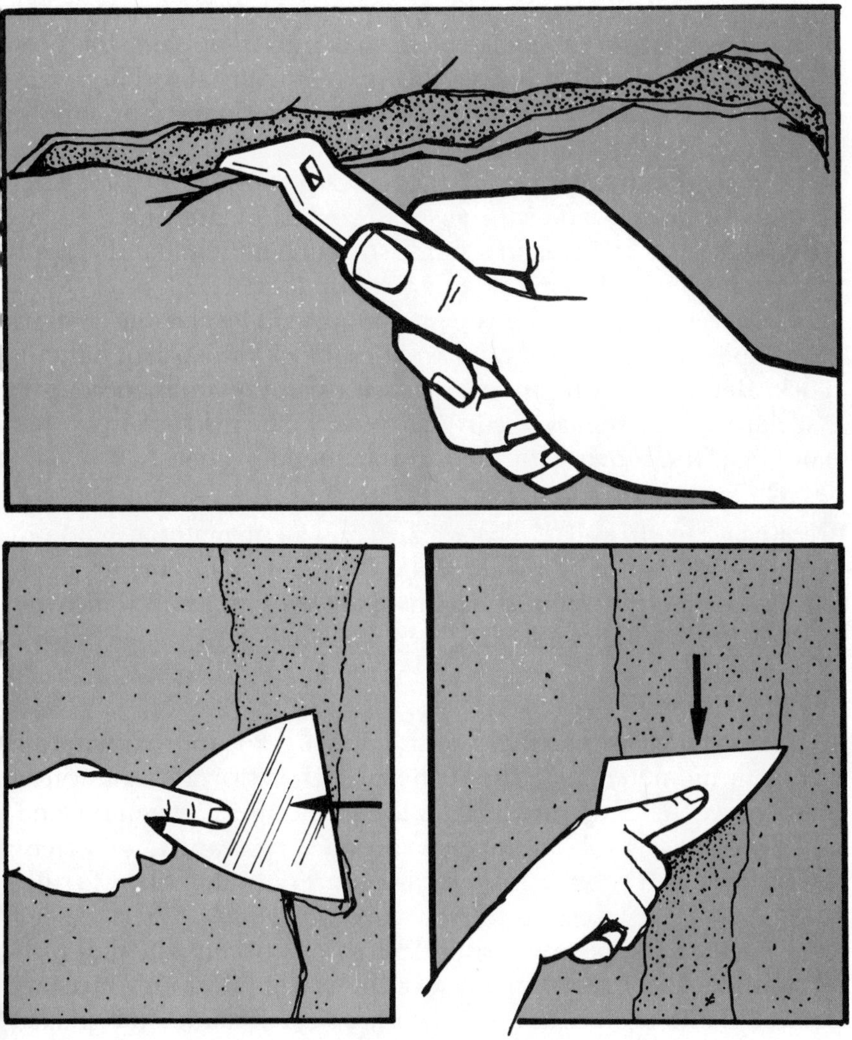

Widen cracks by using the end of a can opener. Apply joint compound or spackling across the surface of the crack at right angles, then smooth and level the repair by drawing the putty knife lengthwise over the filled area.

To fill hairline and other shallow cracks, first use a pointed tool, like the end of a can opener, to widen them enough to accept joint or spackling compound used for wallboard repairs. If possible, undercut the surface of the cracks so the opening is wider inside the crack than at the surface. Brush or vacuum out all debris.

TIP:

Sometimes it is possible to repair areas of loose plaster by injecting construction adhesive through holes drilled in the back of the lath if it is accessible, or the front if it is not. (Construction adhesive comes in cartridges and is applied like caulking compound; the best type to use has a base of acrylic resin.) The plaster must then be pressed against the lath and held with padded boards and a brace until the adhesive dries.

Another method that can be used if the back of the lath is accessible is rekeying. Here, the loose plaster is first braced against the front of the lath as described, then a coat of fresh plaster is applied to the back of the lath to bond with it. Both methods require expertise; amateurs should consult a professional plaster restorationist before proceeding.

Moisten the crack by misting it with water from a spray bottle or a sponge. Allow the moisture to soak into the plaster for a few moments, which will prevent the plaster from absorbing water from the filler and weakening it. Then spread joint compound or spackling over the crack using a putty knife.

Force the material into the crack as you apply it. Then smooth the surface and wipe away any excess by drawing the knife lengthwise over the area in a single stroke. Let the filler dry; apply a second layer if cracking or a depression forms.

If necessary, sand the repair smooth and level using 100-grit sandpaper wrapped around a wooden block or a plastic sanding block. Before covering filled areas with paint or wallpaper, apply a sealer such as shellac according to the filler instructions. Then paint over the repair with the recommended primer.

If a wall has many hairline cracks, consider covering the entire surface with wall canvas or an equivalent material made of fiberglass instead of filling all the cracks before painting or papering. Both covering products are available at paint and wallcovering stores.

Moderate Repairs

To repair larger cracks and holes up to approximately 6 inches in diameter, first check the plaster for overall soundness and remove any loose material. If the plaster flexes when pushed, it has broken away from the lath and must be reanchored or else taken down and replaced. Both procedures are described further on.

Provided the plaster is sound, choose between patching plaster and plaster of paris for making the repair. Both products are essentially the same—powdered, processed gypsum—but plaster of paris hardens in less than half an hour (sometimes in only a few minutes if stirred excessively) and expands more than patching plaster as it sets. Some plasterers feel that the expansion makes plaster of paris bond better to the sides of damaged areas. However, patching plaster, which takes nearly an hour to harden, is easier to use because of the additional working time it provides.

To use plaster of paris or patching plaster, first moisten the cleaned area thoroughly with water, using a spray bottle, sponge, or paintbrush. While the water soaks in, mix a batch of plaster in a container according to the manufacturer's directions. Do not mix more than you can apply before the plaster sets, as once this process has begun, unused plaster must be discarded.

When you have mixed the plaster, wet the damaged area again and immediately apply a layer of plaster to the spot using a drywall-taping knife or a plasterer's trowel. If the damage is deep, apply plaster only to within one quarter of an inch of the surface. When the plaster stiffens, roughen its surface by scratching it in a crisscross pattern with the corner of the putty knife or trowel. Then allow the plaster to harden completely.

The next day or soon after, add a second layer of plaster level with the surface. If several days pass between applications or if the weather is extremely dry, wet the surface of the first layer before adding the second. When the second layer cures, inspect it for cracks. If there are any, fill them with additional plaster.

It is best not to use spackling or joint compound to fill cracks repaired with plaster of paris or patching plaster. Because the synthetic fillers in spackling or joint compound are harder than gypsum, sanding may produce uneven surfaces. When the patch is completely hard and dry, sand it smooth using 100-grit sandpaper and a sanding block. Apply sealer before painting or papering, as described earlier.

Reanchoring Sagging Plaster

If a section of plaster has come away from the lath, it is sometimes possible to reanchor it with drywall screws and dished metal washers called plaster buttons. These are available from plasterers and home renovation suppliers. Install the buttons so their convex side faces out and drive the screws holding them through the plaster and into the lath until the buttons flatten. Use an electric drill or drywall screwgun.

Installing buttons at intervals of about a foot is usually sufficient. Afterward, cover the buttons and screw heads with joint compound or finish plaster (described below) to conceal them. If you are attempting to reanchor loose plaster to metal or gypsum lath, use toggle bolts to fasten the buttons.

Large Repairs

If reanchoring does not work or if damaged areas are larger than 6 inches in diameter, you must take down all loose or cracked plaster and apply a new three-layer finish. For this, you will need base coat and finishing plasters instead of the patching varieties.

Base coat plaster is only sold in large quantities—50-pound bags or heavier. Ingredients for making finishing plaster—lime and gauging plaster—are sometimes available in smaller amounts. All of these materials can be purchased at building supply stores and some home centers.

Start the repair by fastening a piece of new metal mesh lath against any exposed old wooden lath. Use tinsnips to cut the metal lath. The fit should be precise so that the new plaster will be well supported around the edges. Fasten the metal lath to the wood lath with galvanized tie wires, available where you obtain the lath. If you encounter gypsum lath, metal lath can be attached to it with drywall screws.

Next, thoroughly and repeatedly moisten the area in order to soak the existing plaster and wood or gypsum lath. During this time, mix up a batch of base coat plaster by following the manufacturer's instructions. The easiest type to use is a premixed formula with lightweight aggregate. All you have to do is pour it into a bucket of cold water and stir.

Apply the base coat plaster in two layers, each approximately one quarter of an inch thick. After troweling on the first layer, go back and immediately apply the second layer without waiting for the first to stiffen. Plasterers call this process doubling back. The second layer should come to within an eighth of an inch of the surface. Smooth it with the trowel so that no high spots project.

Allow twelve to twenty-four hours for the base coat to harden, then apply the finish plaster. To make finish plaster, obtain gauging plaster and double-hydrated lime. Mix the lime in a bucket with water to form lime putty (the proportions of water to lime are usually printed on the bag) and let the mixture soak for approximately twelve hours until it has the consistency of smooth joint compound. The putty will not harden, so enough for the whole job can be made at one time and kept covered to prevent drying. Lime is caustic, so wear adequate skin and eye protection and a dust mask.

Place a portion of the putty—as much as can be applied in half an hour or so—on a smooth piece of plywood and form it into a doughnut-shaped ring. Fill the center about two thirds full of water, then add gauging plaster to achieve a proportion approximately one part plaster to three parts putty. Mix the materials thoroughly using the trowel until they are smooth and somewhat stiffer than the putty alone.

Spread the mixture in a thin layer over the base coat, pressing it firmly so that the two layers bond. Then double back, smoothing or adding more plaster as necessary to level the surface with the existing plaster. To achieve the smoothest surface possible, mist the plaster lightly, using a spray bottle, as you trowel it.

Wait one to two weeks before sealing and priming the new plaster. If hairline cracks develop, fill them with spackling or joint compound (this is acceptable because finish plaster is harder than plaster of paris or patching plaster) and sand them smooth.

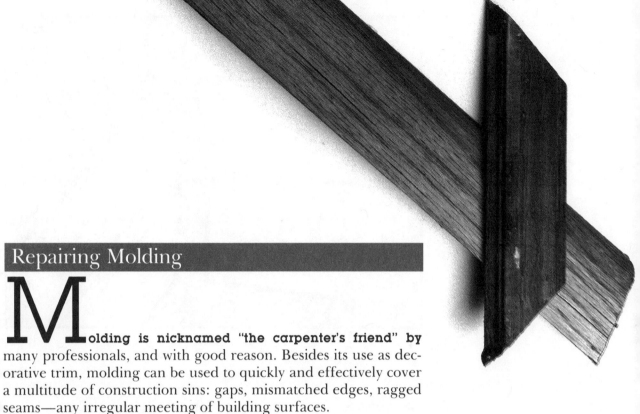

Repairing Molding

Molding is nicknamed "the carpenter's friend" by many professionals, and with good reason. Besides its use as decorative trim, molding can be used to quickly and effectively cover a multitude of construction sins: gaps, mismatched edges, ragged seams—any irregular meeting of building surfaces.

Damaged molding can sometimes be repaired with wood filler or patching compound designed for restoring damaged wood. After the material dries it is sanded level and then may be painted or finished to match the existing molding. However, read labels carefully if you intend to use one of these products on molding that has a clear finish. Some products do not absorb clear finish and so will remain visible despite attempts to blend them into existing molding.

Many repairs require replacing a section of molding. To do this, you must first remove the damaged section from the wall. Use care, as dry, thin molding breaks easily and molding found in older buildings is often difficult to replace.

One method of removing molding is to use a hammer and long nail set to drive the nails fastening the molding completely through it into the wall. Another method is to gently pry the molding away, first with a wide, stiff-bladed putty knife, then with a flat pry bar.

Insert the knife into a crevice between the molding and the wall, and pry gradually along the length of the molding until there is room to insert the bar. Then position the knife against the wall to protect it, and place the bar between the blade and the molding.

In a coped joint, one piece of molding is cut to fit the profile of its partner.

Continue to pry gradually along the length of the molding, but position the pry bar as close as possible to any nails in the molding. If you intend to reattach the molding later, draw the nails out through the back with pliers after the molding is detached.

The reason for care even when removing damaged molding is so that you can use the piece as a guide for making a replacement. However, in case the building has settled since the molding was first attached, also measure the space where the new molding is to go. Remember another saying among carpenters: "Measure twice, cut once."

Coping

Where molding meets at inside corners, the joint is usually coped to fit. That is, the end of one piece of molding is carved with a coping saw to match the profile of its partner at right angles.

To cope a joint where one of the partners is already attached to a wall, begin with a length of molding approximately 4 inches longer than the length you will need. Using a saw, cut one end of the molding at an approximately 45-degree angle so that the molded face is shorter than the back surface of the molding. This exposes the molding's profile, making it more visible for cutting with the coping saw.

Highlight the profile even more by tracing along it with a pencil. Then place the molding upside down in a vise, with the molded face toward you. Holding a coping saw with the handle at right angles to the molding's upper edge when it is in the vise, cut away the mitered portion of the wood by following the traced line.

Afterward, smooth the cut using sandpaper or a half-round file. Without disturbing the edge marked by the pencil line, remove a little additional wood by filing or sanding it at an angle that removes wood from the back of the molding. This will produce a closer fit. The coped end should match the contour of the molding fastened to the adjacent wall and fit tightly against it.

Cope the opposite end of the replacement molding the same way if it, too, forms part of an inside corner. Measure carefully, however. The top edge of the coped molding must fit precisely against the moldings it meets at both ends.

Mitering

Molding that forms outside corners is normally mitered. In a miter joint involving two pieces, the ends being joined are each cut off at an angle equaling half the desired total angle. To miter molding for a 90-degree corner such as the meeting of two walls, the ends must each be cut at an angle of 45 degrees.

The trick is to cut the molding precisely and smoothly, so that the seam between the joined pieces is flawless. To do this, you need a sharp saw with a high number of teeth per inch and an accurate miter box.

Most hardware stores sell saws with eleven to thirteen teeth per inch, adequate for mitering utilitarian molding like baseboard that will be painted or applied in unobtrusive locations. For mitering molding that will receive clear finish or be conspicuously located, obtain a saw with at least fifteen teeth per inch from a woodworking supply store.

As for miter boxes, the metal ones are usually more accurate and durable than wooden models, but are also more expensive. Better designs feature a pivoting frame that holds the saw and allows cuts of any angle to be made.

To miter a piece of molding in a miter box, first place a thin piece of scrap wood in the bottom of the box or on the base, depending on the design. On top of the scrap, place a piece of molding marked with a line for cutting. Be sure that, when cut along the line, the piece will fit precisely between sections of molding it joins at each end.

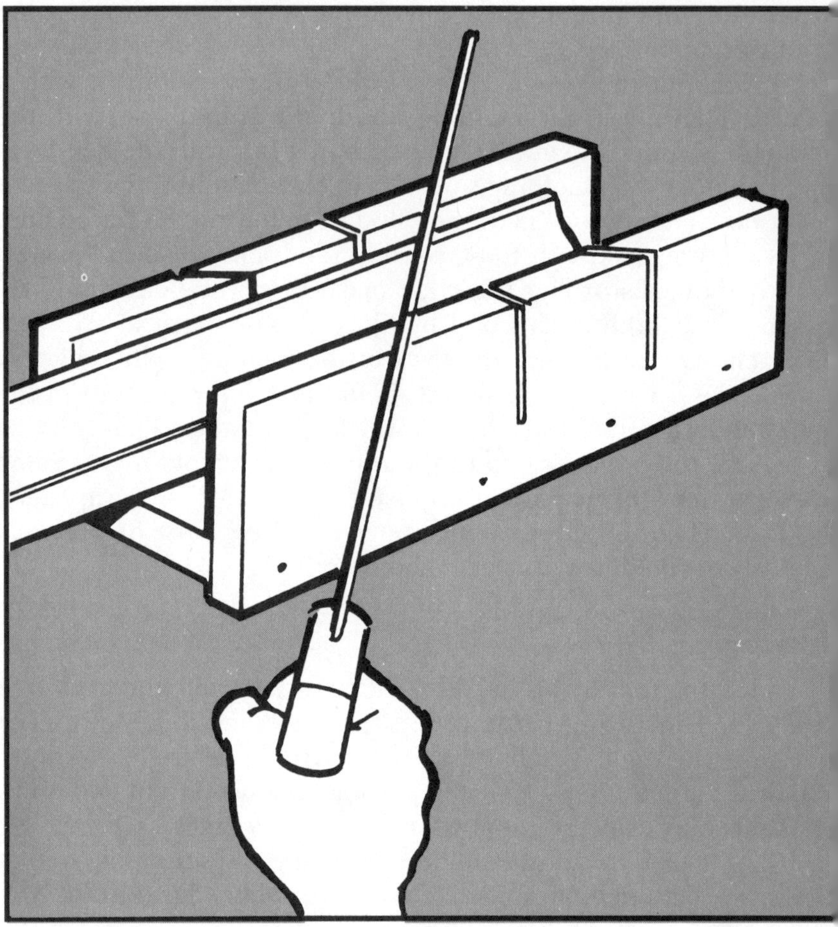

TIP:

Even experienced finish carpenters sometimes must "fudge" mitered corners that do not fit exactly (walls that do not meet precisely at a right angle are a common cause). A little wood putty or caulking compound fills slight gaps and will not be noticed if molding is later painted.

To fill wide gaps (up to about a sixteenth of an inch) or if molding will receive a clear finish, fashion a sliver of wood slightly wider than the gap to slip between the ends of the pieces. Squeeze the sliver in a vise or strike it with a hammer to compress the fibers.

(cont. on opposite page)

Rest the rear edge of the molding against the rear side of the box in the same position the molding will be when installed against the wall or other surface. Align the cutting line on the molding with the slot(s) in the miter box so that the saw blade will cut along the waste side of the mark. Then press the molding firmly against the rear side of the miter box with one hand and cut through the piece by guiding the saw with the other.

If final trimming is necessary, use sandpaper or a sharp hand plane. Trim from the back of the molding toward the front, and avoid marring the edge that will be exposed. To fasten pieces of mitered molding, hold them together and predrill holes for 1½-inch-long finishing nails through each piece. Install the nails at right angles to each other.

Splicing

If only a portion of a long section of molding needs repair, a replacement section may be spliced to it after the damaged part is

Begin a coped joint by cutting the end of one piece of molding at a 45-degree angle (left). Highlight the profile with a pencil, then cut away the waste with a coping saw held so that the blade is perpendicular to the strip.

removed. The splice should occur over a wall stud. Mark the place for the splice, then remove the entire molding, cut the damaged piece out, and fit the replacement section to the original by mitering both pieces so they overlap.

Crown Molding

Crown molding is installed around the top of a room to conceal the seam between the walls and ceiling. Because it flares outward from the wall, joining it at corners is tricky.

Both coping and mitering are best done using a wooden miter box. Mark a line on the base of the miter box, parallel with the sides, whose distance from the rear equals that between the upper front edge of the molding and the corner where the ceiling meets the wall when the molding is installed.

To cope crown molding, place the piece with its front face toward you, upside down in the miter box. Position the piece so that one edge rests against the line and is flat on the bottom of the box and the other rests flat against the box's rear side.

TIP (cont.)

Attach masking tape on each side of the gap. Rub wood glue into the gap with a finger, then press the sliver into place so the end of the grain is visible. Moisture in the glue will swell the sliver for a perfect fit.

Remove the masking tape. After the glue dries, carefully sand or file the sliver to match the molding's contours.

ATTENTION

Align the marked end of the piece with a pair of the box's angled slots. These must be a pair that will cause the end grain of the molding to be visible from the front when exposed by cutting. Saw the piece in two, about an inch from the marked end, and follow the procedure described earlier for completing the joint with a coping saw.

When mitering, pieces must also be placed upside down in the miter box and aligned with the mark on the base as described. Cut the pieces so that their end grain slopes at a 45-degree angle toward the rear of the molding.

Reattaching Baseboard Molding

Baseboard molding is usually covered at the bottom by narrow quarter-round molding called shoe molding and along the top by one or more carved strips called cap molding. To repair baseboard molding, all the pieces must be removed.

To reattach them, start by refastening the baseboard to the wall, using 2½- or 3-inch-long finishing nails. Drive these through the baseboard near the top, into the wall studs. Fasten any cap molding strips using shorter nails. Drive some into the wall studs and others at an angle down into the upper edge of the baseboard.

Predrill holes (or use existing ones) for the shoe molding, then fasten it carefully using 3-inch or longer nails driven into the floor.

Repainting Interiors

Repainting can be a sure, simple way to brighten a room. But to minimize the potential for creating a mess instead, it is important to choose appropriate materials, tools, and equipment and to work in an orderly fashion.

Choosing Paint and Equipment

Naturally, the first step is to select the paint. Latex-based paint is by far the most popular and the easiest to use. Because it is soluble in water, drying takes only about an hour and cleaning up can be done with soap and water.

Alkyd-based paint, the other common type, is formulated with synthetic alkyd resins and vegetable oils. It resists staining (especially from grease) better than latex-based paint, and is also better able to withstand hard scrubbing. For these reasons it is often used in kitchens and bathrooms.

But alkyd-based paint takes longer to dry than latex-based paint and cleaning up involves the use of solvents. Because both alkyd-based paint and solvents are toxic and flammable, numerous health and fire-safety precautions must be observed during application and when disposing of materials.

To ensure even color, buy enough paint in one purchase and make sure that the batch numbers on the containers are the same. Custom colors are best blended at the paint store. Most ordinary housepaint requires no thinning; it should be used as it comes out of the can. No matter what the directions on the paint containers

> **TIP:**
>
> Some hints for selecting brushes:
>
> • The divider in the center of the bristles where they join the handle should be difficult to find. If you can feel it easily by squeezing the brush, the bristles are skimpy. If the bristles separate easily into two groups or if there is a hollow space in the center of the brush, the divider is too large.
>
> • Bristles should feel springy, not stiff, and should fan out evenly.
>
> • When the bristles are bent downward by pressing their tips with the palm of a hand, many should pop up, indicating bristles of varying lengths.
>
> • At the tips, bristles should have the appearance of hair with "split ends." Such bristles are flagged. For more on the advantages of this feature, see page 95.

say, two thin coats are always better than one thick one. More than two coats is seldom necessary, even if you are trying to paint a light color over a dark color. Dark surfaces should first be covered with primer. Primer may also be necessary when applying latex paint over a glossy surface. To determine what type of primer is necessary, check the label on the paint container.

As for tools and equipment, select those of medium price. A minimum assortment for painting a room with plaster or wallboard surfaces should include an ordinary square-edged paintbrush about 2½ inches wide and a 1½-inch sash-painting brush with a longer handle and bristles cut at an angle across the bottom edge.

You will also need a 9-inch-wide roller and one or two roller covers for painting large areas; a 3-inch-wide trim roller for painting narrow areas and behind obstructions (trim rollers and covers are usually one piece); a detachable extension handle that fits both rollers; and a small plastic bucket and a roller tray, each for holding paint. Another handy item is a large, light-colored cloth for wiping spills.

Brushes and roller covers for latex-based paint must be of synthetic material that does not absorb water. For alkyd-based paints use brushes and roller covers of nylon or natural fiber.

General painting with latex-based paint is usually best done with a medium-nap roller cover with ½-inch fibers. This produces a softly stippled surface texture that appears smooth except at close range. For producing a smoother surface (provided the existing surface is also smooth) and for applying alkyd-based paint, use a short-nap roller cover with ¼-inch fibers.

Preparing a Room for Painting

To prepare a room for painting, move out as many furnishings as possible and group the rest in the center of the room. Cover the floor and the remaining items with drop cloths. Light fixtures and plates on electrical outlets can be covered with plastic bags. If you plan to paint behind cover plates or light fixtures, turn off the electricity to the room at the service panel (fuse box) when preparing and painting these areas.

Before removal of fixtures or plates, make sure the power is off by using an inexpensive circuit tester available at hardware stores. The tester consists of a tiny light bulb and two wires and comes with instructions.

Prepare the surfaces to be painted by following the directions printed on the paint cans. Painted plaster or wallboard ceilings in good condition usually need only dusting or vacuuming. Walls of

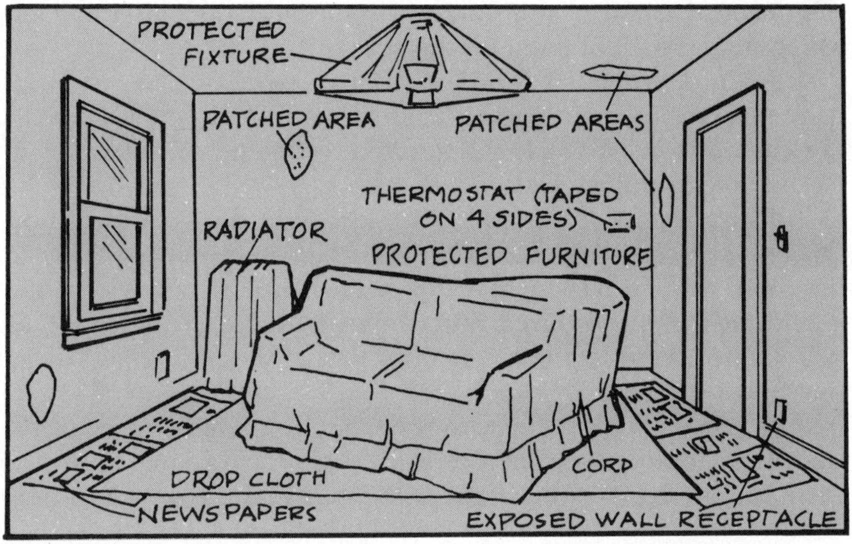

When preparing a room for painting, remove as many items as possible. Cover the rest with drop cloths, plastic sheeting, or newspapers, and mask fixtures with tape.

either material should be washed with strong household cleanser, then rinsed with clear water and allowed to dry. Apply the cleanser with a bristle brush. Use a sponge for rinsing. Latex-based paint can be applied while walls are still damp.

Peeling paint must be scraped away so that new paint will adhere. However, paint applied before 1977 may contain dangerous amounts of lead, posing a health hazard during removal and requiring special disposal methods. If you suspect the presence of lead paint, have it analyzed before proceeding further. Consult a poison control center or call your local health department.

Attach masking tape to the edges of windows, doors, and baseboard molding, unless you plan to use hand-held paint shields to protect them. Leave about 1/16 inch between the edge of the tape and window frames so that paint will seal the edges of the glass. After the paint dries, scrape the excess from the panes using a single-edge razor blade.

Ceilings

Paint the ceiling first. Begin by using the square-edged brush to apply a band of paint—a process called cutting in—around the perimeter and any openings or fixtures that will not be painted.

To cut in a ceiling, start by holding the brush about 2 feet from one of the room's corners (against the seam where the ceil-

APARTMENT OWNERS:

Older urban apartment buildings are particularly likely to contain lead paint. Many cities have created special government agencies to cope with the problem and regulations concerning removal or abatement techniques. Increasingly in such areas, only government-certified professionals are permitted to remove lead paint or carry out other protective measures.

HINT

ing meets the wall). Paint toward the corner, parallel to the seam, depositing a strip of paint on the ceiling.

Do not worry if a small amount of paint gets on the wall, provided you also are going to paint it. But if you must maintain a clean edge instead, use the beading technique described in the section on cutting in walls, below.

Paint in long, overlapping strokes all in the same direction. When you reach the corner, tilt the brush in the opposite direction and draw it back across the painted area in a single stroke. Continue this procedure around the perimeter of the room, always starting the sequence on a dry part of the ceiling and painting into a wet area.

Use the 9-inch roller with the extension handle to paint the rest of the ceiling. Start at a corner of the longest wall. Apply the paint in overlapping rectangular sections each about 4 feet long and 3 feet wide.

To apply paint with a roller, first load it by dipping it in a roller tray no more than half filled with paint. Then roll the roller several times over the tray's sloping portion. When loaded, the roller should be evenly saturated but should not drip.

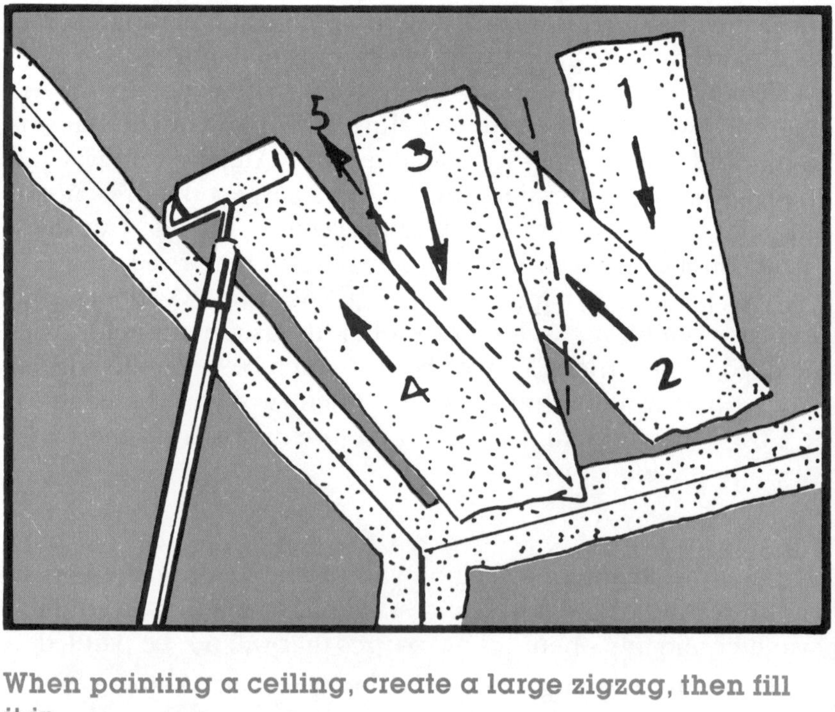

When painting a ceiling, create a large zigzag, then fill it in.

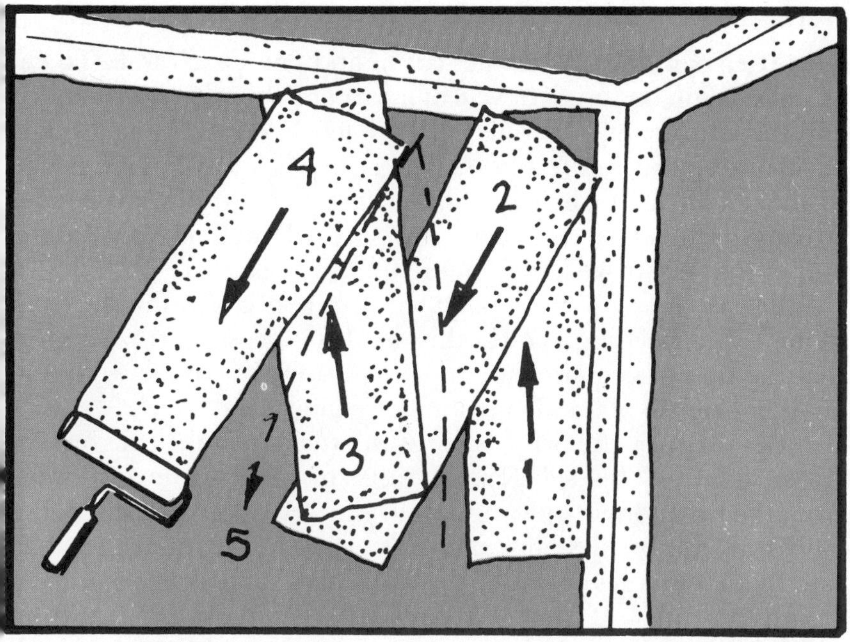

When painting a wall, roll from the corner toward the center. As with a ceiling, create a large zigzag first, then fill it in.

TIP:

Painting without drips takes practice. Hold large paintbrushes like those for cutting in by placing your thumb on one side of the ferrule (the metal band at the top of the bristles) and all four fingers on the other side. Let the handle rest in the crook of your hand between the thumb and index finger. To avoid a mess, paint from a partly filled container, not a full bucket. Dip the bristles no more than a third of their length into the paint, and instead of wiping the brush across the container's rim to get rid of the excess, slap it gently against the inside.

Stand facing the wall and place the roller on the ceiling about 3 feet from the corner of the room. Make the initial stroke by pushing the roller away from you until it reaches the cut-in area. Then using three or four strokes, each about 4 feet long, paint a zigzag-shaped strip leading to the corner.

Fill in between these strokes by crisscrossing the area with additional shorter strokes. The result should be a rectangular painted section measuring about 3 feet wide and 4 feet long. To avoid spattering, do not move the roller too fast. Be sure the roller has stopped moving before lifting it away from a surface.

Work across the ceiling's narrow dimension unless one window creates a strong light source. In that case, orient the longer sides of each section so they are perpendicular to the wall containing the window and apply the sections end to end, working in the direction that light enters the room.

Finish the ceiling by painting any molding separating it from the walls. Use either the square-edged brush or the sash-painting brush. To paint the molding, follow the technique described for cutting in, or the beading technique described below.

Walls

After painting the ceiling, cut in and paint each wall. To cut in walls, begin on the right wall of a corner if you are right-handed and the left corner of a wall if you are left-handed. Using a single backhand stroke, apply a horizontal strip of paint whose top edge is about half an inch below the ceiling line. Apply subsequent strokes forehand, starting from a dry area about 2 feet beyond the end of the last stroke and painting into the wet area.

Before the strip dries, paint the area above it, using the technique called beading. To do this, load the brush and place it so that the tip rests against the unpainted surface, parallel with and about an eighth of an inch from the ceiling seam.

Gently press the brush against the surface so that the bristles curve slightly. This will force a ridge of paint to flow outward from the tip and rise upward to the seam, creating a clean edge.

Draw the brush along smoothly, applying paint at the same rate that it emerges from the brush. A backhand stroke is usually easiest to control. If the brush runs out of paint, start again from a point below the end of the previous stroke and lead the brush back into the position at an angle so the strokes merge.

After completing a strip, blend the beading with the previously applied paint by light brushing with a nearly dry brush, using long backhand and forehand strokes. Finish cutting in a wall by painting the vertical corners and the area above the baseboard.

Rolling paint onto a wall also should be done in rectangular sections starting from a corner, but the pattern can be any that is convenient. Use the 3-inch-wide roller where the larger roller will not fit.

After completing the walls, paint the windows and doors, then the baseboard molding. For all of these, use brushes.

Painting Double-hung Windows

P**ainting wooden double-hung windows—the kind with two** vertically sliding halves known as sashes—is tedious because there are so many components. But the task can be easier and you will be less likely to end up with sticking parts if you use the right equipment and follow a logical sequence.

Double-hung windows are usually painted in two stages. Their interior surfaces are painted with interior-quality paint when the room is decorated; the exterior surfaces with exterior-quality paint when the outside of the house is painted.

Two brushes are required: a sash brush 2 or 2½ inches wide with the bristles trimmed square across the bottom, and a trim brush 1 or 1½ inches wide with the bristles trimmed at an angle. Choose medium-priced brushes with nylon bristles, as these usually offer maximum bristle quality and springiness at the lowest cost.

Each brush should have a relatively long handle for good control, and the bristles should appear somewhat frayed near the tip—"flagged" is the term used by manufacturers—so that they will hold large amounts of paint. Flagging is subtle, so when choosing the brushes, look at the ends closely. The bristles of the sash brush should also taper to a point when viewed from the side. This feature is called a chisel point, and permits painting precise lines and edges.

Use the sash brush on broad surfaces, applying paint with the sides and tip. Use the trim brush for narrow surfaces, applying paint only with the bottom edge. Wipe up drips with a clean rag the moment they occur.

TIP:

For the best control, hold sash and trim brushes as you would a pencil, with the ferrule (the metal band at the top of the bristles) between your thumb and first two fingers.

ATTENTION

To paint the interior of a double-hung window, begin by raising the inside sash to an inch from the top and pulling the outside sash down as far as it will go, or to within an inch of the sill. Using the trim brush, paint all edges of the inner sash that touch the glass. To control drips and make brush strokes less visible, paint the upper horizontal edge first, then the two vertical sides. Paint the lower horizontal edge last.

The paint must seal the seams where the glass and wood meet. For an effective seal, allow paint to overlap the glass surface slightly—about a sixteenth of an inch—on all sides as you paint the sash edges. The border can be applied freehand, after a little practice, by pressing the brush firmly against the sash as you paint it, so that the bristles curve gently toward the glass and fan out slightly over it. If the brush is well loaded with paint, each edge can be painted and simultaneously sealed in one long stroke, with minor touching up in the corners.

Alternatively, use an inexpensive plastic or metal paint shield, available at paint stores, to mask portions of the glass that are to remain free of paint. Hold the shield on the glass at the correct distance from the side of the sash. Then paint the edge of the sash and the small sliver of glass between the shield and the sash. Carefully lift the shield away and wipe it free of paint after each edge is completed.

Switch to the sash brush to paint wide surfaces. Paint the horizontal pieces first, using back-and-forth strokes, then the verticals, with up-and-down strokes. Then paint the underside of the sash.

Do not paint the upper edge where the lock is ordinarily located. Also, try to avoid smearing paint onto the window channels at each side, since heavy accumulations of paint in these areas will cause the sashes to stick.

After painting the inner sash, paint the area of the outer sash that is below it. Begin with the muntins—the partition strips that separate individual small panes of glass; paint the edges that touch the glass first, using the trim brush. If there are no muntins, proceed as already described for the inner sash. Afterward, use the sash brush to paint the perimeter of the sash. Do not paint the underside of the lower horizontal piece.

Before the paint on the outer sash dries, lower the inner sash and raise the upper one by pressing on the unpainted edge of each. Leave an inch of space between the ends of the sash and the top and bottom of the window frame, but be sure the unpainted portion of the outer sash is completely exposed. Paint it, using the techniques and sequence just described.

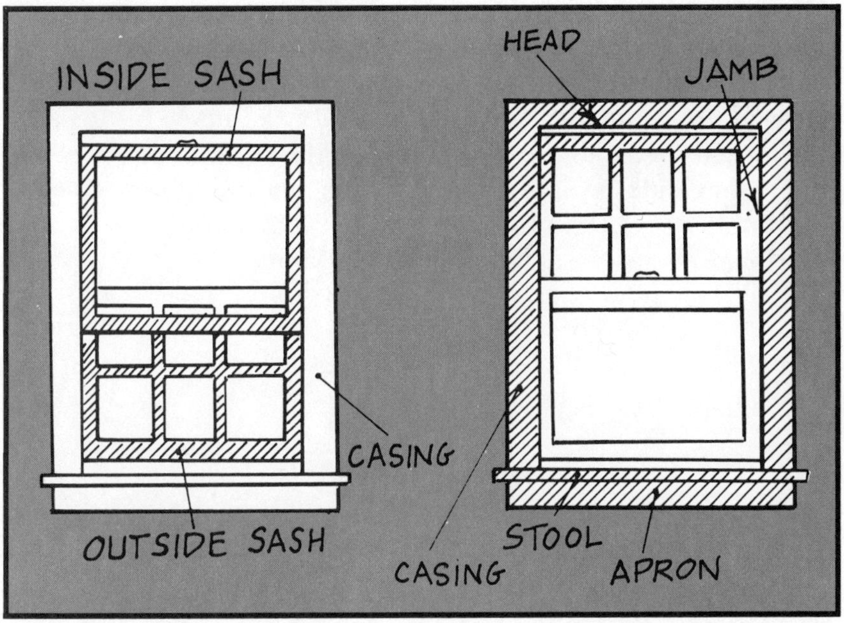

Paint a double-hung window in three stages. In stage one (left), raise the inner sash and lower the outer, then apply paint to the areas shaded in the illustration.

In stage two (right), return the sashes to their normal position and paint the remaining parts of the window (shaded areas in the illustration), including the upper edge of the inside sash. In stage three, after the sashes have dried, close the window and paint the inside surfaces of the jambs and head.

Also paint the upper edge of the inside sash and the interior trim—called the casing—around the window frame. Use the sash brush for both. Paint the sash piece first, then the horizontal casing across the top of the window frame. Then paint the sides, and finally the stool and apron, which are the portions of the sill that face the interior.

After the sashes have dried to the touch, slide them up and down to make sure they do not stick. Close the window and paint all parts of the jambs (sides) and head (the upper horizontal portion of the window frame) that are visible inside the room. Use both brushes, and apply paint as thinly as possible. Do not paint any metal parts or the sash cord.

The procedure for painting the exterior of the window is the same as for painting the interior, except that both sashes must be raised when painting the lower portions of the jambs and remaining portion of the windowsill. After those portions are dry, the outer sash must be lowered to enable painting the upper exterior parts of the jambs and head.

When the jambs are dry, lubricate the surfaces against which the sashes slide by spraying them with silicone lubricant sold at hardware stores, or by rubbing them with paraffin or a white candle, whose wax will not discolor the jambs.

Wallpapering

Applying wallpaper is no longer the tricky, messy task it once was. Stronger paper and slower-drying adhesives have eased the job considerably. However, achieving smooth-surfaced results still depends on preparing the wall carefully before applying the paper.

> **TIP:**
>
> If you plan to repaint molding or trim, do so before repapering.

ATTENTION

Preparing Surfaces

Begin by removing everything from the walls, including electrical outlet covers, shelf brackets, picture hooks, and other fasteners. To simplify replacing fasteners after papering, stick brightly colored pushpins into the wall in their place to serve as markers. Remove these one at a time during papering, but reinsert them immediately.

If the wall is painted with a smooth paint, cover it with a coat of wallcovering primer. A universal type is available that adheres to any sound paint, eliminating the need to determine whether the paint is alkyd-, oil-, or water-based.

Textured paint can be removed with chemical remover formulated for this type; or it can be sanded reasonably smooth, then primed and covered with a layer of wallpaper lining (a thick, patternless wallpaper). For safety reasons, do not sand any paint that may contain lead. If you are not sure about the composition of paint you wish to sand, call the local health department for advice. Most paint applied before 1977 does contain amounts of lead that can pose a health hazard if sanded.

APARTMENT OWNERS:

Lead paint is common in older urban apartment buildings. See note on page 91.

HINT

Another solution for covering moderately textured walls, as well as plaster walls containing many hairline cracks, is to apply a spun fiberglass liner, available at wallcovering stores. Although more expensive than ordinary wallpaper lining, a fiberglass liner produces a smooth surface that is also hard. Special paint sold with the fiberglass liner is required for gluing it to the wall. The paint forms a vapor barrier and also serves as a primer.

Flaking paint must be removed and other damaged surfaces must be repaired before either wallpaper or liner is applied. Precautions concerning lead also apply to removing ordinary paint by sanding, scraping, and the use of heat. If stains on the wall indicate water damage, correct this problem first and cover the stains with primer-sealer containing shellac. This will prevent the stains from discoloring the new wallpaper.

Fill dents and holes with patching plaster or spackling compound and smooth them by sanding. Then cover the patches with wallcovering primer or primer-sealer.

Plaster walls sometimes contain alkali patches (also called hot spots), which result from improperly mixed plaster. Neither paint nor wallpaper adheres well to these. Hot spots can be neutralized by washing them with a solution of one part 30 percent muriatic or acetic acid (available at paint stores) mixed with two parts water.

Apply the acid solution with a sponge and allow it to remain on the spots for the amount of time specified by the manufacturer. Wear rubber gloves, work in a well-ventilated area, and follow all safety precautions printed on the container label. Rinse the treated areas with clear water. After they have dried, cover the spots with primer-sealer.

Before repairing papered walls, tear away damaged paper by folding the loose flaps back and tearing them by rotating your wrist close to the wall—not by pulling the paper outward. This technique feathers the torn edge of the paper, producing a smoother surface.

If no more than two layers of smooth-textured wallpaper are on the wall, a third layer usually can be applied without removing the layers underneath.

The existing wallpaper must adhere tightly. Repaste or patch any areas of loose paper, and also lightly sand seams where paper sections overlap. Covering the paper with a coat of wallcovering primer is recommended; however, ask your wallpaper supplier if this is necessary for applying the type of wallpaper you plan to use.

If the existing wallpaper has a rough texture or is more than two layers thick, it must be removed. Self-sticking paper, meant to be easily stripped, must be removed in any case. To remove self-sticking paper, start by working an upper corner free, then fold the flap back on itself and slowly pull the paper straight down, parallel with the wall.

To remove conventionally pasted wallpaper, the easiest method is to apply enzyme-based wallpaper stripper. The stripper can be applied with a sponge, paint roller, or garden sprayer. Two applications are usually recommended, each followed by a waiting period of fifteen minutes. Afterward, most wallpaper then can be scraped easily from the wall with a putty knife. Washable paper and paper that has been covered with paint should be scored before stripper is applied, using a perforating tool designed for the purpose.

In rare cases where stripper does not work, obtain a wallpaper steamer. Modestly priced small steamers for amateur use are available at hardware and wallcovering stores. Larger steamers can be rented.

Use a wallpaper steamer like a steam iron for ironing clothes. Hold the tool against the wall and move it over a small area to allow steam to penetrate the paper. When the paper loosens, scrape it off.

It is risky to steam wallpaper from wallboard, because the paper facing of the wallboard may melt. In place of enzyme-based stripper (which will not damage wallboard facing), you may be able to strip the paper by scraping it with a hooked paint or wallboard scraper.

In all cases, after the wallpaper is stripped and the wall is dry, apply wallcovering primer before applying new wallpaper.

TIP:

Although relatively inexpensive, spun fiberglass can be irritating to skin if handled without gloves. More expensive liners, producing a less rigid surface but easier to work with, are made of polyester and of gypsum-saturated fabric.

ATTENTION

Planning and Starting Wallpaper

Success in applying wallpaper depends greatly on choosing appropriately patterned paper and arranging a layout of strips that minimizes mismatches in the pattern. When choosing paper, a careful assessment of the walls and trim is necessary. When determining a layout, special consideration must be given to choosing a strategic point in the room from which to start.

If walls have not been previously papered or if you intend to switch from a wallpaper with small designs to a style featuring large designs, the first step is to inspect the walls and trim for construction flaws. A 5- or 6-foot-long builder's level is a useful aid for this; the tool can be rented. If you cannot obtain a level this size, reasonably priced shorter levels are available at hardware stores. To supplement a short level, use a plumb bob, or improvise one by hanging a pair of scissors from a length of string.

TIP:

When marking walls to be papered, use a pencil instead of a pen. The latter may bleed through freshly applied paper, creating a stain.

ATTENTION

Use the long level or the plumb bob to determine whether the walls and trim are vertical. With the level, simply place one of its edges against the surface you are checking and examine the liquid-filled tubes at each end. If the surface is vertical the air bubble in each tube will be centered.

To use a plumb bob, suspend it parallel to—but not touching—the surface you wish to measure. If you are checking walls or the face of trim pieces (the surface parallel to the wall on which it is attached), hang the plumb bob from a pushpin installed in the ceiling. To check the sides of the trim, install the pushpin in the wall, but allow the bob to hang freely.

In both cases, extend the plumb bob to a point just above the floor and allow it to stop swinging. Then carefully measure the distance between the string and the surface at several points. Any discrepancy indicates that the surface is not vertical.

To check whether horizontal trim is accurately positioned, use either the long or short level. Simply set the level on or against the rim and note the position of the bubble in the middle tube as previously described.

Wallpaper strips must be trimmed to fit against nonsquare edges. Small-design wallpaper is usually unaffected by minor misalignments in wall and trim surfaces. However, large-design paper is difficult—sometimes impossible—to apply where surfaces are not square without creating areas where the designs are noticeably mismatched.

As a general guideline, if seams along trim are more than one quarter of an inch out of square and along the corners of walls are more than half an inch out of square, the use of small-design paper rather than large-design should be considered.

Choosing the location for the first strip of wallpaper is crucial. Because strips are usually applied consecutively, one of the edges of the first strip will be likely to form a seam with the final strip, and here a mismatch in the pattern is virtually inevitable.

One of the best locations for the first strip of wallpaper, whether small- or large-patterned, is alongside the room's main doorway. Another good place, if present, is the narrow wall along the least conspicuous side of a floor-to-ceiling projection into the room, such as a fireplace and mantel. (Here, the last strip can meet the first at the seam formed where the narrow wall juts out from the main wall.)

Another method—one especially suitable for use with large-design paper—is to begin by centering the first strip at some well-considered location and then attaching strips on each side. The final strips can still be made to join at one of the inconspicuous locations described.

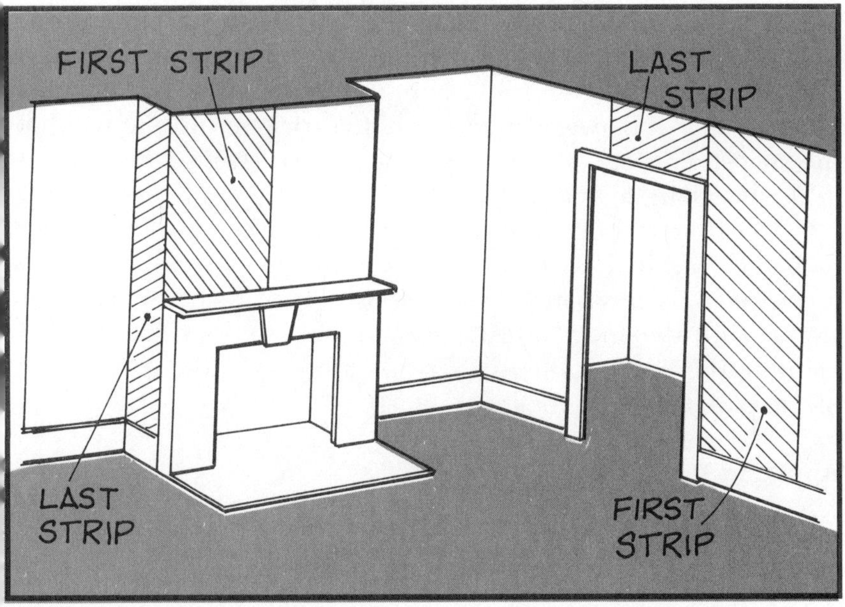

Starting points for wallpaper are against the side of a main doorway or where a short wall of a floor-to-ceiling projection meets the main wall.

TIP:

When allowing extra length for trimming strips, divide the surplus between the top and bottom of the strip. To do this, use a 2-inch-wide straightedge as a guide. Lay its lower edge along the line chosen as the paper's ceiling line (the line to which the paper will be trimmed at the top) and cut off any excess along the tool's upper edge. Then, measure the length of the strip from the cut edge and sever it from the roll along the bottom.

ATTENTION

Centering creates a subtle focal point in a room, reducing the tendency of patterns containing large designs to appear chaotic. First examine several strips of the wallpaper you plan to use. Note where the center of the pattern occurs, and in the case of "drop match" prints—whose designs usually are printed in diagonal rows spanning several sheets—note how many strips must be placed side by side before the pattern repeats.

Take into account the space necessary to display the full pattern of the wallpaper, then mark a spot on the wall indicating the center of the pattern. This will be the focal point. On a strip of wallpaper, locate the center of the pattern (it may not be in the center of the strip) and measure from it to one edge of the paper.

If you measured to the left from the center point of the pattern, measure the same distance to the left of the point on the wall. When you hang the first strip, align its left edge with a vertical line drawn through this mark. Place subsequent strips to the right and left of the first strip, thereby centering the pattern on the focal point.

Continue marking the layout of strips around the room by using a roll of wallpaper as a measuring stick. Hold one end of the roll against a mark signifying the edge of a previous strip, then place a mark at the roll's other end, and so on.

> **TIP:**
>
> Follow the paper manufacturer's instructions carefully for soaking. If the paper requires time to relax (expand), fold wetted strips into thirds with their pasted sides together. This is called booking. Be consistent in overlapping either the bottom edge over the top by about an inch or vice versa; this will tell you at a glance the orientation of the paper and prevent you from accidentally hanging the strip upside down. After booking, paper can be rolled and stored in a large plastic bag to keep it moist and out of the way.

ATTENTION

It is important to complete the layout for an entire room before attaching the first strips, because in a room containing several windows or other interruptions in the walls, you may find that the spaces between them do not correspond to the width of the strips. This creates the need for narrow strips, which can be difficult to handle and align.

Modify a layout that will require cutting strips to less than 6 inches in width. Easy ways of doing this are to plan additional inconspicuous mismatches over doorways or at corners, and to simply shift the entire layout several inches to the right or left by aligning the edge of the first strip—rather than the center point of the pattern—with the initial mark.

Applying Wallpaper

Wallpaper should be cut into strips before it is applied. The strips are usually cut 4 inches longer than necessary to allow for trimming. When cutting strips, keep in mind that the pattern repeats itself: When the strips are applied, the patterns must align.

Prepasted wallpaper, which has adhesive that must be moistened, is easier to work with than unpasted paper. To apply prepasted wallpaper, use a waterbox—a shallow plastic or aluminum trough available at home centers and wallpaper stores. Put it on the floor in front of the spot where you will be working and fill it two thirds full with lukewarm water. If you are using a stepladder, put it in front of the box, with the rungs at right angles to the box.

Roll the precut strip loosely from the bottom, with the pattern inside. Put the roll in the waterbox and let it soak as long as the manufacturer recommends, usually less than a minute.

After soaking, grasp the top edge with both hands and climb the ladder, unrolling the paper from the box as you go. Be sure the pattern faces you. When you can reach the ceiling comfortably, press the upper edge of the paper into the corner where the wall and ceiling meet.

With a smoothing brush—a wide, soft-bristled brush sold for applying wallpaper—press the paper into the corner. Two inches of the strip should extend above the corner for trimming. Descend the ladder, applying short diagonal strokes with the brush to attach the paper lightly to the wall in preparation for smoothing.

Don't worry if small air bubbles form, but be sure the strip is vertical. If wrinkles develop, gently pull the lower part away from the wall, using both hands, until the wrinkle is pulled free.

When you reach the bottom of the wall, use the tip of the brush to press the lower edge of the paper into the corner where the wall meets the floor or baseboard. Allow the remaining paper to extend for trimming.

Now climb back up the ladder to smooth the paper. Working from the top, brush with firm strokes from the vertical center line toward the sides. Force all air bubbles out at the edges and be sure the entire surface bonds to the wall. After the strips on one wall have been applied, wait five or ten minutes for the last ones to dry; then trim them using a metal straightedge and either a wallpaper-trimming knife or a sharp utility knife.

With unpasted paper, you will need a pasting table instead of a waterbox. You can make a table by laying a smooth sheet of plywood half an inch or more thick across a pair of sawhorses. Or you can buy a smooth, unfinished, hollow-core door from a lumberyard or home center. Doors are a better size than plywood sheets, and lighter as well. For most wallpaper, a standard 32-by-80-inch door is sufficient. Pasting tables can also be rented from many wallpaper suppliers and rental centers.

The trick to preparing unpasted wallpaper is to avoid smearing paste left on the table from one strip onto the pattern side of the next strip. If you are papering only a small room, it might be worth the expense to get a roll of kraft or butcher paper and lay each strip of wallpaper on a clean piece of kraft paper while pasting it. Don't use newspaper; the ink will leave stains.

TIP:

Instead of a smoothing brush, a piece of clear plexiglass about 8 inches long shaped like a trapezoid may be preferred. With it, you can exert more pressure on the paper, fit the tool into corners, and check the alignment of even small flaps of paper during smoothing.

ATTENTION

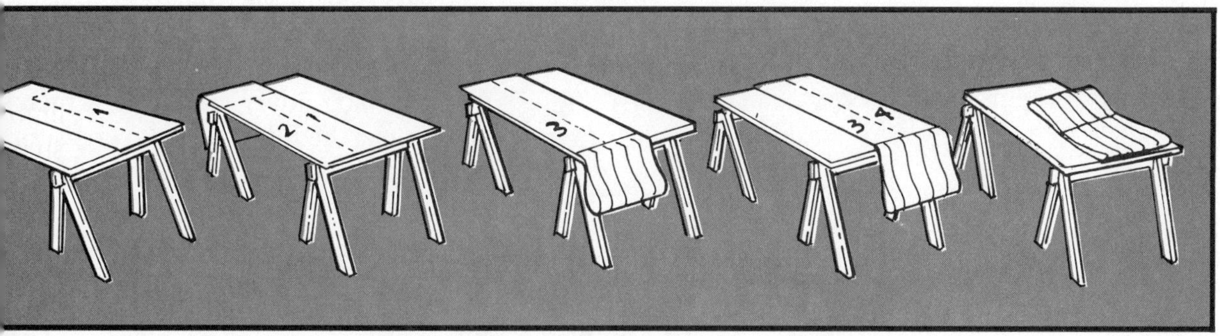

To prepare unpasted wallpaper strips, position the paper on a pasting table and apply paste to the portion marked in the first illustration. Then slide the paper to the other side of the table and repeat the process, as in the second illustration. Continue to apply paste and fold the paper in the sequence shown.

TIP:

When trimming, hold a metal straightedge or wide putty knife against the paper below the knife. That way, if you slip, the paper will not be damaged. Always use a razor-sharp knife; a dull blade easily tears wallpaper and causes it to wrinkle.

ATTENTION

There is an alternative method that does not require kraft paper. First, put a precut strip of wallpaper on the table, pattern side down. Stand at one end of the table and slide the paper away from you so that the top of the strip—the part that will go next to the ceiling—hangs over the far end of the table. The bottom edge should be flush with your end of the table.

Pull the paper toward you slightly and slide it sideways, so the bottom edge and one side of the paper extend about a quarter of an inch beyond the table edges. Apply wallpaper paste to half the width of the sheet, beginning as far forward along the center lines of the paper as you can reach and brushing toward the edges that overlap the table.

Slide the paper to the opposite side of the table and repeat the process to cover the remaining portion that is within reach. Next, step back and pull the paper toward you; reach forward and fold the pasted portion over onto itself—paste on paste—leaving about two thirds of the unpatterned side exposed. Do not crease the paper.

Let the folded portion hang from the near end of the table, bringing the top edge of the paper within reach. Position the remaining unpasted part so the end and one side extend a quarter of an inch beyond the table's far edges; then repeat the pasting process. When finished, fold the paper by bringing the top edge toward you so both ends meet (see Tip on page 106). Then set the strip aside for the amount of time recommended by the manufacturer, usually about five minutes.

To apply the paper, trim the selvages (unfinished edges), if any, along the sides while the strip is folded; once again, be careful not to crease the paper. Be sure the edges of the folded surfaces are precisely aligned, one on top of the other, or the trim will be crooked. Use a trimming knife or sharp utility knife and a metal straightedge; scissors can be used near the folds, to avoid creasing. Then unfold the upper portion of the paper (the larger fold) and attach it to the wall as described for prepasted paper. Unfold and attach the lower portion; then smooth the entire strip. Trim the paper when it is dry.

Wallpapering Around Corners

A basic method can be used to paper an inside corner where two walls meet. First, measure at several points from the corner to the edge of the last strip applied.

Add half an inch to the greatest measurement and cut a strip of wallpaper to this width. Attach the strip to the wall and tap the paper firmly into the corner with a smoothing brush by striking the paper with the ends of the bristles. Paste the extra half inch to the adjacent wall. If the paper's length is greater than the distance from floor to ceiling, slit the paper with a knife above and below the corner to avoid wrinkling it.

Next, measure the leftover waste strip. If it is at least 6 inches wide, it can be used to complete the corner. If it is narrower than 6 inches, substitute a new full-width strip. In both cases, proceed as follows:

Mark the width of the strip onto the uncovered wall by measuring from the corner at any point along its length. Using a plumb line coated with chalk (or an ordinary string coated with chalk and tied at one end to the handle of a pair of scissors), mark a vertical line on the wall. Have an assistant hold the unweighted end of the line against the top of the wall so that the weighted end swings freely a fraction of an inch from the floor. When the string stops moving, make certain it is aligned precisely with the mark on the wall.

While your assistant presses the top end of the string against the wall, stretch the string downward to tighten it and press it against the wall at the bottom with your thumb. Be careful not to disturb the string's alignment.

Using your free hand, grasp the string near the middle of its length, then gently pull the string straight out from the wall about 4 inches and let go. The string should snap lightly against the wall, leaving a crisp, vertical line of chalk from top to bottom.

Paste the strip to the wall along the line. At the corner, the strip should overlap the one previously applied by a half inch.

There are also two specialized ways of papering inside corners. One can be used if the distance from the corner to the last strip applied is very narrow—4 inches or less. The other can be used if the distance is very wide—within 4 inches of the full width of a strip.

In the first situation, subtract from the width of a full strip the longest distance from the corner to the edge of the last strip applied, plus an additional half inch. Using a chalk line, mark a vertical line on the adjacent wall a distance from the corner equal to the measurement.

Then hang a full strip of wallpaper by aligning it with the mark. One side of the paper then should wrap around the corner and overlap the edge of the last strip applied by a half inch.

In the second situation, the procedure is essentially the reverse, but easier. Simply hang a full strip of paper by aligning it with the edge of the last strip applied. Press the paper into the corner and paste the extra against the adjacent wall as described

TIP:

When pasting overlapping strips of vinyl-coated wallpaper at corners, use vinyl-to-vinyl adhesive. Roll the seam with a seam roller; afterward, scrupulously wipe away any excess adhesive.

ATTENTION

TIP:

If the pattern between two adjoining strips meets only along part of a seam, try to adjust the strips so that the best match occurs at eye level; mismatches higher or lower will be less noticeable.

ATTENTION

in the basic procedure. Hang the next strip so that its edge overlaps that of the corner strip by a half inch.

With all three methods, unless the corner where the walls meet is vertical or very nearly so there may be a mismatch of the pattern where the corner strip and the next strip to be applied meet. In the two specialized methods, mismatches will be more pronounced and more noticeable the farther the unaligned edges of the corner strips are from the corner. However, in the basic procedure, the distance from the corner to the seam formed by the next strip is so narrow that mismatching will be slight and most likely will go unnoticed.

To paper an outside corner, like a projection created by a mantelpiece, the basic procedure is first to measure at several points from the corner to the edge of the last strip applied, as described for papering an inside corner. Cut a strip to the width of the longest measurement plus an inch. Align the strip with the edge of the last one applied and attach it to the wall, wrapping the extra amount around the corner and pasting it down. Slit any paper above and below the corner to avoid wrinkling it.

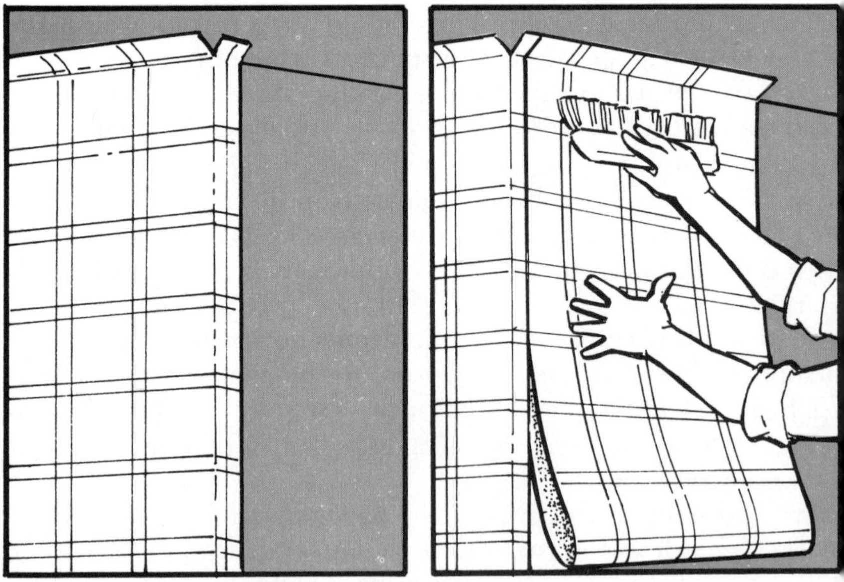

When papering an outside corner, attach a strip that extends 1 inch beyond the corner. Attach a second strip to the adjacent wall so that it overlaps the first strip by ½ inch.

Hold a carpenter's level against the strip's unaligned edge at the top and bottom to check whether or not the edge is vertical. If it is not, loosen it from the wall. Then, using a sponge, reposition the paper on the other side of the corner by dampening and pushing it with the sponge toward the corner. Be careful not to separate the seam between this strip and the one previously applied. Then repaste the loosened portion.

To complete the corner, follow the procedure for attaching the waste strip or a full-width strip to the wall also as described for papering an inside corner. But in both cases add a half inch of the strip's width when marking the wall so that, when attached, the edge of the second strip will overlap the first by that amount.

As an alternative to the basic procedure, if the distance between the corner and the edge of the last strip applied is a half inch or less, or if the strip extends no more than a half inch beyond the corner, simply mark a vertical line on the wall that is an inch less than the width of a full strip. Align the strip with the mark and attach it to the wall so that the extra amount wraps around the corner, overlapping the edge of the strip previously applied.

TIP:

Wallpaper strips may contract slightly as they dry. Recheck seams frequently when hanging; if necessary, force the edges of adjoining strips together with your fingers and press them against the wall with a seam roller.

ATTENTION

Cleaning and Repairing Wallpaper

Wallpaper is either porous or nonporous. To test it, fill a spray bottle with water and saturate an obscure area. If the water soaks in, the wallpaper is porous; if it forms beads and runs down the surface, it is nonporous.

Most nonporous wallpaper can be wiped clean using a cloth or sponge and household spray cleaner or mild household detergent followed by plain water.

Porous wallpaper can seldom be cleaned as completely. To dust it thoroughly, dip a white bath towel in turpentine or mineral spirits (wear rubber gloves to protect your skin from irritation), wring it out, and allow it to dry outdoors. Tie the towel over the head of a dry mop or floor wax applicator, and use it to swab the wallpaper in horizontal strokes, working from ceiling to floor. As the towel accumulates dirt, turn it inside out or replace it.

Smudges on porous wallpaper sometimes can be removed with wallpaper-cleaning dough, available at wallcovering stores. Form the dough into a cylinder and roll it back and forth over the stain. As the dough becomes dirty, knead it to expose a fresh surface.

Grease stains can sometimes be blotted with commercial stain-removing solvents recommended by the wallpaper manufacturer. Another method is to place a piece of blotting paper over the spot and press it with a warm clothes iron for about two seconds. Repeat the process with clean sections of paper until the grease is absorbed.

To mend torn wallpaper, first try repasting it. If this cannot be done because some of the paper is damaged or missing, tear—do not cut—a patch from a spare roll of the same covering (the ragged edge of the patch will be less noticeable against the existing wallpaper than a patch cut with scissors or a knife).

Tear away the damaged paper by folding it back against itself and rotating your wrist close to the wall, not by pulling the paper outward. This tapers the torn edge of the paper to provide a smooth surface beneath the patch.

If the wall itself is damaged, repair it as described for preparing surfaces for wallpapering. To apply the wallpaper patch, coat the back with paste and press it against the area it is to cover. Slide it carefully into place so that it aligns with the pattern, then smooth the patch by rolling it with a seam roller. Wipe up excess paste immediately with a damp sponge.

Maintaining and Repairing Ceramic Tile

Ceramic tiles are admired for their beauty, durability, and moisture resistance. But regular cleaning is necessary to prevent the filler between tiles, called grout, from becoming stained by dirt or mildew, and deteriorated grout or broken tiles must be replaced promptly to prevent extensive damage.

> **TIP:**
>
> To lengthen intervals between regular cleaning of tiled bathroom walls, wipe them dry with a towel or squeegee after showering.

ATTENTION

Cleaning

The key to cleaning tile is knowing which cleaner to use. To remove thin soap film from tub and shower walls and for general cleaning, most nonabrasive household cleaners will do. So will cleaners made for ceramic tile. Never use steel wool or powdered cleansers containing abrasives, as these will scratch the surface. Abrasives can also decrease the tile's moisture resistance.

To remove hard water deposits, use a tile cleaner that has mild acids and is intended specifically for this job. Such a cleaner will usually remove thick soap film also. Home centers and many supermarkets carry the cleaners. For neglected tile with heavy deposits or film, cleaners with strong acids are sold at tile stores.

Follow the manufacturer's instructions carefully, especially with acid products. And with such products, be sure to protect your eyes, wear rubber gloves with cuffs, and provide plenty of ventilation.

To remove mildew, wash tile with a solution of one cup of either borax or household bleach and one gallon of water; commercial products are also made for this. Use the same precautions as with acid cleaners. And never mix bleach or mildew-removing products with any other chemical, including acid cleaners and ammonia. You can be badly injured by the fumes that may result.

Leave the borax or bleach solution on the mildewed area at least two minutes before rinsing it off with clear water. When using a commercial mildew remover, follow the label.

The presence of mildew, which is a fungus, indicates unusually high moisture. This can generally be corrected with an exhaust fan or dehumidifier, or simply by leaving the shower curtain or the tub enclosure open as much as possible. This should keep mildew from returning after it has been removed.

Mildew can also indicate damage or faulty construction that has allowed moisture to accumulate behind or beneath the tile. Without quick repairs, this can loosen and destroy the surfaces below, like walls, floors, and countertops.

When you find mildew, look for places that need repair. Grout may be missing between tiles, or seam sealer may have deteriorated around soap dishes, at tub or sink edges, and in corners. Replace the old material with new—first removing the old if necessary—using the methods described below and at the end of this chapter. Be sure faucets and spouts are tight and not leaking beneath the decorative collars that cover the openings where they go through the tiled surface.

After the tile is cleaned with an acidic cleaner or a mildew remover, and after every five or six cleanings with ordinary household cleaner, it can be given two coats of silicone sealer to preserve its shine, protect it from staining, and make it easier to clean. Sealers, sold at tile stores, are applied by spraying or with a foam applicator.

Repairing Grout

Grout is repaired by replacing it. Regrouting a small area involving only a few tiles is usually easy; regrouting a large area like an entire floor or wall is much more difficult.

Before starting even a small regrouting project, determine the cause of the damage. Two common causes are settling of the building and water damage to the surface beneath the tiles. (This is likely if grout has deteriorated near plumbing fixtures, toilets, and bathtubs.) These must be remedied before regrouting, or the problem will persist. If grout failure is widespread, extensive renovation of the surface beneath the tiles may be necessary; before tackling the repair yourself, consult a professional tilesetter.

Another possible cause is grout that was incorrectly mixed or applied. In that case, regrouting should produce lasting results.

Consider also the type of tile and its condition. Most people should be able to regrout glazed tile in good condition and small reas of unglazed or glazed tile that is old or worn. Large areas should be grouted professionally unless the tile is glazed and in good condition, and you feel confident sealing it as described below.

If grout has crumbled or loosened, the first step is removing it. Use either a grout saw—a short, coarse-toothed blade attached o a curved handle—or a carbide-tipped scoring knife used for utting the cement backer board that is used as a base for ceramic ile. All grouting supplies are available at tile stores.

o remove grout, use a grout knife or a carbide-tipped coring knife. Rake out grout to ¼-inch depth.

Rake out as much grout as possible, to a depth of at least a quarter of an inch. Then scrub the seams with a stiff bristle brush or an old toothbrush to remove loose particles. Wash the area with liquid grout cleaner, following the directions on the container.

There is no need to remove grout that is merely cracked. But do brush and clean it.

If the tile is unglazed or is glazed but old or in poor condition, the next step is to seal it with grout release, following the manufacturer's instructions. Two coats are usually necessary, brushed on from opposite directions. A film will remain; it must be removed by scrubbing with a cleaning solution, also specified in the instructions.

When selecting new grout, especially colored grout, consult tile store employees for advice. Grout that contains sand is usually best because it is strongest.

Wear protective gloves when handling grout; it contains cement, which is caustic. Grout that is already mixed can be applied directly from the container. To mix dry grout, follow the manufacturer's instructions but initially add only three fourths of the liquid called for. It is a good idea to use liquid latex grout additive, which enhances many of grout's characteristics, instead of water.

After initial blending, let the mixture stand for ten minutes and stir it again. Add more liquid only if the grout is so dry it does not stick to the side of the container or a trowel. Correctly mixed, the grout should have the consistency of moderately stiff peanut butter.

To apply grout to a small area, dampen the surrounding tiles. Then spread grout into the seams using a moistened, gloved finger or an improvised flexible applicator like an old credit card. Press firmly to force as much grout as possible into the seams.

When regrouting a large area, complete a section at a time. Work first on an area no more than 10 feet square to learn how quickly the grout hardens. Dampen the tiles. Then spread the grout with a hard rubber grout float. Hold the float at a shallow angle to the surface and make several passes over the tiles to work the grout thoroughly into the seams. Press hard to force out as much liquid as possible.

When the seams are filled, hold the float nearly perpendicular to the tile and scrape off excess grout. Move the float diagonally across the seams so as not to dislodge grout.

Whether regrouting a small area or a large one, wait ten to fifteen minutes; then test the hardness of the grout by wiping a seam gently with a sponge squeezed nearly dry. If this dislodges

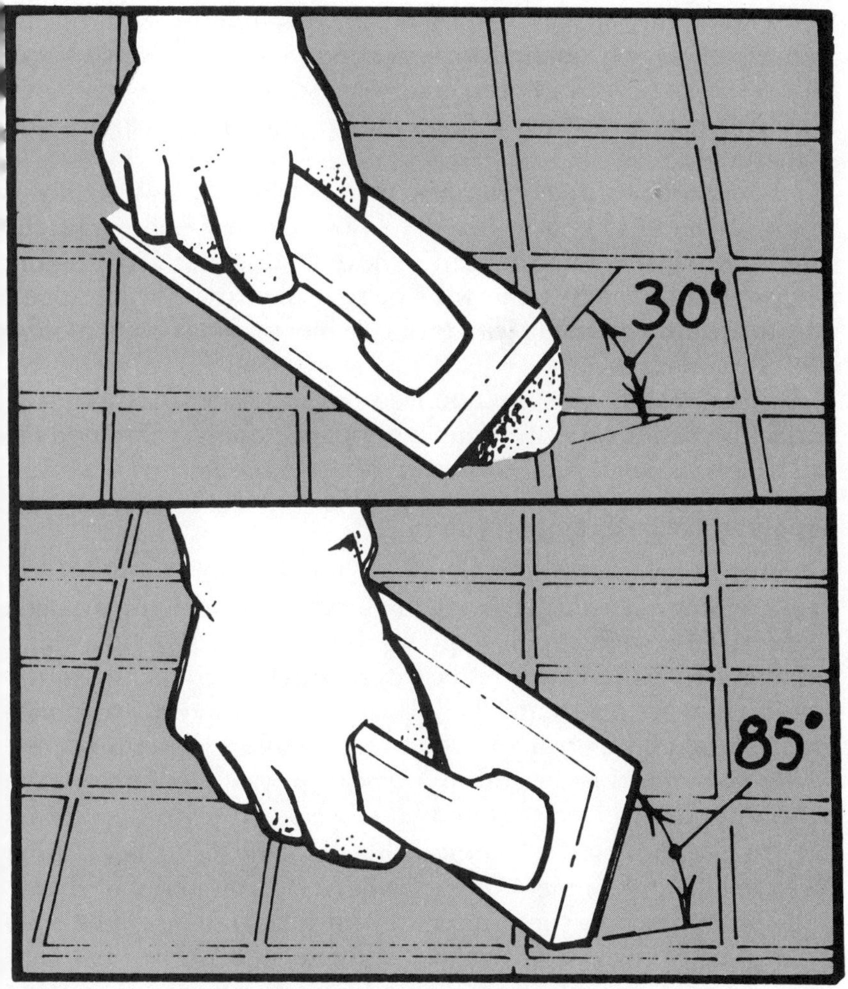

To apply grout over a large area, spread it with a float held at a shallow angle to the floor. After initial spreading, remove excess by scraping across seams with the float held nearly perpendicular.

any grout, replace it and wait a few minutes longer. Otherwise, clean excess grout from the tiles, keeping the sponge as dry as possible throughout.

First, wipe away most of the grout by gently sponging with circular movements. Turn the sponge often and rinse it as soon as its pores are filled. Next, sponge parallel to the seams (covering them with the sponge) to shape the grout level with the edges of the tiles or slightly lower.

Then clean the tile surface again, this time by drawing the sponge very slowly (about a foot in five seconds) toward you over the tiles, being careful not to gouge the seams. Make only one 3-foot-long pass with each side of the sponge before rinsing and squeezing it.

Wait another fifteen minutes, then polish the tiles by rubbing with dry cheesecloth, or with a dry nylon pot-scrubbing pad if the grout has set. It is important to remove all traces of grout before it hardens completely. Otherwise the haze that results will respond only to arduous scouring with grout cleaner and may even require professional removal.

Grout release must be removed within twenty-four hours or as the instructions specify. After seventy-two hours, regrouted tile can be given added protection with two coats of silicone sealer.

Repairing Loose or Broken Tile

If a tile is loose, you must remove it completely to refasten it. Try wiggling the tile by hand, or gently prying it up using a screwdriver or cold chisel. Tapping the prying tool lightly with a hammer may help. However, be careful not to dislodge surrounding tiles that are firmly attached. If you must deliver strong blows, first remove all the grout surrounding the tile (or group of tiles, if you are removing several in a block), so that the force of the blow is not transferred to sound tiles.

Broken tiles can be removed by chiseling (use a cold chisel and a ball peen hammer—not a carpenter's hammer, which may chip) or by striking them directly with a hammer of any type. Wear goggles for eye protection, and use short, sharp hammer blows so that the tile breaks into small fragments, not large chunks.

TIP:

Loose, undamaged tiles can be reused after removing adhesive from their backs. Try scraping it off with a utility knife or hook-type paint scraper. If necessary, soak tiles overnight in water to loosen adhesive.

ATTENTION

If part of a cracked or broken tile extends underneath a fixture such as a toilet that cannot be removed, carefully score around the fixture using a glass cutter or carbide-tipped scoring tool. Striking the scored line with a hammer should cause the tile to break along the line.

After removing a tile, use a putty knife or mason's trowel to scrape away dried adhesive from the space. Also scrape or saw off any grout clinging to the sides of neighboring tiles. Then brush or vacuum away all dust from the surface.

To refasten a removed tile or a replacement, spread a layer of tile adhesive onto the back, keeping the adhesive half an inch away from the edges. Then press the tile lightly into place.

The thickness of the adhesive should raise the tile slightly above the others. Place a board that is longer and wider than the new tile over it, and press down on the board until it rests on the surrounding tiles. This will level the new tile.

Remove the board and carefully scrape away any adhesive that has oozed into the border around the new tile. If the tile is on a wall, tape it securely to its neighbors using masking tape. (Allow the adhesive to cure overnight before removing the tape.) Some tiles have small protuberances—spacing lugs—on the sides to automatically maintain uniform spacing. If no spacing lugs are present, insert toothpicks or other spacers along the bottom edge of the tile to prevent it from slipping even slightly.

When the adhesive has cured, apply fresh grout. If necessary, also apply seam sealer.

Filling Tile Around Corners

Sometimes tiles must be shaped to fit around corners and fixtures. To do this, begin by placing the new tile on top of the

To scribe tile for cutting, use a drawing compass fitted with a grease pencil. Set the span of the compass arms to equal the width of one tile.

TIP:

Before sealing around a bathtub, fill it with water. This expands the joint where the tub meets the walls and will produce a tighter seal. For a neat joint, apply masking tape to the wall and tub at each side of the seam. After applying caulk, strip off the tape by pulling it straight out or up. Smooth with a dampened finger as noted in text.

existing tile that is adjacent to the empty space and parallel to the edge of the corner or fixture against which the new tile will lie.

Next, install a grease pencil or felt-tip pen in a drawing compass and spread the compass arms equal to the width of a full tile. Position the compass so that the point rests against the edge of the corner or fixture and the drawing tip rests on the surface of the new tile. Then move the compass along the contour of the fixture so that its outline is drawn onto the new tile.

With a glass cutter or carbide-tipped scoring tool, score the outline of the fixture drawn on the new tile. Then make many scoring cuts in the waste portion. Using tile biters (these resemble pliers and are available from tile suppliers), nibble ⅛-inch portions of the waste away, working toward the scored outline.

Hold the biters so that cutting is done only with the corners of the jaws. Make practice cuts on spare tile beforehand. When finished, the freshly cut edge of the tile can be smoothed with emery cloth or with a carbide-grit rod designed for sawing.

Round holes for tiles surrounding plumbing are easier to make. Simply rent a carbide-tipped hole-cutting saw and use it with an ordinary electric drill. To cut the tile in half after making the hole (so the tile can be pieced around the plumbing), score the glazed surface and place a long nail beneath the tile, directly under the scored line. Pressing down sharply on the tile on each side of the nail should break the tile cleanly in two.

Applying Seam Sealer

To seal seams between tile and fixtures like tubs and sinks, use silicone sealer meant for the job. The sealer comes in squeeze tubes, and also in cartridges for use in a caulking gun.

Before applying new sealer, remove any old sealer by digging it out with an ice pick or slicing it away with a single-edge razor blade. Scrub the area with a bristle brush dipped in household cleaner or tile-cleaning solution to remove residue, then rinse.

To apply sealer, slice off the tip of the tube or cartridge nozzle at a 45-degree angle. Swab the surfaces of the seam with mineral spirits to remove any soap film or detergent, then hold the tube or caulking gun against the seam at the angle of the tip and push it along the seam while squeezing sealer out at an even rate. Afterward, smooth the seam with a dampened finger.

Replacing Acoustical Ceiling Tile

Acoustical ceiling tiles, which are made of porous wood or mineral fibers, are commonly used to cover new and replacement ceilings. Although they are excellent for absorbing sound, they are also soft, easily broken, and often hard to clean. Damaged or stained acoustical tiles generally must be replaced.

Tiles suspended from a ceiling in metal channels are fairly easy to replace: The old tile is pushed upward and slipped out, and the new one is slipped in. But replacement is a bit more complex for tiles fastened directly to a ceiling or to a framework of narrow boards called furring strips. Such tiles are held by staples or adhesive or both. Most are also joined with interlocking edges.

To remove a damaged tile of this type, wear goggles against flaking tile, dust, or other particles. Old tiles may contain asbestos; unless you are sure the ones you are working with do not, wear a government-approved respirator and remove dust carefully and completely, without contaminating other areas.

Try to put the ladder where you will be reaching forward to the tile being removed. If the ladder is directly beneath the damaged tile, you will have a hard time balancing and will probably be showered with debris.

Using a sharp utility knife, cut the tile into 4-inch squares by making cuts across it between both pairs of sides. Remove the center square, then slide the others one by one into the open space to free them from the flanges of the surrounding tiles.

TIP:

If a rectangular suspended-ceiling tile will not fit easily through an opening in the channel, try pushing the entire tile upward until it clears the channel and then rotating it 90 degrees without turning it on edge. The tile's shorter end should now fit through the opening easily, and the tile can be removed by tilting it downward and sliding it out. To replace the tile, follow the procedure in reverse.

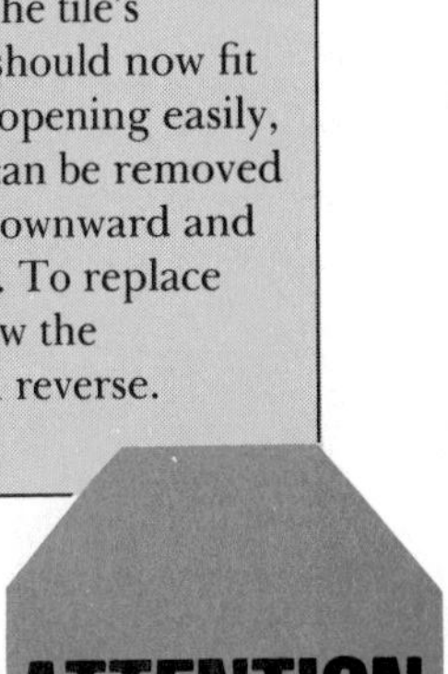

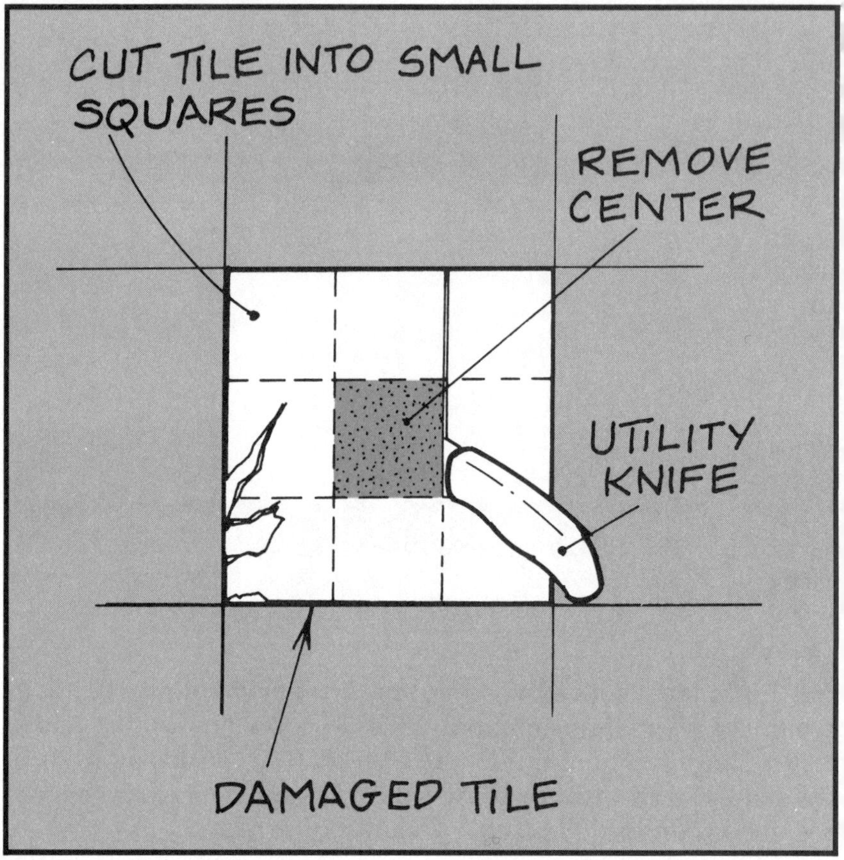

Remove acoustical tile by cutting it into small squares with a utility knife. Pry out the center square first.

Ordinarily, two sides of the tile will be stapled to the ceiling or furring strips above the tongues of adjacent undamaged tiles. Wiggle the pieces free that are stapled, leaving the staples behind if they do not come loose. If any of the damaged tile breaks off and remains stapled, trim it flush with the tongues of the tile below it, but be careful: Preserve as many of the flanges of the undamaged tiles as possible.

When removing several tiles as a group, remove the first tile as described, then slice diagonally between the corners of a neighboring damaged tile. Break the second tile into pieces and remove the fragments by gently tugging and twisting. Do the same with the remaining damaged tiles.

Pry glued tiles away from the ceiling with a putty knife; use the same tool to scrape away any dried adhesive.

Replacement tile is available at home centers, building supply stores, and from tile manufacturers. Builders often leave behind extra tiles for repairs, so check before buying new ones.

To install a replacement tile where only one tile has been removed, first use the utility knife—with a straightedge as a guide—to cut the two wide flanges and one of the narrower tongues from the perimeter of the tile. Then, spread a ribbon of construction adhesive or acoustical tile cement (both are available at hardware stores and home centers) onto the back of the tile, around the three trimmed sides, or where it will contact the ceiling or furring strips.

Hold the tile by its trimmed edges and slide the tongue into the groove of an adjacent tile. Using the tongue as a hinge, press the tile upward so that the glue makes contact. Drive in one or more three-penny (1¼-inch) box nails on the side opposite the tongue to supplement the glue. To avoid accidentally striking the tile while hammering, drive the nails to within an eighth of an inch of the surface; then use a nail set with the hammer to drive them until their heads are flush. Cover nail heads with paint to hide them.

To install a group of replacement tiles, use staples, either by themselves, if the tiles are fastened to furring strips, or with adhesive, if the tiles are attached directly to the ceiling. Leave the flanges untrimmed on all tiles but the last.

To attach tiles with staples alone, slide each tile into place so its tongues enter the grooves of the existing tiles. Then, with a stapling gun, install staples in the two wide flanges that are left exposed.

Tiles must be anchored firmly yet be able to expand and contract with humidity changes. The usual practice for tiles 12 inches on each side (a standard size) is to space three staples evenly in one flange and put one staple at the farthest end of the adjoining flange. For tiles 16 inches on a side, another standard size, use four staples in one flange and one at the farthest end of the other. For double-size tile—12 inches by 24 inches—put five staples in the flange on the long side and one staple in the far end of the flange on the short side. Install staples at an angle to the edges of flanges, not parallel, to increase their holding power.

If a group of tiles is to be cemented in place, apply adhesive or cement to each tile as described. Then fit tiles into place against their neighbors, one at a time. Install two staples in each wide flange to hold the tile until the adhesive hardens.

With either staples or adhesive, install the final tile as described for installing a single replacement.

Caring for Vinyl and Other Resilient Floors

Sheet vinyl flooring is popular because of its appearance, relatively easy installation, and durability. But cleaning and polishing vinyl floors requires care, and precautions also must be taken to avoid damage from heavy furniture. Vinyl flooring can be repaired. If done skillfully, the repairs are often invisible.

The mainstay of vinyl floor care is regular vacuuming or dusting with a dry or damp mop. This should be done at least weekly so that dirt is not ground into the flooring, causing it to lose its shine.

Spills should be wiped up promptly to prevent staining. Soiled floors should be cleaned by sponge-mopping, using either a mild liquid detergent or a vinyl-floor-cleaning solution recommended by the flooring manufacturer. Floor-cleaning solution is suggested if floors are high-gloss or if they must be rinsed with hard water, which causes spotting.

To remove built-up grime, detergents and other cleaning solutions can be fortified by adding half a cup of ammonia per gallon, or as specified by the label instructions, provided the products contain no bleach. Mixing bleach and ammonia produces toxic fumes. Never use undiluted bleach or cleaners containing solvents or gritty abrasives. All three can dull or yellow vinyl flooring.

Floor-cleaning solution will remove most stains if applied promptly. If stronger measures are needed try the following, in order: rubbing with wet powdered cleanser containing soft abrasive like whiting (do not use if floor is high-gloss); rubbing lightly with lighter fluid, turpentine, or mineral spirits; rubbing lightly with a cloth moistened with a mixture of ten parts water to one part liquid bleach. To remove nail polish, rub lightly with a cloth dipped in nail polish remover. To remove rust or grass stains, rub with lemon juice.

Do not mix chemicals. Wait half an hour between applications. Lighter fluid, turpentine, mineral spirits, and some nail polish remover are flammable and hazardous to inhale; when using these, follow precautions listed on the label.

Heavily used flooring may become dull despite regular cleaning. If this happens, apply a liquid vinyl floor finish recommended by the flooring manufacturer. Different finishes are required for standard-gloss and high-gloss floors.

When applying a finish, use a clean sponge mop or liquid floor wax applicator. Do not pour finish directly onto the floor. Instead, pour it into a shallow pan into which the mop or applicator can be dipped. Apply a thin coat of finish and avoid creating puddles. Allow the finish to dry thoroughly for at least half an hour before applying additional coats if any are necessary.

Standard-gloss floors can be polished after cleaning, or after applying finish, using an electric floor polisher equipped with a lamb's-wool buffing pad. Do not buff high-gloss floors; doing so can dull them. High-gloss floors that have been damaged by buffing can usually be restored with a new coat of finish.

Heavy furniture and appliances can tear vinyl flooring or permanently compress it. To prevent this, attach large-surfaced, hard plastic protectors, casters, or glides to furniture legs and appliance bases, even those already equipped with small protectors. Do not use protective items made of rubber; chemicals in rubber can stain vinyl permanently.

To prevent gouging flooring when moving heavy items across it, place thick cardboard on the floor first, and slide or roll the items over it.

Torn or otherwise damaged flooring should be repaired promptly before the damage worsens. To repair minor cuts or gouges, first wipe the area clean with a cloth moistened with mineral spirits. When it is dry, glue the surface material back together with seam sealer recommended for your flooring. The sealer must be applied using a special applicator sold with the product.

Areas damaged more extensively must be patched. Determine the least noticeable places in the design and plan to make cuts there, outlining the damaged area and creating a patch. If the floor's design does not hide cuts easily, a diamond-shaped cutout is usually least conspicuous.

TIP:

Vinyl and other resilient floors do not need frequent washing; in fact, water can seep beneath flooring to loosen adhesive. Do not wash a newly installed vinyl or resilient floor for at least a week. Thereafter, damp-mop only when vacuuming or dry-mopping will not suffice, and sponge-mop only if absolutely necessary—no more than every six weeks on a regular basis. Avoid creating pools of muddy water near entrances where boots or overshoes are removed by spreading an absorbent throw rug over the area.

ATTENTION

TIP:

Before moving very heavy items like kitchen appliances over a resilient floor, cut strips of quarter-inch-thick plywood about 4 inches wide. Lay these on the floor to provide a surface over which to roll the items on their casters or on dollies.

ATTENTION

Either use a piece of leftover material or take material from an inconspicuous spot, like the area beneath an appliance. Trim the piece so it extends about an inch on all sides beyond the area you plan to remove. Place the patch on the floor over the damaged area and align the designs. Tape the patch to the flooring on all sides with masking tape.

With a sharp utility knife, cut through the patch and the flooring along the lines chosen for the cutout. Use a metal straightedge as a guide. Be sure to hold the knife so the blade cuts perpendicular to the floor or the patch will fit poorly.

Remove the tape and the patch. If the damaged flooring is not cemented to the subfloor underneath, lift it out also. Cut several strips of masking tape and, using the point of the knife, slide them sticky side up partly under the undamaged flooring on the perimeter of the opening. Fit the patch into place and press the area with a rolling pin so the patch adheres to the tape. Finish patching by applying seam sealer to the cuts. After the seal dries, apply floor finish.

If the damaged flooring is permanently cemented to the subfloor, use the tip of the knife to carefully separate the surface layer of the flooring from the backing. Then pull it away. Do the same with the patch, but be careful not to damage the surface layer.

Apply a thin layer of vinyl flooring adhesive to the back of the surface layer that will be the patch. Avoid getting adhesive on the edges. Fit the patch into place on top of the backing, then press the area with a rolling pin. Remove any oozing adhesive with a damp cloth. Dry the area with a clean cloth and apply seam sealer. Complete the job by applying floor finish.

A third type of vinyl flooring is cemented to the subfloor but can be pulled completely away. To patch this type, proceed as for noncemented flooring. Instead of using tape to hold the patch in place, simply press the patch against the subfloor with a rolling pin. The remaining adhesive should be sticky enough to secure the patch. Apply seam sealer and floor finish.

Other Resilient Flooring

Other resilient floors—asphalt, linoleum, rubber, cork—also require little maintenance and can be repaired if damaged. Clean them with detergent (fortified with ammonia if necessary), as described for vinyl.

Stains can be removed by most of the methods mentioned for vinyl also, but do not use lighter fluid, turpentine, mineral spirits, or nail polish remover on asphalt or rubber tile, and do not use chlorine bleach on cork.

'o make a patch, tape a spare piece of flooring over the lamaged area and then cut through both layers with a harp utility knife.

'o fasten a patch in non-cemented flooring, position nasking tape partly under the surrounding old flooring ınd press the patch into place with a rolling pin.

'o fasten a patch in cemented flooring, peel off the top ayer and replace it with the top layer of the patch, coated vith adhesive.

Unlike vinyl, other resilient flooring can be rubbed lightly ith No. 00-grade steel wool dipped in any of the cleaners or stain emovers mentioned. To restore glossiness to small areas dulled y rubbing, apply clear nail polish. For larger areas, cover the ntire floor with liquid polish formulated for that type of flooring.

Scratches can often be repaired with paste wax. Spread a mall amount on a soft cloth and rub it lightly over the area of the cratch; then wipe away the excess from the undamaged surface. nother technique that often works is to rub the scratch lengthvise with the rim of a large coin, like a half-dollar, or the handle f a tool like a putty knife.

Afterward, if the scratch remains visible or if the damage is a ut rather than a scratch, lay a doubled thickness of aluminum oil over the area that was rubbed and press it with the tip of a arm clothes iron. Check often to avoid scorching.

Tile and linoleum floors sometimes develop blisters when reas of cement loosen or deteriorate. This can happen if heat is pplied to the flooring material or if the water seeps between the flooring and the subfloor. Before repairing blistered flooring, determine the cause of the damage and repair that if necessary.

To repair the blister, slit it lengthwise with a single-edge razor blade or a utility knife. Try to follow a line in the pattern of the flooring material to make the slit less conspicuous. Extend the cut about half an inch beyond each end of the blister. Place foil over the spot and heat the flooring with a warm iron to soften it. Then force a liberal quantity of flooring adhesive, available at home centers, under both parts of the blister with a putty knife or an old kitchen knife.

Press the blister flat with your hand. If the material has stretched and the sides of the cut overlap, carefully slice along the edge of the overlap, lift it, and remove the trimmed sliver of flooring. Then press the upper piece flat again. Wipe up the excess adhesive; place a weight (at least 20 pounds) over the area and allow the adhesive to cure according to the manufacturer's instructions.

Small tears and holes can be repaired by filling with homemade color-matched putty. To make the putty, use a utility knife to scrape the surface of a spare piece of flooring or a piece removed from an inconspicuous location, such as a closet. Make a paste of the colored shavings by adding tiny amounts of clear nail polish while stirring with a toothpick.

Mask the edges of the blemish with tape. Press the putty into the damaged area using a putty knife with a flexible blade. Then lay foil over the repair and press with a warm clothes iron to melt the shavings. Avoid scorching.

Allow the putty to dry at least an hour, then carefully remove the tape and rub the repaired surface with No. 00-grade steel wool. Apply a thin coat of clear nail polish for gloss.

Large tears and holes must be patched; a damaged tile must be replaced either with a spare or with one removed from an inconspicuous area. If you remove an undamaged tile to use as a replacement, buy a new tile to fill the space (it needn't match if the old came from an inconspicuous location).

To remove a tile, soften it by heating with an iron placed over foil. When the tile becomes pliable, lift it with a putty knife and grasp a corner with your fingers. Pull the tile upward while cutting away adhesive clinging to it.

Reheat the tile as necessary until the task is complete. Allow adhesive remaining on the subfloor to harden; then scrape it off.

To install a replacement, first apply a thin layer of flooring adhesive to the subfloor using a notched trowel designed for spreading adhesive. Place the new tile so one edge is against an adjoining tile; then lower the new tile carefully into place. Rub the tile all over with your palm to press it down; place a heavy weight on it until the adhesive cures.

To repair damaged sheet flooring, follow the directions for cutting a patch for vinyl flooring. If a layer of tar paper covers the subfloor, remove it and replace with fresh 15-pound building felt, available at home centers. Spread a thin layer of flooring adhesive over the subfloor and place the felt patch over that.

The flooring patch should be set on top of a thin layer of adhesive applied to the subflooring or the felt. Press the material all over so it lies flat; place a doubled piece of foil over the seam and heat with a warm iron as described for repairing scratches and cuts. Finally, place a heavy weight on the area until the adhesive cures.

Caring for Wood Floors

Finished wood floors are durable and easy to care for. With regular maintenance, they will retain their original appearance for many years.

Frequent dusting is essential. At least weekly, vacuum floors or sweep them with a dry dust mop to pick up dirt and grit before it becomes embedded by foot traffic. Vacuuming does the most good because it lifts dirt from crevices and seams.

A mop dampened with a little water can be used for dusting if the floor is in good condition and has been finished with penetrating sealer, polyurethane, or a resin-based finish (sometimes called a Swedish finish). Use a damp mop also for wiping up spills and for general cleaning.

Avoid using more water than this on a wood floor, regardless of its finish. Never wet mop or wash a floor with a cleaning solution containing water. Remove spills promptly. If the floor is in poor condition or is unprotected by sealer or the types of finish mentioned, forgo even damp-mopping except in an emergency.

WARNING:

Do not apply wax to floors with polyurethane or other "no-wax" finish. Doing so will prevent recoating the floor with a similar finish at a later time to renew it. Most stains and other blemishes can be removed from these floors by applying a special floor cleaner made for the finish and available at floor dealers.

ATTENTION

Removing Stains

The problem with water—besides warping and roughening the grain of wood—is that it causes stains. To remove a light-colored water stain, rub the spot gently with No. 2-grade steel wool until it disappears. Then apply new wax to the area as described further on.

Dark stains may be caused by dirty water or some other substance. To remove these, first rub the spot with No. 2 steel wool dipped in mineral spirits; then lay a cloth dipped in distilled household vinegar over the area. Allow the vinegar to remain on the stain for about ten minutes, then wipe the area with a cloth dampened in mineral spirits. If the treatment has worked, apply fresh wax.

If vinegar fails to lighten the stain, make a stronger bleaching solution by mixing oxalic acid crystals (available at hardware and paint stores) in very hot water. When the crystals no longer dissolve, the proportions are correct. If you cannot obtain oxalic acid crystals, use a laundry detergent containing it, such as Oxydol. Wear rubber gloves, as this solution will irritate skin.

Saturate a clean cloth with the solution and allow it to remain on the stain for one hour. Then sponge the area with clear water and promptly blot it dry. Apply fresh wax after the area has dried completely. If this treatment fails, consult a professional floor or furniture refinisher.

Stains caused by alcohol—these too may be light-colored—can usually be removed by rubbing the area with a cloth dipped in liquid wax containing cleaner for removing old wax, or in silver polish containing whiting (a fine abrasive). If this does not work, try rubbing with a cloth dipped in ammonia and squeezed almost dry. Afterward, apply fresh wax if you have rubbed through to the finish; otherwise, simply buff the area by hand with a clean cloth to restore the floor's sheen.

To remove black heel marks or those left by furniture casters, rub with No. 00 steel wool dampened with mineral spirits and squeezed nearly dry. Apply fresh wax.

To remove oil and grease stains, saturate a gauze pad with hydrogen peroxide and place it over the stain. Saturate a second pad with ammonia and place it over the first. Wait about fifteen minutes, then check the results. Repeat if necessary. After the floor is dry, apply fresh wax.

TIP:

Chewing gum and candle wax can be removed by applying ice (held in a plastic bag) to freeze the material. When it becomes brittle, either scrape it from the floor with a kitchen knife or pour about a tablespoon of mineral spirits around the material (not on it). The fluid will seep beneath the gum or wax, loosening it. Afterward, if necessary, treat as for removing oil and grease stains.

Crayon marks can be removed by the same method, or try rubbing them with a cloth dipped in toothpaste. To remove mildew stains, wash with cleaning fluid.

ATTENTION

Waxing

Floors with a wax or wax-covered finish benefit from one or two coats of wax per year. More frequent waxing is advisable in heavily trod areas where wax wears thin sooner. Wax helps prevent serious damage from stains by forming a barrier over the floor that slows or keeps spills from penetrating the finish. Wax also enhances the appearance of wood.

Paste wax is the most durable floor wax, but the solid kind that comes in a can is strenuous to apply. Liquid paste wax avail-

TIP:

Giving polyurethane and other "no-wax" floors a cleaning equivalent to rewaxing is accomplished by wiping the entire floor with a cleaner formulated for the finish, mentioned in the note on page 101. Buffing afterward is often not necessary, but can be done using an electric buffer or polisher fitted with a lamb's wool buffing pad.

TIP:

Provided wax has never been applied, a polyurethaned or other "no-wax" floor hazed by scratches can be renewed simply by roughening the surface with steel wool or an abrasive screen and then applying a fresh coat of similar finish.

able from floor dealers is easier to use. Many brands contain a cleaner that removes much of the previous wax, slowing discoloration due to accumulation of old wax and enhancing the bonding of new wax to what remains of the old.

When selecting a liquid wax containing cleaner, check to see that it is solvent-based. Water should not be listed on the label as an ingredient, and rinsing the floor with water should not be suggested.

Wax can be applied by hand or with an electric floor polisher. The latter can be rented and is worthwhile if you intend to apply paste wax or to buff the floor after waxing. Rent a polisher with a pad that is 12 to 16 inches in diameter and have store personnel demonstrate how to use the tool before you take it home.

To apply wax, follow the manufacturer's instructions. When applying liquid wax containing cleaner, change applicator pads frequently to avoid reapplying dirty wax that the cleaner has removed.

With both solid and liquid paste wax, a thin coat is best. This dries to a harder film than a thick coat—providing more protection against grit—and can be buffed to a higher gloss. It is also less slippery.

If floors seem dull despite waxing and buffing, stripping them to remove all built-up wax is probably necessary.

To strip a waxed floor, apply solvent-based liquid dewaxer or deglosser, available at hardware stores and home centers.

Apply the liquid using cloths and No. 2 steel wool pads, squeezed dry or changed frequently. A floor polisher can also be used but is messy unless you are experienced. Follow all safety precautions listed on product labels and supply plenty of ventilation. All these liquids are flammable and dangerous to health.

After stripping, apply two thin coats of paste wax. Follow by thorough buffing, using a floor polisher for best results.

Refinishing

When a wood floor becomes so badly worn or stained that no amount of floor finish or wax will improve its looks, the solution is to sand the floor down to bare wood and refinish it.

Sanding a wood floor is not too difficult, but it is dusty, noisy and time-consuming. If the floor is thickly covered with paint, consider having it chemically stripped by professionals first, to reduce the amount of sanding necessary. (Paint applied before 1977 may contain hazardous amounts of lead; in some communities, removal of even thin coats must be by professionals. For advice, and to have paint tested for lead, contact the local health department.) Also consider professional treatment if the floor is ornately patterned, or if the floorboards measure less than 5/16 inch thick.

To sand a floor, you will need a drum sander and an edger, two power tools available from rental centers. When sanding, wear goggles, ear protectors, and a dust mask. These you can get at a hardware store.

A drum sander resembles a large upright vacuum cleaner. Its main components are a horizontal cylinder—the drum—around which sheets of sandpaper are attached, and an electric motor that spins the drum at high speed over the floor.

Be sure the sander you select operates on ordinary household current (120 volts) unless a 220-volt outlet—such as for a clothes dryer—is conveniently located. Models with a slotted drum or that take belts of sandpaper rather than sheets are easier to load and use.

An edger is a smaller machine, without a long handle, for sanding where the drum sander cannot reach. It uses disks of sandpaper rather than sheets or belts.

Sandpaper is usually supplied when you rent the tools. Customarily, unused sandpaper is returnable. Have the representative demonstrate the operation of both sanders, and also how to change sandpaper.

Most floors are sanded in three stages. First, a coarse grade of sandpaper (20-grit for a painted floor, 36- or 50-grit for a clear-finished floor) is used to remove the finish. Then a medium (80-grit) and a fine grade (100-grit) are used to remove scratches. Sometimes more than one sanding with coarse-grade paper is necessary before moving to the finer grades.

When sanding a clear-finished floor, begin with 50-grit sandpaper unless the finish is very thick. If the sandpaper clogs quickly, switch to 36-grit. If the 50-grit paper performs adequately—removing the finish down to bare wood—the second sanding with 80-grit sandpaper can sometimes be omitted.

On parquet floors, begin with 80-grit paper. If it removes the finish, follow this with 100-grit paper to complete the job. However, if the 80-grit sandpaper clogs, switch to 50-grit paper and perform all three sandings.

Before sanding, prepare the floor and the room carefully by removing all items and sealing all openings to the rest of the house against dust. Cover cabinets and appliances that cannot be removed. Extinguish stove pilots. Leave windows and outside doors open for ventilation.

Scrupulously inspect the floor for protruding items, especially nail heads. Use a hammer and nail set to drive these at least

APARTMENT OWNERS:

See note about lead paint on page 91.

HINT

TIP:

Old sheets or other cloths are better for sealing doorways than plastic sheeting. Cloth is less likely to be moved away from an opening by stray air currents, and due to a lower degree of static electricity does not attract as much dust.

ATTENTION

an eighth of an inch below the surface. Remove items like staples and old carpet tacks; refasten loose floorboards and repair large cracks or splinters. Just before sanding, vacuum the floor.

Begin each stage of sanding with the drum sander. Place it against a wall parallel to the floorboards so you can sand them lengthwise. Leave at least 6 feet of space behind the sander for maneuvering it. (It is a good idea to mark this point with a line of chalk across the floorboards to the opposite wall.)

On a parquet floor, the first sanding should be at a 45-degree angle to the room's length. The next sanding should be at a 45-degree angle across the first, and the last sanding should be parallel to the room's length.

Operating a drum sander without gouging the floor is tricky. The cardinal rule is to never let it remain stationary—nor start or stop the motor—with the drum touching the floor.

Begin with the drum raised and the cord either draped around your shoulders, so that you do not run over it, or clipped to your belt. Be sure the dust bag on the sander is out of the way.

Turn on the motor. When it reaches full speed, gently lower the drum while pushing the sander forward.

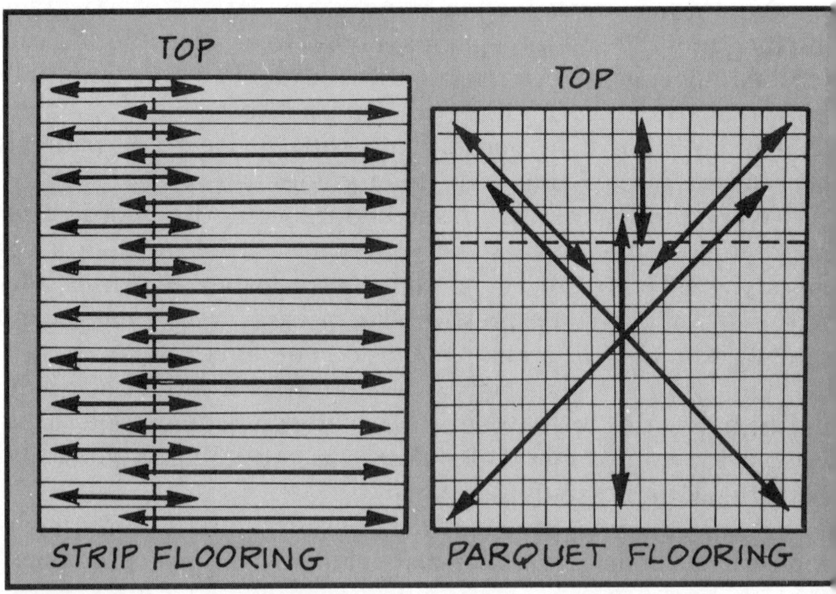

When sanding ordinary floors, follow the back-and-forth pattern shown. For parquet floors, follow the pattern showing diagonal passes.

Take small, slow steps to prevent the sander from moving forward too fast. Keep the tool moving at an even rate and in a straight line.

Raise the drum before the sander strikes the wall at the end of the floorboards. Begin walking backward, and lower the drum again as you do so. Draw the sander over the path it has just taken. When you return to the starting point, raise the drum just as the sander crosses over it.

Maneuver the sander to the side so that the drum overlaps about half of the previous pass. Then begin the second pass, guiding the sander as before.

Continue across the room until you reach the wall opposite the starting point. Then turn the sander around and sand the remaining part of the room on the other side of the chalked line.

Renew the sandpaper when it dulls, tears, or clogs. Empty the dust bag when it fills more than halfway.

Use the edger in areas missed by the drum sander. Move the tool parallel to the floorboards or in small, overlapping clockwise circles. Do not press down or you will gouge the floor; the weight of the tool supplies sufficient pressure.

If you make a mistake with either sander and gouge the wood, sand back and forth over the spot, widening it gradually until it blends with the rest of the floor. Sometimes, sanding at a 45-degree angle to the damage erases it more quickly; however, be sure to finish by sanding in the direction of the wood grain.

After rough sanding, vacuum the floor and fill any cracks or holes with wood putty made by mixing sanding dust and lacquer to any desired consistency. Wear a painter's respirator when working with lacquer.

For the remaining sanding stages repeat the process. After final sanding, use a hook-style hand scraper (available at hardware stores) to scrape areas missed by the edger. Then smooth the scraped surface by hand-sanding.

TIP:

Filler can be made by mixing water-based floor sealer with sanding dust. As with lacquer-based filler, wearing a respirator is advisable.

ATTENTION

Buffing

Before applying finish, rent an electric floor polisher and buff the floor with a 120-grit abrasive screen to blend the final sanding marks. To buff, stand perpendicular to the floorboards and sweep the machine back and forth, parallel to them. Practice with the buffer first, using just the pad, because the machine can get out of hand and bump into walls. When buffing with a new screen, start in an inconspicuous area. The sound of the machine—coarse at first, then smoother—will tell you when an area is sufficiently buffed. After buffing, vacuum the floor thoroughly.

TIP:

Water-based floor finishes have replaced many solvent-based varieties in recent years. Besides emitting lower levels of volatile organic compounds into the air, water-based finishes are easier to apply than some oil- and solvent-based finishes, and do not alter the color of the wood. Cleaning up is easier, too: Only soap and water are needed.

However, water-based finishes are not harmless. Rubber gloves and a painter's respirator should be worn when applying them, and plenty of ventilation is also required.

Staining

Stain enhances the contrast between light-grained and dark-grained wood. Oil-based and water-based stains are available; either can be used beneath any finish. To apply stain, follow the manufacturer's directions. Usually, the procedure is to spread stain onto the floor with one cloth, then wipe off the excess with another a few moments later. The interval between spreading and wiping must be uniform across the floor, otherwise staining will be uneven. For this reason, have a helper do the wiping while following you at a prescribed distance as you apply the stain. Allow at least twelve hours for stain to dry before applying finish.

Applying Finish

There are many varieties of floor finishes, each with its own characteristics and application methods. In general, use a natural-bristle brush when applying oil- or resin-based finish and a synthetic brush that does not absorb water when applying water-based finish. Always brush from a dry area into a wet one to avoid lap marks, and overlap each pass 3 or 4 inches with the next one.

To view the finish while applying it, work away from strong light sources, not toward them. To avoid splashing, take short, slow strokes with the brush; for the same reason, use a very dry brush when painting projecting edges like stair nosings. Pick up dust particles you encounter, rather than brush over them.

After completing the first coat and allowing it to dry, repair any blemishes by scraping and hand-sanding. If necessary, use colored putty (available from flooring suppliers) to match the color of a repaired spot to the surrounding area.

Buff the floor with a 150-grit screen before applying the second coat of finish. (Hand-sand with 100-grit sandpaper areas the buffer cannot reach.) Apply the second coat as you did the first, then apply a final coat after buffing the second.

Be very careful when applying the final coat to brush in the direction of the wood grain and to pick up any dust particles. Otherwise, brush marks and blemishes will remain visible. Do not buff the final coat. Wait two or three days for it to harden before waxing it and moving furniture back into the room.

Cleaning and Repairing Blinds and Shades

Spring cleaning traditionally calls to mind beating carpets and clearing attics. However, sprucing up venetian blinds and window shades is probably a more common activity.

> **TIP:**
>
> When using absorbent gloves to clean venetian blinds, moisten the fingers with furniture polish to remove thick dust and leave a smooth surface.

ATTENTION

Cleaning

Of course, dusting blinds and shades regularly keeps them from becoming so dirty that thorough cleaning is necessary. Brushes and tools designed especially for cleaning the slats of venetian blinds are available at department stores and many supermarkets. Slats can also be cleaned by running your fingers over them while wearing absorbent cotton gloves or by wiping the surfaces with a dampened towel.

To dust shades, simply unroll them all the way and vacuum them on both sides or wipe them with an absorbent cloth.

When thorough cleaning of blinds does become necessary, washing is usually the best answer. However, there are a few exceptions. Wooden blinds should not be washed, because the slats will absorb moisture and warp. Instead, wipe each slat with furniture cleaner or mineral spirits and immediately wipe dry. To clean canvas or other nonwashable shades, try wallpaper-cleaning dough, available at wall covering and paint stores.

Metal and plastic blinds are most easily washed outdoors or in a bathtub. Outdoors, lay the blinds flat on the grass, a drop cloth, or newspapers. Sponge or scrub the slats on both sides with a solution of household detergent (or wax-free car-washing deter-

TIP:

Small smudges often can be removed from shades by rubbing them with a soft pencil eraser or art gum.

ATTENTION

gent) and warm water, then hang the blinds from a clothesline. Rinse them by spraying with a garden hose. Allow the blinds to dry completely before rehanging them.

To wash blinds indoors, extend them fully and arrange them in a bathtub filled with warm water and detergent. Let them soak for about half an hour, then sponge or scrub. Drain the tub after washing and refill it with clear water. Sponge the slats again to rinse them.

To dry the blinds, spread newspapers over the rim of the tub and on the floor. After making sure the shower curtain rod is fastened securely, hang the blinds fully extended from the rod.

If you cannot hang the blinds from the shower curtain rod, wrap each one in a towel to carry it and rehang it from its window brackets. Spread newspapers on the floor to catch drips.

If you must leave the blinds in place to wash them, follow this method: Use two buckets. Fill one with a solution of grease-cutting household detergent, and the other with plain water. Spread plenty of old newspapers beneath the blinds to absorb drips. Extend the blinds fully and adjust them so the slats are horizontal. Starting from the top of the blind, wash and rinse both sides of each slat, first using a sponge dipped in detergent, then a separate sponge dipped in plain water. When you are finished, dry the slats individually using a soft towel.

To clean shades, unroll them before taking them down and lay them flat on absorbent material. If the shades are washable, sponge them with detergent solution followed by clear water. Avoid wetting the rollers and metal parts at the ends. Dry shades by hanging them unrolled.

Repairing blinds

Occasionally, blinds and shades also need repair. If blinds pull unevenly, extend them fully and adjust the lift cords by repositioning the buckle clasping them so that their lengths above the buckle are equal. If cords jam, remove the blind and untangle them from above.

Broken blind cords and the tapes that hold the slats can be replaced with kits from department and hardware stores. To replace a broken tilt cord (the cord that adjusts the angle of the slats), simply cut off the ends, pull it out of the blind from above, then thread a new cord in its place by passing it over the pulley that rotates the tilt mechanism.

To replace a broken lift cord (the cord that raises and lowers the slats), first untie the ends. On some blinds these are found beneath the bottom rail, concealed by plastic caps that can be ɔried out with a penknife. On others, the bottom rail is hollow ınd made up of an upper and lower half. Pry off the caps at each end of the rail and slide the halves apart. The ends of the lift cord ıre tied beneath the underside of the rail's top half.

Draw the cord upward, pulling it through the slats but not nto the upper portion of the blind, called the headbox. Remove he slats. Don't worry if they get mixed up; their order is inter- changeable.

Thread one end of the new lift cord into the headbox from below, into one of the holes from which the old cord still emerges. Use the old cord as a guide for threading the new one. As you work the new cord into place, remove the old cord a little at a time by drawing it out through the top of the headbox.

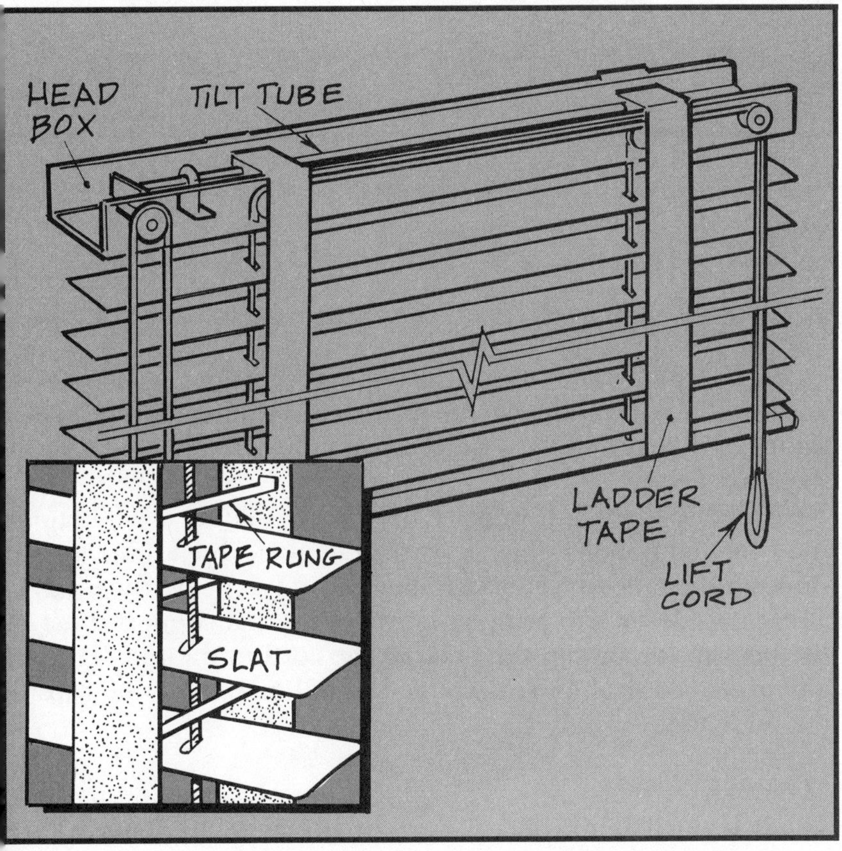

If a venetian blind jams, check for tangled cords in the headbox. When installing a new lift cord, thread it on alternate sides of the rungs.

TIP:

A quick way to wash metal blinds is to take them to a coin-operated car wash. Spread the blinds on the floor, wash both sides with detergent, then rinse. Do not apply wax. Place wet blinds in plastic garbage bags to transport them home for drying.

ATTENTION

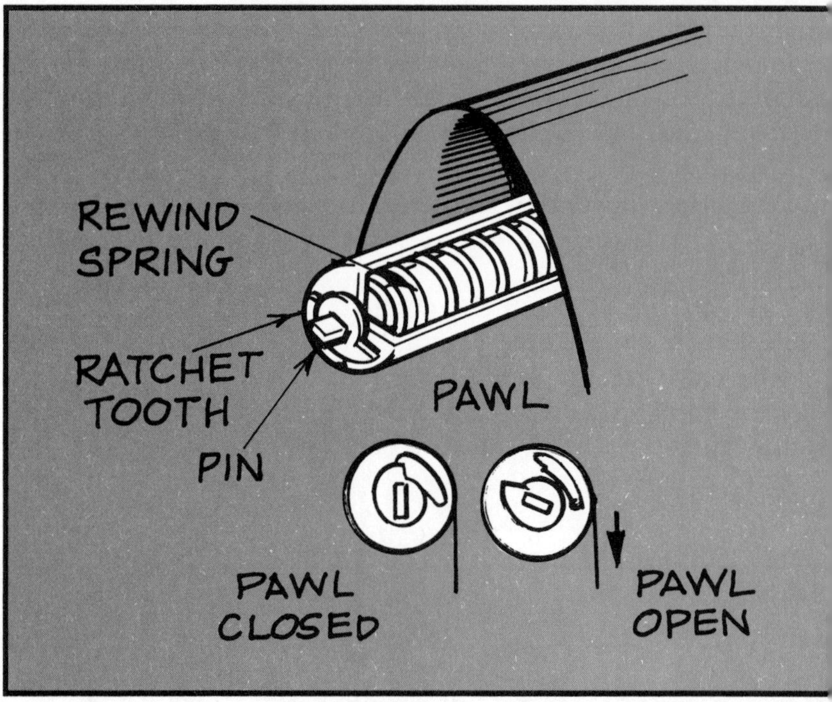

The spring inside the roller controls the action of the window shade. The swiveling pawl at the end prevents the shade from rolling back up after it is drawn.

Use enough cord so that the ends reach below the bottom ra when the blind is fully extended. Also leave a loop at one side c the blind long enough to be reached conveniently when raisin the slats.

Rehang the blind. Replace the slats by sliding them betwee the twine or ribbon rungs on each side, then thread the lift cor through the holes in the slats, being careful to weave the cords o alternate sides of the twine or fabric rungs that support them. A the bottom, tie or clip the ends of the cord to the rail. Trim of any excess cord, then reassemble the rail or replace the caps o the underside.

Repairing Shades

It is possible to conceal worn or permanently stained lowe portions of shades by removing the material from the roller an reattaching it upside down. To do this, unroll the shade, remov it from its brackets, and remove the staples that hold the materia to the wooden roller at the top. Also remove the narrow slat fron the hem at the bottom of the shade and snip off or untie the pull ring. Open the seam of the hem so the material lies flat.

Form and sew a new hem in the upper edge of the shade, wide enough to create a new sleeve for the slat. Attach the pull ring. Refasten the shade to the roller using staples, carpet tacks, or a long strip of cloth utility tape after carefully positioning the original bottom edge of the material along the roller so the long edges of the material are perpendicular to it.

Always rehang shades in the same position—rolled, semi-rolled, or unrolled—as when you removed them to avoid altering the roller-spring tension that controls the shade. However, if shades are accidentally rolled or unrolled between hangings, or gradually fail to operate properly, they can be adjusted as described below.

If the shade retracts too swiftly, remove it from the brackets, unroll it about 24 inches, and rehang it. If the shade won't roll up fully or the spring seems weak, remove the shade from the brackets, roll it up several turns by hand, and rehang. If a shade that was removed in the rolled position accidentally unrolls before being rehung, roll it up by hand a few turns, then twist the flat-sided pin at one end of the roller clockwise using a pair of pliers until some tension is felt. Release the pliers carefully to make sure the pin does not suddenly unwind. If it does, tap the end of the roller gently to close the pawl inside and repeat the process until it catches. Rehang the shade and adjust it further if necessary.

Sometimes the roller spring becomes so tightly wound that the shade cannot be pulled down. If this happens, take the shade down, grip the flat-sided pin with pliers, and twist clockwise firmly a partial turn to open the pawl. Release the pliers quickly. Repeat until the pin rotates swiftly counterclockwise, indicating that the roller spring is unwound. Then readjust it as for an accidentally unrolled shade.

TIP:

Brackets that hold shades are often fastened to the wall or window frame with short nails. If these frequently pull loose, replace them with screws 1 inch long or longer.

ATTENTION

Mapping Electric Circuits

By making a map of your home's electrical circuits, you can know at a glance which paths or wiring routed throughout the house serve which outlets. A map can also help you determine whether any circuits supply too many outlets and are thus overloaded.

Creating a circuit map is easy but time-consuming. Start by drawing a floor plan of the home using a pencil and notebook-size sheets of paper. Include all areas served by electricity, even the attic, basement, garage, and outdoors. Drawing to scale is not necessary, but draw large enough so that you will have room to add notations and small diagrams later. Write the name of each room or area inside its outline.

Using standard electrical symbols or symbols you devise yourself, add to the plan all electrical outlets including receptacles, switches, ceiling and wall fixtures, baseboard heaters, and permanent appliances. Don't forget items like bathroom ventilator fans and kitchen range hoods. And be sure to investigate closets and other obscure areas.

Using standard electrical symbols will allow the map to be understood easily by an electrician should the need arise. Most household wiring carries 120 volts. The symbol for a 120-volt outlet is a circle containing two parallel vertical lines. Large appliances such as kitchen ranges, furnaces, and some clothes dryers and air conditioners are served by 240-volt wiring; the symbol for a 240-volt outlet is a circle containing three parallel vertical lines.

APARTMENT OWNERS:

In an apartment building, monitoring electric circuitry is usually the job of the building's superintendent or engineer, and maps of all circuits probably already have been made. If a service panel (described in the text) is located inside your apartment, you can map the circuits leading from it. But before doing so, it may pay to ask the superintendent if such a map already exists.

HINT

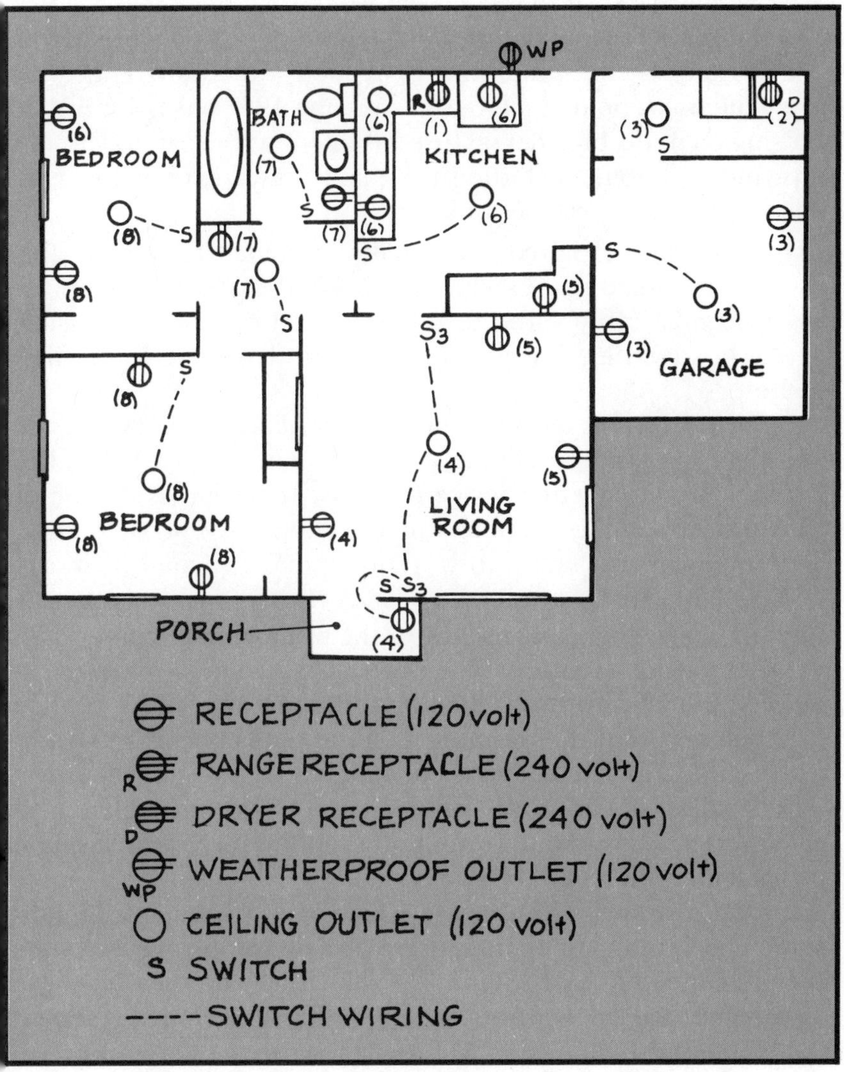

On this example of a circuit map, symbols identify outlets and show their locations. The numbers beside the symbols indicate the circuits supplying those outlets and correspond to numbers on the service panel or fuse box.

Examine an outlet if you are not sure of its voltage. Ordinary-looking receptacles carry 120 volts. Receptacles delivering 240 volts have slots that are shaped differently from 120-volt receptacles. If an appliance is wired directly to a circuit and no receptacle is present, a nameplate on the appliance should supply voltage information. Indicate switches on the plan, and link them with dotted lines to the outlets they control.

APARTMENT OWNERS:

Service panels for individual apartments in a building are usually subpanels—branch-service panels connected by electrical cable to a main panel located where the power supply enters the building.

HINT

As you leave each room or area, switch on several items. Then go to the service panel or fuse box, where power delivered from outdoors enters the home and is divided into the circuits that supply the household. Each circuit carrying 120 volts is controlled by a single circuit breaker or fuse installed in the panel. Circuits supplying 240 volts, including the main power supply, are controlled by breakers or fuses linked in pairs.

Fuses that are paired are usually located inside removable plastic boxes, called fuse blocks, installed in the panel. To view the fuses you must remove the fuse box. Paired breakers are visible and easily identified by the small plastic bar that joins their switches.

Attach a durable label or small square of adhesive tape beside each single or paired device. Write a number on each label to represent the circuit the device controls. If the breaker pair or fuse block governing the main power supply is not already labeled, use the word "main" instead of a number to identify it.

Now you can begin mapping. Start by tripping a breaker or removing a fuse that controls any of the numbered circuits. Then find the room or area to which power has been disconnected—that is, where items you switched on earlier are now off.

When you find the room, test all the outlets nearby. To test fixtures and appliances, try their switches. To test receptacles, plug a small desk lamp into each socket. Check thoroughly. Circuits often serve areas on several floors, and in rare cases, a single receptacle may be served by two circuits.

If you cannot find outlets to which power has been disconnected, check individual appliances. Circuits supplying 240 volts serve only one item each. Some 120-volt circuits do the same.

Assume that all nonfunctioning outlets you find are served by the disconnected circuit. On the plan, write the number of the disconnected circuit next to the outlet symbols you drew earlier.

When you think you have found and recorded all nonfunctional outlets, reconnect power to the circuit and check your work. The outlets whose symbols you numbered should function. If you find any that do not, circle their symbols on the plan.

Repeat the mapping process for all numbered circuits. When you are finished, all symbols on the plan should be accompanied by a number corresponding to a circuit.

If any symbols remain unnumbered, the process of elimination generally will identify the circuits supplying those outlets. Those outlets that do not function when power is restored may have been disconnected during renovation, or there may be a problem that should be checked by an electrician.

TIP:

Safe methods for handling circuit breakers and fuses are described on pages 22–23.

ATTENTION

Make a photocopy of the circuit map, and place it in a plastic
lder that can be stored near the service panel. File the original.

You can use the map to identify overloaded circuits. To do
is, examine everything connected to an individual circuit and
ote its wattage, a number labeled "Watts" or "W," that is printed
n the item. If instead of the wattage you find an amperage rating
abeled "Amps" or "A"), list the figure separately.

Add the wattages for all the items. Then divide this figure by
e number of volts supplied by the circuit, either 120 or 240.
dd any individual amperage ratings you listed separately. The
sult is the total number of amps carried by the circuit. For ex-
mple, a 120-volt circuit to which ten 150-watt items are con-
ected has a total amperage of 12.5 amps.

Compare this number with the amperage rating printed on
e fuse or circuit breaker governing the circuit. If it is the same
r greater, the circuit is probably overloaded. You will either have
disconnect some items or consult an electrician to see if you can
fely install a larger fuse.

TIP:

Instead of adding every electrical item in a house or apartment to calculate the amperage drawn through circuits, it is possible to estimate the figures. For circuits supplying only lighting and convenience receptacles (these supply power to clocks, radios, and other items not considered appliances), first determine the square footage of floor space served by the circuit and multiply the figure by 3 watts. Then, to find estimated amperage, divide the answer by the circuit's voltage as described in the text. Lighting and convenience circuits in typical rooms draw 5 to 7 amps each.

The following are approximate amperages for some common appliances: coffee maker, 6 amps; hair dryer, 8 amps; portable electric heater, 10 amps; 100-watt incandescent light bulb, 0.8 amps; microwave oven, 5 amps; television (color), 3 amps; toaster, 9 amps; vacuum cleaner, 9 amps.

ATTENTION

Upgrading Electric Wall Receptacles

APARTMENT OWNERS:

See note on page 21.

HINT

If your home has old-fashioned, ungrounded two-slot electric wall receptacles, you can easily determine whether the wiring will accommodate newer, more convenient, and safer three-slot grounding models. You can also perform the replacement if local codes permit. (To find out, contact a building inspector.)

Begin by inspecting the wiring. Get an inexpensive circuit tester—a tiny light bulb from which two wires protrude—from a hardware store. Insert the wires in the pairs of slots in the receptacle; if the receptacle works, the test bulb should glow brightly.

Next, insert a wire into one of the receptacle's shorter or narrower slots and touch the other wire to the central screw in the cover plate (scrape the screw first so the wire touches bare metal). If all the receptacle's slots are the same size, perform the test as described further on, after removing the cover plate.

If the bulb lights brightly, the outlet box (inside the wall) containing the receptacle is grounded. This indicates adequate wiring to accommodate a three-slot receptacle.

If the bulb does not light or only glows, the box is not grounded; therefore the wiring is not adequate and installing a three-slot receptacle may be a code violation.

Instead, to use three-prong appliances in a two-slot receptacle, install an external plug adapter. These have two prongs at one end that fit the receptacle and three slots at the other for the appliance. They also have a metal tab that must be fastened beneath a screw in the cover plate to provide grounding. Although

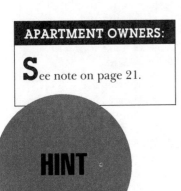

TIP:

Safe methods for handling fuses and circuit breakers are described on pages 22–23.

ATTENTION

ot as safe as a functioning three-slot receptacle, adapters are ccepted by most codes and provide more protection from shock ian an ungrounded receptacle. (The safest solution is to install a round-fault circuit interrupter—a GFCI—in place of the two-ot receptacle. A GFCI offers even greater protection than a iree-slot receptacle, but at several times the cost.)

Assuming that the wiring is adequate, the next step is to turn ff the power to the circuit supplying the receptacle. Do this by emoving the fuse or tripping the circuit breaker controlling the ircuit at the service panel (the "fuse box" where power enters the uilding and is connected to the household circuitry).

Back at the receptacle, again insert the wires of the tester into ach pair of outlet slots to make sure the power is off. The bulb hould not light at all. If it does, do not proceed until you have ound and disconnected the source of the power reaching the eceptacle.

When the power is off, remove the cover plate to expose the eceptacle and the wires attached to it. If you were unable to test he wiring earlier because all the receptacle slots were the same ize, test them now by restoring the power and carefully touching ne probe of the tester to a black wire connected to a brass screw n the receptacle and the other probe to the metal outlet box.

If the bulb lights brightly, the box is grounded. If the bulb oes not light or only glows, the box is not grounded and the viring will not support a three-slot receptacle.

With the power to the circuit off, remove the screws at the op and bottom of the receptacle and withdraw it from the box, ogether with the wires attached to it. You may find a bare copper r green-insulated wire attached inside the box. This is the rounding wire that allows a three-slot receptacle to function as it hould. Often, however, metal-sheathed cable attached to the box as no grounding wire (the sheathing provides grounding) or the vire is wrapped around the connector that joins the cable to the ox.

In any case, make a diagram of how each wire is connected to he receptacle. Then, loosen the screws and disengage the recep-acle from the wires.

Three-slot receptacles are sold at hardware stores. For ordi-ary use in homes with standard 120-volt circuitry, purchase re-eptacles stamped "15A/125V." Be sure they carry the UL logo of Jnderwriters' Laboratories, Inc.

Also purchase plastic wire caps for joining wires, metal rounding clips, and a short length of No. 14-gauge copper wire you will need approximately 6 inches per receptacle), preferably

TIP:

When adding to previously spliced wires, a larger wire cap may be needed. Also, see tip on page 25.

ATTENTION

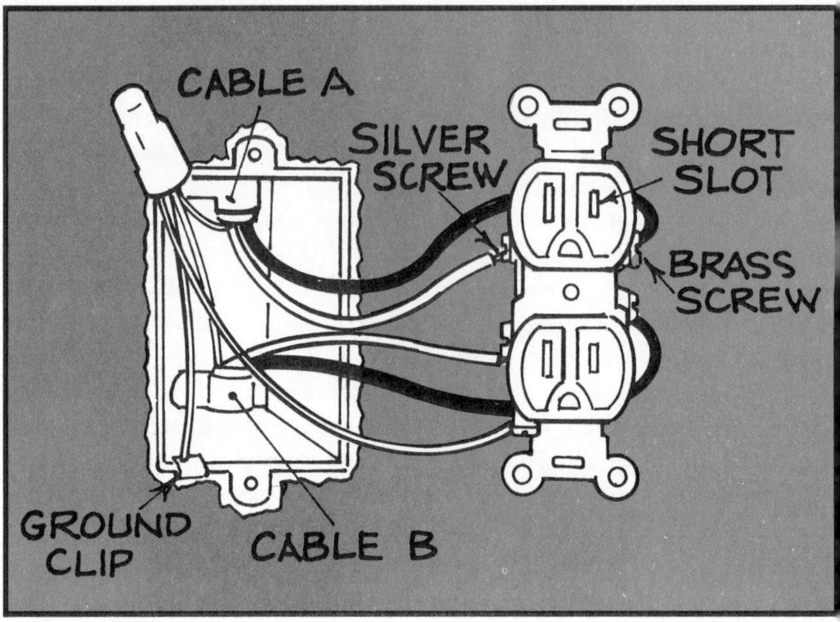

Wiring for a three-slot receptacle in the middle of a circuit run. Use a grounding clip to fasten a single ground clip to an outlet box. A wire cap joins multiple grounding wires.

sheathed with green insulation. If green wire is not available, purchase bare (unsheathed) wire.

To install the new receptacle, fasten the wires to it in their original positions. Black or red wires are always attached to the side of the receptacle fitted with brass screws; white wires always to the side fitted with silver screws.

Wrap the wires clockwise around the screws so that as you tighten them the wires are drawn beneath the screw heads. Do not let any bared portions of separate wires touch. Also be sure the bared wire around each screw does not overlap itself; otherwise it may loosen.

Now strip three quarters of an inch of sheathing from each end of the 6-inch green-insulated or bare wire. This will be the grounding wire. If similar grounding wires (green or bare) enter the box, snip the 6-inch wire in half and strip those ends, too.

Fasten one end of the wire to the green terminal screw on the new receptacle. If there are no other grounding wires, fasten the other end beneath any screw in the box or clamp the end to the box using a grounding clip. To install a grounding clip, place the end of the wire against the side of the box, even with an edge, and force and clip over both.

If other ground wires are present, loosen them from their connection to the box. Straighten their ends and place them with the end of the green wire attached to the receptacle and with one end of the remaining 3-inch segment of wire you purchased.

With pliers, twist the ends of all the wires together clockwise, as you would an end of rope. Then insert the twisted ends into a wire cap and twist it clockwise also, until it is tight.

Fasten the remaining end of wire to the box either with a screw or a grounding clip.

Reinstall the receptacle by gently folding the wires and pressing it back into the outlet box. Reattach the screws at each end, then replace the cover plate.

Restore the power and check your work with the tester. First insert the tester wires into each pair of slots to check whether current is flowing. Then check the receptacle ground by inserting the wires into the shorter slot and semicircular opening of each outlet. Finally, check the grounding to the box by inserting one wire into a short slot while touching a bared cover plate screw. In each case the bulb should light.

TIP:

After testing to make sure they work, it is a good idea to wrap two or three clockwise turns of electrician's tape around receptacles and wall switches to cover the terminal screws. This protects against short circuits in case a wire loosens inside the outlet box or in case a terminal screw touches the side of the box should the receptacle or switch be handled while the power is on.

Replacing Electrical Wall Switches

Replacing a faulty wall switch is not as difficult as it might seem. In most cases, all you will need are a screwdriver, long-nose pliers, a replacement switch, and a voltage tester, which consists of a small light bulb in a plastic holder with two insulated wire probes extending from it.

As in any electrical repair, the first step is to shut off the power—but before you do, make sure the tester works. Insert the probes into the slots of a wall outlet, and if the tester is working, the bulb will light.

Now, go ahead and shut off the power. To be completely safe, it's best to shut off the entire power supply to the house or apartment. However, if you can positively identify the circuit supplying the switch, removing the fuse or tripping the breaker to that circuit alone is sufficient.

After you have shut off the power, unscrew the cover plate from the wall. Most plates are easily removed by loosening the screws visible on the front. Avoid touching any metal, either on the switch itself or the outlet box in the wall until you have made doubly sure no electricity is flowing to the switch. More on this in a moment.

Beneath the plate you will see two screws that fasten the switch to the outlet box. Loosen these; they cannot be completely removed from the switch. Then gently pull the switch out of the box to expose the wires connected to it. Avoid touching the wiring or the screws on the sides.

APARTMENT OWNERS:

See note on page 21.

HINT

> **TIP:**
>
> **S**afe methods for handling fuses and circuit breakers are described on pages 22–23.

ATTENTION

Most household switches contain two brass screws, called terminal screws, installed in the plastic portion of the switch (the switch body). Newer switches also have a small green terminal screw for a ground wire.

Some switches contain three or even four terminal screws. The type with three screws is known as a three-way switch and is used in pairs to control a light from two different locations; the type with four screws is a four-way switch and is used between two three-way switches to provide an additional point from which the light can be controlled. Other switches contain no terminal screws; instead, the wiring enters the switch body through holes in the rear. Most switches contain both holes and screws, but the wiring is attached by means of only one or the other.

Three-way switches contain one terminal screw that is significantly darker in color than the other two, or if the switch has holes in the rear, one of them is marked "common."

Four-way switches seldom have terminal holes, and all of the terminal screws are identical in color.

Now it's time to use the voltage tester. Touch one of the probes to the metal outlet box and the other, in turn, to each of the brass terminal screws or into each of the terminal holes. If the outlet box is plastic instead of metal, touch one probe to any one of the bare copper wires (these are ground wires) visible inside the box while touching the other probe, in turn, to the terminals. If the tester bulb lights or even flickers, power is still flowing to the switch. Proceed no further until you are absolutely certain the power is off.

When you are sure the switch is safe, you may remove it for replacement. If only two wires are connected to the switch body, their positions need not be marked. Just loosen the terminal screws and remove the wires. If the wires enter terminal holes, insert the tip of a screwdriver into the slot near each hole. This will release an internal clip, allowing the wire to be pulled out.

If there are more than two wires, put masking tape on each, and mark on the tape the terminal to which the wire was connected.

To install a new switch, position it so that when the handle points down the switch is off. Using long-nose pliers and working clockwise, wrap the bared end of each wire two thirds to three quarters of the way around the shaft of the appropriate screw. Then tighten the screw firmly.

Tightening the screws should cause the wires to tighten around the shafts. Make sure that no bare wire is exposed—this could cause a dangerous short circuit—and that ends of wires do

TIP:

For more about aluminum wiring, see the section covering aluminum wiring beginning on page 27.

ATTENTION

not wrap completely around the screws, overlapping bare wire and causing a poor connection.

To ensure a better connection when installing wiring in terminal holes, clip off the existing bare wire ends. Now strip the insulation from the wire, using as a guide the groove marked "wire gauge" or "strip gauge" on the back of the switch. Then press the wires into the appropriate holes, making sure that no bare wire is exposed. Do not use the terminal holes if your wiring is aluminum or if you are not sure of its composition; the wires may work loose from this type of connection.

With switches having only two terminal screws or holes, it makes no difference which wire is connected to which terminal. On all other switches, replace the wiring exactly as it was on the old switch, using your masking tape markings as a guide.

Connect a short length of bare copper wire or green insulated ground wire to the green terminal screw on the new switch. If bare copper wires are present in the outlet box, add the new wire

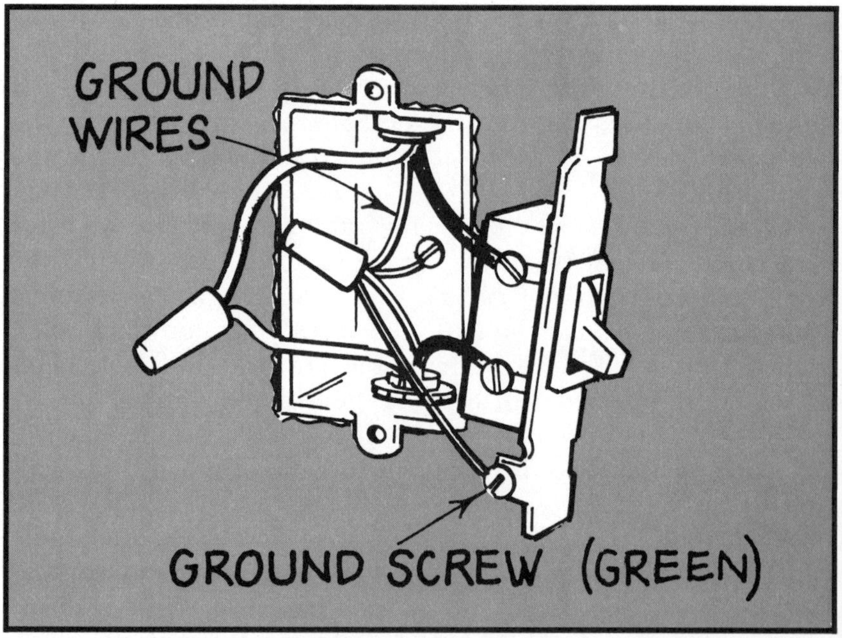

Wiring for a simple switch. Although it makes no difference which black wire is attached to which terminal, the switch should be positioned so that when the handle points down, the switch is off.

TIP:

When adding to previously spliced wires, a larger wire cap may be needed. Also, see tips on pages 25 and 147.

ATTENTION

to them. To do this, unscrew the plastic cap, called a wire nut, that links the copper wires, twist the end of the new wire around those already joined, then replace the cap. If no bare wires are present, attach the end of the new wire firmly to any metal part of the outlet box.

Press the reconnected switch into the outlet box, being careful not to disturb the wiring. Adjust the switch so that it is vertical, then tighten the two screws that fasten it to the box. Restore the power and test the switch. If it works, replace the cover plate.

Sometimes a four-way switch will fail to work even though the wiring has been faithfully reconnected. To remedy this problem, shut off the power again, then reverse the positions of the wires on one side.

Repairing Doorbells and Chimes

When a doorbell malfunctions, the problem is usually easy to diagnose and correct. Most systems consist of only three main parts and the wiring that links them.

Here is how an ordinary doorbell works:

At one or more doors, push buttons are attached. Each of these has a pair of thin wires connected to it. One of the wires links the button to the bell or other signaling device. The other wire links the button to the power source, a transformer connected to one of the household electric circuits.

A third wire is connected between the transformer and the bell.

At the transformer, high-voltage household current (120 volts) is reduced to low-voltage current (usually less than 16 volts), which is all that is required to power the system. Because of their low voltage, doorbell components and wiring are safe to handle even when electricity is flowing through them.

However, do not touch the wiring until you have tested the strength of the current at the push button or bell, as described below, and do not handle live doorbell components or wiring if you wear a pacemaker.

Current from the transformer flows to each push button, where pressing the button permits it to continue flowing until it reaches the bell, causing it to sound. The current then flows back to the transformer via the third wire, completing the circuit.

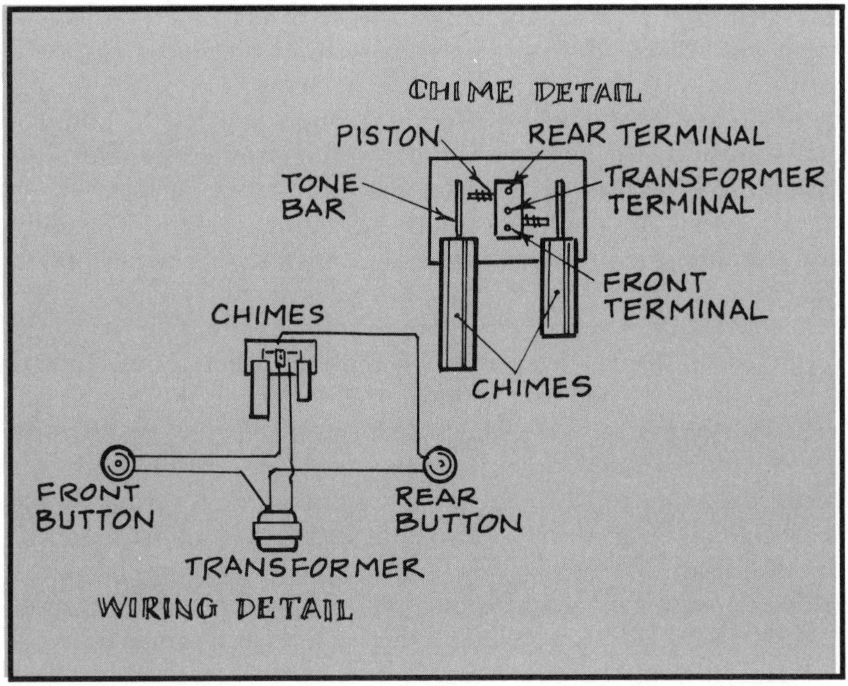

Doorbell wiring is simple to trace and safe to handle even when connected. Pressing button(s) causes pistons to strike the tone bars, sounding the chimes.

If pressing the push button on a single-button system fails to sound the bell, or if only one button of a two-button system produces results, the problem is most likely a faulty push button.

Remove the button carefully from the wall without touching the wires. Before going further, test the strength of the current by touching the probes of a circuit tester (an inexpensive device consisting of a bulb and two wires, available at hardware stores) to the terminals on the button to which the wires are connected.

The test lamp requires ordinary-strength household current to operate. Therefore, if the bulb lights, too much current is flowing to the terminals, indicating a faulty transformer and a serious shock and fire hazard.

Without touching the wires, immediately shut off the power to the doorbell as described below. Before restoring it, replace the transformer.

If the test lamp does not light, disconnect the wires from the button by unscrewing the terminals. Then touch one wire to the other. If the bell sounds, the push button is faulty.

Clean the terminals by sanding them with fine-grit sandpaper. Renew the connections by clipping off the dirty wire ends

TIP:

Other hints for quick troubleshooting:

- If a doorbell sounds continuously, either the push button is stuck or the wires attached to the button are touching, causing a short circuit.
- If a new doorbell is barely audible, the transformer may be mismatched. Check labels on the transformer and the bell. The voltage output of the transformer must vary no more than 2 volts from that required by the bell.
- If chimes fail to complete a full sequence, the inside of the bell is probably dirty.

ATTENTION

and stripping away about half an inch of insulation to expose fresh wire. Next, attach the wires by wrapping each one clockwise around its terminal and tightening the screw. Retest the button by pushing it. If the bell still does not sound, replace the button.

If pushing the button produces a hum or other peculiar noise inside the bell (you can detect the sound by placing your ear to the bell while an assistant pushes the button), remove the cover and examine the interior for dust, lint, or poor electrical connections.

To test the current if you have not already done so at the push button, touch the probes of a circuit tester to any pair of terminals on the bell that includes the one marked "Tr." This is the wire that leads back to the transformer.

Then, provided the wiring is safe, use a cotton swab and vacuum cleaner to clean the parts. With chimes, a spring should be visible on each of the pistons that strike the tone bars. Search the unit if any are missing, or obtain replacements at a hardware store. Lubricate parts with powdered graphite or silicone spray, but do not use oil. Restore and tighten the wiring connections.

If touching the wires together does not cause the bell to sound, splice them temporarily by twisting them together—this will free you from having to make repeated trips to press the button—and then go to the transformer and test the entire system.

The transformer is a rectangular metal-and-fiber device about 3 inches long, 2 inches wide, and 1 inch thick to which thin wires are attached. Generally it is fastened to a junction box mounted on a floor beam in the basement. If you cannot find it, search instead for the wires leading out of a push button. Following these will lead you to it.

When you find the transformer, check the circuit breaker or fuse governing the household circuit to which it is attached. Reset the breaker or replace the fuse, if necessary. If the bell still does not sound, shut off the power by tripping the breaker or removing the fuse; then open the junction box and examine the wires inside connecting the transformer to the circuit. Make sure all the connections are tight by removing and replacing the threaded plastic caps—the wire nuts—that splice the wires together.

If these wires are satisfactory, replace the cover of the box, then restore the power and test the transformer. To do this you will need either a volt-ohm meter or a second circuit tester designed to test low-voltage current. Both are available at electronics supply stores.

Touch the probes of the meter or tester to that part of the transformer terminals where the thin wires are attached. If the transformer is working, a meter should show about the same voltage as that printed on the transformer. A tester should light.

If the transformer is faulty, install a new one. If the transformer works, clean and tighten the wiring and repeat the test at the bell. Power there indicates that the bell unit is defective and must be replaced. If no power is detected, the wiring is faulty.

Sometimes broken wires can be spliced. However, installing new wires is usually the simplest solution.

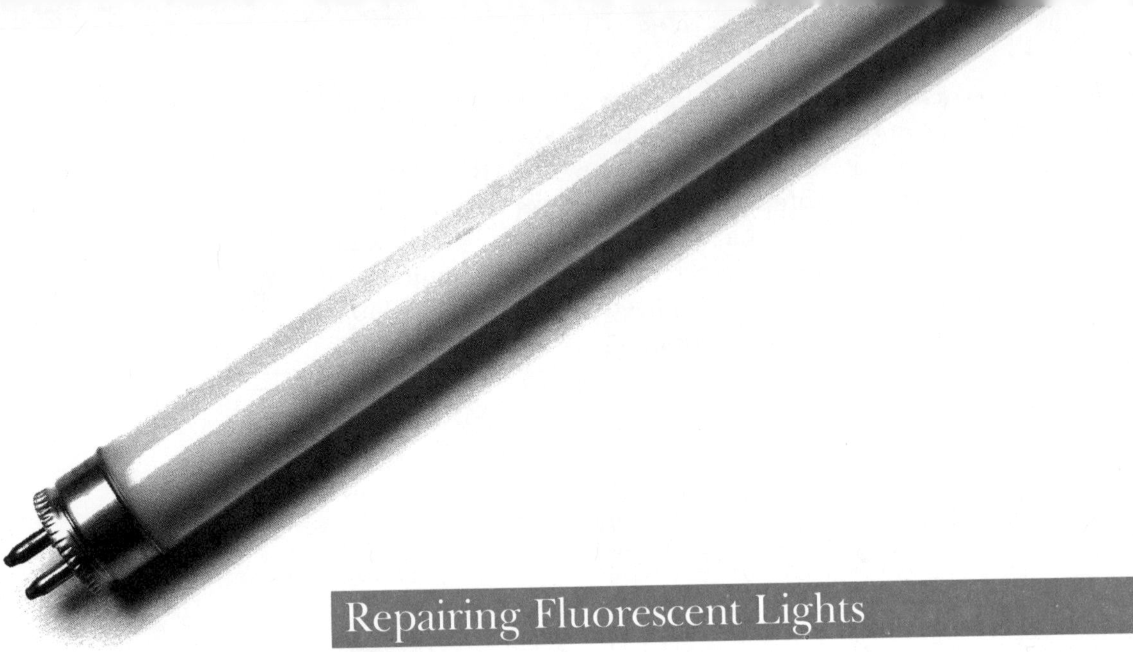

Repairing Fluorescent Lights

TIP:

When choosing a replacement ballast, select an electronic model. These are more efficient than older electromagnetic types and will result in both brighter lighting and less flicker.

ATTENTION

Fluorescent lights are more efficient than incandescent ones, but also more complicated. As a result, simply replacing the "bulb"—actually a tube—when a fluorescent light develops problems will not always remedy the situation. Fortunately, however, troubleshooting fluorescent lights is not too difficult, and repairs are usually easy to make.

If a fluorescent tube neither lights nor flickers when switched on, first check to see that the fixture is plugged in and that no fuse has blown or circuit breaker has tripped.

If this does not help, try wiggling the tube gently in its sockets by rocking it back and forth and from side to side. This will scour away minute deposits of corrosion or dust that can sometimes hinder the flow of electricity. Be sure to do this when the light switch is turned off.

It is normal for the light in new fluorescent tubes to flicker or appear to swirl in the first one hundred hours of operation. If an older tube exhibits these symptoms, turn off the switch, remove the tube, then clean the ends thoroughly. Socket shapes vary, but the tube-removal process is the same. To remove a straight fluorescent tube, rotate it a quarter turn in either direction and pull the tube straight down out of the sockets. If the tube is circular, simply unsnap it from the brackets supporting it and pull it free from the single socket.

To clean the ends of a tube, scrub the pins projecting from them with fine-grit sandpaper, then wipe away all dust with cloth or a paper towel. If any pins are bent, squeeze them gently with needle-nose pliers to straighten them.

When inspecting the ends, examine the glass portions. A brownish tint is normal on tubes that have been in use for some time. Tubes whose ends are blackened usually are wearing out.

If only one end of a tube appears blackened, reverse the tube end-for-end and reinstall it after cleaning the pins. If the tube is blackened only along one side, rotate it after cleaning and reinstall it so that the blackened portion is turned 180 degrees from its former position.

Tubes that are blackened at both ends still may last a considerable time. So, if a tube still malfunctions after you have cleaned and repositioned it, check the condition of other components of the light before shopping for a replacement tube.

The first component to check is the starter. This is a small cylinder approximately 2 inches long and usually silver-colored. Its purpose is to accumulate current briefly when the light is switched on and then release it after the tube is lighted.

The starter is responsible for the momentary delay in lighting when some fluorescent tubes are switched on. If it is faulty, it can also be the cause of initial flickering as the tube warms up, or of failure to light at all.

Not all fluorescent lights have starters, but if yours does it will usually be located near a tube socket. Lights with more than one tube have a separate starter for each. If you do not find a starter, unplug the light or shut off the power, then remove the deflector above the tube and look there, or disassemble the base if the light is a desk or floor model.

To remove a starter, press it inward and twist it counterclockwise a quarter turn; it should pop out. There is no way to tell if it is malfunctioning except by replacing it, and since starters are available at hardware stores for less than a dollar, it is worth the gamble. Take the old part with you to obtain a duplicate.

Fluorescent lights designed without starters are called rapid-starting lights, and this designation is usually printed or stamped on them. With these, dirt on the tube can sometimes prevent lighting or can cause flickering.

The cure is to remove the tube and clean it by wiping with a cloth dipped in dish detergent, and then by a cloth dipped in plain water. Be careful when handling tubes. They are fragile and if smashed may explode into shards.

If a fluorescent tube blinks on and off—a slower and more distinct process than flickering—the fault may lie in loose wiring connections or another component, called the ballast. The ballast

TIP:

If a fluorescent tube breaks, clean up carefully without touching any of the debris with bare hands. Mercury inside fluorescent tubes is poisonous, and the glass can cause cuts and splinters.

ATTENTION

TIP:

Ballasts typically last more than a decade. However, a sure sign of a faulty ballast is black resin dripping from it, caused by overheating.

ATTENTION

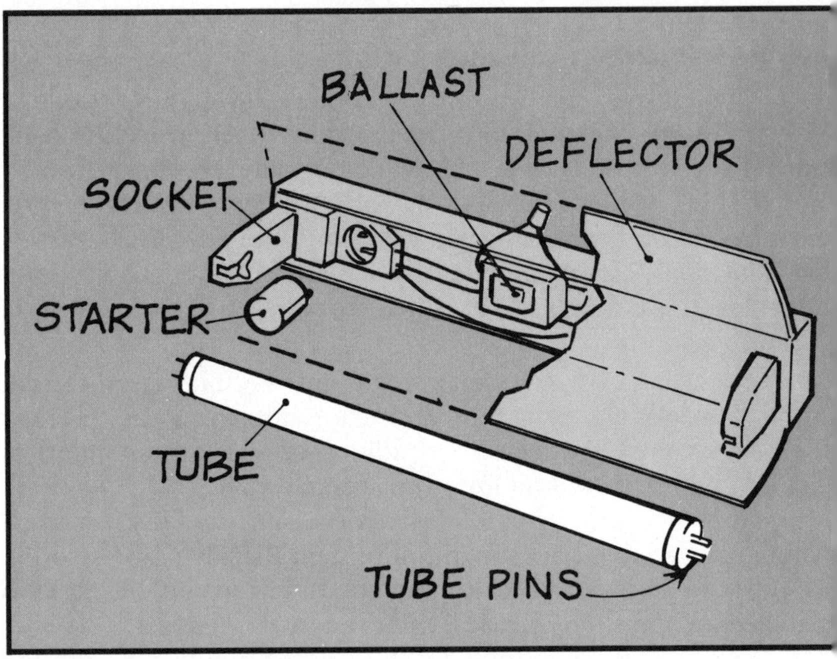

Older fluorescent lights like the one shown have removable starters. On newer models, the starter and ballast are combined in a single component.

is almost always to blame if the fixture hums during operation.

To inspect the wiring and ballast, remove the deflector o disassemble the base, as well as any other parts necessary to ex pose the tube sockets and wiring.

Check that the plastic twist-on connectors (wire nuts) joinin the wires are firmly tightened and that the ground wire—usuall green—is fastened tightly to the metal body of the fixture. N exposed wires should be present. A wire that appears discon nected probably is, and should be reconnected. The sockets, a well as other components, should also be firmly in place.

The ballast is a rectangular metal or plastic component re sembling a small box with wires issuing from both ends. To test i install a working fluorescent tube and a new starter. If the ligh malfunctions, the ballast is at fault and must be replaced.

Mark the ballast wires and the wires leading to the socket wit pieces of tape so that they are paired to simplify reinstallation then unfasten the wires from their connectors and unscrew th ballast from the fixture. Take the ballast to a hardware or electri cal supply store for replacement.

TIP:

When squeezing pins with pliers to straighten them, squeeze each pin separately. Pinching both together can break them and may also break the end of the tube.

ATTENTION

If noise is the only problem, obtain a low-noise ballast. If the light is operated in temperatures below 50 degrees Fahrenheit (another cause of blinking and flickering), obtain a low-temperature ballast.

When shopping for a new fluorescent tube, compare lumens (brightness), wattage, and life expectancy. Most manufacturers print this information on the cartons. Bulbs typically last for at least a year, often much longer.

The life expectancy of tubes is based on the number of times the tube is started.

TIP:

Be sure that the wattage of replacement fluorescent tubes matches that of the transformer, otherwise tubes may work poorly and fail prematurely. Usually, buying new tubes the same length as the old assures a match. Tubes labeled as pre-heat are for use in fixtures having starters, but ordinary tubes can also be used with somewhat less efficiency.

Cool-white tubes are least expensive but deliver harsh bluish light that may be objectionable. Light from warm-white tubes more closely resembles that of incandescent bulbs. Tubes containing rare-earth phosphors are the most expensive; they come in many degrees of cool and warm, all of which produce light that is superior to ordinary fluorescents in their ability to render color.

ATTENTION

Rewiring a Lamp

A **malfunctioning desk or floor lamp can be dangerous** as well as annoying. If a lamp flickers, won't light, requires delicate positioning to operate, or has a frayed cord, it should be repaired immediately or not used.

Most lamp repairs are easy to perform. Tools and replacement parts are inexpensive and available at hardware stores. However, if disassembly of a valuable lamp is necessary or if the lamp's components are not like those described here, consider having the lamp professionally repaired.

If a lamp will not light, even after replacing the bulb with one that operates in another lamp, check the wall outlet by plugging into it an appliance that you know works. If the appliance now does not work the trouble is in the outlet or the electric circuit supplying it. Unless you know how to repair household wiring and are permitted to do so by local building codes, call a licensed electrician.

If both the bulb and the outlet work, the trouble is in the lamp. Unplug it and remove the bulb, lamp shade, and harp (the wire framework that supports the shade). Using the tip of a screwdriver or nail file, or a piece of fine-grit sandpaper, clean the metal strip at the base of the socket by scraping it until it shines. Blow out the dust, pry the strip upward slightly, and try operating the lamp again.

If it still does not light, inspect the plug and cord. A plug that has been mishandled or damaged or that requires wiggling to operate should be replaced. First, cut off the plug and about 2 inches of the cord.

If the cord is the light-duty kind—two copper wires running side by side, each sheathed in rubber insulation that is uniformly textured and colored on the outside—you can replace the old plug with a self-connecting plug that requires no tools. There are several styles.

One common variety has a small lever or cam on top. To attach a cam-equipped plug, merely lift up the cam, insert the cut end of the lamp cord, unstripped, into the slot at the side of the plug, then close the cam to lock the cord in place.

Another type is assembled by squeezing the prongs together. To attach one of these plugs, thread the cord through the hollow

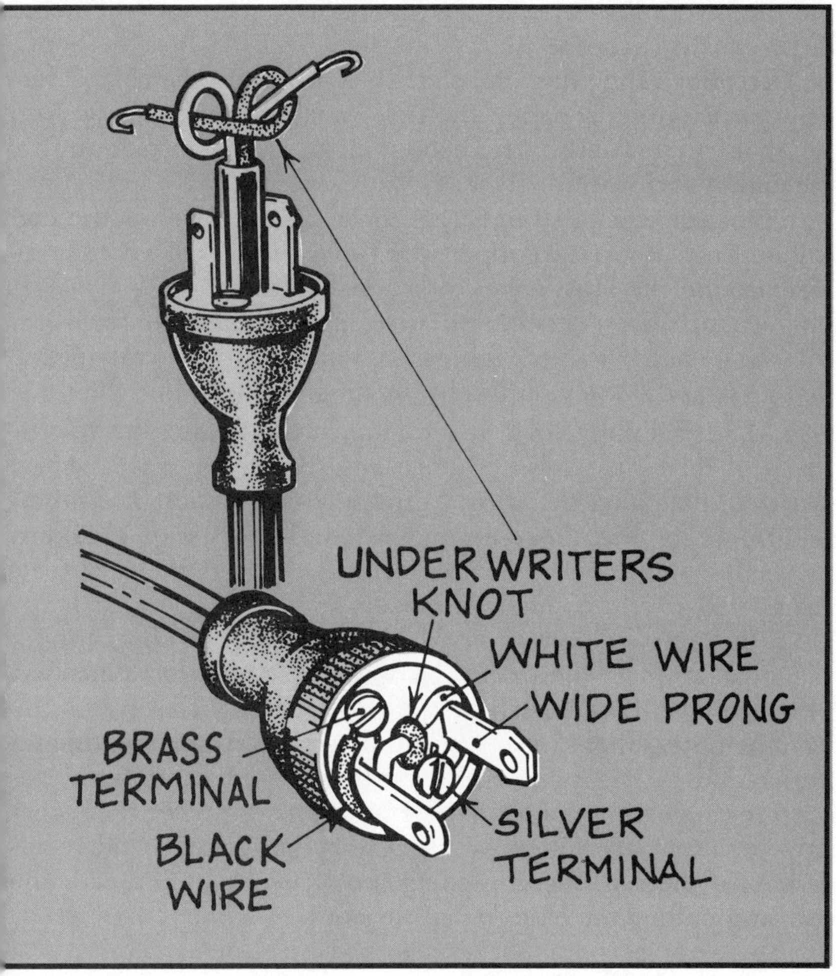

Polarized plugs and plugs for heavy-duty cords have terminal screws. Tie an underwriters knot in a heavy-duty cord to prevent strain on the ends.

TIP:

To remove a light bulb that is stuck in a socket, unplug the lamp or shut off power to the fixture. Squirt penetrating oil into the socket, wait a few moments for the oil to work, then try unscrewing the bulb. Apply more oil or wait up to fifteen minutes longer if necessary.

To remove the base of the bulb that has broken off in a socket, unplug it or shut off the power as described, then grasp the filament or base of the bulb with long-nose pliers and turn counterclockwise. Apply penetrating oil if necessary. Sometimes it is possible to remove a broken bulb by pressing against the base with a tennis ball while unscrewing it.

ATTENTION

cover and into the body of the plug, to which the prongs are attached. Squeeze the prongs so that they are parallel and press the body into the cover.

If the lamp cord has separate copper and silver-colored wire or if the insulation around one wire is white or ribbed while the other is black or smooth, the lamp is wired for a polarized plug. This kind has one prong that is wider than the other and it will only fit into wall outlets with corresponding wide and narrow slots. This is safer than the light-duty wiring, but requires care when repairing.

Buy a replacement plug that is labeled "polarized." Disassemble the new plug by unscrewing it or by separating the body of the plug from the cover with a screwdriver, following the manufacturer's instructions.

To attach the plug, first slide the cover onto the cord. Then using a penknife, separate the two wires that make up the cord for about an inch. Also strip about half an inch of insulation from the end of each wire.

Twist the metal strands that make up the wires so the ends will not fray. Wrap the copper wire three quarters of a turn clockwise around the brass-colored terminal screw on the body of the plug. Wrap the silver-colored wire similarly around the silver-colored terminal screw. Tighten both screws firmly, making sure that no strands loosen. Finish by pressing the insert into the cover.

Cylindrical plugs for heavier lamp cords are also attached by means of terminal screws. But because these plugs are seldom polarized, matching the wires to the screws is usually not necessary. Do tie the wires together in an underwriters knot, as shown in the drawing. This prevents strain at the end if the cord is mishandled after the plug is installed.

If the lamp still fails to work after replacing the plug, unplug it again and replace the socket. To remove it, find the spot marked "press" along the seam where the shell of the socket meets the base, then press there with your thumb while twisting and pulling the sections apart. Remove the cardboard insulating sleeve beneath the shell, then loosen the terminal screws to free the socket body from the wires. Remove the base by untying the underwriters knot if there is one, loosening the set screw underneath the base, and pulling the base free of the cord.

Buy a replacement socket stamped with the same electrical rating as the old one. Install it as you would a plug with terminal screws.

If the lamp cord has copper and silver-colored wires and the plug is polarized, match the wires to the appropriate terminal screws on the socket. Tying an underwriters knot is not necessary.

Reassemble the socket by sliding the insulating sleeve down over the terminals and pressing the shell and base together. The lamp should now operate.

A lamp cord, too, can be replaced if it is old or if you wish to convert it to polarized wiring. To replace a cord, cut it off about a foot from the base of the lamp and untie any knots along the length of the remaining piece (these are used to keep the cord taut). Strip about 3 inches of insulation from the wires of both the attached old cord and the replacement, then twist the bared ends of both cords together to splice them.

Wrap the splice with electrical tape several times, taking care not to enlarge greatly the circumference of the cord. Then pull the old cord up through the top of the lamp, simultaneously threading the replacement cord. Cut the new cord below the splice and wire it to the socket.

Glue the felt lamp base back in place, if necessary, after tightening the lamp parts and making sure the new cord is free of kinks.

Repairing a Toilet

As unpleasant as the prospect of repairing a toilet may seem, it is not as bad as living with a toilet that needs repair. Fortunately, most toilet problems are relatively easy to fix.

Blockages and Leaks

If water in the bowl simply swirls when the toilet is flushed, remove the tank cover and watch the tank refill. If the water does not rise to the height of the waterline marked on the tank, adjust the float mechanism inside the tank until it does (this procedure is described in the section on tank troubles). Containers of cleaner or other devices that take up space and are designed to reduce the amount of water in the tank also can hinder the toilet's flushing ability.

Another item to check is the vent hole (there may be more than one) in the base of the toilet bowl. Probe the hole with a wire to clear it of mineral deposits or other debris. When cleared, if there are no other blockages and the water supply is adequate, the toilet should flush normally.

If the toilet's drain—the large opening—becomes blocked, causing the bowl to fill with water or to overflow, try using a flange-type plumber's plunger to clear it. This type has a cup with a funnel-shaped projection that fits snugly into the drain opening at the bottom of the bowl. Never use chemical drain cleaner which can cause injury if splashed onto skin.

Begin by putting on rubber gloves and mopping up any overflowed water. Clear the bowl of solid material. Place the plunger over the drain opening and pump vigorously about a dozen times. Then remove the plunger.

If plunging pumps out the water in the bowl, or if remaining water drains normally when the plunger is removed, the blockage probably has been dislodged. Add water to the toilet from a bucket until the bowl is nearly full and begins to flush. Insert the plunger again and pump rapidly. The bowl should empty normally and the extra water should clear the drain completely. Repeat the process if the toilet empties sluggishly and you have already checked the vent hole.

If initial plunging does not significantly empty the bowl, bail out the contents with a nonbreakable container. Inspect the inside of the drain passage, which slants upward, by placing a hand mirror in the bottom of the bowl at an angle while shining a flashlight against it.

If you spot a blockage, use a bent coat hanger to pull it out. If the passage appears clear, suggesting that the blockage is farther inside the toilet, you will need a closet auger, available at hardware stores.

The auger is a metal cable with a crank at one end and a corkscrew-shaped tip at the other. The cable is enclosed in a metal or plastic tube with a curved lower end. Draw the cable out of the tube until the tip is against the tube's lower opening. Place the auger into the toilet so that the curved part of the tube rests on the bottom of the bowl and the tip enters the drain opening.

Holding the tube upright, twist and push the cable into the tube to feed the cable into the drain. When you encounter the obstruction, snare it with the tip by turning the crank handle clockwise, then pull on the handle to withdraw the cable from the drain.

Repeat the process until the blockage is removed or no resistance to the auger is felt. Remove the material drawn by the auger, then plunge the toilet with water from a bucket, as described. If the toilet is still blocked, you may need to call a plumber: Removing it from the floor may be the only way to reach the obstruction.

Moisture on the floor or on the outside of the toilet may be the result of condensation or loose connections. If you are not sure, open the tank and add a tablespoon or so of food coloring to the water, enough to color it substantially. Wipe the moist area dry, then wait without using the toilet until moisture reappears. Blot the area with a white paper towel. If the moisture is colored, the tank is leaking. If not, the moisture is probably condensation.

To cure a leaking tank attached directly to a toilet bowl tighten the bolts at the bottom. First drain the tank by shutting the valve in the supply pipe leading to it (turn the valve clockwise and flushing the toilet. Then, with a wrench, tighten the nuts underneath the rear of the toilet, holding the bolts stationary by inserting a screwdriver into their slots inside the tank. Do not tighten the nuts more than a quarter turn beyond hand tight otherwise you may crack the tank or bowl.

Also try tightening the nut beneath the tank that secures the flushing mechanism inside. Hold the mechanism with one hand to prevent it from rotating and use a wrench to tighten the nut up to a quarter turn.

If tightening the tank bolts doesn't work, remove them and replace the rubber washers beneath the bolt heads. If leaking persists beneath the flushing mechanism, replace the washer at its base. You may also have to replace the mechanism.

Another source of tank leaks is the flush valve, the large opening at the base of the tank. To tighten the nut securing the valve or to replace the gasket sealing it, the tank must be removed from the bowl. Again, this may be a job for a plumber.

To repair a leaking wall-mounted tank, use a spud wrench to tighten the connections at both ends of the pipe that joins it to the bowl. If this doesn't work, drain the tank and loosen the leaking nut or nuts. When loosening the nut beneath the tank, hold the flush valve steady inside to keep it from turning.

Slide the nuts onto the pipe, remove any packing material (usually twine or putty), install new packing, then retighten the nut or nuts.

If the problem is condensation, you need to keep the tank from dropping below room temperature. Buy a toilet tank lining kit of ½-inch-thick plastic foam sheets and adhesive. The sheets insulate the tank from the cold water inside.

To install toilet tank lining, first drain the tank and dry it completely with paper toweling and/or a hair dryer. Then cut the foam to fit around the inside of the tank and attach it with the adhesive, following the instructions supplied with the kit. Allow the adhesive to dry overnight or as specified by the instructions before refilling the tank.

If undyed water that does not seem caused by condensation accumulates around the base of the toilet, suspect a leaking bowl. This, too, may best be repaired by a plumber.

Tank Troubles

When a toilet runs continuously, makes noises, or fails to flush completely although unblocked, minor adjustments to internal parts can often cure the problem. With most toilets, these parts are inside the tank. With tankless toilets that operate by means of a pressurized flush valve (common in apartment buildings), the parts are inside the valve.

To diagnose a problem in a toilet with a tank, remove the cover, flush the toilet, and observe the results. Operating the handle should raise the rubber flush valve at the bottom of the tank, visible under the water. The water in the tank should then drain quickly through the hole beneath the valve and enter the bowl, flushing the toilet. As the tank empties, the flush valve should close automatically and the tank should refill.

The tank is refilled by the flushing mechanism, usually located on the left side. On older toilets, a float ball attached to a horizontal rod governs the refilling process. As water empties from the tank, the ball drops. This opens a valve inside the mechanism, and water enters from the supply pipe connected underneath the tank.

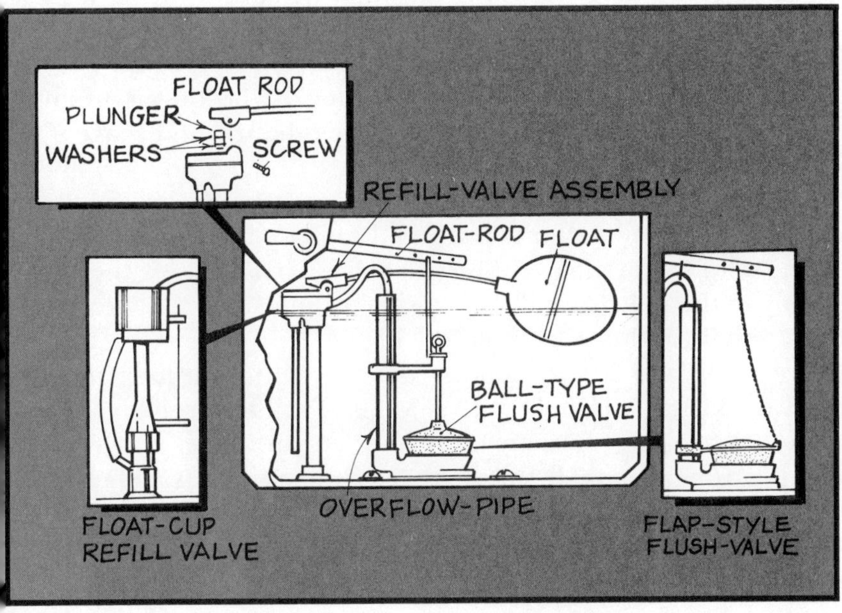

Because toilets function rather simply, most problems are easy to remedy. Older models usually feature a float-rod assembly and a ball-type flush valve. These can be replaced with a newer, simpler, float-cup refill valve and a flap-style flush valve.

TIP:

Instead of marking the water level inside the tank, testing for a leaking flush valve can be done with dye. Simply add enough food coloring to the tank water to color it, then observe whether water in the bowl also become colored. If it does, the flush valve leaks.

ATTENTION

On newer toilets, the flushing mechanism has no horizontal rod. The float is a hollow plastic cylinder called a float cup that slides up and down on the mechanism itself.

An opening in the flushing mechanism directs water into the tank. Another, connected to a small tube, fills the bowl by directing water into the vertical overflow pipe beside the flush valve. As water fills the tank, the float ball or cup rises, gradually closing the refill valve. This stops the flow of water into the tank and bowl, completing the flush.

A loose handle can cause parts linking it with the flush valve to be misaligned. To tighten the handle, simply tighten the nut that holds it against the inside of the tank.

If water rises above the top of the overflow pipe, it will spill into the pipe and enter the bowl, causing the toilet to run continuously. Often a hissing noise develops, because the float cannot rise high enough to close the refill valve completely.

To fix this problem, flush the toilet, and while the water is rising, bend the float rod slightly in the middle so the ball no longer rises as far before the valve closes. On float cup mechanisms, reduce the float's travel by squeezing a clip on the side.

The refill valve should close when the water in the tank is about half an inch from the top of the overflow pipe. Incomplete flushing means the water level is too low.

On float ball mechanisms, if hissing is the only symptom, check for a leaking float. Unscrew it from the rod and shake it. If water has entered, get a new float.

If the problem continues or if water sprays upward from the mechanism when the toilet is flushed, replace the rubber washers or the diaphragm sealing the refill valve. First turn off the water supply to the toilet, usually by closing a shutoff valve beneath the tank, and flush the toilet to empty it.

Remove the screws holding the top of the flushing mechanism (including the float rod) and remove the assembly. If the valve has a plunger, remove the washers around it and replace them with new ones. If the valve has a diaphragm separating its two halves, remove that. Scrape away sediment with a penknife or scrub the parts with a toothbrush dipped in vinegar. After reassembling the flushing mechanism, adjust the float if necessary.

If the toilet runs even though water does not spill into the overflow pipe, if jiggling the handle sometimes remedies running or hissing, or if the toilet fills but begins to hiss a short time later, suspect a leaking flush valve.

To check, flush the toilet and let the water rise in the tank. As soon as the refill valve closes, mark the water level on the inside

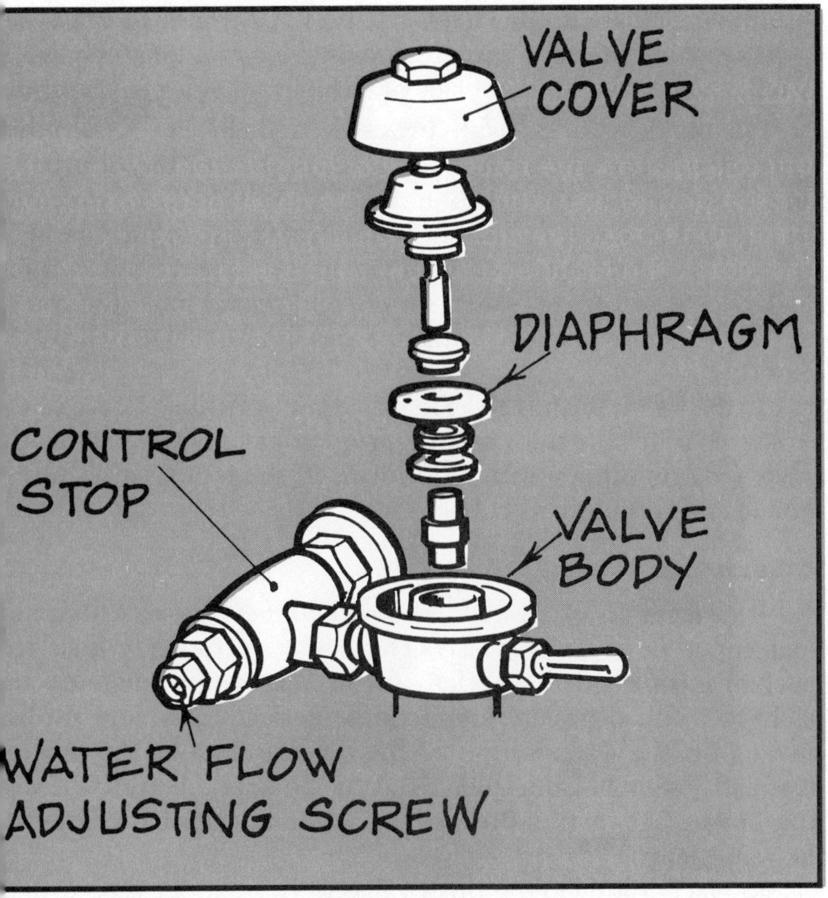

n a pressurized flush valve, turning the adjusting screw egulates the amount of water per flush.

the tank with a pencil. Wait approximately half an hour and spect the tank again. If the water level has fallen, the flush valve aks.

Flush valves consisting of a rubber ball at the end of a metal nkage can be adjusted by loosening their screws, repositioning e parts, and tightening the screws. The valve must drop presely into the tank opening. Also, scrub the parts and the valve pening with steel wool to smooth their surfaces.

Flush valves consisting merely of a flap of rubber with a bulb n the underside should be replaced.

If you cannot perform adjustments or repairs because of corded parts, or if symptoms persist, consider replacing the flushg mechanism, flush valve, or both with modern, trouble-free equipment. Float cup mechanisms and flap-style flush valves se dom need attention. They are inexpensive, reasonably easy t install, and can be fitted in place of virtually all older mechanism

On tankless toilets with pressurized flush valves, turn th brass adjusting screw located in the control stop, the fitting th joins the valve to the supply plumbing. Turn it clockwise to reduc the amount of water in a flush, counterclockwise to increase it. I the flow is insufficient even with the screw turned fully counte clockwise, shut off the water supply and disassemble the top c the valve with a wrench. Replace worn internal parts with ne ones sold as a kit.

If the valve flushes too long or does not shut off, clean th bypass channel (in the diaphragm on some models and in th valve body on others) with a thin wire. If the handle leaks, disa semble it and replace its rubber seal.

Modernizing

Replacing an old-fashioned float ball mechanism with a ne float cup type is usually easy. Hardware stores carry float cu mechanisms designed especially for installation by amateurs an packaged with complete instructions. Basically, the job involv turning off the water supply to the toilet, unbolting the existin float ball assembly from the base of the tank, and bolting the ne unit in its place. A trial flush or two is then necessary to regulat the water level.

Replacing a ball-type flush valve with a flapper type usuall requires separating the toilet tank from the bowl. This is cumbe some and requires care to avoid breaking the tank while loosenin or tightening the fasteners and valve parts. If you are reasonabl experienced and can get someone to help you with lifting, th procedure is not difficult. If not, the job is better left to a license plumber.

Replacing a Toilet

Replacing a toilet is a major repair or remodeling project, but in most cases is not as difficult as might be imagined. The hardest tasks are usually selecting a new toilet and removing the old one. This chapter deals with replacing the most common variety of toilet, the freestanding type mounted on the floor.

Choose a new toilet carefully. Be sure to find out from the dealer whether existing plumbing will have to be modified, a job for a licensed professional plumber. Also ask a building inspector what the plumbing regulations are in your area.

Toilets range in price from less than $100 to well over $1,000. Most better-quality toilets are one piece and have an oval-shaped bowl and a siphon-jet flushing action. This produces higher water velocity during flushing than standard toilets, which usually come in two pieces and have a round bowl and reverse-trap flushing.

To save water, you should look for a toilet that requires only about 1½ gallons of water for flushing. Called ultra-low-flush toilets, these can save a family of four as much as 14,000 gallons of water a year, even compared to ordinary water-saving toilets which typically use 3½ gallons per flush.

To remove an existing toilet, first turn off the water supplying the tank by closing the shutoff valve at the rear of the toilet; turn the handle clockwise. Then remove the tank cover, flush the toilet, and sponge the tank dry. Also use a plumber's plunger to force as much water as possible out of the bowl.

APARTMENT OWNERS:

Before undertaking to replace a toilet, check with your building's maintenance supervisor, as plumbing chores may have to be performed by professional plumbers. In addition, municipal water-conservation requirements in your area may stipulate installing only a low-flush toilet.

HINT

TIP:

Whether in new or renovated construction, communities increasingly require that all new toilets be ultra-low-flush models. Be sure to check local requirements before purchasing and installing a new toilet, especially if it is not an ultra-low-flush type.

ATTENTION

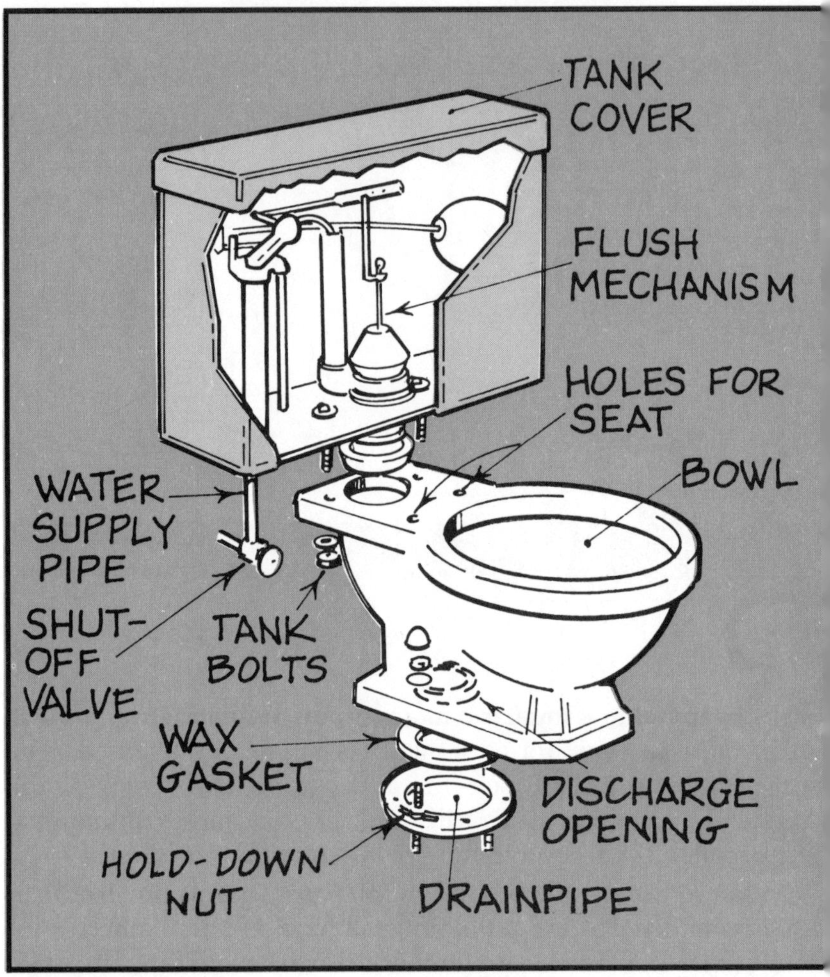

The parts of a conventional toilet. Before setting a new toilet on the drainpipe flange, get new hold-down nuts and a new wax gasket.

Next, unscrew the nut fastening the supply pipe to the underside of the tank and disconnect the pipe. If the nut is corroded and cannot be loosened, unscrew the nut connecting the pipe to the shutoff valve instead and replace the pipe with a new one, available at hardware stores.

If the toilet tank is removable, separate the nuts and bolts that fasten it to the bowl. The nuts are usually in recesses at the rear of the toilet, accessible from underneath the tank. However, these also may be too corroded to budge. If so, go on to the next step. The toilet can be removed with the tank attached, but its weight will be approximately 100 pounds.

After removing the tank, or if the toilet is a one-piece type, remove the bowl from the floor. To do this, pry off and dispose of the porcelain or plastic caps covering the hold-down bolts at the base of the bowl, then unscrew the nuts. If necessary, apply penetrating oil to them and use a snug-fitting open-end, box-end, or socket wrench rather than an adjustable wrench. If this fails, either cut the fasteners apart with a hacksaw (the bolts are usually soft brass) or break the nut with a tool called a nut splitter, available at automotive and hardware stores.

Spread an inch-thick layer of newspapers near the bowl to set it on, because the trap system may still contain several ounces of unsanitary water. Then, with a helper, rock and twist the bowl to loosen it from the wax gasket and sealing compound underneath, and lift the bowl off the drain opening, holding it as level as possible to minimize leakage.

Set the bowl on the newspapers right side up for draining water. Or drain the bowl immediately by placing a disposable pie pan on the newspaper, then lifting and tilting the bowl so that water empties from the drain opening.

Remove the hold-down bolts (unless they are in good condition and are screwed into the flooring) and any wax or sealant clinging to the drainpipe flange attached to the floor. Then stuff a large rag into the flange opening to block odors and keep small parts from falling in. If there are any shims on the floor that have been used to level the toilet, save them for use with the new one.

To install a new toilet, first install new hold-down bolts if the old ones are ruined. These are available at hardware stores and come in two varieties, usually packaged together. Those with wood-screw threads at one end and machine-screw threads at the other are the strongest but can only be used if the floor beneath the flange is wood. The other type has a flat bolt head that slides into grooves in the rim of the flange. Washers and nuts that come with the bolts hold both types in place.

Remove and dispose of the rag from the flange opening and replace it with a new wax gasket or other sealant specified by the local plumbing regulations. Set the gasket into the top of the flange so that the plastic sleeve on the gasket extends into the drainpipe.

Then lift the bowl and position it carefully so that the rim of the drain opening fits inside the gasket and the hold-down bolts protrude through the holes in the bowl's base. This is easiest to do if a helper guides the work by watching underneath the bowl as it is lowered.

TIP:

Take advantage of having removed an existing toilet by repairing the flooring surrounding it if necessary. Water leakage often causes subflooring around toilets to rot and floor tiles to lift.

Press firmly on the top center of the bowl to settle it. Then check it by holding a carpenter's level on the bowl, across it and from front to back. If necessary, slip improvised shims of wood, metal, or tile under the base of the bowl to level it. Fasten the bowl to the floor by threading a second pair of washers and nuts that come with the bolts onto them and tightening them evenly and snugly. Avoid overtightening as this can break the bowl.

When you are finished, bolt the new tank to the bowl if necessary, following the manufacturer's instructions. Install the flushing mechanism included with the new toilet or obtained separately (instructions accompany these parts, too). Then reconnect the water supply pipe to the base of the tank and reopen the shutoff valve.

Flush the toilet to check for leaks and to make final adjustments to the flushing mechanism. Then apply a ribbon of adhesive bathtub and tile sealer around the base of the bowl using a caulking gun. Attach the toilet seat. Finally, tighten the hold-down bolts again slightly and press new caps (supplied with the toilet) over the nuts.

Unclogging Sink and Bathtub Drains

Sluggish drains in sinks and tubs rank high among house- old annoyances. However, remedies for drain woes are usually mple. If the problem is addressed early, restoring a sluggish rain to full effectiveness or even clearing a drain that has become ompletely clogged seldom requires much skill or effort, and may e done using only a few tools.

Of course, the best defense is to prevent clog-causing debris om accumulating in the first place: Refrain from pouring liquids ntaining grease down kitchen drains, and make sure the basket r strainer over a sink or tub drain remains in place and is cleaned ter each use.

Each week, pour half a cup of baking soda followed by half a ıp of vinegar into kitchen drains and others that are frequently sed. Allow about ten minutes for the mixture to work, then pour kettle of boiling water into the drain to flush it.

Instead of this treatment, you can also use chemical drain eaner. Because it is stronger you need apply it only once a onth. However, drain cleaner is dangerous, so follow the man- facturer's instructions faithfully. Avoid using drain cleaner fre- ıently if your home's plumbing is connected to a septic system.

When a sink or tub drains slowly or not at all, the first place check is the portion of the drain nearest the fixture. Kitchen ıks usually have a removable drain basket that lifts out to give cess to the drainpipe below. However, inside the pipe there is ten a smaller strainer. To remove this, hold a pair of pliers with the jaws upward and insert the ends of the handles in two of th strainer openings. Then put a large screwdriver horizontally be tween the handles just below the jaws and use the screwdriver t twist the pliers counterclockwise, unscrewing the strainer.

Bathroom sinks generally are fitted with a pop-up stoppe held in place inside the drainpipe by a linkage of rods or othe parts connected to a knob or handle between the faucets. T remove a pop-up stopper, first raise it by means of the knob c handle. Twist the stopper half a revolution in whatever directio it will turn to free it from the linkage, then lift the stopper straigh up.

If this does not work, examine the linkage under the sink Usually you will find a single horizontal rod entering the drain pipe. Removing the rod will free the stopper.

To remove a bathtub pop-up stopper, you must first deter mine what type it is. If a strainer is fitted at the entrance to th drain, the mechanism is the trip-lever variety: The stopper is plunger that slides vertically in the overflow drainpipe, and it ma become clogged with hair. To remove the plunger, unscrew th

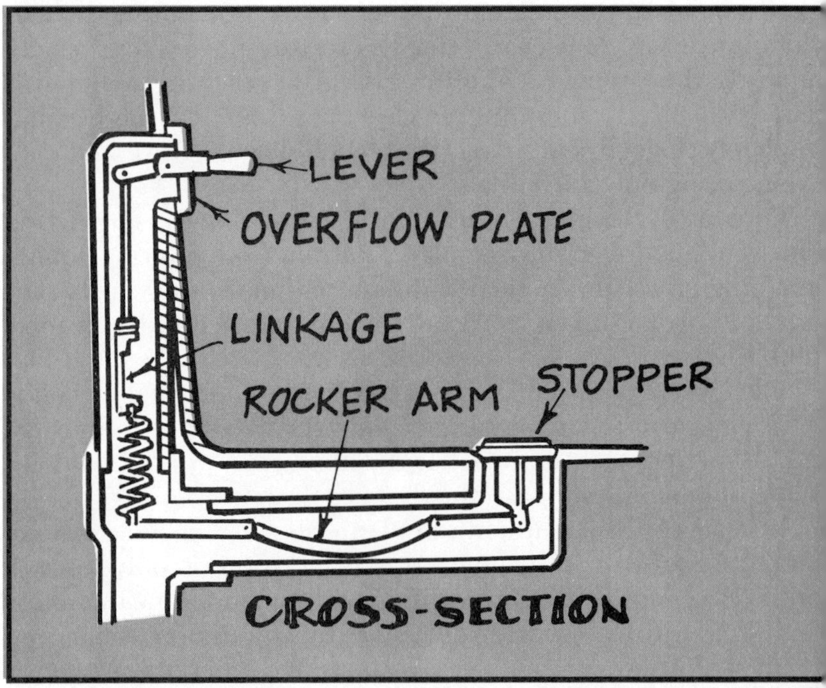

Disassemble a clogged strainer with a screwdriver and pliers. To remove the stopper assembly, pull out the stopper and rocker arm; remove the cover of the overflow vent to withdraw the remainder of the linkage.

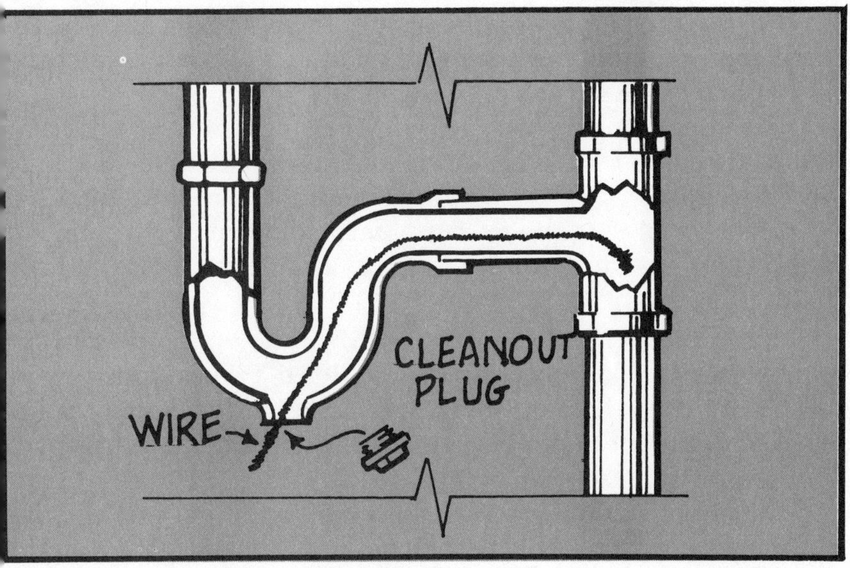

To clear a sink trap, remove the plug, drain water, and probe for blockage with a wire.

plate covering the overflow vent near the top of the tub. Grasp the lever protruding from the vent cover and withdraw it, along with the linkage and the plunger, which is attached to the end.

If you want to probe the horizontal pipe beneath the strainer that connects the tub to the drain, unscrew the strainer using pliers and a screwdriver as described above.

If there is a stopper in the drain instead of a strainer, the stopper is the pop-up kind. To remove it, grasp it with your fingers and wiggle it up and out, along with the attached linkage parts; then unscrew the plate covering the overflow vent and withdraw the remaining linkage, including the large spring at the end, which may have become clogged. Do not disassemble either section of the linkage further. Doing so will alter the adjustment of the parts and may cause the stopper to leak.

Scrub the parts clean, then run water down the drain. If the drain is still sluggish but not blocked, pour a kettleful or two of boiling water into the pipe (or use the baking soda and vinegar remedy), wait approximately ten minutes, then flush the pipe with hot water from the tap.

If the drain still empties slowly after this treatment, or is blocked, use a plumber's plunger to unblock it. Do not use chemical drain cleaner. Should the cleaner not work, you would then

TIP:

Before plunging a sink to whose drainpipe a dishwasher is attached either directly or via a garbage disposer (the connection is usually visible beneath the sink), seal the hose connecting the nearest of these devices to the drainpipe. To do this, sandwich the hose between two blocks of wood and tighten the assembly with a C-clamp.

ATTENTION

have to use the plunger or disassemble the plumbing anyway, and then you would have to cope with quantities of caustic water that if splashed or spilled could cause injury.

Use the plunger this way: With wet rags, plug any overflow holes in the sink or tub and, in the case of double sinks, any additional drain openings. Have enough water in the sink or tub to partly cover the plunger cup. Smear the rim of the cup with petroleum jelly so it will seal tightly against the bottom of the fixture.

Then place the plunger directly over the drain opening and plunge the handle vigorously up and down a dozen times, exerting effort while both pushing and pulling. Don't give up if a blocked drain does not clear after the first set of a dozen strokes. Try several more sets, up to ten.

When the drain does clear, flush it for a few minutes with hot running water from the tap, then apply the baking soda and vinegar remedy or chemical drain cleaner according to the manufacturer's instructions. Reinstall the stopper or strainer.

If plunging will not clear the drain, try cleaning out the trap beneath the fixture if it is accessible. The trap is a section of U- or J-shaped pipe. Because the trap contains water, you will need a bucket under it, and you may prefer to don rubber gloves. (On bathtubs either the trap is not accessible or there is a metal plate in the floor nearby that gives access to an old-fashioned drum trap, which can be cleaned with an auger.)

First inspect the underside of the trap. On kitchen sink traps, there is often a cleanout plug, which can be unscrewed with a wrench or pliers. (Wrap the jaws of either tool with electrician's tape to prevent marring polished metal plumbing surfaces.) Let the water drain from the trap after you remove the plug, then poke inside the trap through the cleanout hole using a hooked length of coat hanger wire or a plumber's snake to find and withdraw the blockage.

If there is no plug, unscrew the large slip nuts that join the ends of the trap to the drainpipe. Pull the trap free, empty it, and replace it. (Should the seams covered by the slip nuts leak afterward, replace the rubber gasket under each nut and wrap the trap threads with Teflon plumber's tape before reassembling.)

If you can't locate a blockage in the trap, the problem lies farther along in the drainpipe, or may signal a different problem altogether. If you have a plumber's snake, try probing the pipe farther before reassembling the trap or replacing the plug. If you still find nothing, it's time to call a plumber.

Repairing a Pop-up Drain

Pop-up drains, the kind operated by raising a vertical rod in ıe center of the faucet, are common on bathroom sinks. Al- ıough convenient to use, these drains clog easily because the pening in the bottom of the sink cannot be screened. Also, the lug mechanism frequently slips out of adjustment.

If the drain is sluggish or if operating the lift rod is difficult, ogging may be the problem. Try removing the plug by simply fting it straight out of the opening or by rotating it a partial turn hile lifting. Then clean the plug by washing it and clear the lumbing by using chemical drain cleaner or a plumber's snake, r by removing and cleaning the U-shaped trap pipe beneath the nk. A safer alternative to chemical drain cleaner is to pour half cup of baking soda down the drain, followed immediately by alf a cup of vinegar. Allow the mixture to work for at least ten ıinutes, then pour a kettleful of boiling water down the drain to ush it.

Some plugs cannot be removed except by disassembling the rain mechanism. This is described further on.

Reinstall the plug and test the drain. If the lift rod is still ifficult to operate, if the plug fails to seal the drain opening, or the drain malfunctions in other ways, the problem is with the lug mechanism.

Repairing or adjusting the mechanism is easy but requires orking beneath the sink, usually an awkward location. You will so need an assistant to operate the drain from above while you fix it from below. For comfort, prepare the area before you begir by removing items that may get in your way and by spreading ar old throw rug or blanket beneath the sink for padding.

Slide under the sink. Take a flashlight with you that can be hung or positioned where you want it, leaving both your hands free. You will also need a pair of channel-type pliers, and if the mechanism parts are rusty, an aerosol can of penetrating oil.

The jaws of the pliers should be wrapped with adhesive tape to prevent them from marring plated parts. The oilcan should be the type with a tiny tube that allows focused spraying of smal items from different angles.

Locate the setscrew that joins a vertical flat rod with holes ir it to another vertical rod above it. The rod with the holes is callec the clevis rod. The upper rod is the lift rod that protrude through the faucet and is pulled or pushed to operate the drain.

Loosen the setscrew by turning it counterclockwise with your fingers or the pliers. If the screw is stuck, do not force it. Instead apply penetrating oil to the threads, wait a few moments for the

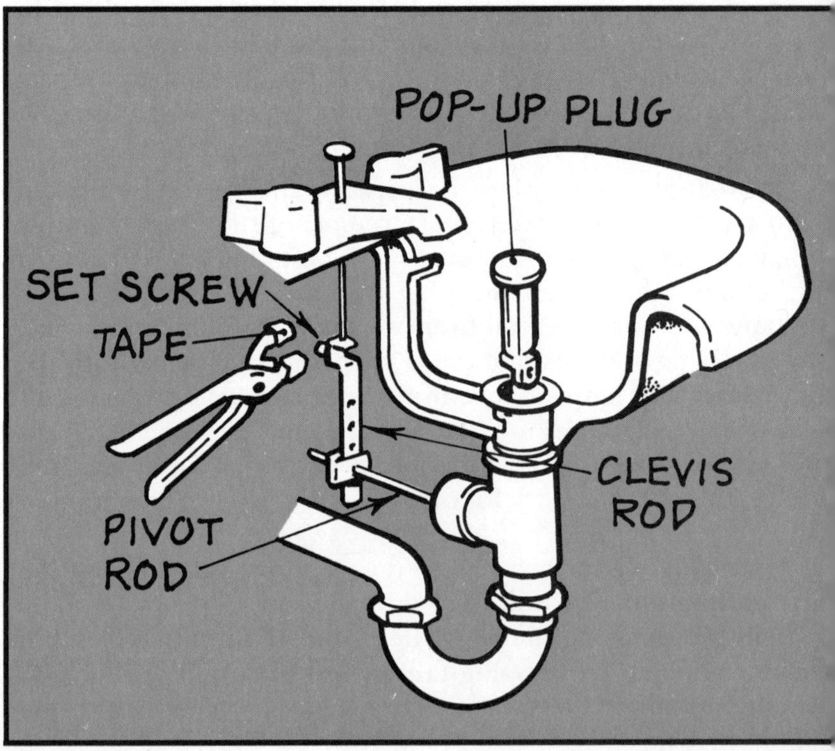

Most pop-up drain problems can be cured by cleaning the plug and adjusting the rods. On some models, the pivot rod must be removed to withdraw the plug.

ɔil to work, then try again. If the setscrew does break, a replace-
nent can be obtained from a hardware store.

With the setscrew loosened, have someone press the drain ɔlug firmly into the drain so that it seals. From underneath the ·ink, push the lift rod up as far as it will go without separating it 'rom the clevis rod. Then retighten the setscrew with the rod in his position.

Test the drain again. If there are still problems, adjust the ɔivot rod. This is the rod connected to the clevis rod at right ıngles. To loosen the rod, squeeze the spring clip that secures it. Then slide the rod out of the hole in the clevis rod and insert it hrough the next higher hole.

You will have to move the spring clip upward to the new ocation also. Try the drain again. If necessary, readjust the clevis ·od or repeat both procedures.

If the lift rod does not stay raised when pulled up, thus causng the plug to rise from the drain when the rod drops, the retainng nut surrounding the pivot rod where it joins the drainpipe nay be loose. The nut can be tightened by turning it clockwise. This should increase the resistance felt when the lift rod is operıted. Tighten the nut gradually until the resistance is sufficient to ɛeep the rod from dropping by itself. Overtightening will make he rod difficult to operate.

Tightening the remaining nut should also cure any leaking hat occurs from the spot. If it does not, or if you must disassemble he drain mechanism to free the drain plug, loosen the nut instead ınd slide it along the pivot rod out of the way.

You should then be able to withdraw the pivot rod from the lrainpipe. Do so gently, taking care to note the position of any vashers or gaskets that come loose with it.

If you cannot slide the rod completely free of the drainpipe, queeze the spring clip at the other end of the rod at the same ime. This will allow the pivot rod to slide through the hole it is ecured to in the clevis rod. Withdrawing the pivot rod will permit emoving a drain plug that cannot be lifted out otherwise.

To cure leaking, obtain new washers or gaskets and a new ·all fitting to replace the one on the end of the pivot rod. To be ure of obtaining duplicates for the old parts, take them with you o the hardware store when shopping for new ones.

Before reassembling the drain mechanism, clean the inside ·f the drainpipe by swabbing it with a twisted rag. Then insert the ıew washers or gaskets. If the drain plug is the type that can be emoved only by withdrawing the pivot rod, place the plug in the lrain opening, aligning it so that the hole in the base of the plug an receive the end of the rod when it is inserted.

Slide the new ball fitting onto the pivot rod and position the fitting so that the end of the rod projects at least halfway into the vertical portion of the drainpipe. Lubricate the ball with a dab of petroleum jelly, then slide the rod into place.

Test whether the rod passes through the base of the drain plug by having someone lift the plug from the drain opening slightly while you hold the rod. You should be able to feel the tug. Then wrap two or three turns of plumber's thread-sealing tape clockwise around the threads of the opening through which the pivot rod enters the drainpipe. Reinstall the retaining nut securely; if necessary, adjust the clevis rod and pivot rod.

TIP:

Brown and green stains on porcelain caused by dripping water can usually be removed by applying chlorinated cleanser and scrubbing with a damp scrub brush. Wear rubber gloves to avoid irritating skin. If further treatment is necessary, cover the stain with liquid chlorine bleach (by partly filling the sink or by placing a cloth saturated with bleach over the stain) for half an hour. Then apply cleanser and scrub. Rinse with plenty of clear water. Other remedies include using stain-removal chemicals sold at plumbing supply stores and marble companies.

ATTENTION

Repairing Bathroom and Kitchen Faucets

Dripping or leaking faucets are among the most exasper-ating household annoyances. Not only is the dripping sound a nuisance, but the amount of water that flows uselessly (and expensively) down the drain can be appalling. In porcelain sinks, basins, and bathtubs, constant contact with water also causes stains.

Repairing most faucet leaks, however, is simple and inexpensive. The first step always is to halt the water flowing to the faucet by turning a shutoff valve on the supply pipe beneath or near the fixture. Turn the valve clockwise. Single-handle faucets that provide both hot and cold water have two supply pipes and two shutoff valves. If you cannot find a shutoff valve at this location, look for one elsewhere, between the fixture and the water meter. If your plumbing system has no shutoff valves, you will have to turn off the main water supply by closing the valve at the meter.

Single-lever faucets show other signs of needing repair besides leaking. These are difficulty in adjusting the water temperature, hot water entering cold water outlets such as toilet supply lines, and inadequately heated water at some faucets. The last symptoms occur because hot and cold water supplies come together at single-handle faucets, thus a malfunctioning faucet can permit water of one temperature to enter the pipes of another.

Hardware stores carry replacement parts for virtually all faucets. The repairs in this chapter cover the most popular types of faucets. Yours may not match these exactly, but the procedure for repairing them will almost always be similar.

TIP:

When disassembling a faucet or other item with many small parts, lay the parts down in the order that you remove them. This will ease reassembly.

ATTENTION

Compression Faucets

Compression faucets are probably the most common type Certainly, most older faucets are likely to be this variety. If wate drips from the spout after the faucet is turned off, the problem i usually a worn-out stem washer inside. If water leaks from arounc the faucet handle, the problem is usually deteriorated packing o a worn O-ring.

To repair the faucet, first remove the screw that fastens th handle to the central shaft called the stem. If the screw is no visible on the top of the handle, you will most likely find it b removing the decorative cap that is there instead.

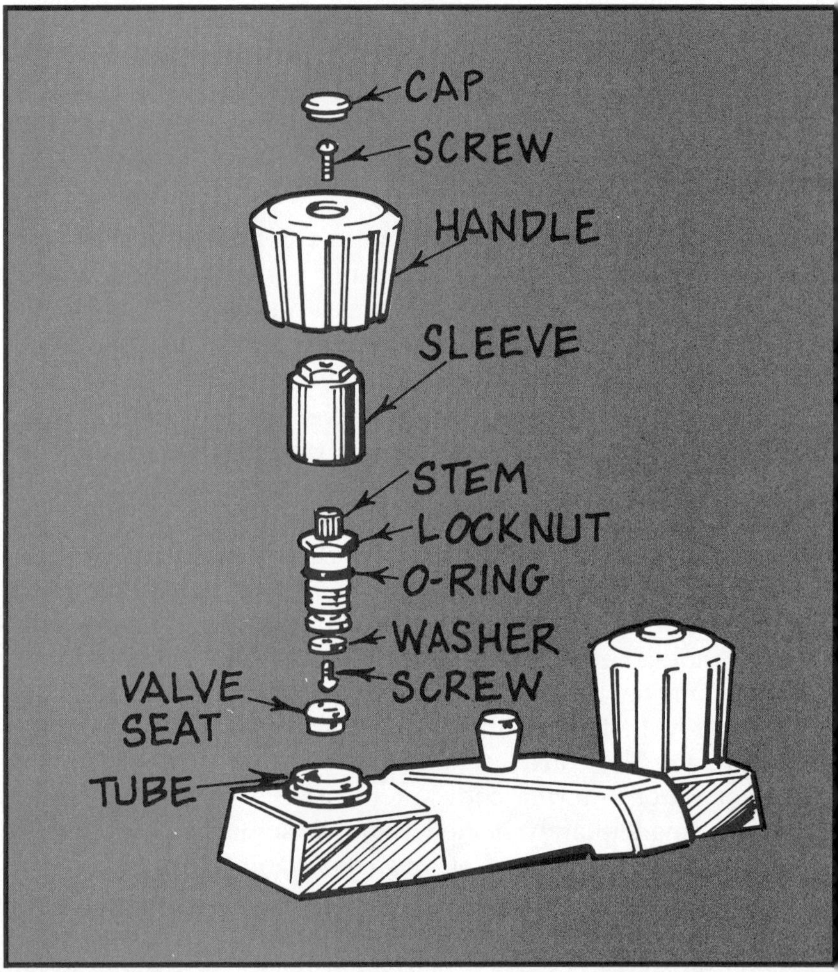

Compression faucets can develop drips when the washer at the base deteriorates. Replace the washer.

Knurled caps, whose edges resemble the rim of a coin, can usually be unscrewed using pliers. Wrap the jaws of the pliers with adhesive tape to prevent scratching finished surfaces. If the edge of the cap is smooth instead, pry it up with a thin-bladed screwdriver. After removing the screw, lift the handle off the stem.

Beneath some faucet handles—usually contemporary-styled deck faucets that incorporate the faucet handles and a central spout into a single unit—is a metal or plastic sleeve. Slide this also off the stem. If a metal sleeve sticks due to corrosion, apply penetrating oil like Liquid Wrench or WD-40 to free it. Never strike the sleeve hard, otherwise you may ruin the stem.

On faucets without sleeves, the next step is to remove the packing nut that holds the faucet assembly in place while allowing the stem to turn. This is a large cone-shaped nut with a hexagonal base designed for turning with a wrench or pliers. If you do not see a packing nut, it may be hidden beneath a decorative metal housing called a bonnet. This usually slides easily off the stem.

Sometimes on faucets mounted on a wall instead of a sink or other fixture, the packing nut is recessed into the wall behind the bonnet. To reach it you will need a special socket wrench, available at hardware and plumbing supply stores.

After removing the packing nut, withdraw the stem assembly by turning it counterclockwise, as if turning the faucet on. If it will not turn easily, reinstall the handle on the stem (there is no need to install the screw at the top) to obtain greater leverage.

Faucets with sleeves usually have a thin locknut instead of a packing nut. To remove this, turn the stem as if opening the faucet a half turn, then unscrew the nut.

At the base of the stem you will find the stem washer, held in place by a screw. If no washer is present, the faucet is not a compression type. Most likely it is still easy and inexpensive to repair; take the stem assembly to a hardware store and obtain the necessary replacement parts.

To free the washer, remove the screw. If corrosion makes this difficult, cut the washer out using a penknife, then apply penetrating oil to the screw and remove it with pliers. A replacement screw is easily obtained if the original is damaged.

When removing the screw, avoid clamping the stem in a vise or locking pliers, which can damage the stem. If a better grip is necessary, reinstall the handle temporarily as described.

In an emergency, a leaking faucet can be repaired by reinstalling the old washer upside down. But to do the job right, replace the washer with a new one that fits tightly into the brass cup at the base of the stem. New stem washers are cone-shaped; install them with the cone side exposed. Then reinstall the screw.

If the washer you removed was damaged, the inside surface —called the valve seat—of the faucet may be flawed. To repair a valve seat, first examine the inside of the faucet with a flashlight and determine whether the opening at the bottom is octagonal. If it is, you may be able to remove the seat by unscrewing it with either a large allen wrench, a wide-bladed screwdriver, or a special inexpensive wrench made for the purpose. If the seat is removable, simply replace it with a new one and the repair is made.

If the opening appears round, the valve seat is not replaceable. Obtain a valve seat grinding tool instead; it is also inexpensive. Following the manufacturer's instructions, lubricate and insert the tool into the faucet opening and twist it a few times. This will grind the valve seat smooth. Clean the filings from the opening using a cloth.

Reassemble the faucet by reversing the disassembly procedure. When you are finished, restore the water supply and test the faucet.

If leaking beneath the handle has been the problem, or if leaking develops after reassembly, first try tightening the packing nut a half-turn or more. If this does not work, if you must tighten the packing nut so tightly that the faucet handle becomes difficult to turn, or if there is no packing nut, you must replace the sealing material around the stem.

On faucets with packing nuts, use packing twine. Wrap a length of the material two or three times clockwise around the stem underneath the packing nut, then tighten the nut down over it to compress the twine and seal the seam between the stem and the nut. There is no need to remove old packing.

Where no packing nut is present, replace any rubber or synthetic O-rings around the stem. To install new ones, lubricate them first with petroleum jelly, then roll them over the stem into place.

Rotating-Ball Faucets

Rotating-ball faucets are a common kind of single-handle variety supplying both hot and cold water. They are distinguishable by the dome-shaped base of the handle.

To repair a rotating-ball faucet, begin by shutting off the water supply and lifting the faucet handle to release water remaining in the spout. Then close the drain or cover it with a saucer to prevent losing small parts.

At the base of the faucet handle, find the tiny hole containing a setscrew that secures the handle to the faucet body. Loosen the

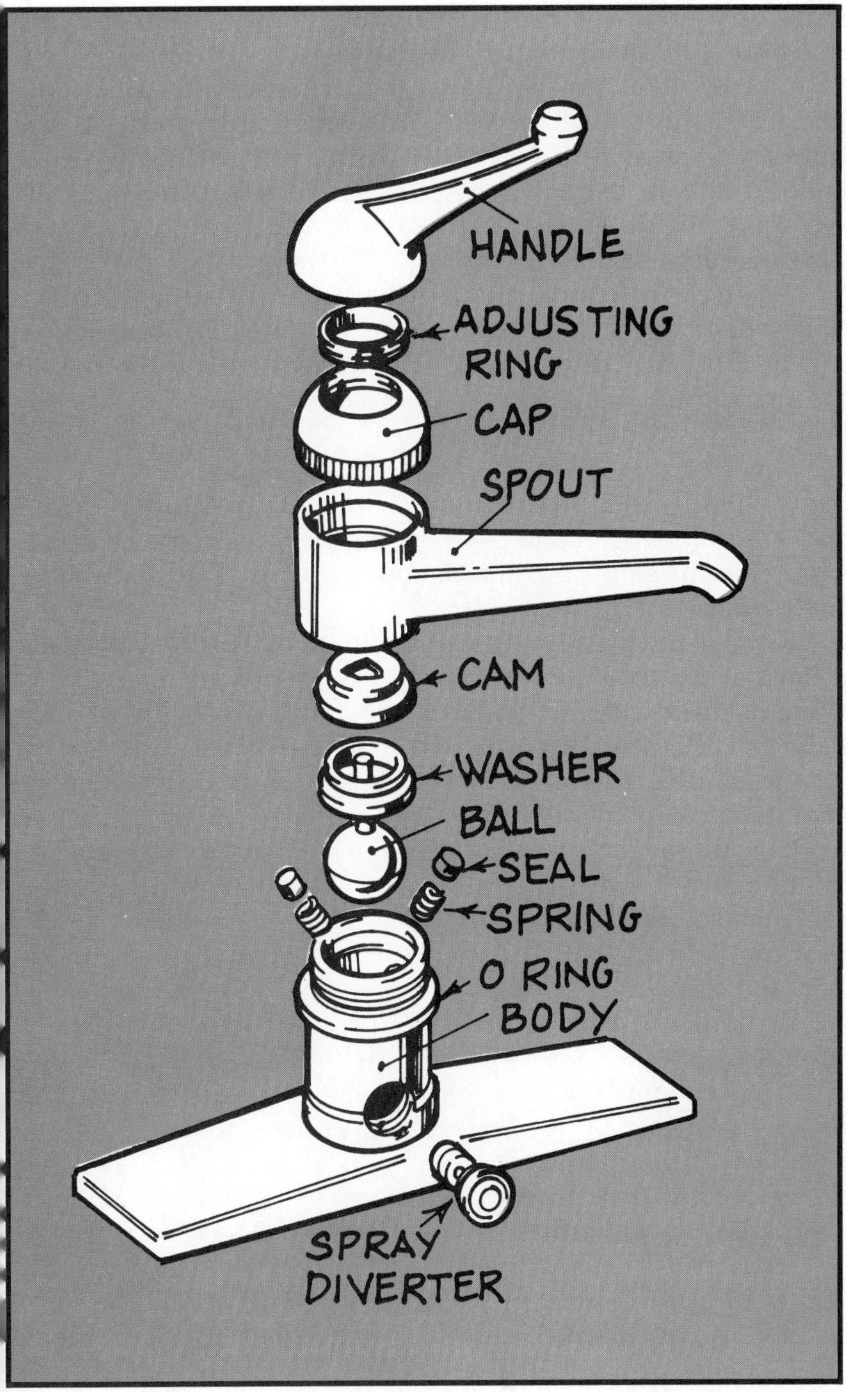

Rotating-ball faucets contain numerous small parts. Seals, springs, and O-rings are most likely to require replacement if the faucet malfunctions.

screw using a hex or allen wrench, but do not remove it as it is easily lost. Lift the handle off the faucet.

This exposes the adjusting ring, a threaded washer with notches in the top. If the only problem with the faucet is that leakage occurs beneath the handle, use the blade of an old kitchen knife to tighten the adjusting ring. To do this, place the knife across the ring so that the blade enters two of the slots. Then turn the ring clockwise.

Reattach the handle and test the faucet. If partial success is achieved, try tightening the ring further. However, if leaking persists or if other problems must be corrected, remove the ring by turning it counterclockwise and proceed with the steps that follow.

Unscrew the faucet cap beneath the adjusting ring using channel-type pliers. To prevent marring the cap's chrome edges, first wrap the jaws of the pliers with electrician's tape or Band-Aids. After lifting off the cap, remove the plastic cam and rubber cam washer underneath.

Remove the ball also, which is now exposed. It may be made of brass or plastic. Beneath it, at the openings in the faucet body where hot and cold water enter, find two tiny rubber rings called seals, and beneath them, tiny metal springs. Some faucets may have pairs of ceramic disks and rubber O-rings instead. Remove all of these components using long-nosed pliers.

Now lift off the spout. Usually you will have to twist it while pulling upward with some force, as it fits tightly over the faucet body, compressing two rubber O-rings in between. When the faucet is removed, pry the O-rings off from around the faucet body using the blade of a screwdriver.

If the faucet is equipped with a sprayer hose, the diverter valve that causes water to flow through it will be visible in the side of the faucet body. It can be removed by pressing or unscrewing. Pry off its rubber O-ring and replace it with a new one.

Check for deposits or roughness between the diverter's plunger and its seat. To get rid of them, try twisting the plunger against the seat a few times to smooth both surfaces.

If this doesn't work, disassemble the valve and clean it with a moistened brush dipped in powdered cleanser, or boil the valve for about twenty minutes in distilled white vinegar mixed with an equal amount of water. If deposits remain or if the valve is corroded, replace it.

Replacement parts are usually available in kits containing everything needed except the ball, which is sold separately. Repair kits often also include a hex wrench for the faucet handle setscrew and a special tool for turning the adjusting ring.

Before reassembling the faucet with the new parts, clean the faucet body thoroughly inside and out. Use a moistened brush dipped in powdered cleanser. Scrape sediment from openings in the base of the faucet with a penknife, then smooth their surfaces by sanding lightly with 440-grit sandpaper. Afterward, rinse the faucet thoroughly with water to remove grit.

Reinstall the cleaned diverter valve if there is one (equip it with a new O-ring), or with a replacement. Next, use petroleum jelly to lubricate the new O-rings that fit around the faucet body and roll them into their grooves.

Reinstall the spout by pressing it down over the faucet body and rotating it until the bottom of the spout's collar rests against the plastic ring at the base of the faucet body.

Install the new seals and springs, or disks and O-rings. Long-nose pliers can be used for this, or the cylindrical parts can be installed by slipping them over the point of a pencil that is then inserted in the opening. Using a fingertip or the tip of a screwdriver, hold the parts in place in each opening while withdrawing the pencil.

Insert the ball by aligning the slot in its side with the pin inside the faucet body. Then replace the cam washer and cam, being sure that the projection on the underside of the cam fits into the notch cut for it in the upper edge of the faucet body.

Reinstall the faucet cap by screwing it down by hand and tightening it about a quarter turn with pliers. Avoid overtightening, otherwise the faucet will operate stiffly and the seals beneath the ball may be damaged.

Install the adjusting ring by screwing it into the top of the cap and tightening it until light friction can be felt while operating the ball shaft.

Finally, replace the faucet handle by aligning the setscrew's hole so that it is directly above the spout. Using the hex wrench, tighten the setscrew firmly.

Restore the water supply and test the faucet. If it leaks beneath the spout, tighten the cap further with the pliers. If leakage occurs beneath the handle, or if tightening the cap produces a leak there, follow the procedure for tightening the adjusting ring.

Cartridge Faucets

Cartridge faucets are another single-lever variety. These feature only one major internal component—the cylindrical metal or nylon cartridge—instead of many small ones. Usually, cartridge faucet woes mean that the rubber O-rings inside the faucet or surrounding the cartridge have worn out, or that passages within the cartridge have become clogged. Repair consists of replacing the O-rings and, if necessary, the cartridge.

Before disassembling the faucet to get at the cartridge, shut off the water supply and lift the faucet handle to let any remaining water out. Then cover the drain hole in the sink so that small items like screws cannot fall in.

Carefully pry up the decorative cap or cover from the top of the faucet using a thin-bladed screwdriver. Beneath should be a screw that holds the faucet knob or lever in place. Remove the screw and lift off the parts that come free.

Faucets with a swiveling spout usually have a round retainer nut sandwiched between the handle and the spout. The rim of the nut is visible even when the faucet is assembled and is grooved like the edge of a coin. Remove the nut by unscrewing it with channel-locking pliers (wrap the jaws of the pliers with tape to avoid marring the nut's edges). Then remove the spout by lifting and twisting.

Beneath the spout, visible after it is removed, is the cylindrical faucet body, usually surrounded by two O-rings. If leaking has occurred around the base of the spout, replace these with duplicates.

With the handle removed—and the spout also, if necessary—the top of the cartridge should be visible, held in place by a horizontal metal clip resembling a long staple. Remove the clip by pulling it with long-nose pliers.

To remove the cartridge, first try pulling it out by gripping the stem with padded pliers. However, if the cartridge sticks (which is likely), use either a cartridge-pulling tool available at some hardware stores and from plumbing suppliers, or—if the stem has a hole through it near the top—the following method:

To provide a fulcrum, place a small block of wood behind the faucet body (or above it if the faucet is mounted horizontally, as in a shower). The top of the block can be even with or as much as an inch higher than the top of the cartridge.

Next, insert a large nail through the hole in the stem so that approximately an inch of the nail protrudes on each side. Rotate the stem so that the nail and the block are parallel.

Hold a pair of pliers by the jaws and slip the ends of the handles under the nail and onto the top of the block. The handles should straddle the stem. Then pry the cartridge out by pulling upward on the jaws of the pliers.

Inspect the cartridge after removing it. If it feels smooth and the passages inside seem clear, simply replacing the O-rings may be sufficient. To install new O-rings, lubricate them with a dab of

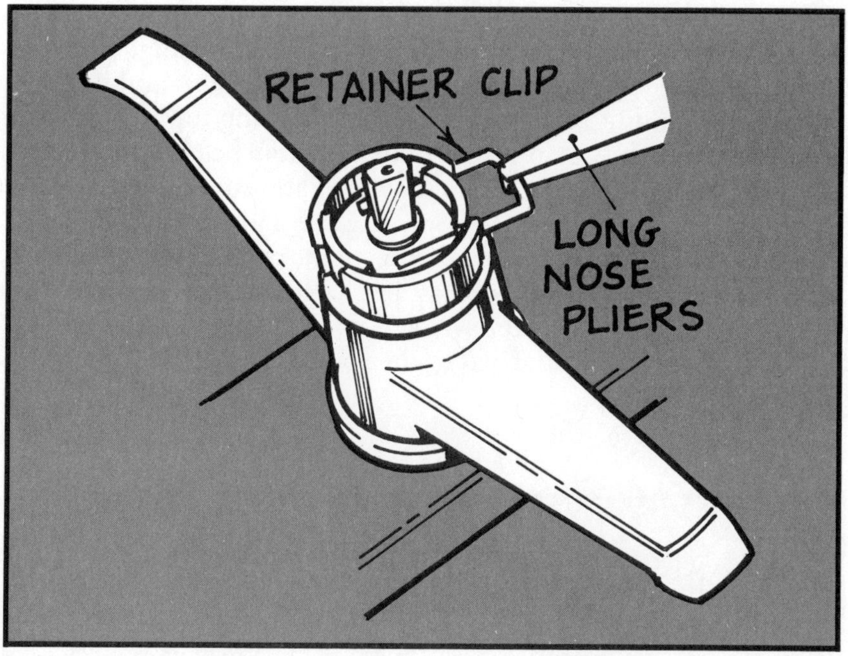

To remove cartridge, withdraw the retainer clip using long-nose pliers, then lift the cartridge from the faucet body.

petroleum jelly and roll them into place over the cartridge body, into their grooves. If the cartridge is clogged, corroded, or damaged, replace it with an identical new one.

To reinstall a cartridge, first pull the stem out as far as possible. Then slide the cartridge into the faucet body by pressing against the cartridge rim. It is normal for water to appear around the stem when the cartridge is inserted.

With the pliers, rotate the cartridge until the small tabs—called ears—at the top align with the slots in the faucet body that permit installing the retainer clip. While pressing the cartridge into the faucet body, replace the clip by inserting it beneath the cartridge ears and into the slots. Use pliers to press the clip fully into place.

On faucets controlled by a knob, rotate the stem until the notch at the upper end points away from the sink or tub floor. Reinstall the handle parts, screw, and decorative cover or cap to complete the repair.

On faucets controlled by a lever, point the notch in the opposite direction. If necessary, first install new O-rings on the faucet body as described earlier. Then reinstall the spout and retainer nut.

To reinstall the lever, hold it facing the sink. Hook the back of the handle ring (located inside the handle housing, which is attached to the lever) over the top of the retainer nut and into the groove surrounding it. Lower the handle housing toward you and press it down firmly so that the underside touches the top of the cartridge stem. Reinstall the handle screw and cover the cap.

Restore the water supply. Moving the faucet control to the left should deliver hot water; to the right, cold. If the positions are reversed, remove the knob or lever. Rotate the stem 180 degrees and reassemble. If the water flow seems restricted, remove and clean the aerator attached to the spout.

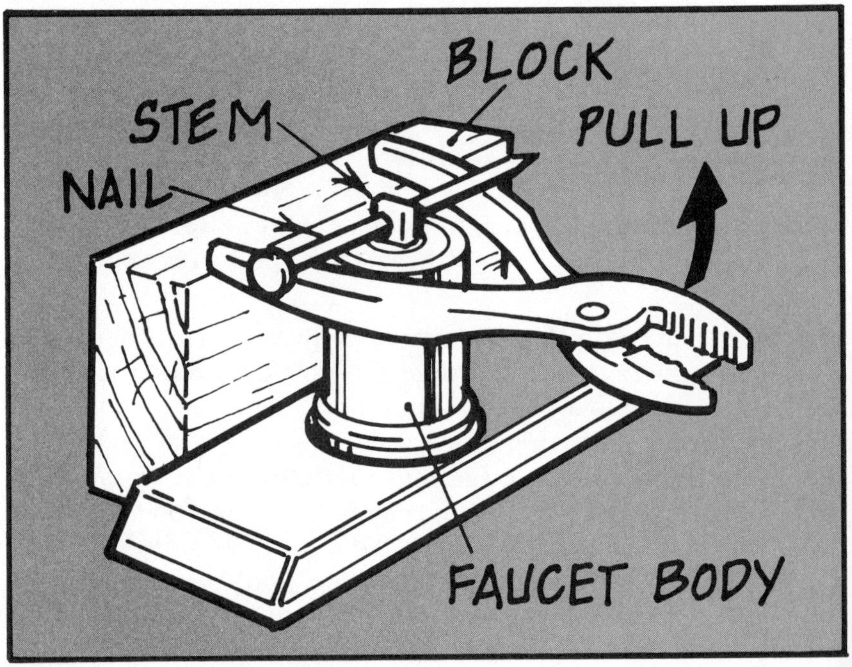

To loosen a stubborn cartridge, insert a nail through the hole near the top of the stem and pry upward using pliers as levers. A small wood block serves as a fulcrum.

PART 4:

Summer (June Through August)

CONTENTS

HIGHLIGHTS

Readying an Air Conditioner

Room air conditioners will perform better and last longer if given simple maintenance before the cooling season begins and again about midway through the summer. Both tune-ups consist chiefly of making sure that nothing interferes with the passage of air around and through the unit.

Begin by uncovering the air conditioner or turning off and unplugging it if it has been in use. Vacuum the front grille and any accessible components, then dust the surfaces with a soft cloth, or wipe them using a cloth and a bottle of spray cleaner. Air conditioners draw air from a room into the machine. Therefore, the front of an air conditioner often collects large amounts of lint and dust, which can clog vital parts.

Next, remove the grille to check the air filter, which is usually just inside. Most grilles are either held in place by screws or are made of flexible plastic and pop away from the air conditioner housing when pressed along the top. Models differ; if you are not sure how to remove the grille, consult the owner's manual.

Dirty air filters are a common cause of air conditioner problems and inefficient operation. Most filters need cleaning every four to six weeks and should be replaced each year.

Before removing the filter, notice how it is held in place so you can reinstall it correctly. Many filters simply slide in and out or are sandwiched between the grille and the front of the air-conditioning unit. However, with some, a particular side of the filter must face the room. To clean a filter, wash it in warm soapy water, then squeeze it until it no longer drips. Let the filter dry completely before reinstalling it. New filters are available at appliance stores.

APARTMENT OWNERS:

Air-conditioner servicing in an apartment building may be handled by the maintenance supervisor. But if you are performing service yourself on a large unit, you will probably find that with the grille removed, the entire unit can be slid forward into the room while the exterior cover remains outside, attached to its supports. Have a helper on hand to assist; such units are usually too heavy for one person to handle safely.

HINT

While the filter is out, check the condition of the evaporator fins. These are normally exposed by removing the filter. Warm air drawn into the air conditioner passes through the filter and then over these fins, where it is cooled and blown back into the room. A filter that is dirty, torn, or improperly installed can admit dust to this area, causing poor cooling if the fins become coated or the spaces between them become clogged.

Vacuum the fins carefully, using a soft brush attachment. Fins are delicate, so be careful not to bend any. If damaged they will block the flow of air and may also produce a whistling noise when the air conditioner is running. If any fins are bent, straighten them by inserting the blade of a putty knife between them and twisting gently.

Examine the base of the air conditioner cabinet. Beneath the fins or where there is access to the partition behind them you will normally find a small drain hole at the bottom of the partition.

This opening is designed to conduct water that condenses on the evaporator fins to a drip pan in the rear of the air conditioner. Poke a wire or straightened paper clip through the drain hole to clear it, especially if you notice water beneath the evaporator fins or in front of the hole.

Cleaning and maintenance will improve performance of an air conditioner. Wash or replace the air filter at least twice during the cooling season.

TIP:

Most foreign noises coming from an air conditioner during operation are caused by loose screws or bolts, resulting in vibration of the parts they fasten. Rhythmic noises are an indication that something (perhaps the thermostat's sensor bulb) is striking one of the two fans, or that a fan is brushing against the housing surrounding it. To check and adjust the position of the thermostat sensor, remove the filter. The other two problems can often be solved simply by tightening all accessible fasteners and by slightly repositioning the air conditioner in the window.

ATTENTION

TIP:

Oily water in an air conditioner's drip pan may indicate a refrigerant leak. Call for service, especially if the air conditioner does not cool effectively.

ATTENTION

Any standing water should then drain out. If it doesn't, use carpenter's level to check whether the air conditioner is mounte correctly in the window. The unit should slope downward towar the rear at least a quarter of an inch.

In very humid weather, water dripping from the outside o an air conditioner is normal. It indicates that condensed water i overflowing the drip pan because evaporation cannot carry it awa faster than it accumulates.

However, a musty smell coming from the air conditioner is sign of mold or bacteria growth in the pan. If the smell persist after the drain hole has been cleared and water ceases to dri from the outside, professional servicing is usually necessary t disassemble the air conditioner and clean the drip pan.

Inspect, dust, and lightly lubricate other visible component inside the air conditioner such as louver assemblies that direct ai flow. Then replace the filter and grille and examine the outdoo part of the unit.

For maximum cooling efficiency, the exterior of an air con ditioner should be shaded from the sun. Trees, shrubs, or a awning can be used to provide shade, but these must not com near enough to block warm air escaping from the machinery. I necessary, trim foliage back about 2 feet in breezy locations, mor in corners where air is still.

Clean and straighten the external fins at the rear of the ai conditioner. These dispel heat removed from the indoor air and like the evaporator fins, must be free of debris and damage t function effectively.

Finally, examine the seams and weatherstripping around th air conditioner and along the window frame. Much cool air ca pass through faulty seams and seals.

See that the filler panels on both sides of the air conditione fit snugly against the sides of the window frame. Apply new foan weatherstripping in places where existing strips have come loose Renew crumbling putty or caulk around windows and frames.

When reconnecting the air conditioner, make sure that nei ther drapes nor heavy furniture obstruct air flow in front of th grille. A venetian blind or roller shade is best for covering th window above the air conditioner.

Appliances sharing the same electric circuit while the air con ditioner is operating can drain current, causing poor cooling an possibly damaging components. If an extension cord is used, b sure it is the proper size and as short as possible. Ordinary exten sion cords are not adequate.

Preparing and Repairing Window and Door Screens

With the arrival of warm weather comes the rush to reinstall window and door screens. However, screens usually require cleaning and sometimes repair before being ready for another season's use. Screens provide more than just ventilation; they also keep out insects. Because of this, screens should not be allowed to develop holes and tears, particularly during late summer and early fall, when insects are seeking winter quarters.

Cleaning

To clean screens, simply wash them by scrubbing both sides with a solution of household detergent and warm water. Use a stiff bristle scrub brush. Rinse by spraying with a garden hose. If you must do the job indoors, wash the screens in a bathtub and rinse them by sponging with clear water.

Repairing

To repair a tiny hole in plastic or fiberglass screen, dab clear household cement over it using a toothpick. If the screen is plastic (vinyl is common), read the label first or test the cement on spare screen to be sure it will not melt the material.

To mend tears, align the torn edges and hold them in place by pressing a strip of masking tape against one side. Then spread cement over the tear on the other side. After the cement dries, gently remove the tape.

Holes too large for gluing can be covered with a patch. For plastic and fiberglass screen, cut a square of spare screen larger than the damaged area. Spread cement thinly around the border of the patch, then place it over the area so that the mesh of the patch and the screen aligns.

For metal screen, press-on patches are available at hardware stores. These snap into place when pressed against the existing screen.

To make your own metal screen patches, use scissors to cut a section of new screen large enough to cover the damaged area. Unravel the edges of the patch to form a fringe about an eighth of an inch wide on all sides, then bend the strands at right angles. Install the patch by pressing it against the screen so that the bent strands pass through the mesh. Fold the strands flat on the other side to fasten the patch in place.

To darken new metal-screen patches so that they are less conspicuous, spray them with gray or matte-finish black enamel before reattaching them.

Screens that have torn loose or are extensively damaged must be replaced. Metal replacement screen is more durable than plastic or fiberglass, and usually not much more expensive. If the damaged screen is held in place by a spline (a thin strip of plastic or rubber) around the frame, replacement screen should be cut about 2 inches longer and wider than the frame opening. To install spline-held screen, get an inexpensive tool called a spline roller.

First, free the damaged screen by prying up one end of the spline; then carefully pull the entire spline from its groove. The screen can now be lifted away. Place the frame on a flat surface and center the new screen over the opening. Attach it with tape to the frame in two or three places.

Cut off the corners of the new screen at a 45-degree angle using a straightedge and a sharp utility knife. To do this, place the straightedge so that it touches the inside edge of the groove at each corner of the frame and remove the screen beyond it.

Next, starting at one of the shorter sides, remove any tape and use the convex-edged disk of the spline roller to press the screen into the groove. Place the tool on the screen over the groove and gently roll it back and forth, working with short strokes from the center toward the ends. Pressing the screen into the grooves stretches it, which is desirable. However, avoid pressing hard, or the screen may tear. Repeat the process along the opposite side, then along the two longer sides.

With the screen seated in the groove, replace the spline. Place one end of it at a corner and lay the rest, untwisted, over the groove. Press the spline into the groove with the concave-edged

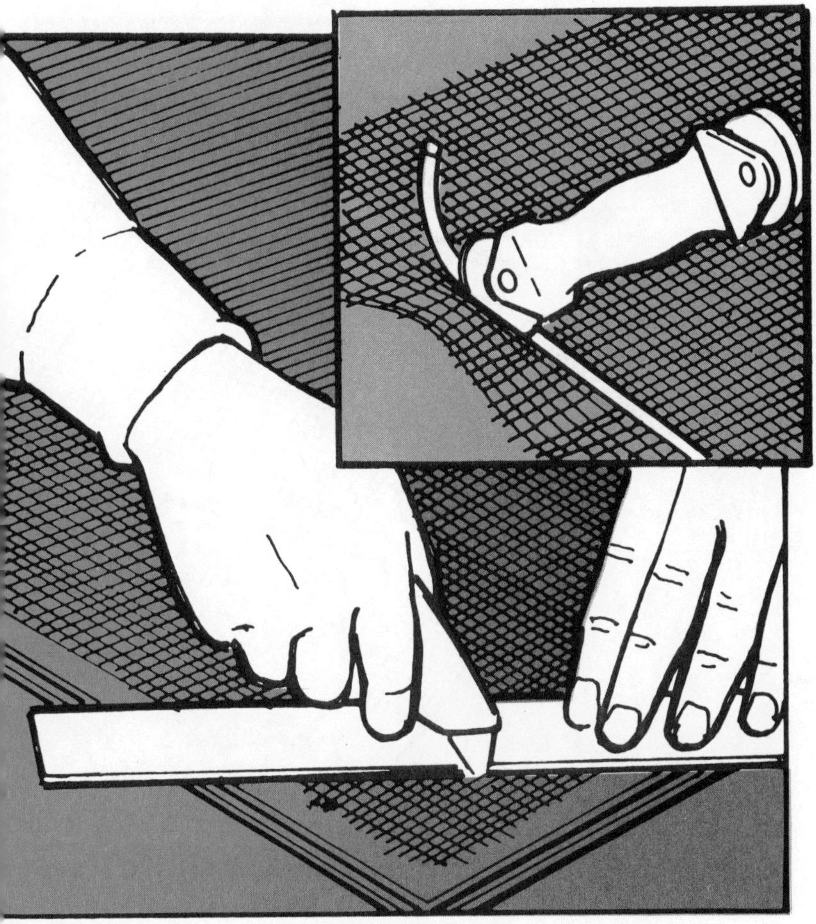

rim the corners of a spline-held screen to a 45-degree ngle. Install the screen and spline using a spline oller.

lisk of the roller, using the technique just described. Try not to tretch the spline.

At the corners, press the spline into place with the tip of a crewdriver. When you are finished, trim the spline if necessary, o the ends meet. Then trim away any excess screen.

Screen in wooden frames is generally held in place by staples or tacks hidden beneath strips of molding. To replace it, carefully pry up the molding using a putty knife, then use long-nose pliers o withdraw the nails or staples holding the screen.

Replacement screen should be about 2 inches wider than the rame opening and about 18 inches longer. Staple or tack the creen to the frame across the opening's bottom edge, allowing an nch or two of material to extend past it. Work from the center

When attaching a screen to a wood frame, fasten the bottom edge and wrap the top around a board. Press down on the board to stretch the screen.

toward the ends to avoid wrinkles. Then wrap the opposite end o the screen around a flat board about 5 inches wide and at least a long as the screen's width.

Rest the lower edge of the board against the top edge of th frame and press down on the board to stretch the screen. Stapl or tack the screen across the top of the opening, then fasten i along both sides. Replace the molding using new nails inserted i the original holes. Trim away the excess screen.

Frames

Metal frames for screens seldom need attention. But woode frames for windows and doors should be given a fresh coat o paint or other finish when necessary, and their corners should b tightened. Mitered corners can be tightened by installing eithe

›rrugated metal corner reinforcements or metal fasteners called ıevrons. Both are usually available at hardware stores.

To install, clamp or wedge the frame pieces tightly together ıd be sure the corners form right angles, either by holding a ırpenter's square against them or by measuring between corners ıat are diagonally opposite. If the angles are correct, both mea-ırements will be equal. While the pieces are clamped, hammer ıe fasteners into the wood so that they cross the seam of each int. One or two fasteners should be enough for each corner.

Corners of all types can also be tightened with metal corner :aces—flat, L-shaped steel plates about 2 inches long on each de with holes for screws. Clamp the frame so the joints are tight nd square, then fasten one plate against each corner using flat-ead wood screws. If more strength is needed, turn the frame ver and repeat the process on the other side.

A more difficult but less visible way to reinforce corners is by ıstalling wooden dowels. Choose dowels whose diameter equals bout one third the thickness of the frame pieces.

To install, clamp the frame, then drill one or two holes the iameter of the dowels into the edge of the frame at each corner. 'he holes must penetrate both pieces of each joint. Apply wood-orking glue to the dowels and tap them into the holes with a ammer. After the glue dries, trim the projecting ends of the owels with a saw, then sand them smooth and apply finish.

'ooden Screen Doors

Wooden screen doors sometimes sag. To correct this, first try ghtening the hinge screws. If any have pulled loose, replace ıem with longer screws. If the problem persists, install a sturdy ye screw on the inside of the door at the top corner of the hinge de and another at the bottom corner of the latch side. Fasten ne length of metal picture wire or cable to the top eye, and one › the bottom eye. Join the two ends at the middle of the door ith a 3- or 4-inch turnbuckle, an adjustable fastener with an eye :rew at each end. Tighten the turnbuckle until the door swings 'eely.

TIP:

To stretch the large screen of a wooden screen door, place the door horizontally on long boards supported by sawhorses. Insert ¾-inch-thick boards beneath the ends of the door, then use C-clamps to tighten the middle of the door against the long boards, bowing the door upward. Attach the screen to the door in this position; when unclamped, the door will straighten, stretching the screen.

ATTENTION

Freeing Stuck Double-hung Windows

Although double-hung windows—the kind with uppe and lower sashes that slide vertically—have been popular for cen turies, all-wood models usually become stuck eventually, fron warping or accumulated layers of old paint.

Before assuming a window is stuck, be sure it is unlocked an that there are no hidden fasteners preventing the sashes fron moving. Then, if a window appears to be sealed shut by pain first score with a utility knife along the seams where the sashes f into the tracks, and also at the top and bottom of the windo frame. Follow this by forcing a wide, stiff-bladed putty knife int the seams. Insert only a corner of the blade, then tap the end o the knife handle gently with a hammer. Be careful of the glass.

While hammering, pivot the blade until its entire edge i embedded. Drive the blade approximately an inch deeper, then wiggle the knife back and forth to widen the seam and break loos any paint inside.

Perform this procedure around all four sides of the windo if necessary. Be careful not to mar the edges of frame parts. Also unless the sashes are stuck partly open, drive the knife blade int the seam between the sashes where they meet in the middle of th window.

This treatment should free the sashes. If they remain stuck or if they bind because of warping, obtain a block of wood ap proximately a sixteenth of an inch thicker than the width of th window tracks. Place the block against a track as close as possibl to the binding sash and hammer it in.

Remove the block and repeat the process on the opposite side ·f the window. Hammer the block into the tracks elsewhere along heir length also, if necessary. This will widen each track by preading its sides. Afterward, the sashes should slide freely.

If neither of these methods work, and you have access to the xterior of the window, go outside and pry upward on the underide of the lower sash using a wide pry bar. Protect the windowsill vith a piece of thin plywood and slip the blade of a putty knife etween the end of the pry bar and the underside of the sash to void marring it also.

An alternative to this technique is to drive a wedge such as an x blade between the sash and the sill. Always strike a metal wedge vith a wooden mallet or light sledgehammer, not an ordinary arpenter's hammer, which might splinter.

To free a lower sash that you cannot reach from outside, or o free a stuck upper sash regardless of its accessibility, remove he molding strips from around the window frame. To free a ower sash, remove the side strips on the frame's interior. Use a tiff, wide-bladed putty knife. Insert it into the seam between the nolding and the frame, perpendicular to the sashes.

A cure for stuck sashes is to force a putty knife between he sash and the molding strips. Hammer with care near panes.

Pry the strips away from the frame gently, working graduall along their entire length to avoid breaking them. Because th strips are usually mitered at the top, you may also have to loose or remove the horizontal upper molding strip.

The lower sash then can be pulled away from the fram However, before you do so, detach the sash cords, chains, an balance mechanisms from the sash sides.

When unfastening sash cords or chains, secure each one to screwdriver or long nail before letting go. Otherwise, the counte weight attached to the other end will drop, carrying the cord o chain out of sight into the wall cavity housing it.

Balance mechanisms can be unscrewed from the sashes. Be cause their springs are under tension when the sash is down, gri each one firmly as you free it, and allow it to retract gradually.

To free an upper sash from the outside, pry away the oute molding strips. If you must work from the inside, your only re course is to remove the center strips of molding—called the par ing strips—from the frame instead. These divide the sides of th frame into two tracks, one for the lower sash and one for th upper.

Unfortunately, the parting strips are usually inset in a groov cut into the window frame. To remove them, first remove th lower window sash. Next, score the paint along the edges wher the strips meet the frame, using a utility knife. Then grip eac strip near the lower end with a pair of pliers and pull it towar the center of the window. With luck, the strips will come awa from the groove, nails and all. However, if they break, you wi have to obtain replacements at a lumberyard.

With the sashes removed, you can recondition the window s that they glide smoothly when replaced. First, scrape away a accumulated paint from the tracks, sash edges, and sides of mol ing against which the sashes rub. Use a small hook scraper for th job. Pay particular attention to removing paint from the corne where the parts of the window tracks meet.

Afterward, sand the scraped surfaces smooth, using fine-gr sandpaper. Because of the danger that old paint may contai hazardous amounts of lead, wear a dust mask during the entir operation to avoid inhaling particles, and dispose of all paint chi by collecting them in a bag and depositing it in the trash.

Then apply a coat of primer to any bare wood, followed by thin coat of finish paint to the window tracks and sash sides. D not apply finish paint to the edges of the sashes. This is also good time to install weatherstripping in the window tracks to re duce drafts.

After the paint dries, rub a candle against the track surfaces o lubricate them, or spray the tracks with silicone or Teflon lu- ricant.

To reinstall the sashes, fit the upper one into place first and eattach its sash cords, chains, or balance mechanisms. Then rein- all the parting strips if they were removed, or else the outer olding strips. Finally, install the inner sash and molding strips nclosing it.

When reattaching molding, leave a tiny amount of space be- veen the strips and the sashes to prevent binding. An easy way o do this is to insert an old credit card or the blade of a putty nife between the molding and the sash while hammering.

Replacing Sash Cords

Many double-hung windows, especially older ones, are equipped with counterweights that assist in raising the sashes and also prevent them from sliding downward when released.

The weights are inside cavities on each side of the window frame. They are attached to the sashes by cords that pass over pulleys set in the side pieces of the frame, called the jambs. Lowering the sashes raises the weights and vice versa. The system is effective and simple, but the cords eventually break and repair involves disassembling the window.

When a sash cord breaks, it is prudent to replace all of them at the same time, using flat-link sash chain instead of rope. Sash chain is available at hardware stores.

However, the cavities are sources of heat loss in buildings that are otherwise well insulated. If the window is installed in a wall containing insulation, you should consider instead replacing the entire counterweight system with a more modern window balance system that does not require the cavities. The cavities can then be filled with insulation to supplement that already in the wall.

In both cases, start by removing the lower window sash. Use a sharp utility knife to score along the edges of one of the two strips of stop molding that form the indoor sides of its channels (the tracks the lower sash slides in). Then use a wide, stiff-bladed putty knife to carefully pry the strip away from the jamb to which it is attached.

Work gradually up and down the length of the strip when rying. Afterward, use pliers to remove the nails from the strip by ulling them out through the back. When reinstalling the strip, se new nails.

Pivot the sash toward the inside of the room and wiggle it ree from the opposite channel. Then detach the cords from the ash (they may be held in place by small nails) and allow them to rop into the cavities.

If you have access to the outside of the window, the easiest ay to remove the upper sash is to pry off the stop molding that orms the outside of one of its channels, following the directions or removing the lower sash. If you must work from indoors, use liers to pull free one of the parting strips—the molding that ivides each jamb down the center—instead.

Grip the strip at the bottom to start, and gradually work upard. Pull toward the center of the window opening, parallel to ne glass. If the strip breaks, you can obtain a new one from a umberyard. Remove the sash and detach the cords as described.

Open the cavities by removing the access plate at the base of ach jamb. Usually the plates are made of wood and may be fasened with screws or nails. If they are covered with paint, score round their outlines first, using the knife, or remove the paint by craping or with remover.

When scraping, wear a dust mask to avoid inhaling particles n case the paint contains lead. For the same reason, dispose of all aint chips by sweeping them into a bag and throwing it out with ne trash. Water-based paint remover that does not contain harsh hemicals or produce harmful fumes is now available at most ardware stores.

If no access plates are present or if you are planning to fill ne cavities with insulation, open the cavities by prying away the ndoor trim on each side of the window.

Remove the weights and cords. If appropriate, fill the cavities ith fiberglass insulation, reclose them, and proceed with installng a new balance system as described further on. If you are nerely replacing the sash cords, free the old ones from the eights and attach new ones. Use an unbroken old cord as a guide or cutting new cords or chains to length, or measure from a ulley to the base of a channel and add 6 inches.

Feed each new cord or chain over a pulley and push a long ail through the upper end to prevent it from falling into the avity. Attach the lower end to a weight. Tie knots in cords; to asten chains, wrap soft copper wire through the links.

TIP:

Welded sash chain is stronger than flat link chain but harder to find. To secure it to a sash weight, pass it through the hole, then insert the end link through one of the other links to form a loop. Attach a thick piece of wire to the emerging part of the end link to keep it from slipping out. To attach the chain to the sash, obtain special clips resembling small springs. Screw the clip onto the chain, then insert the clip into a circular hole drilled for it in the side of the sash.

ATTENTION

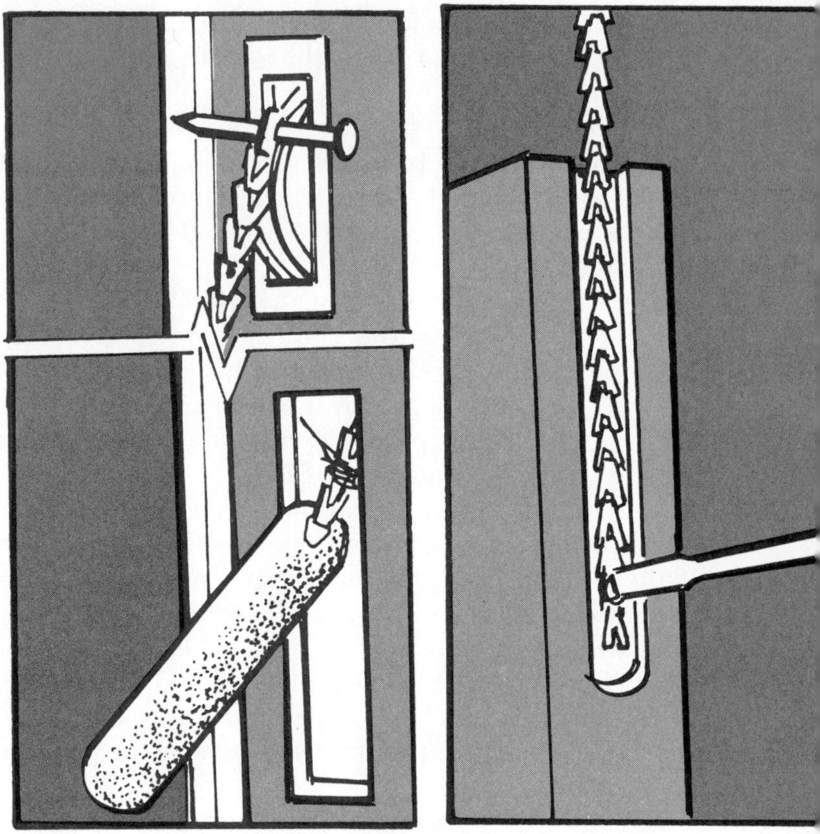

A long nail prevents the sash chain from falling into the cavity while being fastened. To attach the chain to the weight, wrap soft wire through the links. Attach the chain to the groove in the sash.

Replace the weights in the cavities and fasten the cords chain to the sashes, starting with the upper one. Set the sash the windowsill, pull the appropriate pair of cords or chains un their weights rise to the pulleys, then reposition the nails to kee the weights from falling.

Attach the free ends of the cords or chains in the sash slo using small screws or nails. Then remove the long nails, set th sash in place, and slide it upward as far as it will go. If the weig strikes the base of the cavity, shorten the cord or chain by 3 inche

Reinstall the stop molding or parting strip, then attach th lower sash by following the same procedure.

The two most common modern window balance systems a the spiral type and the clockspring type. Both are availab through window repair companies and some home centers.

Installing spiral balances requires cutting grooves in the sides of the sashes with power tools. Unless you are experienced, this is a job for a professional carpenter. However, clockspring balances usually can be installed by amateurs. Be sure to obtain balances appropriate to the size and weight of the sashes.

To install clockspring balances, remove the pulleys and their brackets from the jambs. Then insert the clocksprings in their place and fasten them to the jambs with the screws provided.

Attach the brackets for the spring ends inside the grooves of each sash, also with the screws provided. Slip the ends of the clocksprings onto the hooks on the brackets, then reinstall the sashes in the tracks, beginning with the upper sash.

Replacement window channels are also available. These fit against the jambs and cause the sashes to fit more tightly in the window frame, lessening draftiness.

The friction of the channels is sufficient to hold windows in place, and with lightweight windows balances are not needed. Heavier windows require balances designed to accompany the channels.

Amateurs can install replacement channels fairly easily. Installing the balances requires cutting grooves in the sashes and so usually is a job for a professional.

Installing Replacement Window Channels

Balky or drafty double-hung windows can often be repaired and sealed quickly by installing replacement window chan nels. Various styles are available, the simplest being shallow meta troughs that fit vertically on each side of the window frame, cre ating smooth, close-fitting channels in which the sashes can slide

Replacement window channels do away with the need fo sash cords, chains, and counterweights characteristic of older win dows. Some replacement channels have built-in spring balance: Others can be used with coil-spring lift and spiral-lift balance found on modern or restored windows, or accept special sprin balances designed for them and added after the channels are i place.

Usually, the most difficult part of installing replacemen channels is removing the window sashes. If the window has spira lift balances, the first step is to unscrew the tubes containing th spirals from the top of the window frame, then unscrew the bo tom of each mechanism from the underside of the sash.

Next, pry off the interior stops. Do this also if the window ha another type of balance that cannot be removed until the sash freed from the frame. The interior stops are three strips of mold ing around the inside of the window frame. The two side strip form one side of each channel for the lower sash. The third stri extends between them across the top of the window frame.

The stops must be reinstalled later, so to avoid breaking hem, use a utility knife to slice through the paint covering the eams between the stops and the window frames. Then inspect he stops for screws holding them in place and remove any that 'ou find.

Insert a stiff putty knife between one of the side stops and he window frame, and gently pry it away. Start near the middle nd work gradually up and down along the entire length of the top until it comes away. If the top is mitered, carefully bend it in he middle and slip it free from the upper stop. Remove the upper top next, also by prying.

Before removing the remaining side stop, pivot the lower vindow sash toward the inside of the room by pulling on the side f the frame from which the stop was removed. If a sash cord, hain, or clockspring (another type of balance mechanism) is fasened to the edge of the sash, remove it along with any fasteners iolding it.

The sash cord and chain can be released and allowed to drop o the bottom of the cavities that house the counterweights on ach side of the window frame. (Before installing the replacement hannels, the cavities can be filled with fiberglass insulation to educe drafts.) Clockspring tapes and other balance mechanisms nust be removed by unscrewing them from the sides of the winlow frame.

Slide the window sash free of the frame, and while resting it n the sill, remove the balance mechanism from the other side. Then set the sash aside and remove the remaining stop. Withdraw ll nails from the stops and sides of the frames.

To remove the upper sash, first remove any spiral-lift mechnisms. Then use pliers to grip the base of each parting strip—he narrow piece of molding that divides each channel vertically—and pull it out; these strips will not be reused. Do not remove he parting strip spanning the top of the window frame.

The upper sash can then be lowered and tilted out of the rame. Unfasten any balance mechanisms, then remove the sash nd set it aside.

Some contemporary or restored double-hung windows have emovable metal window channels. To remove the sashes from his type, together with the channels that are to be replaced, slide he sashes together so that they meet in the middle of the frame. Disconnect any spiral-lift mechanisms, then remove the fasteners ttaching the channels to the window frame at the top and botom. With a helper, tilt the sashes and channels as a unit inward rom the top, then lift the assembly out of the frame.

TIP:

Old paint on window sashes may contain hazardous amounts of lead, requiring careful removal. Wear a dust mask when scraping or sanding, and dispose of all paint chips by collecting them in a bag and depositing it in the trash.

ATTENTION

With a helper, install the replacement channels and sashes as a unit into the window frame.

Next, prepare the window frame for the replacement chan nels by scraping or sanding the sides of the frame smooth and removing any pulleys or other hardware from them. If the in structions with the replacement channels specify, use a sharp chisel to shorten each end of the upper parting strip by half an inch.

To install the new channels, place the upper and lower sashes together, one in front of the other, and set them upright on a chair so that their sides extend beyond the seat. Be sure that both ashes are right side up and that the lower sash is nearest you. Fit he replacement channels against the sides of the sashes so that he angled end of each channel points downward with the long edge away from you.

With a helper, lift the sashes and channels together as a unit and set them into the bottom of the window frame. Then tilt the assembly upward into place.

Before fastening the channels, test the sashes. Each should operate smoothly when pressed gently against the parting strip. f a sash feels too tight, bend the channel edge slightly away from he sash on one or both sides of the window using a putty knife. f too loose, bend the edge toward the sash.

When the sashes slide smoothly, use flathead wood screws to asten the channels to the sides of the window frame. Screws permit easy removal for cleaning or repair. (Replacement channels rom which sashes can be removed are available, but installing hese requires professional skill.)

Finally, replace the interior stops. To do this, hold the blade of a putty knife between the channel and the inside edge of each stop to act as a spacer. Then attach the stops to the window frame with small finishing nails.

Repairing Casement Windows

Casement windows, which open and close by pivoting o hinges, generally develop fewer problems than double-hung windows, whose two sashes slide in channels. But casement window can become hard to close because of insufficient lubrication, dirt clogged parts, or a worn cranking mechanism. Usually, casemen windows are easy to repair, and the work can nearly always b done from indoors, safely and without a ladder.

If a casement window squeaks or the crank is difficult to turn first try lubricating the moving parts. Use any lightweight household oil or silicone spray lubricant. Open the window as far a possible, then apply lubricant to the hinges and the ends of th metal extension arms.

Casement windows that are hinged at the top and bottom an open to the right or left have only one extension arm at the bottom of the window. Awning windows, which are casement windows that open from the bottom, are hinged at each side an usually have two arms, also at the bottom, or a scissorslike assembly of four arms. A third type of casement window, which open from the top, has hinges at the sides and no extension arms o operating mechanism.

Lubricate all areas where parts rub together. Then crank th window open and closed several times to distribute the lubricant If this does not solve the problem, check for dirt or paint in th extension arm tracks or on other surfaces that may be causin parts to bind.

To clean the tracks and other parts, open the window fully and unhook the extension arms or arm assembly by sliding the guide at the end of each extension arm out of its track. Then, using a wire brush and a whisk broom, scrape away any dirt that has settled in the tracks or in the sides of the window frame.

Apply a thin layer of lubricant to the inside of the track. Avoid applying too much, otherwise the lubricant will attract dirt and soon become gummy.

Lumps of hardened paint or other deposits that resist brushing can be chipped off using the tip of an old screwdriver. Pay particular attention to the areas of the window and frame that come in contact with each other when the window is shut, especially if the window closes smoothly except for the last inch or so.

Sometimes one or more of the extension arms becomes bent or one of the fittings that joins the arms or slides in the tracks becomes damaged. You may be able to remove bent parts, straighten them with pliers or by hammering, and then reinstall them, but usually the best solution is simply to replace them with duplicates available at hardware stores or from the window manufacturer.

If none of these remedies work, then the cranking mechanism is most likely at fault. The problem is often that grease inside it has stiffened with dirt, making cranking difficult. But sometimes the gears that mesh when the crank is turned are misaligned or damaged.

To remove the cranking mechanism for greasing or replacement, find and remove the screws holding it.

If the latch does not close the window tightly, installing a thin cardboard or plastic shim can help.

To examine the mechanism, remove it from the window. To do this, first disengage the extension arms from their tracks, then find the screws holding the mechanism to the inside of the window frame. The screws may be visible or they may be hidden beneath a removable strip of molding fastened across the bottom of the frame.

If the screws are visible, simply remove them using a screwdriver. Then pull the mechanism toward you while sliding any extension arms through the slot in the window frame.

If the screws are hidden, carefully pry the molding away from the base of the window frame using a putty knife. You should find the screws, installed vertically, beneath the molding. Remove these and the mechanism and extension arms should slide out of the window frame.

Examine the gears inside the cranking mechanism by turning it upside down or inspecting the open end that fits against the windowsill. If the gears appear worn or broken, obtain a replacement mechanism. Be sure the new unit opens the window in the same direction (either to the right or to the left as viewed from inside the house) as the old one.

If the mechanism is not worn, soak it in kerosene or charcoal-lighting fluid (never gasoline, which can explode) for a half hour, then scrub out the old grease with a discarded toothbrush. Relubricate the gears by lightly coating them with petroleum jelly, white all-purpose grease, or graphite powder. Turn the crank handle a few times to spread the lubricant.

If the crank handle is loose, tighten the setscrew that anchors it to its spindle. These screws are frequently damaged. If necessary, take a damaged setscrew to a hardware store and obtain a replacement. Then reattach the cranking mechanism to the window.

One other problem sometimes develops with casement windows: The latch eventually fails to close the window tightly enough to seal out drafts. To remedy this, unfasten the latch from the window by removing the screws holding it. Cut a piece of cardboard or an old credit card to fit between the latch and the window frame and pierce or drill holes through this shim to let the screws pass.

Replace the latch with the shim sandwiched between it and the window frame. This will move the latch slightly inward (toward the inside of the room), causing the latch to draw the window more tightly against the frame.

The shim must not be too thick, otherwise the hooked portion of the latch will not enter the slot intended for it in the window. If more tightening is needed, attach strips of adhesive-backed foam weatherstripping to the surfaces of the window frame that contact the window. Weatherstripping will also help seal gaps if the window frame is twisted or warped.

Replacing Broken Window Glass

Replacing broken window glass is not too difficult. But knowing how to proceed and working in a safe, orderly fashion helps assure the best results.

The first step is to remove the broken glass. Wear heavy work gloves for this. Place a cardboard box near the window, then wiggle the shards free and carefully deposit them in it. To avoid injury in case a fragment of glass falls, work from the top of the window to the bottom.

If the glass is only cracked and the shards cannot be picked out, press strips of masking tape gently across the pane in a crisscross pattern. Then, if possible, remove the sash from the window and place it flat on several thicknesses of newspaper.

With a glass cutter—inexpensive ones are available at hardware stores—score around the perimeter of the pane about an inch from the edge. Strike the glass gently on the scored lines with the cutter. The glass should break into sections held together by the tape; they can then be gathered up and discarded. Remaining glass can be freed during later steps.

On all wooden windows and some metal varieties, glazing compound is used to seal the glass against the exterior side of the sash. To replace the glass, the compound must be removed.

Loose compound can usually be pried away from the sash with a putty knife or a chisel. A glazier's knife, which is made for the purpose but is often hard to find, also can be used; some glass supply stores carry them.

To remove hardened compound, use heat from a hair dryer or a heat gun designed for softening housepaint. The latter can be rented. Hold either tool close to the compound and wave it back and forth. As soon as a section softens, quickly pry it up with a putty knife.

Try not to blister nearby paint; toxic fumes can be produced if the paint contains significant amounts of lead, as does much of the oil- and alkyd-based paint manufactured before 1977. As a precaution, wear a government-approved respirator rated for protection against lead fumes. These are available at hardware and paint stores. Of course, paint that does blister can be repainted after reglazing is completed.

On wooden windows, glass is held in place by small triangular metal chips, called glazier's points, embedded in the sash beneath the glazing compound. To remove these, rake them out with a small hook scraper designed for scraping paint.

Afterward, remove any remaining shards of glass and smooth the recessed part of the sash (into which the pane fits) by sanding it lightly. Be careful not to round over the edges.

TIP:

Although neither a hair dryer nor a heat gun should generate enough heat to start a fire, keep a fire extinguisher handy when using either of these devices. Never use a torch for softening putty or removing housepaint.

ATTENTION

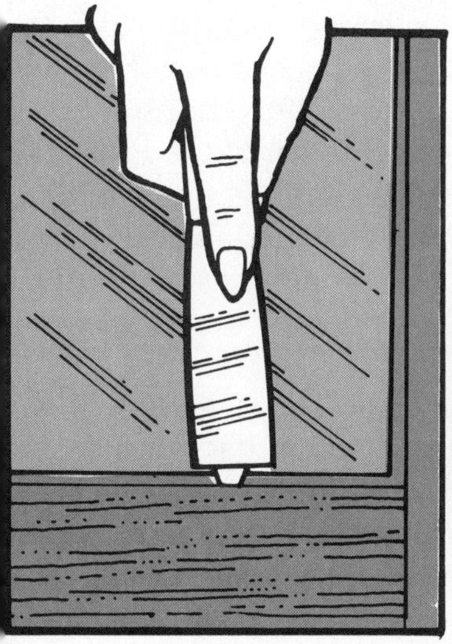

Secure the new glass with glazier's points pressed into the sides of the sash with the tip of a putty knife.

To smooth and trim the outer glazing compound, hold a putty knife at a 45-degree angle to the sash to leave a beveled surface.

Metal windows may have removable clips beneath the glazing compound. Windows without compound usually have removable rubber gaskets or molding strips that hold the panes in place.

Once the glass has been removed, measure the opening for a new pane. Hold a tape measure between the outside edges of the recess—from top to bottom and from side to side—in several places. Then subtract ⅛ inch from each measurement to allow slight clearance.

Replacement glass can be purchased at most hardware stores. Two types are usually available: single strength (3/32-inch thick) and double strength (⅛-inch thick). Single strength is sufficient for most windows, but get double strength for storm windows and for lower panes in vulnerable locations. Stronger glass for use in patio doors, shower and bathtub enclosures, and doors likely to receive impact is available from glass companies.

To install replacement glass in wood sashes or in metal sashes requiring glazing compound, first seal the surface of the recess. With wood sashes, brush on a light coat of wood sealer, thinned exterior primer, or linseed oil. On metal windows, apply primer formulated for metal.

Next, apply a continuous ribbon of glazing compound, about an eighth of an inch in diameter, around the inside of the recess. Compound that comes in a cartridge is easiest to apply; load the cartridge into a caulking gun, snip off the tip of the nozzle, and insert a long nail into the cartridge to break the seal inside, then squeeze the compound onto the sash. One cartridge is usually sufficient for glazing both panes of a large double-hung window.

Next, set the glass in place by pressing it against the compound. On metal windows equipped with them, reinstall the clips. On wooden windows, install new glazier's points, which are available at hardware stores.

To install points, place them around the perimeter of the opening at intervals of about 6 inches. Lay them flat on the glass. If the points have a small ledge on one side, it should face up. Then, with the tip of a screwdriver or putty knife, press the points into the sides of the recess, up to about half their length.

Cover the points or clips and seal the glass with additional glazing compound. This should be applied in a wider and thicker ribbon than before, around the rim of the glass and against the sides of the recess. To prevent the compound from being visible through the glass, do not allow any to spread beyond the width of the sash's recessed surface.

Smooth and trim the compound using a putty knife. Hold it so that a corner of the blade touches the glass while part of the blade's tip touches the sash. Tilt the knife handle away from the sash at a 45-degree angle, then draw the blade along each side of the sash opening to slice away excess compound and leave a smooth, beveled surface.

Let the compound dry for one week or as the instructions on the label specify. Then apply a thin coat of exterior paint over it, extending the paint onto the glass and sash 1/16 inch to seal the seams.

To replace glass in metal windows having gaskets or molding strips, simply remove the broken pane, install a new one, and reassemble the fittings.

Repairing Rotting Windowsills

W**ooden windowsills receive a great deal of abuse from** weather. Even though they are designed to shed moisture, snow and rain often accumulate on them and remain for long periods of time, fostering decay. This eventually destroys the sill and can also cause damage to adjacent window parts and walls. Further moisture entering walls as a result of deteriorated windowsills can cause interior paint to peel and plaster or wallboard to crumble.

Ideally, badly rotted windowsills should be replaced, but this requires skilled carpentry. Too, replacement lumber for sills in older homes (particularly those built before World War II) is often difficult to find.

There are two solutions to the problem. Moderately rotted sills can be patched with wood hardener and filler—relatively new products designed to be used together—then treated with wood preservative and waterproofing compound. And badly damaged sills can be sheathed with aluminum flashing after being repaired and treated as described.

Patching and Preserving

Hardener and filler are available at home centers and some hardware stores. The most common and least expensive variety is polyester based.

Before application, strip the old paint from the sill using paint remover. Apply the hardener first. Hardener may be brushed onto sound-looking but decaying wood and allowed to penetrate, or holes can be drilled in the wood and hardener poured into them, following the manufacturer's instructions.

Where the surface of the wood is decayed, the damaged wood should be scraped away with a penknife or chisel and hardener applied to the sound wood underneath as a base for the filler.

Allow the hardener two to four hours to dry. Then mix the filler by blending its two components: resins and another variety of hardener sold with it. Mix only as much filler as can be applied in less than ten minutes.

Apply the filler by spreading it onto the damaged portions of the wood with a disposable plastic applicator. These are available where you buy the filler and also at automotive stores for use with auto body patching compound. An applicator can also be made by cutting a section from a plastic milk carton.

Before the filler hardens, shape the repairs as well as possible with the applicator, leaving their surfaces slightly higher than their surroundings to permit finishing. After hardening is complete, in about half an hour, smooth the repairs level with the surrounding surface using medium-grit sandpaper followed by fine-grit sandpaper.

Saturate the repaired sill with two coats of wood preservative. Copper or zinc naphthenate varieties, available at home centers, are the safest and can be applied with a brush. Both will also accept paint. Follow the manufacturer's instructions for applying preservative. Afterward, apply paint.

TIP:

Although both copper and zinc naphthenate preservatives are manufactured in compliance with the latest antipollution regulations, a new preservative formulation is even safer. This type lists a carbamate as the active ingredient.

ATTENTION

Sheathing

To sheath a windowsill after restoring it and applying preservative, use standard (.019-inch-thick) aluminum flashing, available at hardware and building supply stores. To avoid mistakes when cutting the sheathing, make a template first using brown wrapping paper.

With scissors, cut the paper so a single sheet covers the entire exposed surface of the windowsill including the underside. Allow extra material at the ends for folding.

If the window is equipped with built-in aluminum storm and screen windows, the template material need only butt against the horizontal bottom edge of the storm window frame, which rests on top of the sill.

But if no storm windows are present, the template must extend between the jambs (sides) of the window frame to the edge of the interior windowsill, called the stool. Cutouts must be made in the template so that it fits around any molding that forms the sides of the window tracks attached to the jambs.

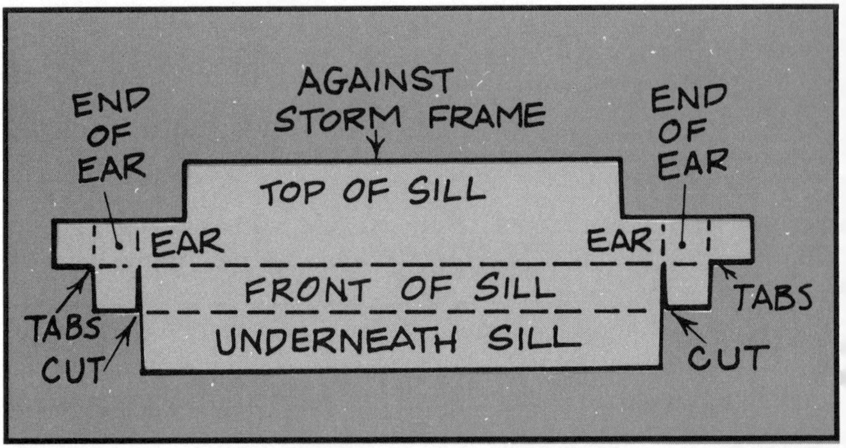

To cut sill sheathing, make a template using heavy paper. Note the cuts separating the tabs at the ears from the front of the sill. Dashed lines indicate folds.

To attach sheathing, fasten the top edge first, then bend and fasten the tabs. Fold the remaining sheathing over the sill's front edge and fasten it to the underside.

Use the template to scribe the outline of the sheathing onto the flashing. To do this, lay the flashing on a smooth surface and attach the template to it with a few short pieces of tape.

Then use a nail or an awl and a ruler to scratch the outline of the template onto the flashing. Afterward, carefully cut out the sheathing with metal-cutting shears or tinsnips.

To attach the sheathing, first apply caulking compound around the sill wherever the edges of the sheathing will touch it. Use butyl caulking or another type designed for use with metal and wood.

Carefully position the sheathing on top of the sill. Next, using inch-long aluminum trim nails, fasten it at intervals of about 4 inches along the edge of the metal where it meets the storm window frame or stool.

Then bend the metal downward and underneath at the ends (called the ears) of the sill and around the corners in front. To bend metal evenly, use a rubber mallet to hammer it gradually to the desired angle along the entire length of the seam.

Do not fasten the metal at the ends of the ears; instead, fasten it underneath the sill and against the front edge.

Then fold the remainder of the sheathing carefully down over the front edge of the sill, over the ears, and under the bottom. Fasten the edge of the sheathing with nails on the underside.

Finish the job by filling small gaps with caulking compound. Include the gaps where the sheathing is folded over each ear at the front of the sill. Paint the sheathing if desired. Usually a two-week weathering period is required before new aluminum can be painted. Prepare the metal with a primer formulated for aluminum.

TIP:

Thin metal like aluminum flashing can also be bent by hand. Start in the center and press the metal firmly against the edge of the sill. Work gradually toward the ends first, then repeat the process until the metal is evenly folded around and under the sill.

ATTENTION

Maintaining and Repairing Aluminum Siding

Aluminum siding requires no maintenance to prolong its life span. But to keep it looking its best many manufacturers recommend washing siding twice a year, and more often in areas with severe air pollution. Naturally, damaged siding should be promptly repaired.

For washing, a hard spray from a garden hose is usually sufficient. If necessary, siding can be washed with a solution of strong, nonabrasive household detergent mixed with water. Follow the manufacturer's instructions. Usually one cup of detergent added to one gallon of water is adequate.

The easiest way to apply the detergent solution is to use a long-handled brush or power sprayer designed for attaching to a garden hose. These are available at home centers. After washing, rinse the siding thoroughly by spraying it with clear water.

If spots resembling soot remain on siding, they may be caused by mildew. To find out, dab some spots with a cloth dipped in full-strength chlorine bleach. If this lightens or removes them, the spots are probably mildew.

Mildew killer is sold at home centers and paint stores. Follow the manufacturer's instructions carefully, and wear goggles and rubber gloves with cuffs to prevent contact with the solution, which can cause chemical burns.

A mixture of 1 cup of borax and 1 gallon of warm water is not as harsh as commercial mildew killer and is often effective. Wearing rubber gloves and goggles, apply the mixture to mildewed areas after washing with detergent. Let the mixture remain for fifteen to thirty minutes, then rinse with water.

To repair scratched siding, sand the area down to bare metal sing fine-grit sandpaper, then apply primer formulated for alu- ıinum. After the primer dries, apply latex exterior housepaint ıat matches the color of the siding around it.

Dents can be repaired with automotive techniques and prod- cts. If the dent is roughly circular, drill a ⅛-inch hole in the enter, at the deepest part of the dent. For dents of other shapes, rill a row of ⅛-inch holes about 1 inch apart along the deepest art of the dent.

Install a ¾-inch-long self-tapping sheet metal screw in each ole, with two flat metal washers under each screw head. Tighten ıe screws, then grip them one at a time with pliers and gently ull. This should raise much of the dented surface.

Remove the screws and washers. Sand the area, then wipe it ith a cloth dipped in deglossing liquid, available at paint and ardware stores.

Fill the area with two-part epoxy automotive filler, which can e found in auto supply and department stores. Follow the mixing ıstructions, and apply the material with a plastic spreader sold ɔr this purpose.

Smooth the filler as much as possible before it hardens, using he spreader. Afterward, smooth it further by sanding. Apply alu- ninum primer over the filler and surrounding siding. After the ɔrimer dries, apply latex exterior housepaint to cover the repair ompletely.

Often it is easier to replace badly damaged siding than to epair it. With a sharp utility knife, remove the lower part of the lamaged piece by slicing it lengthwise along the centerline (or ıbout 1 inch above the centerline on pieces that simulate a double ow of siding).

You will get the best-looking repair job if you remove a strip hat is the full length of the siding. But you may wish to cut out he damaged part by making vertical cuts about 12 inches from he edge of the damage on each side, then slicing horizontally ɔetween the cuts. In all cases, leave the upper portion of the siding ntact to provide a gluing surface for the replacement piece.

Take a new piece of siding and cut off the upper edge con- aining the slots for fasteners. The new pieces should extend 3 nches beyond the end of the damaged piece, or 6 inches if it is a hort patch to cover only part of a piece.

Spread a generous amount of roofing cement or adhesive :aulking compound over the surface of the damaged siding that emains on the house and onto the ends of siding panels next to he damaged one.

To replace damaged siding, remove the lower part but leave the upper edge. Apply adhesive, then press the trimmed replacement against it.

To replace a corner post, remove the exposed part, leaving the flanges behind. Remove and discard the slotted strips from a new post. Fasten the new post to the flanges of the old one with adhesive and blind rivets.

Fit the new siding into place so that it covers the cemented surfaces. The trimmed upper edge of the new siding should fit behind the hooked lower edge of the overlapping siding above it. The lower edge of the new siding should fit over the top edge of the siding underneath. Press the entire surface of the new siding to spread the adhesive. Siding is thin, and the new layer of siding will not be conspicuous even though it has a partial layer of damaged siding beneath it.

To supplement the cement, you may wish to fasten the new siding further by installing blind rivets (also called pop rivets) along the upper edge. To do this, drill ⅛-inch-diameter holes at 16-inch intervals through the new siding and the strip of old siding it overlaps, just below the lower edge of the next higher row of siding. Then use a blind riveting tool to insert and tighten the rivets. Blind riveting tools and rivets are available at hardware stores. If necessary, install a rivet in the center at each end of the new siding section to flatten it.

A corner post can be replaced, but the procedure is more difficult. Start by slicing vertically along each side of the post to remove the exposed part. Leave behind a flange of metal on each side, projecting at right angles from the house. From a new corner post, cut off and discard the outer edges containing the fastening slots.

Apply roofing cement or adhesive caulking compound along the outside of the flanges attached to the house. Press the replacement corner post against them so that the flanges of the new section overlap those spread with adhesive.

On both sides of the corner, drill ⅛-inch holes through the overlapping flanges at about 18-inch intervals. Install blind rivets in the holes to fasten the flanges together.

Repairing Vinyl Siding

Vinyl siding is extremely durable and nearly maintenance-free, but if it is damaged it may have to be repaired or replaced. And when work has to be done on walls covered with siding, it must be removed and reinstalled.

Working with vinyl siding requires modest carpentry skills and a zip tool—a special hand tool for separating and refastening the interlocking edges of horizontal sections. A zip tool is inexpensive and consists of a thin steel blade resembling a hacksaw blade. One end is bent to form a hook, and the other is a handle.

Not many home centers or general-purpose hardware stores carry zip tools. Building supply stores that sell siding and cater to professionals sometimes carry them, as do siding distributors and wholesalers. These are listed in the Yellow Pages.

Removing siding with a zip tool is simple. Start near one end of a section. Insert the tip with the hook up, between the interlocking edges where two sections overlap. Pull the tool down and away from the wall to separate the edges. Slide the tool farther along the siding and repeat the process.

After the overlapping edge is loose, carefully lift it upward, but don't bend it too far or it might break. Put a flat-bladed pry bar against the siding to be removed and pry out the nails holding it. Try not to damage any building paper or insulation underneath; if any does tear, patch it with waterproof utility tape (duct tape), which is sold at hardware stores.

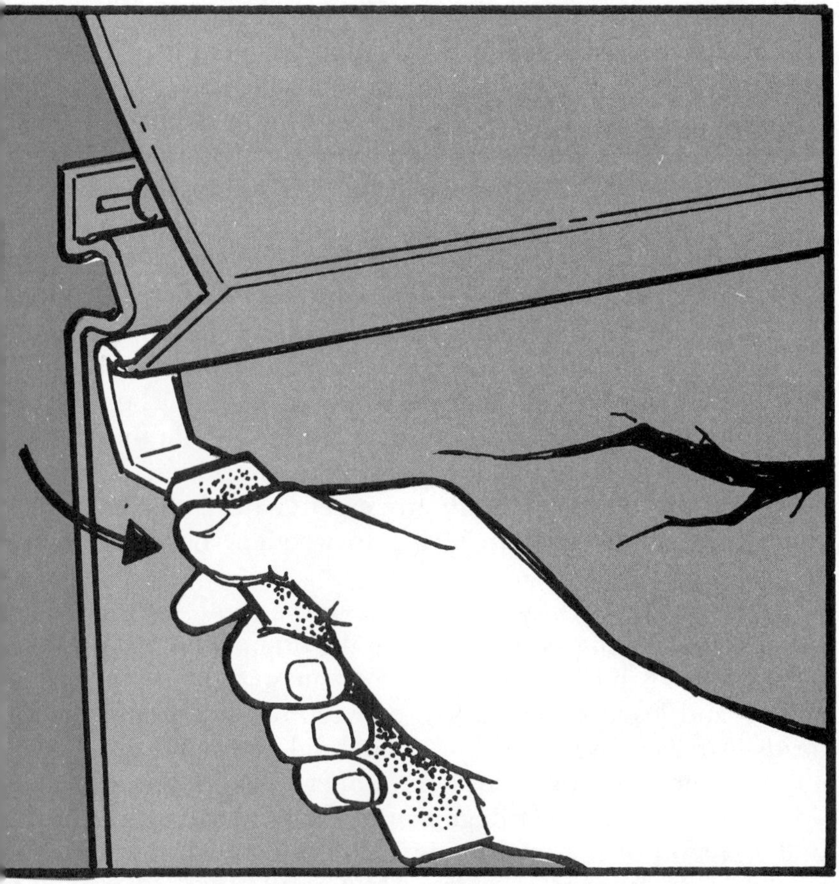

o remove vinyl siding, use a zip tool to unlock the edges. ook the tip of the tool between overlapping edges and ull down and out.

After removing the nails, press down on the siding to disen- ıge its lower edge from the section below.

If a section is broken and pieces are missing, replace it. To atch it, use spare siding if any has been saved. If not, remove ›me undamaged siding from an inconspicuous spot—behind ırubbery, say—and use it. The patch can be replaced with new ding, even if it doesn't quite match.

Use the damaged siding as a pattern for cutting replacement ding. Mark the replacement with a sharp pencil and cut it to the ›rrect size with metal-cutting shears or tinsnips.

Cracked siding can easily be patched from behind using a rap piece. Use shears, snips, or a sharp utility knife for cutting atches. A patch should be as long as the crack in the siding and at least an inch wide. Fasten it with pipe joint cement (PVC ce ment), which is used to join plastic plumbing and is sold at hard ware stores.

First use PVC cleaner-primer, sold with the cement, to clea the patch and the area surrounding the crack on the back of th siding. Put cement on the patch and the siding, and press th patch into place, covering the crack. Hold the pieces together fo about thirty seconds until the cement hardens.

To reinstall siding, reverse the removal procedure. First pres the lower edge of the removed siding against the upper edge o the section below, locking them together. Then lift the lower edg of the section above and nail the removed piece to the wall. Us broad-headed roofing or siding nails, either aluminum or galva nized steel, like the ones that were removed. The nails must b long enough to pass through any exterior insulation and pene trate three quarters of an inch into wooden sheathing or wa framing.

Put the nails as close as possible to the center of the siding' prepunched nailing slots, but not in the original holes. Install th nails 16 to 18 inches apart. Drive them straight in—not at a angle—and leave a 1/8-inch gap between the siding and the na heads. After nailing, the siding should slide back and forth freel

Use the zip tool to lock the upper edge of the reinstalle siding against the lower edge of the siding above it. To do thi pull a section of the upper siding downward with the tool, ove the lip of the reinstalled siding. Holding the tool in place, pres the pieces together with the heel of your other hand. Continu sliding the zip tool along the edge, pressing with the heel of you hand as you go, to snap the entire seam together.

It is also possible, but more difficult, to replace damaged viny corner posts. These posts have a vertical nailer strip on each side and the replacement involves removing the damaged post fron its nailer strips, which will remain attached to the building. The the nailer strips are removed from a new corner post, which i attached to the old strips.

To remove the damaged post, use a sharp utility knife t score both sides of the post vertically, just beneath the edges tha overlap the siding. Be sure the flanges that join the old post to it nailing strips remain as wide as possible. Use pliers to grasp th portion of the post that overlaps the siding, and bend it back an forth until the post breaks on the scored lines.

Repeat the scoring and bending procedure on the replace ment post, this time discarding the nailing strips. Cut close to th strips, so that the flanges remain connected to the post.

Overlap the flanges of the new post with the flanges of the ·d nailing strips. Fasten the flanges together using blind rivets lso called pop rivets), spaced about 10 inches apart.

To install blind rivets, first drill holes through the flanges, .en insert and fasten the rivets with a blind riveting tool. Most ind riveting kits include instructions; they are inexpensive and ·e sold at hardware stores.

Maintaining and Repairing Wood Shingles

Wood shingles, whether used for roofing or siding, are durable and generally trouble-free. But because wood is susceptible to rot and other damage from moisture and insects, regular inspection and maintenance is necessary, and repairs should be carried out promptly.

Maintaining wood shingles consists of keeping them free of dirt and mildew, as well as moss and other growths that can trap moisture. For protection in humid climates, shingles should be coated every three to five years with clear penetrating sealer containing wood preservative, or with stain containing both preservative and sealer.

To clean shingles of dirt and most growths (except mildew), start by brushing the surface with a stiff-bristle brush or a push broom. It is best to do this after several days of warm, sunny weather so that debris will be dry and easy to remove.

Often, brushing alone about once a year is sufficient cleaning. However, to remove extensive dirt and growth, rent a pressure washer—a hose and compressor that delivers a powerful water spray—and wash the shingles.

Using a pressure washer is not difficult, but you must be careful not to aim it at doors, windows, vents, or foliage. Wear safety goggles for eye protection and follow the instructions supplied with the washer.

To wash siding, begin at the top and work downward in horizontal strips about 5 feet long. Hold the spray nozzle perpendicular to the shingles and about 18 inches from them.

To wash roof shingles, use the same technique but start at a ar corner from the ladder and work backward, so that you always tand securely on dry roofing. Wash raised surfaces like dormer oofs first, then wash the main roof in strips running at right ngles to the ridge. When you reach the last section on each side f the roof, wait for the washed area to dry so you can stand there o wash the final sections.

To remove most stains from shingles, wash them with a solu-on of 1 cup strong household detergent to 1 gallon of warm ater. Use a scrub brush for individual shingles; for larger areas

o cut through nails beneath shingles, use a hacksaw lade wrapped with tape at one end.

TIP:

When you find damaged shingles, try to discover the cause; other repairs may be necessary to prevent shingle damage from recurring or other problems from developing.

Rotten, spongy, or warped shingles—the most common damaged varieties—usually indicate decay or insect damage, almost always due to the presence of moisture behind them. The source of the moisture may be gutter or flashing damage, especially if shingles are stained blue or black. Poor air circulation due to excessive foliage is another possibility.

use a pressurized garden sprayer. Afterward, rinse the shingle with plain water.

To remove mildew stains, substitute 1 cup of borax for th detergent in the solution above, and apply it the same way.

For all stains, except rust, that do not respond to the solution above, apply a mixture of 1 cup trisodium phosphate (TSP— cleaning powder available at most hardware stores) per quart o laundry bleach and 3 quarts of warm water. When using eithe

To attach a shingle beneath an overlapping row, slide th shingle nearly into place and drive two nails upward at a 45-degree angle, just below the shingles in the row above Then drive the new shingle into place by striking it with a hammer and wooden block (as shown opposite).

he borax solution or this one, wear goggles and rubber gloves for protection, and avoid spraying foliage.

Rust stains can be removed by treating them with oxalic acid olution, available at paint supply stores. Wear goggles and rubber gloves, and follow the manufacturer's instructions carefully. Rusty nail heads should be covered with sealer after rinsing and drying, otherwise stains will reappear.

Replacing a damaged shingle is fairly easy. Begin by splitting it into pieces by driving a chisel into the shingle's bottom edge, called the butt. Then wiggle the pieces out from beneath the overlapping shingles. When removing a group of shingles, start at the top of the area and work downward.

Generally, nails fastening shingles of one row are hidden beneath the shingles in the overlapping row. To remove hidden nails, wrap one end of a hacksaw blade with tape (for a handle) and slide the other end beneath the overlapping shingles. Saw the nails off flush with the surface and pry them out, so that replacement shingles can be easily slid into place.

New shingles are available at lumberyards. Choose grade 1 or 2 for exposed shingles and grade 3 or 4 to use beneath exposed shingles where two layers are applied.

To determine the length of shingles to buy, measure the length of a removed piece. To determine the width, measure an undamaged shingle.

You should have no trouble obtaining shingles of the correct width. However, if it is necessary to trim a replacement shingle to length, fit it into place and measure the distance it extends below the butt of an existing shingle in the same row. Then remove the replacement shingle and draw a line across the tapered end to mark the measurement.

Cut the shingle by scoring it along the line with a utility knife and then breaking it, using a carpenter's square as a straightedge.

To fasten a group of replacement shingles, begin at the bottom of the area. Align the butts of the new shingles with those of the neighboring shingles in the same row.

If only one layer of shingles covers the surface, fasten each new shingle with three-penny (1¼-inch) rust-resistant box or shingle nails. Install two nails per shingle, about half an inch from each edge and an inch above the line formed by the butts of shingles in the next higher course.

To fasten a shingle in a row that is overlapped by existing shingles, slide it into place until it is about half an inch below its final position.

Install two nails in the shingle at a 45-degree angle pointing upward, just below the butts of the overlapping shingles. Drive the heads of the nails below the surface using a nail set.

Then place the block of wood against the butt of the new shingle and drive it upward the required distance by striking the block with a hammer.

If there are two layers of shingles, fasten those of the bottom layer with a single three-penny nail in the center, above the tips f the shingles in the row below. Install five-penny (1¾-inch) nails n the shingles of the top layer, about 2 inches above their butts.

These nails remain visible below the butts of overlapping hingles. They should penetrate the upper portions of the shingles in the row below.

hakes

Shakes are similar to shingles but larger. Also, because they re usually made by splitting wood, they are coarser than shingles, which are sawn. Maintaining and repairing shakes is the same as or shingles, except that a wider space is left between shakes laced side by side (usually half an inch; for shingles the distance s a quarter of an inch) and longer nails are used for fastening.

Repairing Clapboard Siding

W**ooden clapboard siding, also called bevel siding, is**
very old style that is still popular. When made of carefully selecte
seasoned wood and installed properly, it is durable and effecti
and can be maintained in excellent condition for as long as
house stands. But cracks, warping, and decay can occur. Whe
they do, prompt action is needed.

If the edges of a crack meet precisely, it usually can be r
paired with waterproof wood glue. First, gently pry the loose pie
away from the rest of the clapboard using a putty knife or flat p
bar. Then spread glue along both edges and press the piece ba
into place. Clamp the seam by driving a row of six-penny (2-inc
long) finishing nails into the undamaged clapboard underneat
just below the lower edge of the glued piece.

To avoid splitting the undamaged clapboard, first blunt th
nail points by striking them with the hammer two or three time
After the nails are in, bend them up to exert pressure. After th
glue dries, remove the nails and fill the holes with waterpro
putty or paint.

To flatten the end of a warped clapboard, renail it to the wa
stud behind. Use a single seven-penny (2¼-inch-long) galvanize
siding nail. Because such nails have a larger diameter than finis
ing nails, drilling a hole will prevent splitting more effectively tha
blunting the points. Drill a ⅛-inch-diameter hole for the na
through the clapboard, but not deep into the stud.

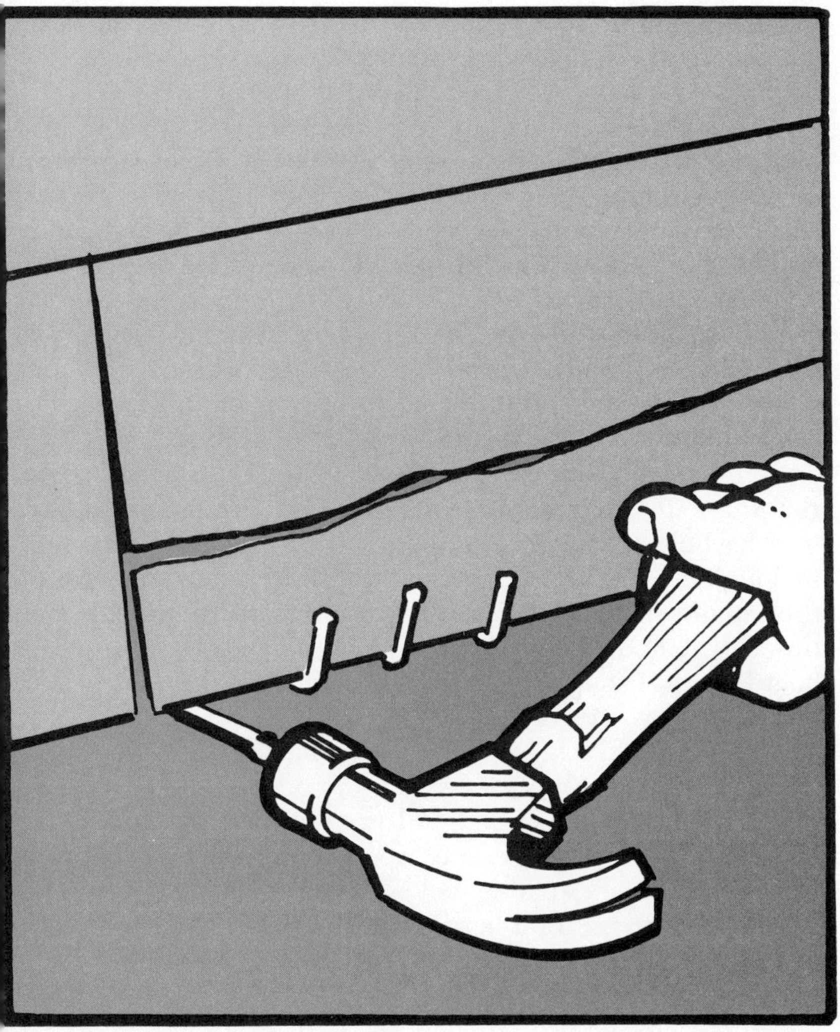

Repair cracked clapboard with waterproof glue. Clamp the seam with finishing nails installed below the board and bent upward.

If the clapboard is finished with stain, drive the nails flush with the surface. Then touch up the area with fresh stain and apply caulking compound to the seam where the ends of adjacent clapboards meet.

If the clapboards are painted, drive the nails about an eighth of an inch below the surface using a nail set. Fill the area above each nail with waterproof wood putty, allow it to dry, then repaint and apply caulking.

If there is no stud behind the end of a warped clapboard, o
if a section of clapboard is too badly damaged to repair, it shoul
be replaced. Clapboards are available at lumberyards.

To replace a section of clapboard, first drive small wedges o
scrap wood beneath the damaged clapboard to raise it from th
one below. Then, using a backsaw (a handsaw having a rectangu
lar blade rather than a tapered end), saw across the exposed po
tion of the clapboard on each side of the damaged area.

Make the cuts far enough apart so the replacement sectio
can be nailed to studs, which are usually spaced at 16-inch inte
vals. When replacing the end of a clapboard with no stud behin
it, also remove the end of the adjacent clapboard. Cut both bac
to the midpoints of the nearest studs.

To saw through the remainder of the damaged clapboar
reposition the wedges to raise the clapboard overlapping it. Switc
to a keyhole saw (a small handsaw with a pointed blade and
handle like a pistol grip). Attach the saw blade upside down o
the handle so that when cutting the end of the handle poin
upward. Slide the pointed end of the saw beneath the raised cla
board to cut through the concealed portion of the damaged cla
board. Remove the wedges.

The nails fastening the section still must be withdrawn.
they are visible in the exposed portion of the siding, insert a fl
pry bar beneath the section and pry the piece upward as far
possible. Place a piece of scrap wood beneath the pry bar to pr
vent marring the clapboard below. Then remove the pry bar an
strike the raised section hard using the palms to force it back
its original position, leaving the nail heads protruding. Use th
bar to pry them out.

If nails in the overlapping clapboard pass through the dam
aged section, remove them the same way. The section then shoul
slide out easily.

If the nails are concealed beneath the overlapping clapboar
and cannot be pried out, cut through them with a plunge-cuttir
hacksaw (its handle holds the blade only at one end) or an ord
nary hacksaw blade wrapped with utility tape at one end to crea
a handle.

Start by splitting off the exposed portion of the damage
section using a hammer and wood chisel. Then insert the hacksa
blade beneath the remaining portion and slice through the nail
When you are finished, the remaining section should slide out.

To install a new section, cut it to fit snugly. If it is more tha
48 inches long, cut it a sixteenth of an inch too big. Coat its end
and the ends of the pieces on each side, with primer.

When the new section is dry, slide it beneath the overlapping clapboard until it is even with the pieces on each side. If the section is oversize, bend it when setting it into place so the center bows out slightly. The section will straighten when released and press tightly against each side. To move the section up into position, hold a scrap block against the section's lower edge and strike the block with a hammer.

Fasten the section by installing a single seven-penny siding nail at each end and where the nails will penetrate studs (drill holes first to prevent splitting). If the exposed surface of the clapboard is less than 4 inches wide, install nails so they pass through the upper edges of clapboard underneath. This lessens chances that the clapboard being fastened will split if the hammer strikes it accidentally. However, if exposure is more than 4 inches, it is better to sacrifice this advantage and position nails so they pass above the clapboard underneath. This allows free movement of the clapboards in response to changes in humidity. Recess the nails if necessary. Apply finish and caulking.

TIP:

Before repainting stucco, wash the surface with hard spray from a garden hose to clean off dirt and to remove loose particles. (Some experts recommend using a pressure washer, but on cracked stucco this tool has enough power to erode the surface and also to force water behind it.) Always start at the bottom of a wall and work upward, saturating the surface as you go so that dirty water running down the walls does not cause stains that paint will not hide.

Besides latex paint, cement-based paint designed for stucco is an obvious choice. When using latex paint, choose an alkali-resistant type and wait four weeks before painting over new stucco.

ATTENTION

Repairing Stucco

Stucco is a type of plaster that differs from conventional wal plaster chiefly in that it contains Portland cement instead of gyp sum. Because cement is virtually waterproof when cured, stucc can be used outdoors, where it provides a hard, durable surfac that is also fire-resistant and impervious to rot and fungus.

However, moisture penetrating stucco through cracks cause by expansion and contraction of building materials, or imprope application of the stucco, can lead to serious damage.

Hairline cracks in stucco—cracks that are shallow and no accompanied by loosened material—need not be repaired. This i fortunate, because stucco repairs generally are difficult to conceal For the sake of appearance, hairline cracks can be covered b painting the stucco with latex housepaint.

To repair deep cracks and those surrounded by loosene material, first widen the crack with a stiff-bladed putty knife or a pointed can opener. Cut away all loose stucco and try to angle th sides of the crack so that the opening is wider inside than at th surface.

Fill the crack with silicone or latex caulking compound, o with premixed stucco repair compound. A tinted caulking com pound may match the color of the stucco; otherwise select a typ that can be painted.

Tinted and plain stucco repair compound, both of which can be painted, come in cans and are available at paint and masonry supply stores and some home centers. To apply them, dampen the damaged area with fine spray from a garden hose, then press the compound firmly into the crack with a putty knife or mason's trowel. Allow the compound to cure according to the instructions printed on the container.

To repair larger areas up to about 6 inches in width, use stucco repair compound or obtain dry mortar mix for bricks, available in bags at hardware and building supply stores. To apply mortar mix, blend it with water according to the directions on the bag, then follow the directions for applying stucco repair compound. Cure the mortar according to the instructions on the bag.

If desired, obtain powdered pigment from a paint or masonry supply store to add to the mortar mix to color it. Count on having to make several test batches. As a general rule, the new stucco should appear darker-colored when wet than the old. As it dries, the color will lighten.

To repair holes larger than 6 inches, proceed as if applying new stucco. This involves applying three layers with time for curing allowed between. Only two layers are necessary if the building material beneath the stucco is masonry or concrete.

Begin by chipping away all loosened stucco. Use a hammer and cold chisel and wear goggles and heavy work gloves for protection. If any reinforcing material beneath the stucco is damaged, replace it by fastening metal mesh stucco lath (available from building and masonry supply stores) over it, using galvanized staples. These are installed by hammering, not with a staple gun. Masonry and concrete usually do not require reinforcing material. Blow or brush away all dust and other particles.

If three layers of stucco are to be applied, prepare stucco for the first layer by combining one part Type M cement (a mixture of Portland cement and lime, available in bags) and three parts masonry sand with enough water to produce a smooth, easily spread material that neither crumbles when squeezed nor slumps when troweled into a mound.

Mix the stucco in a wheelbarrow. Measure dry ingredients using a coffee can or marked bucket, and blend them by stirring with a shovel or large mason's trowel before adding water. Use only clear water suitable for drinking. Add it gradually while continuing to stir until the correct mix is achieved. Wear rubber gloves when mixing and applying stucco, as Portland cement is mildly caustic.

Spray the prepared area with water as described. Avoid soaking. Apply the stucco by pressing it into the mesh with a mason's trowel. Cover the mesh completely, filling the area to within a quarter of an inch of the surface.

TIP:

Lath for stucco should be installed so that it stands about a quarter of an inch away from the surface. Self-furring lath contains bumps in the weave that accomplish this, allowing the use of conventional fasteners.

ATTENTION

Apply the first layer of stucco within ¼ inch of the adjoining surface. After thirty minutes, scratch to roughen.

Apply the second layer the next day. Fill the area level with the surface, then smooth and compact it.

The finish layer is mixed differently than the previous layers. Apply it ⅛-inch thick, using either a float or a brush.

Wait about thirty minutes until the stucco stiffens. Then thor oughly scratch the surface horizontally with a nail or a garde rake to a depth of about an eighth of an inch. Afterward, allov the stucco to harden overnight while keeping it damp by occa sional spraying (one spraying after dark and one early in th morning is usually sufficient).

The next day, dampen the stucco and apply a second coa mixed the same as the first. Fill the area level with the surround ing surface. If only two layers of stucco are to be applied, begi with this one and apply it after dampening the masonry or con crete to which it will be applied.

Before the stucco hardens, scrape away any excess by sawing back and forth across it with the edge of a long board. Ther smooth and compact the surface by rubbing it with a mason's trowel or a smoothing tool called a float.

Dampen the stucco two or three times daily while it cures fo forty-eight hours. Then wait five additional days for complete curing before applying the finish layer.

To mix stucco for the finish layer, blend two parts white Portland cement; three parts clean, light-colored sand; and powdered pigment if desired. Then add clear water while stirring until the mixture is the consistency of smooth peanut butter.

Dampen the area thoroughly and apply the finish layer an eighth of an inch thick with a float or large paintbrush. Work from the top of the repair toward the bottom.

If desired, add texture to the finish layer to blend the repair with its surroundings. Flicking stucco from a brush produces a spattered texture; other textures can be achieved with creative use of a float, a trowel, or even a sponge. Allow the finish layer to cure without dampening it further.

Repointing Crumbling Brickwork

The mortar joints in nearly all brickwork eventually deteriorate. Prompt repair is essential, because even small cracks and crumbled areas let moisture in between bricks, setting the stage for major damage.

The process of restoring mortar joints is called repointing or tuck pointing. It consists of chiseling away most of the old mortar and replacing it with new material. Because mortar is easiest to work with and cures best when temperatures are between 50 degrees and 80 degrees Fahrenheit, late spring or early summer is a good time for major repointing projects, especially those involving outdoor construction.

Repointing only a few joints usually can be done using improvised tools—an ordinary cold chisel no wider than the joints, a heavy ball peen hammer or a small sledgehammer for striking the chisel, a gardener's trowel for mixing and applying fresh mortar, and an old kitchen spoon for smoothing the restored joints.

However, for large jobs use a plugging chisel and a cape chisel instead of a cold chisel, and proper masonry tools described further on. All are available at hardware and masonry supply stores.

Whether using improvised tools or not, wear goggles for protection against brick and mortar particles and heavy work gloves to ward off errant hammer blows. Never use a carpenter's claw hammer for striking a metal chisel. The head of the hammer may chip or even shatter, sending out dangerous metal splinters.

TIP:

Besides a spoon for smoothing joints, a short section of pipe can also be used. This creates a concave mortar joint that is best for shedding water.

ATTENTION

Repoint areas approximately 3- to 5-feet square at a time. Use the plugging chisel, which has as thin blade trimmed at an angle across the end, for loosening the mortar, and the cape chisel, which has a thicker blade that tapers to a point in the center, for digging the loosened mortar out of the joints. Cut a square-sided groove—not V-shaped—about three quarters of an inch deep between the bricks and expose bare brick on at least one side of each joint.

After chiseling, either brush the joints free of dust using a whisk broom or a wide, thin brush with coarse bristles like the kind used for applying wallpaper, or wash the joints clean with hard spray from a garden hose.

Next, apply new mortar. Dry mortar that requires only adding water is available in bags from building supply stores, home centers, and many hardware stores. This is the easiest type to use. An 80-pound bag is sufficient for repointing more than one hundred bricks.

For larger jobs, mixing your own mortar from separate ingredients is usually more economical. Conventional proportions for mortar are one part Portland cement, one part hydrated lime, and six parts sand, or one part masonry cement (a packaged mixture consisting of Portland cement and hydrated lime plus additives) and three parts sand. Specify clean masonry sand.

Before repointing brick that is more than one hundred years old, consult an experienced mason. Modern mortar mixed in conventional proportions is often harder than old brick and can cause it to crack or flake.

To mix mortar, use a coffee can or marked bucket for measuring the ingredients. Mortar becomes too hard to use after approximately two hours, so mix only small batches at a time. Place the dry ingredients in a wheelbarrow. Mix them thoroughly with a large mason's trowel, then add small amounts of clear water and continue mixing until the mortar forms peaks that hold their shape when the mortar is spread upward with the trowel.

Some masons advocate first adding only enough water to make a stiff ball of mortar, then waiting about twenty minutes before adding more. This process, called rehydration, may reduce the tendency of the existing mortar to draw moisture away from the new mortar, which weakens it.

To fill the joints you will need a small mason's trowel sometimes called a pointing trowel. First, wet the joints with fine spray from a garden hose, dampening them thoroughly but not soaking them. Then scoop up mortar on the back of the large trowel and hold it against the wall as a palette and to catch excess mortar falling from the joints as they are filled.

Use a margin trowel to apply mortar to the horizontal joints.

Finish repointed joints by smoothing and compressing with a jointer.

TIP:

When working with acid, wear eye protection and rubber gloves. If acid or acid solution and water must be mixed, always add the acid to the water, not vice versa. Water added to acid can cause the mixture to splatter onto skin. An acid solution can be neutralized by adding baking soda (sodium bicarbonate).

ATTENTION

Use the back of the pointing trowel to pick up mortar from the large trowel and press it tightly into the brickwork's vertical joints. After filling these, use the same technique to fill the horizontal joints. However, because the horizontal joints are longer, it is often easier to repoint them using a long, narrow tool called a margin trowel.

After about an hour, when the mortar has stiffened enough to retain a thumbprint when pressed, scrape off excess amounts with a mason's trowel and finish the joints by smoothing and compressing them with a curved tool called a jointer.

Smooth the vertical joints first, then the horizontals. If possible, duplicate the shape of the surrounding joints. However, keep in mind that joints with concave surfaces shed water best and are easiest to make. After smoothing, move on to the next section.

Keep repointed joints damp by spraying them often until the mortar cures fully, usually in about four days. After twenty-four hours, excess mortar particles can be swept from the edges of the smoothed joints using a whisk broom. Large pieces should be left to harden completely, then knocked off by striking them with the edge of the large mason's trowel.

Stains left by mortar can sometimes be removed simply by scrubbing the brick with a stiff-bristle brush after the mortar has hardened. If that doesn't work, wash the wall with a mild solution of muriatic acid, available at building supply stores and many home centers. Follow the precautions printed on the container for using the acid. Afterward, wash the brick thoroughly with clear water.

Exterior Paint Problems

Before repainting or making repairs to exterior house- paint, it pays to examine deteriorated areas and eliminate their causes. Otherwise, the problems may recur, sometimes quickly. Here are some flaws in exterior painted surfaces that appear frequently.

Moisture blisters. These are blisters that reveal bare wood when cut open. They are usually caused when water vapor escaping a building becomes trapped under the paint. The cure is to reduce the amount of vapor trying to pass through the walls and to provide increased ventilation for vapor that remains.

Techniques for preventing the passage of vapor are described in the chapter "Curing Indoor Condensation," beginning on page 383. To ventilate remaining moisture, install small circular ventilator plugs in the siding on exterior walls. Plugs designed for the purpose and tools for installing them are available at home centers.

If moisture blisters are localized near the base of siding, the cause may be shrubbery growing close to the spot. This can keep the siding permanently damp by preventing air circulation. Removing the shrubbery should cure the problem.

Rainwater can also splash from the ground onto the siding, then rise because of capillary action. For this, the cure may be adding additional gutters or modifying the landscaping around the building to improve drainage.

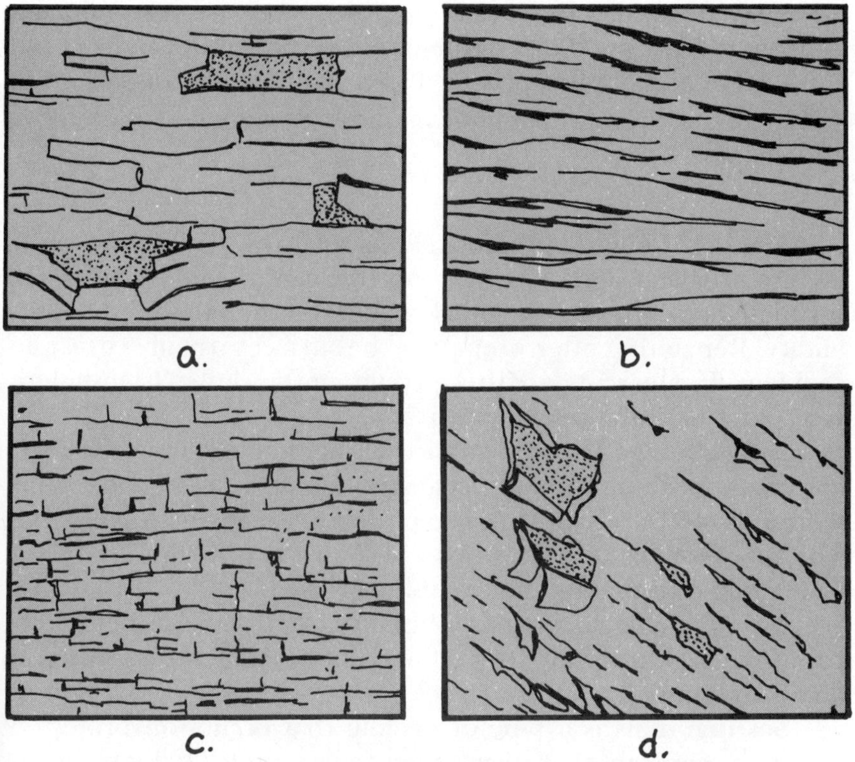

Frequently encountered flaws in exterior paint jobs include peeling (a), flaking (b), alligatoring (c), and scaling (d).

If the condition occurs near the roof, suspect faulty gutters or roof elements. Repair these where necessary. Around windows, doors, and other trim, check for gaps between pieces, and fill them with caulking compound.

Solvent blisters. If cutting open blisters in oil-based or alkyd paint reveals wet paint, chances are it was applied in direct sunlight or when temperatures were greater than 90 degrees Fahrenheit. Under these conditions, fresh paint rapidly forms an outer skin that traps paint solvents before they can evaporate. To prevent solvent blisters, follow the paint manufacturer's application instructions carefully.

Peeling. When this accompanies blistering, it usually has the same causes and cures. At other times, peeling may mean the flawed paint was applied to an improperly prepared surface. Paint will not adhere well to surfaces that are dirty, greasy, glossy, or covered with "chalk"—the naturally occurring residue of deteriorated paint (see below). Peeling may also occur when paint is applied to a surface that is already heavily painted, usually with three or more coats.

TIP:

Surfaces with three to five coats of old oil-based paint on them can usually receive an additional coat or two of oil-based paint before complete stripping down to bare wood is necessary. However, applying latex paint over so many layers is not recommended: The earlier coats should be removed.

ATTENTION

The cure in all cases is to remove the previously applied paint —down to bare wood if possible—before repainting, and to wash the surface and apply a primer if necessary. To do this correctly, follow the surface-preparation methods described at the end of this chapter.

Flaking. Long, approximately parallel rows of narrow peeling are usually a sign of aging paint that can no longer stretch or shrink to accommodate seasonal changes in the siding due to humidity. Repainting after preparing the surfaces usually cures the problem. If it persists, moisture could be the cause, so installing vent plugs in the siding may help.

Alligatoring. The appearance of many interconnected shallow cracks, with or without peeling, is usually caused when paint is applied too thickly or to a surface that is already heavily coated. The condition also occurs when a second coat of paint is applied over a first coat that has not completely dried.

To avoid alligatoring, strip heavily coated surfaces before repainting. Also, carefully follow the paint manufacturer's application instructions.

Scaling. This is a type of peeling that occurs on protected surfaces—beneath roof overhangs, for example. It looks much like flaking but is more random, not appearing in rows, and produces very small flakes. It is caused by air pollutants and other chemical deposits left by evaporation that are not washed away by rain or neutralized by sunlight.

Repainting after properly preparing the surface will correct the problem. To prevent it, wash the surface two to four times a year, or when necessary.

Chalking. "Chalk," the powdery product of eroded paint, is natural. Most exterior paint is formulated to gradually deteriorate on the surface, so that rain washing away the residue takes with it dirt and grime.

To remove excess chalk, scrub the painted surface with detergent and water, using a scrub brush. Then rinse with plain water. Before repainting a severely chalking surface, apply a coat of recommended primer.

Mildew. Paint that appears soot-covered or dirty—especially in warm, humid, and shady locations—may actually harbor a fungus. Applying household bleach to the spot is a sure test: If the discoloration disappears, mildew is the culprit.

Techniques for removing mildew are described below. When repainting areas where mildew is chronic, use mildew-resistant primer and paint.

Preparing Surfaces for Repainting

For exterior housepaint to last as long as its manufacturer advertises, the surface to which the paint is applied must be carefully prepared. The good news is that new, unpainted wood requires only coating with a recommended primer, which is usually specified in the instructions for the paint you plan to apply.

The bad news is that preparing surfaces that have been previously painted can be the most arduous and time-consuming part of house painting; and new findings concerning the dangers of lead and mercury in paint complicate the process further.

To prepare previously painted wood, first determine whether the existing paint contains lead, a serious and common health hazard. Virtually all housepaint applied before 1950 contained lead and the practice continued into the 1970s.

The only way to determine the presence of lead in paint is to have the paint tested. Community services involving lead testing and abatement vary. For advice on how to proceed in your area, contact the state or local health department.

If previously applied paint does contain lead, removal by a professional who specializes in lead abatement may be mandatory. In any case, it is the safest procedure. The techniques used by the professional should minimize the production of airborne particles and fumes and include the removal of all paint chips and debris from the ground and other surfaces.

If the paint does not contain lead, you can safely prepare the surface yourself. Remove all loose paint with a scraper or by sanding. A hot-air paint remover, resembling a hair dryer, is useful for softening thick layers of paint for scraping, but avoid using a torch with an open flame, which can easily start a fire.

Sand areas of sound but shiny old paint to produce a rough surface that new paint will adhere to more easily. When removing paint by any method, wear goggles and a dust mask approved for protection against damaging airborne particles.

Next, or if the paint is in good condition and removal is unnecessary, wash the surface thoroughly. Use household detergent mixed with water according to the manufacturer's instructions, and rinse by spraying with plain water from a garden hose.

If mildew is present, adding 1 cup of borax per gallon of water to the detergent mixture should remove it. If stronger treatment is necessary, apply a liquid mildew remover containing bleach, available at paint stores. For both treatments, wear goggles and rubber gloves for protection against harsh chemicals.

Countersink protruding nails using a hammer and nail set and cover the nail heads with waterproof putty. Apply fresh caulk-

TIP:

Washing wood, aluminum, or vinyl siding with a pressure washer saves time and gives excellent results. Keep the nozzle pointed away from yourself and others, as well as from windows, shrubbery, and other items that can be damaged by hard spray. Wear eye protection.

ATTENTION

ing. Coat stains and areas where paint remains powdery even after washing by brushing with a stain-blocking primer-sealer. Cover all other bare spots with primer suited to the paint you plan to use.

Finally, if removing loose paint results in baring large areas, or if the new paint will be a very different color from the old, priming the entire surface to be painted is recommended.

To prepare aluminum siding for painting, remove loose paint by sanding or brushing with a wire brush. Lead in the paint is unlikely. Afterward, wash and rinse the siding as described for wood. Often washing and rinsing alone is sufficient.

Vinyl siding can be painted to change its color, provided the new coat is not significantly darker than the original (the sun's heat may warp dark siding). Preparation consists of washing with detergent and rinsing. Sanding or using a wire brush is unnecessary and will scratch the siding.

To prepare unpainted concrete, brick, and stucco surfaces, scrub the surface with a wire brush to remove loose particles. Then rinse by spraying with a garden hose and allow thorough drying. The same procedure can be used to remove old, peeling paint from these surfaces. However, unless you are certain the paint contains no lead, have testing and professional removal carried out as described earlier.

Unpainted or fresh concrete, brick, and stucco must be coated with an alkali-resistant primer before finish paint is applied. Previously painted surfaces in good condition usually need only wire brushing and rinsing before painting. Surfaces with paint in poor condition, particularly paint that remains powdery even after scrubbing and rinsing, first should be coated with masonry conditioner. This is a type of sealer available at paint stores.

Depending on the kind of paint to be applied, masonry conditioner can sometimes be mixed with the paint and the two applied as a primer. Afterward, a second coat of paint containing no conditioner is applied.

Metal downspouts and gutters that may be coated with lead paint should be tested and replaced or professionally stripped if necessary. If previously applied paint is free of lead, preparing these surfaces for repainting consists of sanding or scouring away loose paint and applying a coat of rust-resistant primer. Rust spots should be sanded down to bare metal before primer is applied.

Primer is not necessary for galvanized metal in good condition. However, new unpainted galvanized surfaces should be washed with detergent to remove oils that may be left from the galvanizing process. Afterward, rinse with plain water and allow the surfaces to dry before applying paint.

TIP:

Before painting aluminum siding, prime bare spots with primer formulated for aluminum. The best type of paint for aluminum siding is acrylic latex. Use flat rather than glossy paint if the siding is dented —imperfections will not be as visible.

ATTENTION

TIP:

Some latex paints suitable for concrete, brick, and stucco are formulated to resist alkali. This type can be used without alkali-resistant primer.

ATTENTION

Replacing a Doorsill

The wide board called the sill, which is visible beneath the narrower threshold in an exterior doorway, receives much wear and frequently develops rot. Sometimes mildly decayed sills can be repaired using two-part wood hardener and filler available at home centers. Worn and badly decayed sills must be replaced.

Begin replacing a sill by removing the door from its hinges. Also remove the threshold, either by prying it up if it is wood or by removing the screws that fasten it to the sill if it is aluminum. Save the threshold for reattaching, or get a new one.

If the door frame is old, it is a good idea to brace it so that it does not move while you are taking out the old sill and installing the new one. Should the frame be disturbed, the door may bind or rub when rehung.

To brace the frame, cut a length of two-by-four lumber to fit between the doorjambs (the sides of the frame), then place it a few feet from the bottom of the doorway and drive a wedge between one end of the brace and the jamb to hold it securely.

Examine the sill carefully. If it appears to extend beneath the jambs—what you are seeing in most cases is the sill fitting into a groove in the sides of the jambs—pry off the strips of doorstop molding before proceeding further. Use a wide-bladed putty knife or scraper, followed by a flat pry bar.

Start by inserting the putty knife or scraper into a seam near one end of a strip and gradually prying it away from the jamb along its entire length. Then insert the pry bar and wide-bladed

A doorsill's sloping upper surface aids drainage and reduces drafts beneath the door. The replacement sill must be notched to fit between the jambs.

tool together into the seam and repeat the process. Hold the bladed tool against the doorjamb and use it to protect the wood of the jamb from the fulcrum of the pry bar.

To remove a sill that does not extend below the jambs, it is usually possible simply to pry it up with the pry bar. If this can be done, try to remove the sill in one piece so that it can be used as a pattern for making the new one. However, to remove a sill that extends beneath the jambs or into grooves, either saw it crosswise nto three sections, using a handsaw, and then remove the sections by prying and twisting, or split the sill lengthwise into inch-wide strips with a chisel.

When removing a sill or section by prying, it often helps to raise the piece slightly; then flatten it again by striking it with a hammer. This leaves the heads of nails in the piece projecting enough so that they can be gripped by the pry bar or hammer claws.

Nails that cannot be withdrawn while removing a sill must be cut off flush with the framing below using a hacksaw. Blade holders that grip a hacksaw blade at one end and allow sawing in tight places are available at hardware stores.

For the new sill, obtain a piece of sill stock from a lumberyard. Sills are usually made of oak or fir, and come shaped to standard dimensions. You will have to saw the sill to length and cut notches at each end that conform to the contours of the door opening.

If you can, trace around the old sill by setting it on top of the new stock. If the old sill was sawn into sections, those at the ends can be used as patterns and the space required between them measured and marked onto the new stock by using a yardstick or framing square.

If no part of the old sill can be used, you will have to create an outline for the new sill by measuring the length and width of the opening into which the old sill fit.

Make a cardboard template using the measurements and trim it until it fits easily. Then trace the outline of the template onto the new stock. Cut the new sill carefully using a handsaw.

Slide the sill into place to test the fit. Tap it gently with a hammer if necessary, but do not strike hard blows. If the sill does not fit smoothly, remove it and trim it with a plane, sharp chisel, wood rasp, or file.

When the sill does fit, mark it in two or three places near each jamb for installing nails. To avoid splitting the wood, predrill holes for these by removing the sill and drilling through it using an electric drill and a drill bit slightly smaller than the nails you plan to use. These should be eight- or ten-penny (2½- or 3-inch-long) galvanized finishing nails. Drill the holes at an angle pointing toward the ends of the sill.

Brush or vacuum the area beneath the sill free of debris and grit before installing the sill permanently. Also apply a generous bead of caulking compound to the surface as weatherstripping.

Slide the sill into place and nail it securely. When nailing, be careful not to mar the jambs by accidently striking them. Remove or relocate the brace installed earlier, if it is in the way. When the nails have been driven to within half an inch of the surface, use a nail set to drive them beneath the surface approximately an eighth of an inch.

Fill the holes with waterproof wood putty, then sand the area and apply paint or clear finish to the wood before reinstalling the threshold.

When replacing doorstop or other molding strips, remove the old nails and attach the strips with new nails to avoid damaging the wood. Withdraw the old nails by pulling them completely through the molding and out the back. An easy way to do this is to grip the nails with channel-type pliers and lever them out, using the back of the molding as a fulcrum for the jaws.

When installing the new nails, use a nail set to sink the heads below the surface. Then fill the holes with wood putty, sand the areas smooth, and apply paint.

Position doorstop molding carefully when reattaching it. With the door closed, you should be able to insert a credit card between the molding and the door's outside surface.

Caring for Outdoor Decks

Outdoor decks are built to withstand exposure. Nevertheless, to look their best and remain sturdy, they should be cared for when necessary and inspected at least once a year.

Cleaning

Simple washing will remove general grime and brighten a deck for a new season's use. In most cases, scrubbing the wood with a bristled scrub brush dipped in a solution of warm water and ordinary household detergent is sufficient. For stronger cleaning, scrub with a solution of trisodium phosphate (a powdered cleaner available at most hardware stores) and warm water. Wear rubber gloves for protection.

More expensive, but milder and often very effective, is acid-free and bleach-free teak cleaner made for boats. It is available at marine supply stores. With all the cleaners mentioned, rinse the deck afterward by hosing it with clear water.

Home-care products labeled as deck cleaners are mildly caustic powders designed to be mixed with water. They will clean wood that has become gray or discolored and will brighten the surface of stained wood by etching away the surface layer.

To apply deck cleaner, follow the directions and precautions on the container. Wear rubber gloves, sturdy shoes, goggles, long trousers, and a long-sleeved shirt. Mix the cleaner, then apply it with a mop, paint roller, or sprayer. Allow the cleaner to work undisturbed for about fifteen minutes. Then scrub the deck with a scrub brush or sweep it with a stiff broom.

Rinse the deck and surrounding area thoroughly by spraying with a garden hose. Two or more treatments may be required to achieve a uniform color and remove deep stains.

Deck cleaner may darken some types of wood, particularly redwood. To lighten them, rinse the wood to dampen it, then mop it with a 5 percent solution of oxalic acid, available at hardware and paint stores. Afterward, rinse the wood thoroughly again.

Wood that has been treated with deck cleaner needs further protective coating. If the deck has been a natural wood color or has been stained within the last three years, apply clear water-repellent sealer containing preservative and a mildew killer. Clear sealer remains durable for about two years, but will not prevent wood from graying naturally, which occurs with exposure to sunlight.

Stain lasts about three years and is more resistant to scuffing than clear sealer. If you wish to stain the deck, use a stain containing preservative and sealer. To avoid a muddy appearance, apply stain no more than once every three years.

Nails and other ungalvanized steel fasteners often cause rust stains in decking. To remove these, try scrubbing with an oxalic acid solution after treating the deck with deck cleaner. To prevent further staining, drive nail heads at least an eighth of an inch below the surface using a hammer and nail set, then swab the heads with water-repellent sealer and fill the depressions above them with stainable waterproof putty or with putty the same color as the wood.

Repairing Floorboards and Joists

Loosened deck parts should be retightened as soon as they are detected. This prevents wobbling, which eventually can cause breakage. If the loose parts are bolted together, retightening the bolts is usually all that is required.

Parts that have been nailed together or are loose because of inadequate fastening can be strengthened with galvanized metal reinforcing plates or with construction anchors (these are available in many shapes and sizes at building supply stores), or with wooden blocks. When using blocks, treat them with preservative prior to fastening them in place.

An aggravating problem that also can be hazardous is a warped floorboard whose end(s) protrude above the level of the deck. Installing additional nails or even screws to flatten the board may work. If it doesn't, try prying up the board, turning it over, and refastening it with screws.

If this solution doesn't work, replace the board with a new ›ne. When selecting a new floorboard, sight along the length of ts wide faces to make sure it is not bowed, and along the length ›f its edges to make sure it is not crooked. Also, try to find a board vhose growth ring segments—visible at the ends of the board— ıre straight and perpendicular to its wide faces. Though rarely ound due to modern sawmill practices, a board with this pattern s not likely to warp later on.

If you must select a board whose segments are curved, fasten t so the ends of the segments point up. Although the board will nevitably warp, when it does the ends will tend to curve down- vard, against the joists.

Reinforce a decayed joist by treating it with water- epellent preservative to prevent further damage. Fasten a ıew joist alongside it.

If inspecting the deck reveals decay, try to replace the af fected parts. Where this is not feasible—for example, with floo joists—treat the wood thoroughly with a preservative to preven further damage, then reinforce the part if necessary.

One way to reinforce a weakened joist is to fasten a new jois section on each side of the damaged area. To do this, obtain tw pieces of new, preservative-treated lumber the same width an thickness as the damaged joist, each 4 to 6 feet longer than th damaged area.

With a helper, temporarily nail one section to each side of th weakened joist, centered over the damage. Drill a zigzag patter of 7/16-inch-diameter holes at 10- to 12-inch intervals through al three boards, then install 3/8-inch-diameter carriage bolts with fla washers and nuts in the holes. Tighten the nuts with a wrench.

If a floorboard has decayed, you need replace only the dam aged section. Saw it out flush with the inside edges of the joists o each side and treat the remaining ends of the floorboard wit preservative. Nail a two-by-four or larger piece of treated lumbe to the inside faces of the joists to act as supports. The top edge of the supports must be even with those of the joists. Cut the nev floorboard section to the same size as the damaged one. The treat the ends with preservative and fasten the board to the sup ports with screws.

Repairing Posts

Where vertical posts supporting decking enter the ground o are set in concrete, decay often damages the wood at ground leve The only repair is to replace the post. Saw through the post a ground level and unbolt it or pry it loose from the deck above Then, if the remainder of the post is buried in the ground, exca vate to remove it. Instead of replacing the post with a duplicate construct a pier of concrete and install a shorter post as follows.

While removing the remainder of the buried portion of th post, dig a hole about 8 inches in diameter at the top and abou 12 inches in diameter at the bottom. The depth of the hole should be 6 to 8 inches below the frost line, which is 24 to 48 inches in most of the United States. A local building inspector can give you the frost line depth for your area.

Shovel gravel or small stones into the hole to a depth of 6 inches. Then insert a cardboard form 8 inches in diameter (avail- able at building supply stores) in the hole so that it extends about 6 inches above ground level. Mix and pour concrete into the hole until it is level with the top of the form.

While the concrete is wet, embed the threaded anchor bolt of post pedestal (a type of construction anchor) into the top. The edestal will elevate the post above the concrete and prevent ecay from recurring. Allow the concrete to cure according to the anufacturer's recommendations (usually about six days), then ttach the pedestal and a new post, cut to fit between the deck and he pedestal.

Sometimes the buried portion of a decayed post is set in con- rete and cannot be removed. In that case it may be possible to ap the existing pier with fresh concrete and install a new post as escribed. Or you can install a new pier and post next to the old ne.

Repairing Metal Porch Railings

Metal porch railings need proper care to preserv their appearance and sturdiness. Many newer railings are mac of aluminum, which needs little maintenance. But steel an wrought iron railings are prone to rust and require close atter tion.

Regular cleaning, inspection, and painting are the keys maintaining metal railings. To clean painted railings, use a clot or sponge to apply strong household detergent and water, the rinse. Brass or other bright metal features can be kept shiny wit an appropriate metal polish applied according to the manufactu er's directions.

As an alternative to commercial polish with its harsh chem cals, brass or copper can be cleaned with a solution of equal par of distilled white vinegar and table salt. Heat them to dissolve th salt; then dip half a cut lemon into the solution and use it to ru the metal until it shines. Rinse the metal afterward with plai water. To clean aluminum or chrome, simply wipe it with a clot dipped in heated vinegar, then rinse with water.

Car or paste wax can be applied to handrails and to polishe parts to keep them smooth and prevent tarnishing.

Inspect railings at least once or twice a year for loose or dan aged fasteners and chipped paint. Repairs and retouching shoul be done as soon as possible.

Loosened bolts and screws that fasten railing parts togethe can usually be tightened with a wrench and screwdriver. If corr sion prevents turning a fastener, apply penetrating oil to it, wa ıpproximately fifteen minutes for the oil to work, then try again. Riveted parts may have to be professionally repaired (railing companies are listed in the Yellow Pages), or you may be able to ubstitute a short bolt and nut for the broken or missing rivet.

The most serious and difficult railing problems are loosened asteners that join railings to masonry, and the rusting apart of posts attached to porch steps.

Loosened masonry fasteners generally cannot be retightened. nstead, the fastener and its anchor (also called a sheath or shield) nust be removed and replaced. Use a wrench to unscrew damaged bolts, or a claw hammer or pry bar for nails.

The anchor is embedded in the masonry. Anchors that hold nails generally overlap the outside of the railing's mounting fixture and may come out of the masonry when the nail is withdrawn. If not, they can be pulled out with pliers.

Anchors holding threaded fasteners are usually covered by he fixture. To expose them for removal, detach the fixture from

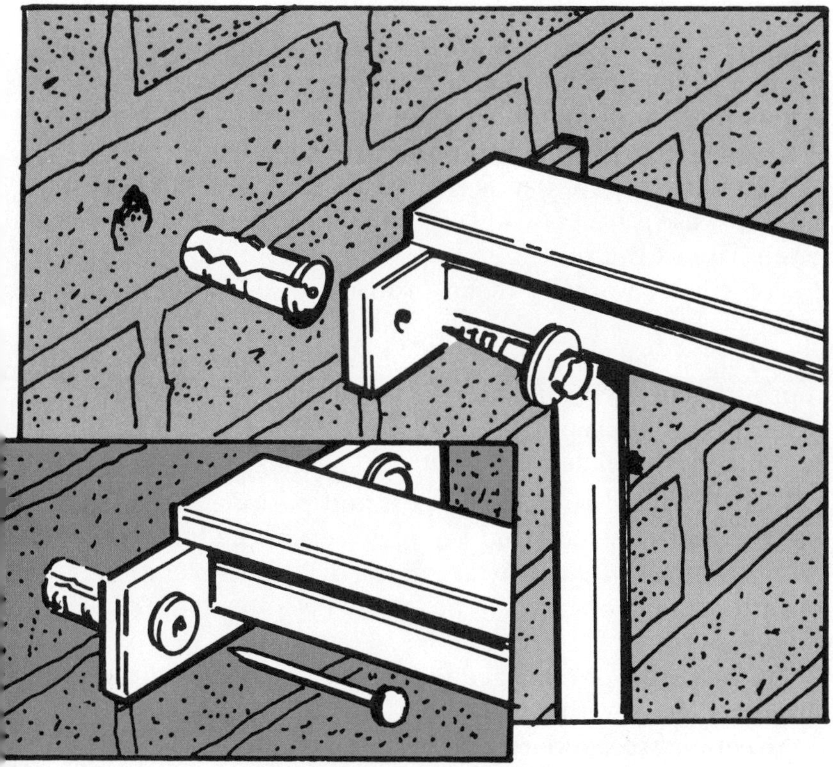

ew anchors for bolts are usually covered by fixtures. nchors for nails usually overlap fixtures.

the masonry by removing all the fasteners holding it. These can be reinstalled as long as the anchors are not loosened in the process.

The railing and fixture then must be moved out of the way so the loosened anchor can be pulled from the masonry with pliers. To do this, you may need to take apart the section of railing attached to the fixture.

There are two ways to install a replacement fastener. If possible, get a similar fastener that is either longer or wider. You will probably have to enlarge the hole into which the anchor fits, using an ordinary electric drill with a carbide-tipped masonry bit the same diameter as the anchor. If a more powerful drill is needed, rent an electric hammer drill.

If a fastener the same size as the original must be used, clean the anchor hole by blowing out loose particles and fill it with slow-curing epoxy. Allow the epoxy to stiffen but not harden completely. Then, to install a nail and anchor, reposition the fixture, insert the fastener through it and into the epoxy-filled hole, then drive the nail into the anchor with a hammer.

To install a bolt and anchor, drive the anchor into the hole first, then reposition the fixture and install the bolt by tightening it with a wrench. In both cases, scrape away any excess epoxy with a putty knife and wipe the masonry clean with a dampened piece of rough cloth. Allow the epoxy to cure completely.

To repair a post that has rusted apart or broken where it joins the steps, use a hacksaw to cut away the rusty or damaged metal. If the base of the post is embedded in a hole drilled in the step, saw or chisel away any metal protruding above the step so the surface is level.

From a railing company or railing supply store obtain an appropriately sized slip shoe—a metal plate with a socket in the center that will accept the end of the trimmed post. The slip shoe has holes in the plate for fasteners.

Fit the slip shoe onto the post and position the assembly so that the post is vertical and the plate covers the hole in the step. Using the holes in the plate as guides, drill new holes into the step for fastener anchors. Install the fasteners to attach the slip shoe to the step.

If the rusted or damaged post is already fitted with a slip shoe, simply replace it with a new one.

Keeping steel and iron railings well painted is the only way to prevent them from rusting. To treat minor rust spots before painting, scrape away all the rust, then apply a good grade of rust-resisting primer. Where rust has already taken hold, scrape away loose rust only, then apply rust converter, followed by primer. In both cases, cover the primer with high-quality rust-resisting paint.

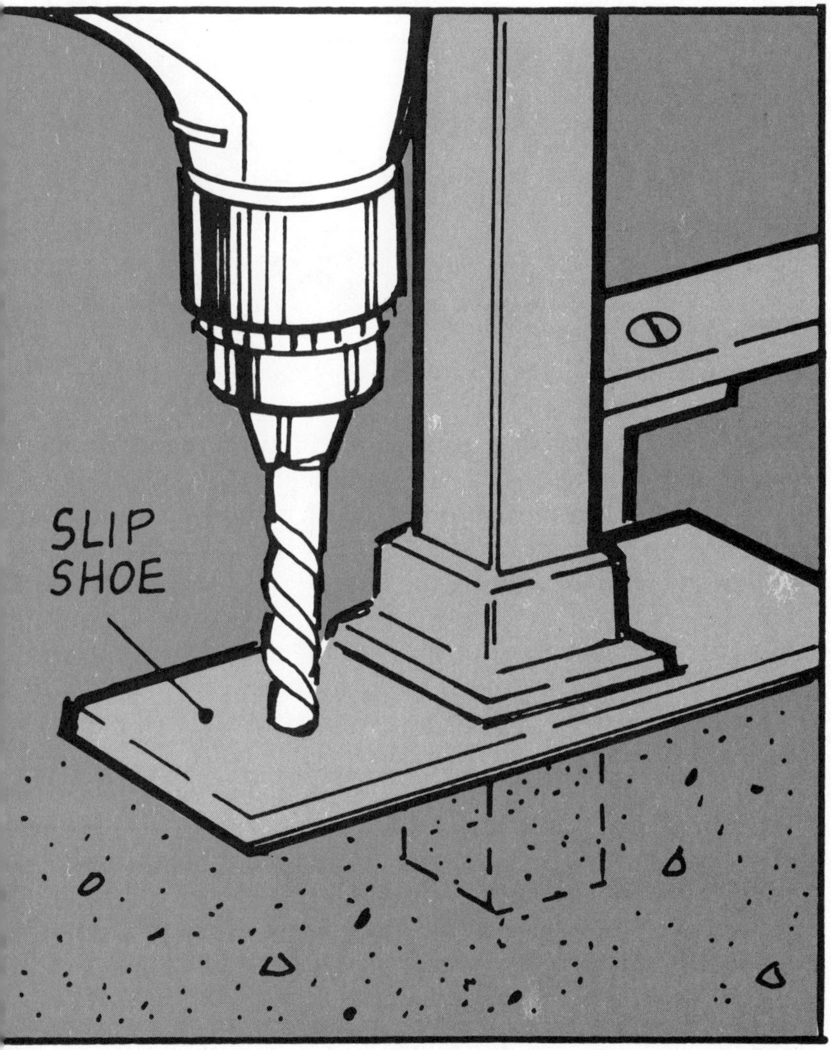

After sawing off the rusted end of a post and trimming the stub projecting from the step or porch, install a metal slip shoe on the end of the post and attach it to the step or porch with masonry fasteners.

Repairing Sliding Patio Doors

TIP:

Lithium grease, available at auto supply stores, is an excellent lubricant for sliding doors. The grease is virtually transparent when thinly applied, and stands up well to moisture and hard wear.

ATTENTION

D**uring warm weather, traffic through patio doors i**
creases and doors that stick or are difficult to slide become nu
sances. Fortunately, most problems with sliding patio doors ca
be fixed relatively easily.

Cleaning and lubricating the bottom track may be sufficien
Open the door and use a whisk broom to remove accumulate
debris from the corners and ridges of the track that are expose
If there are small holes drilled in the outside of the track to drai
water, clear these with a piece of wire or a straightened paper cli
Then vacuum the track to rid it completely of dirt.

Wipe the track next, with a cloth dipped either in a solutio
of detergent and water, followed by clear water, or in miner
spirits. Wear rubber gloves when using mineral spirits and avoi
inhaling fumes.

Afterward, lightly lubricate the rail (the protruding part o
the track) by rubbing it with a waxy door lubricant or with
candle. Close the door and repeat the process to clean and lubri
cate the remaining portion of the track.

If the door still does not slide smoothly, try adjusting th
rollers. These are located in the base of the door and each can b
raised or lowered by turning an adjusting screw found along th
door's lower edge. On some doors the adjusting screws are a
the ends of the door. On others the screws are installed along th
inside face.

o ease a sticky patio door, try adjusting the rollers until ıe door sides are parallel to the door frame.

First, determine whether or not the door rests squarely in the oor frame. To do this, open the door so that there is a gap of bout an inch between it and the vertical section of the frame next) it. If the door is mounted squarely, the edges that define the ap will be parallel.

If the gap is wider at the top than at the bottom, retract the oller nearest the gap by turning its adjusting screw counterclock-ise using a screwdriver. This will lower the door on that side, ausing the top of the door to tilt toward the gap.

Alternatively, extend the roller that is farthest from the gap y turning its adjusting screw clockwise. Doing so will raise the oor on that side, causing the same result.

You may have to adjust both screws if one has reached its mit. If the gap is wider at the bottom than at the top, reverse the rocedure.

When the door is positioned squarely, slide it again. If it fee tight, turn both adjusting screws counterclockwise to retract th rollers an equal amount until the door slides more smoothly.

If the door wobbles or seems to drag along the bottom, rais the door by turning both adjusting screws clockwise an equa amount. If a helper can lift the door to take the weight off th rollers, turning the adjusting screws will be easier.

If a door is very difficult to slide, inspect beneath the bas with a flashlight to check whether the rollers have slipped off th rail. If they have, retract the rollers fully, then lift the door whil sliding it. This may set the door back on the rail.

If it doesn't, remove the door and rehang it as describe below. The rollers of doors that are difficult to slide also may nee cleaning or replacing, or else the track may require repair.

Methods for removing sliding patio doors vary and so d procedures for removing rollers. With many models, removin the door is done by sliding it toward the middle of the track, the lifting the door to push its top edge into the upper track as far a it will go. This raises the bottom edge of the door clear of the rai allowing the door to be tilted from the bottom toward the insid of the house. The door can then be lowered to free it from th upper track.

On other doors, removal is by detaching a strip of molding a the top of the door frame. Then the door can be tilted toward th inside from the top and lifted clear of the rail.

To remove rollers from some doors it is only necessary t loosen one or more obvious screws, including the adjusting screw With others, the lower section of the door must be detached fro the sides and the rollers slid out of openings in the ends.

To do this, lay the door flat on a table or on sawhorses an unfasten the screws joining the lower section to the sides. The tap against the section with a hammer and wood block to separat it from the glass.

The screws that fasten the lower section to the sides may als fasten the rollers. If not, the rollers may be fastened to the sectio by screws located in the groove that fits over the glass.

In both cases, after removing the screws, pry against the rol ers with a screwdriver to slide them out of the section at each enc

To clean rollers, soak them in kerosene, charcoal-lightin fluid, or mineral spirits. Use an old toothbrush to remove gumm deposits. Wear rubber gloves and work where there is plenty o ventilation. If any parts of a roller are damaged, obtain a replace ment roller from the door manufacturer or from a window an door company.

After cleaning, dry the rollers and lubricate them lightly with licone spray or household oil. Reinstall rollers and doors by re-ersing the removal procedure. After rehanging a door, adjust e rollers until they move smoothly.

The most common kind of track damage is a crushed rail. ometimes a rail that is only slightly misshapen can be raightened with pliers or by placing a wooden block on one side f it and striking the other side with a hammer.

However, in most cases the best solution is to obtain a metal placement rail, U-shaped in cross section, that snaps into place ver the damaged original or in its place after the original has een pried off. Like rollers, replacement rails usually must be rdered from the door manufacturer, but are sometimes available om window and door repair companies.

To install a replacement rail, cut it to length and use a ham-er and wood block to tap it gently over the existing rail. If the xisting rail is badly crushed, you may have to file its sides first to arrow them so that they will fit the groove in the replacement il.

TIP:

Dampness on basement walls that appears to be due to leakage may instead be due to condensation. To test, tape a piece of aluminum foil about a foot square to the wall, sealing all four sides. Leave the foil in place for at least three days. If moisture forms on the outside of the foil, the problem is condensation, which generally can be cured by proper ventilation (see pages 383–85). If moisture forms on the inside, the wall leaks. Both problems can occur at the same time.

ATTENTION

Sealing Basement Leaks from Outside

Basement leaks are cured most effectively by making repairs on the exterior side of the foundation walls. Unfortunately this is usually a major undertaking, not because of the patchin procedure (which in most cases is simple), but because of th excavation that must be done to expose the areas requiring treat ment.

Before deciding to perform exterior repairs, make certai they are necessary. Eliminate gutter and downspout problems poor landscaping (the ground should slope away from the foun dation on all sides), and indoor condensation. Then, if dampnes or leakage persists, determine whether the problem is localized— for instance, due specifically to visible cracks—or covers larg areas of one or more walls.

Localized repairs require less excavation than areas needin widespread treatment, and you may decide to do the diggin yourself. However, where exposing more than 10 feet of a wall i necessary, consider having the job done by professionals. Dr summer weather is the best time for excavation and repairs.

To patch a cracked foundation, begin by excavating along th length of the crack. Expose approximately 2 feet of the wall o each side, and dig away from the wall at least 3 feet to allo climbing into the hole. Dig all the way to the footing (the base o the foundation) unless the crack clearly ends well above it. Th excavation must expose approximately 1 foot of the wall belo the crack.

Near the footing, be careful not to damage any drain tile made of clay or fiber that may be laid at the base of the wall. Together with a layer of gravel that should also be present, the drain tile is meant to carry away water accumulating against the foundation. If you do not encounter any drainage material, consider adding it. If existing tiles are damaged, replace them.

For protection against cave-ins, brace the sides of holes deeper than 4 feet by placing planks of wide lumber or sheets of plywood vertically in the hole, against the side opposite the wall. Wedge them using horizontal lengths of two-by-four lumber pressed between the wall and the bracing.

After excavating, scrub the cracked portion of the wall with water and a scrub brush to expose clean concrete. If the crack is large enough to accept the blade of a cold chisel, use the chisel and a ball peen hammer to widen the crack and undercut the sides so the crack is wider inside than at the surface. Wear goggles when hammering. If the crack is merely a hairline, only brush it free of dust so the pores of the concrete are open.

Use hydraulic cement to fill the chiseled crack or to spread it over the hairlined area. Hydraulic cement hardens very quickly and expands as it cures, creating an extremely strong bond with existing masonry. The material is available at home centers, and is mixed with water and applied using a mason's trowel. Follow the instructions printed on the package.

After the cement has hardened, apply asphalt or one of the newly developed geosynthetic foundation coatings over the repaired area. Asphalt foundation coating, which resembles roofing cement or tar, is available in cans at home centers. It is troweled or brushed on with a mason's trowel or a wide disposable brush. Spread the coating in a layer approximately ⅛ inch thick over the cemented area and at least 8 inches on all sides. Geosynthetic coating can be troweled on or sprayed on; it is also available in sheets for attaching to foundation walls with adhesive.

You may encounter a layer of building felt—tar paper—covering the exterior of the foundation wall. This functions as a type of waterproofing; moisture problems mean damage somewhere to the paper. When you locate the problem, brush the area clean, then apply a layer of foundation coating over it. Before the sheet hardens, press new sheets of 30-pound grade building felt (available at home centers) against it. Lay the sheets side by side, overlapping the seams by at least 4 inches. Smooth the felt free of wrinkles and air bubbles using the edge of a board. Allow the first layer of coating to harden; then apply another layer over the felt to protect it from sharp pieces of fill.

TIP:

For more on the methods professionals use to correct foundation leaks from the outside, see the note on page 70.

ATTENTION

Regardless of the type or number of layers that are applied, after foundation coating has hardened, you may complete the repair by refilling the hole and then grading the surface of the ground so that water will drain away from the foundation. However, for state-of-the-art protection, consider placing panels of drainage board (these consist of plastic, nylon mesh, or other synthetics) against walls after the foundation coating has been applied and has hardened. Drainage board creates a vertical channel between the soil and the foundation wall so that water near the area is conducted more quickly to the drain tile. Hydrostatic pressure against the foundation—a major cause of basement wetness—is also relieved. In the absence of building paper, drainage board also prevents damage to the foundation coating during filling-in.

Filter fabric of either polyester or polypropylene should be placed against the drainage board to prevent soil particles from clogging the board. For best results, gravel should be poured to the desired height around the footing and drainpipe first, then the filter fabric attached to the wall and spread over the gravel to protect it from clogging also. Afterward, filling-in with earth can proceed, followed by grading.

For waterproofing an entire wall or even an entire foundation, follow the same procedure, but on a larger scale. If long runs of new drainpipe must be installed, it is a good idea to add cleanouts—angled extensions of nonperforated pipe leading to the surface—so that they can be cleared with an auger every few years.

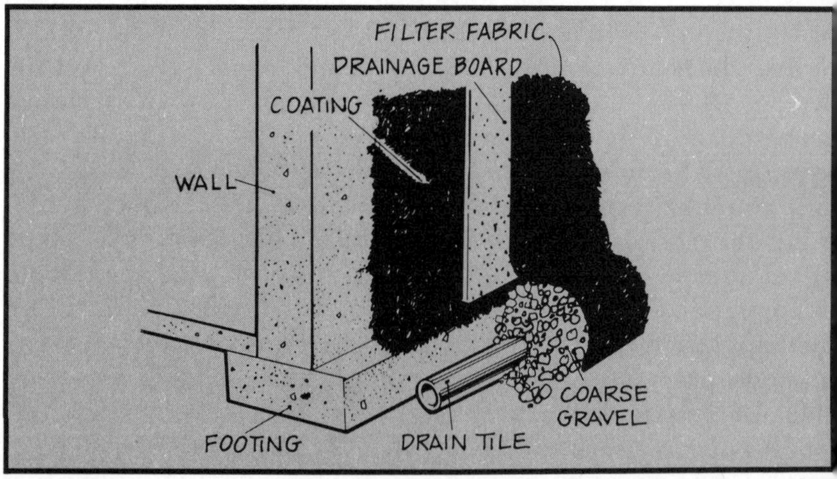

Full-scale exterior waterproofing should include wall coating, drainage board, and filter fabric, as well as drain tile at the footing, embedded in gravel.

Repairing and Sealing an Asphalt Driveway

Asphalt driveways should be kept in good condition and coated with sealer every three to five years to protect them from moisture, chemicals, and the effects of weather. Because many repair compounds and most sealer must be applied when temperatures remain above 50 degrees Fahrenheit even at night, summer is the best time for the job.

Repairs

Cracks, holes, and other damage should be repaired promptly as soon as seasonal temperatures allow, and in any case before sealing. To repair cracks less than half an inch wide, fill them with liquid crack filler made for driveways. Crack filler is available at hardware stores and home centers, as are virtually all products needed for driveway care. Instead of liquid filler, a type resembling caulking compound can also be used. It comes in a cartridge and is applied with a caulking gun.

To enhance adhesion of the filler, dampen all cracks and the surrounding driveway surface before applying it, unless the filler instructions specify otherwise.

Cracks should be filled level and examined the next day for settling. If necessary, more filler should then be added. Normally, filler hardens within twenty-four hours. Although the driveway can be used during this time, avoid parking on freshly filled areas. Sprinkling sand over the filler will prevent it from sticking to tires.

TIP:

To remove oil and grease spots from asphalt, cover them as soon as possible with baking soda or cat litter dampened with water. Spread plastic over the material to keep it from drying out; allow the material to remain for twenty-four hours to absorb the stain.

ATTENTION

TIP:

To save on crack filler, pack deep cracks with sand to within about half an inch of the surface. Apply the filler over the sand.

ATTENTION

Patch narrow cracks in an asphalt driveway with liquid crack filler.

To repair cracks that are wider than half an inch, use crack-patching mastic, also formulated for driveways. This material resembles thick tar and consists of asphalt and fibers. It comes in a can and is applied with a putty knife or mason's trowel. Crack-patching mastic can also be used to fill shallow depressions. Avoid disturbing large patches of mastic until they are dry. Small areas can be treated as described for crack filler.

For potholes or to replace large areas of crumbled pavement, use cold-mix asphalt patching compound. This is a mixture of asphalt and gravel and comes in bags. Mixing is not required.

To fill a pothole, first remove all loose material from the hole and use a pick to chip away any crumbled pavement around the edges. To remove an area of pavement, first cut around its outline with a rented pavement saw—essentially a chain saw with a circular abrasive blade. Then break up and remove the material inside with a pick.

If the hole or prepared area is more than 4 inches deep, fill it to that level with gravel and tamp it firmly using a wooden post or a rented tamping tool.

With a disposable masonry paintbrush, apply a thin coating of asphalt primer (emulsified asphalt, sold in cans) around the edges of the hole and on the surrounding surface. Then shovel enough patching compound into the hole to create a 2-inch-thick layer when tamped.

Fill the hole a layer at a time, tamping between layers, until it is overfilled by about an inch. Then place a wide, thick board on the repair and roll a vehicle over it a few times to flatten and compact the compound as much as possible. Allow twenty-four to thirty-six hours for the patch to harden.

TIP:

For coping with driveway cracks that reopen, patching material of asphalt-coated polypropylene fabric like that used for highway repairs is available at some hardware stores and home centers. Although more expensive than crack filler or mastic, applying it is easier: just cut the patch to size, peel off the paper backing and press it over the crack. The fabric is self-adhering and can be driven over or walked on immediately. Sealing the driveway after applying patches is recommended for appearance.

Sealing

When preparing a driveway for sealing, first complete any repairs necessary. Trim grass or weeds from the sides of the driveway, then sweep the surface thoroughly with a stiff broom and spray the driveway with hard spray from a garden hose to rid it of loose particles.

While the driveway is still damp, scrub any areas stained by oil, gasoline, or other chemicals. Use a stiff-bristle scrub brush dipped in strong industrial detergent or driveway cleaner. Follow the instructions printed on the container and wear rubber gloves if their use is recommended.

Afterward, or if the driveway is not stained, wash the entire surface with a mixture of detergent or driveway cleaner and water. Unless the manufacturer's instructions specify otherwise, use 1 cup of detergent or cleaner to 1 gallon of water.

The most convenient tool for washing is a long-handled scrub brush. Following washing, remove standing water from the driveway with a long-handled squeegee. (This tool is also required later for applying sealer.)

There are several grades of driveway sealer. All consist of emulsified coal tar with various protective compounds added. The best grades require little stirring and produce a surface that provides traction even when wet.

Sealer comes in 5-gallon containers and is best applied with a disposable combination push broom and squeegee sold for the purpose. A good grade of sealer will cover about 300 square feet of a badly weathered or unsealed driveway. The same grade will cover about 500 square feet of a driveway in excellent condition that has been previously sealed.

After repairing a hole by filling it with fresh asphalt, flatten the spot by placing a board over the repair and rolling a vehicle over it.

To apply sealer, start at the end of the driveway nearest the garage. Pour sealer in a ribbon 8 to 10 inches wide across the width of the pavement and gently spread it along the length of the driveway until a strip about 3 feet wide is covered. Then use the squeegee to level the sealer and spread it to an even thickness of about an eighth of an inch. Maintain this thickness even in depressions, as sealer that is too thick sometimes will remain permanently sticky. Avoid splashing sealer onto walls, sidewalks, or other surfaces.

Repeat the procedure until the driveway is covered. For the best appearance, follow a consistent pattern of spreading and leveling. On inclined areas, a light sprinkling of sand over the sealer will improve traction. Excess sand that does not adhere to the sealer can be swept away later.

When you finish, use the empty sealer container(s) to block the entrance to the driveway. Allow sealer to dry without walking or driving on it for at least twenty-four hours, even longer if the weather is cool or very humid. Do not apply sealer if rain is expected within twenty-four hours; the rain may wash it away.

Tools and soiled gloves, clothing, and shoes can be cleaned if washed immediately in warm soapy water. Before entering the house, it is a good idea to thoroughly check clothes and shoes worn during the sealing so that sealer will not get on furniture and floors.

Spread driveway sealer in a layer about ⅛-inch thick, using a combination push broom and squeegee. Avoid applying sealer too thickly, otherwise it may not harden.

Repairing Concrete Steps

Concrete outdoor steps are durable and ordinarily will last the life of a house. However, concrete is inherently brittle, and as a result, corners and sharp edges of steps are vulnerable to chipping. Cracks that permit water to enter are most damaging. When the water freezes, it expands with sufficient strength to force apart even large slabs.

To keep out moisture, coat steps annually with liquid penetrating sealer. This can be applied with a paintbrush or, with some brands, by attaching the container to a garden hose. One coat per application is usually enough. Allow up to four hours for the sealer to dry before using the steps.

A small, cleanly broken chip from the corner or edge of a step can usually be glued back with epoxy. First, brush the broken surface of the step and the fragment free of loose particles. If grease or oil is present, clean the surfaces also, using detergent; then rinse.

Let the surfaces dry by themselves, or dry them with a hair dryer. Mix the epoxy according to the manufacturer's instructions. Liberally coat both surfaces, then press the fragment into place.

Brace the repair with a brick or with some other support for about fifteen minutes. Clamping is unnecessary. Protect the repair from moisture and avoid stepping on it for twenty-four hours while the adhesive cures completely.

For filling holes and cracks, and for resurfacing roughened areas, use vinyl or acrylic latex concrete patching compounds. These are sold as powders for mixing with accompanying liquid or with plain water. The instructions specify mixing proportions. Patching compound contains Portland cement, which is caustic. When mixing or using it, wear rubber gloves and goggles to avoid irritation.

To repair concrete with patching compound, first chisel away all cracked and crumbling concrete from the damaged area. Widen cracks for better penetration of the compound and, if possible, slope the sides of cracks and holes so that they are farther apart at their base than at the surface. This process is called keying.

Brush away all loose particles and remove any grease or oil. The instructions for some patching compounds recommend using solvent such as paint thinner for this, rather than detergent and water. Afterward, dampen the area with water, then apply the compound with a putty knife or mason's trowel.

Press with the knife or trowel when applying compound to ensure complete contact with the damaged surface and to squeeze out excess air. When resurfacing an uneven area, first apply compound in a low spot, then spread it outward gradually until the surface is level.

Patching compound can also be used to restore missing chips or larger pieces from corners and other areas. But because it is relatively expensive, and because some kinds can only be applied in layers an inch thick at a time (with intervals for curing allowed between layers), ordinary concrete is often a better choice.

Premixed concrete requiring only the addition of water is available in small bags from hardware stores and home centers. To enhance the bonding of the fresh concrete to the damaged surface, also obtain liquid bonding adhesive.

To reinforce the repair from within, drive masonry nails into the damaged surface at 1- to 3-inch intervals. For strength the nails must penetrate at least three quarters of an inch. However, they may have to be driven deeper to be concealed by the fresh concrete. Wear safety goggles and use a ball peen hammer or small sledge for hammering. An ordinary carpenter's hammer may splinter, sending off metal shards.

To create the shape of the missing corner, and to support the concrete until it hardens, you will have to build a wooden form around the area to be repaired. Use either solid lumber or thick plywood. Cut the pieces so they fit against the step and so their top edges are even with the step's horizontal surface. This will aid smoothing the step after the repair is completed.

TIP:

To calculate the amount of concrete needed, measure the length and width in feet of the area to be repaired, and the thickness in inches. Multiply all three numbers together, then divide by 12. This is the volume of concrete needed, expressed in cubic feet. (For example, an area measuring 3 feet long, 2 feet wide, and 4 inches deep has a volume of 2 cubic feet.) An 80-pound bag of premixed concrete contains about three fifths of a cubic foot.

ATTENTION

Coat each board's inside surface with used motor oil or wrap each board in a single layer of plastic sheeting to prevent the concrete from sticking to it.

Assemble the boards to create the form, then attach them to stakes driven into the ground to support them. The tops of the stakes must not protrude above the top of the form.

For restorations where little concrete is used, the boards comprising the form can be held in place by bricks or other heavy weights instead of stakes.

Mix the concrete in a wheelbarrow or large, shallow container, by adding water to the dry ingredients according to the instructions on the bag. Brush and clean the damaged surface, apply liquid bonding adhesive with a paintbrush, then shovel the concrete into the form.

To settle the concrete, stab it several times with the point of the shovel or a trowel. To level the repaired surface after the form

To level a large patch, drag a board on edge across the top of the form while the concrete is still wet. Slide the board from side to side.

is filled, drag a board on the edge across the top edges of the form while moving the board from side to side with a sawing motion.

Let the concrete stiffen for about an hour, until an impression made with a thumb no longer fills with water. Then smooth the surface by rubbing it lightly with a wood block.

If desired, round off sharp edges of the repair before removing the form, using a metal edging tool inserted between the edge of the concrete and the form.

Remove the form after twenty-four hours, but keep the repair moist for about five days or as long as the instructions for the concrete specify. During this time, stay off the step.

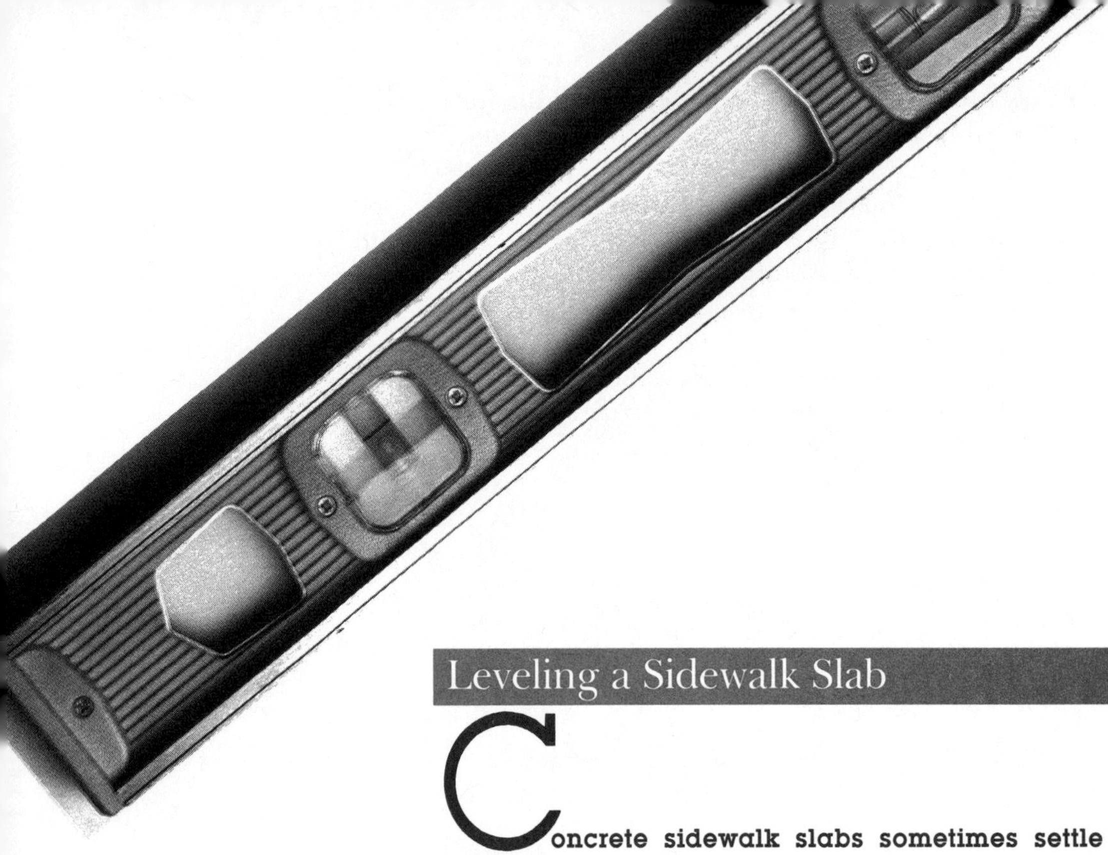

Leveling a Sidewalk Slab

Concrete sidewalk slabs sometimes settle unevenly if soil beneath them compacts or is washed away. Not only is the problem a safety hazard, but you may also be legally at risk if you fail to maintain sidewalks on or bordering your property.

If a slab has tilted more than 3 inches away from level, or if it has also broken, the easiest repair may be to pour a new slab of concrete over the old one or to replace it altogether. However, if a slab has tilted less than that amount and is intact, it may be more easily leveled than covered, by filling the area beneath it with fresh concrete.

First, cure whatever problem has caused the slab to shift. Don't bother with this if the slab has not changed from its tilted position for many years, but if shifting has been recent or is ongoing, locate the cause—usually improper drainage—and remedy it before leveling the slab. Otherwise, the slab will probably continue to shift, usually at the same rate as before.

When you are ready to level the slab, the first step is to pry it up and prop it securely so that concrete can be poured underneath. You will need at least one helper (a 4-inch slab of concrete measuring 2 feet on each side weighs about 200 pounds), plus a shovel, a heavy-duty steel pry bar approximately 5 feet long (this can be rented), and an assortment of two-by-four or larger lumber scraps to use as support blocks.

Dig a hole at each corner of the tilted slab on the side away from the curb, if there is one. Make the holes somewhat wider than the shovel's blade and deep enough to expose the slab's bottom edge. Set a thick board in or across the hole, then insert the pry bar underneath the slab and press downward to pry the slab up. The lumber acts as a fulcrum for the pry bar.

If the slab does not rise easily, loosen the soil along the entire side between the holes, then try prying at the other corner. Work back and forth until the slab loosens. Once you are able to raise the slab even slightly, have your helper place blocks underneath it near the pry bar to keep it raised. Be careful when doing this. If the slab or pry bar should slip, injury can result.

Repeat the process at the other corner, then alternate between corners until enough blocks have been inserted to support the slab so its bottom edge—on the side where you are working—is 6 or 8 inches above ground level. This will allow enough room to pour and spread the concrete.

Next, after making certain that the slab is securely supported, insert a 1- to 2-foot length of lumber under the slab, positioning it as close as possible to the center. This piece creates a pivot point as well as a central support for the slab, so that after the concrete is spread underneath and the support blocks at the sides are removed, the slab will rest on the pivot at a height equal to that of the adjacent slabs. The block prevents the slab from sinking under its own weight into the wet concrete and also allows the slab to be adjusted by rocking it at the corners.

For a slab tilted approximately 2 inches below the slabs adjacent to it, a length of two-by-four lumber is of sufficient thickness. Use a thinner board if the slant is less than 1 inch, and a thicker board if the slant is close to 3 inches. The block does not have to be precisely centered beneath the slab. To prevent the block from shifting during the application of concrete, it is best if you can wedge it tightly between the underside of the slab and the soil.

If you wish, test the pivot by removing the support blocks at the corners and attempting to level the slab at the correct height. Forgo this step if raising the slab was difficult.

With the slab raised and the pivot in place, mix and pour the concrete. Use bags of dry concrete mix containing gravel, available at home centers, and either a shallow concrete-mixing tray (this can be rented) or a wheelbarrow. To determine the amount of concrete you will need, hold a ruler vertically against the edge of a slab adjacent to the one that has tilted, midway between the point at which the tilted slab is level with the adjacent slab and its deepest point, to measure the approximate average depth that

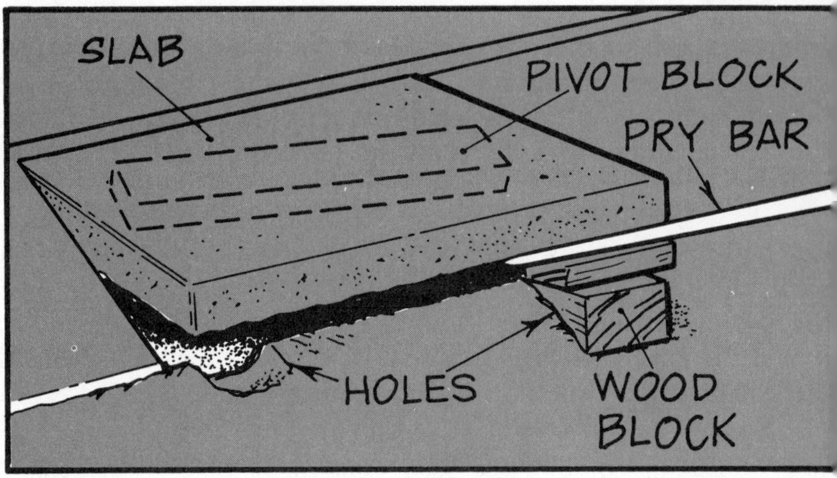

Use a pry bar and wood blocks to raise the tilted slab. Put a lumber pivot block under the slab to support it while the concrete cures.

the slab has sunk. Then add half an inch to allow for settling of the fresh concrete.

Multiply this total by the area in square feet of the slab (found by multiplying the length in feet of two perpendicular sides) then divide by 12 to derive the number of cubic feet of concrete necessary to level the slab. Compare this amount to the volume of concrete obtained per bag (an 80-pound bag yields about three fifths of a cubic foot) to determine how many bags of concrete are needed. To level a 3-foot-by-4-foot slab that has sunk an average of 1 inch, approximately 1½ cubic feet of concrete are necessary ((3 x 4 x 1½) ÷ 12 = 1½)—roughly the contents of two and a half 80-pound bags.

Mix and spread the concrete one bag at a time. When mixing use as little water as possible (this creates the strongest concrete) but use enough so that the material can be easily poured and spread beneath the raised slab. Pour the concrete beneath the slab and push it as far toward the rear as possible, using the end of a board. Stop pouring when the level of the concrete reaches or slightly exceeds the height of the pivot block.

Then remove the support blocks carefully and adjust the pitch of the slab by pressing on the corners. It should float level on the freshly poured concrete or tilt slightly toward the curb to promote good drainage. Pour approximately one quarter of the last batch of concrete (you should have this much left over) beneath the side of the slab opposite the one that was raised, and force the mixture beneath the slab using a narrow board.

Finally, wash away any concrete that has spilled on or around the slab. Fill in the holes, then erect a barrier to warn off passersby. Allow the concrete to cure for twenty-four hours before walking on the slab.

Setting and Repairing Wood Fence Posts

Wobbly wooden fence posts should be promptly repaired before they cause other fence parts to loosen. Posts that have been in the ground for less than five years usually wobble because of improper installation; ordinarily, tightening these is fairly easy. But in older fences, decay is a more likely culprit. Although strengthening a decayed post sometimes works, the best solution is to replace it.

Wooden fence posts should be of a kind that is naturally decay resistant (locust, cedar, or redwood, for example) or should be commercially pressure-treated with preservative. The tops of fence posts should be sawed off at an angle to prevent water from collecting on them.

To install a fence post, use either a clamshell posthole digger —a hand tool with long handles and spoon-shaped digging blades, resembling large tongs—or a gasoline-powered auger. Both can be rented.

Dig holes about 2½ feet deep and about 6 inches wider than the diameter of the post. Make the bottom of the hole about twice as wide as the top; the wider section should begin about a foot from the bottom.

Shovel about 4 inches of crushed stone into the bottom of the hole. (Crushed stone is available from building supply stores and brickyards; ordinary stones 2 to 3 inches in diameter, from any source, will also do.)

Compact the stone by tamping it with the post or a piece of umber. Then put a larger flat stone on top of the crushed stone o support the post and help prevent it from settling. Instead of a lat stone, you can also use a brick or a fragment of concrete.

Set the post in the hole. While a helper steadies it, hold a :arpenter's level against one side of the post and then 90 degrees away, on another side. Adjust the post until the level indicates that t is vertical at both locations.

Then shovel more crushed stone into the hole and tamp it to within about 8 inches of the surface. Finish filling the hole with oil, tamping each 2-inch layer.

Using soil to top up the hole costs nothing and allows posts o be removed easily if necessary. But in sandy soil or where flood-ng or frost heaving is a problem, post holes should be filled above he crushed stone with concrete. Above ground level, the concrete should slope away from the post to aid drainage.

Quick-setting concrete for fence posts is available at building upply stores. For setting several posts, the cheapest product is high-strength early-setting concrete. It hardens in about an hour, which lets you install posts in the morning and fencing in the afternoon.

So-called instant concrete products are about twice as expen-sive, but they harden much faster—in as little as five minutes—and allow fencing to be attached after about an hour.

For fence posts made of four-by-four lumber (or posts whose ends can be trimmed to that size), an alternative installation method is to use post supports, available from fence suppliers. These are steel sockets that taper to a point. They can be driven nto the ground with a sledgehammer or embedded in concrete. Afterward, the fence post is driven into the socket.

To repair a wobbly but undecayed post set in soil, saw a 4-foot length of two-by-four lumber into four 2-foot-long wedges first cut the 4-foot length in half, and then cut the two sections nto wedges). Each wedge should measure about 1½ inches square at the thick end. Soak these for twenty-four hours in copper naph-thenate wood preservative, available at home centers. Drive the wedges into the ground along each side of the post, then bind the wedges and post together by twisting metal wire tightly around them.

If a post set in soil wobbles because it has decayed below ground, dig a hole alongside it. Shape the hole and add stones as described. Install a short length of new post beside the rotten one. The new post should be treated with preservative and angled across the top, and it should rise about a foot above ground level.

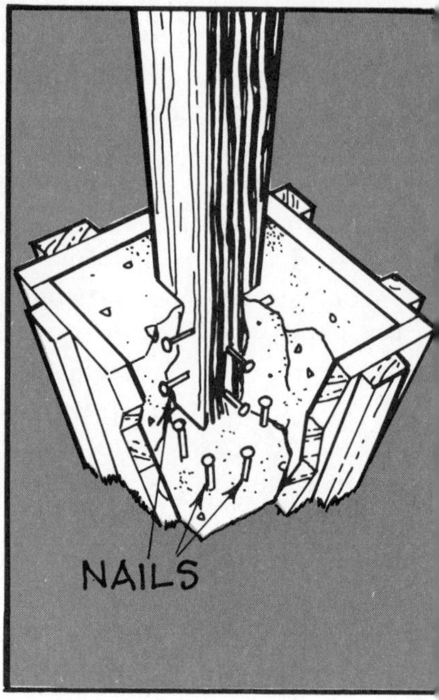

To steady a decayed post set in soil, install a new section of post in the ground next to it. Then join the two posts with bolts.

To strengthen a wobbly post set in concrete, pour new concrete atop the old. Use a homemade wooden form to hold the concrete until it sets.

Drill two to four holes ⅜ inch or more in diameter through both posts using an electric drill with a long drill bit. Bolt the posts together with galvanized carriage bolts having wide, flat washers. Fill the new posthole with soil, stones, or concrete; then saw through the decayed post below the bolts to slow further deterioration.

To strengthen posts set in concrete, cast an above-ground extension of the concrete base. If the post is decayed inside the old concrete, first drill half a dozen ¾-inch holes slanting from the lowest areas of sound wood downward toward the center of the post. Fill the holes with copper naphthenate preservative to halt advancing decay.

Clean and roughen the top of the existing concrete using any strong detergent and a stiff brush; rinse thoroughly with clean water. Drive several 2-inch masonry nails partway into the concrete to provide a grip for the new concrete. And drive several nails into the sides of the post 3 to 5 inches above ground. Wear goggles when hammering.

Using plywood or boards, build a four-sided bottomless box about 8 inches high around the post as a form for the new concrete. The inside of the form should be at least 2 inches from the post on all sides.

Place the form on top of the existing concrete and anchor it by nailing it to stakes driven into the ground. Wipe the inside of the form with fresh or used motor oil to prevent the concrete from sticking.

Mix new concrete. For extra strength, instead of adding water to the ingredients, blend them with a mixture of equal parts water and a liquid concrete bonding agent containing acrylic or other plastic (available where concrete is obtained).

When the new concrete is ready, dampen the existing concrete with water and coat it and the lower portion of the post with full-strength bonding agent. Immediately pour the fresh concrete into the form. Tamp the concrete thoroughly and slope the surface away from the post. After the concrete hardens, remove the form.

A type of post support called a repair spur can be used to repair wobbly 4-by-4-inch posts set in concrete. Saw through the post where it emerges from the concrete, drive the spur into the embedded wood, then insert the post into the spur's socket.

Closing a Summer House

Preparing to vacate a summer home shouldn't dominate your stay, but as the season ends, a well-planned buttoning up will help ensure that you have a summer home to come back to and that you won't spend the greater part of next year's stay setting to rights the home you left in disarray this year.

Map out a closing-up strategy that addresses these three goals: securing the house inside as well as out against the elements; preventing damage from pests, dampness, and poor air circulation; and minimizing the likelihood of burglary and theft. Some jobs must wait practically until you start the car, but others can be done as the summer tapers.

Outdoor chores can usually be done furthest in advance. Overall, this means seeing that external maintenance is up to date. Restore caulk and weatherstripping to keep out weather and pests. Give priority to inspecting and, if necessary, repairing the roof and chimney.

Clean the gutters and prune back branches that might hit the house in windstorms or heavy snows. Trim branches also to keep squirrels away from the roof. Inspect and repair screened attic vents to repel bats and insects. Patch screens and repair broken windowpanes.

Inspect all masonry, especially the foundation. Fill seams and cracks with caulking compound or patching cement to stop leaks and pests, and especially to prevent further damage from freezing and thawing. Buy rodent shields—metal collars available from hardware and farm supply stores—and install them around pipes entering the house.

Remove all trash and edibles, including garden vegetables and orchard fruits, from the area around the house, and thoroughly scrub garbage cans. Be sure no bags of salt from ice-cream-making sprees, or leather items like harnesses, ball gloves, boots, or shoes remain where animals can find and gnaw them. Store garden tools in a safe place; porcupines and other pests will munch on sweat-permeated wooden handles. In desperation animals will also eat candles, soap, sponges, and even self-striking matches (which can cause a fire).

Be sure that outdoor fixtures—television antennas, shutters, awnings, doors on outbuildings—are secure against storm winds. Check that no objects like patio furniture, yard equipment, or toys lie loose to blow around during storms, or, if the house is by a lake or seashore, be lost should the water rise.

Indoor preparation usually must wait until the final days. Clean out closets and cabinets. Leave doors and drawers open and place chemical dehumidifiers in areas prone to dampness. Take as many clothes and linens with you as you can; clean those you leave and hang them in airy, sunlit rooms in open-bottomed plas-

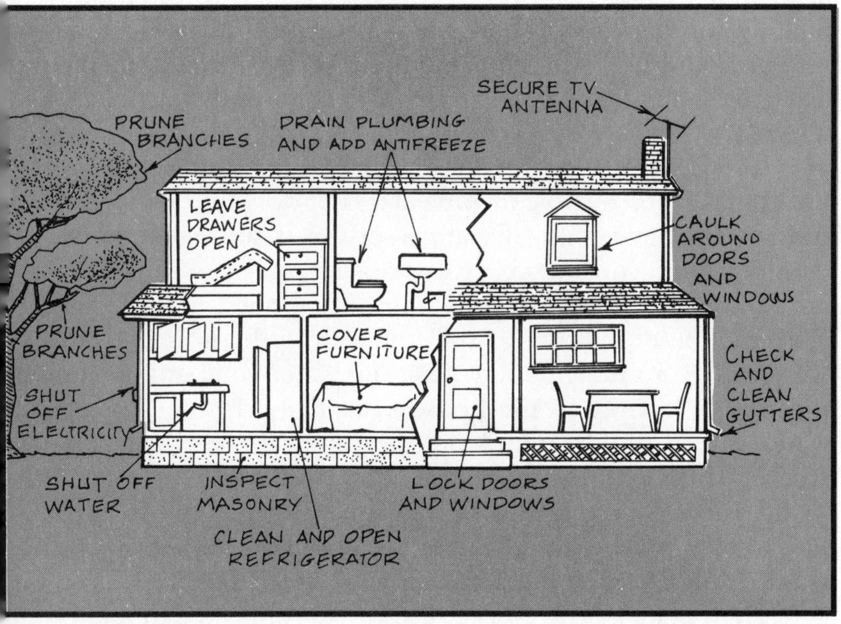

Protection against weather, pests, and burglars is basic when closing a summer house.

tic bags (the kind dry cleaners use) to protect them from dus Strip beds and upholstered furniture, vacuum them, then pro up the cushions, mattresses, and box springs to expose them t sun and air. Cover items loosely with plastic or old sheets agains dust.

Remove all food and, if you intend to shut off heat, any othe items that may be damaged by freezing. Clean the refrigerato freezer, stove, washers, and all other appliances, and prop thei doors or lids open. Place a box of baking soda in each, as well a in kitchen cabinets (leave their doors open, too) to absorb odors Leave baking soda or odor-absorbing cat litter in kitchen, bath room, and poorly ventilated utility areas to keep them fresh.

Unless the house will be frequently checked by someone wh can respond to a power failure, all utilities must be shut off, an the plumbing must be drained to prevent the pipes from burstin in a freeze.

To turn off the electricity, switch off the circuit breakers a the service panel (the indoor "fuse box" where the power compa ny's wires enter). Unplug all power cords, including those to ap pliances. Next year you will have to plug them in again, which wi assure that you notice any winter damage to them.

Bottled propane gas is easy to shut off also; merely close th valve outdoors on the line from the tank to the house. To shut of oil and gas services, however, it is usually best to call a utility o heating company technician unless you have been shown the cor rect procedure. Try to have these services performed the day yo leave, or soon after if you can be sure the job will be done in you absence.

It's nicer not to have to drain the plumbing at the last minute but it makes for terrible inconvenience if done too soon. Keepin utilities on year-round (if you can afford it, and if the house ca be monitored) considerably eases closing up.

To drain the plumbing if water is supplied from a well, firs close off the pipe leading from the well to the house. If water i supplied by a municipal line, ask the water company to turn of the supply leading to the house instead. Both steps ensure tha water in the underground pipe leading to the house does no freeze. (If the pipe is buried below the frost depth for your regio —the water company can supply this information—it is usuall safe to turn off the water simply by closing the main water suppl shutoff valve located indoors near the water meter.)

Then open all the faucets and valves connected to the plumb ing and let the water remaining in the pipes run out. Save a bucke or two of water for last-minute or unexpected cleaning. Drain th vater heater also, so that the water inside does not stagnate. Leave he indoor faucets and valves open, but close the outdoor faucets o prevent insects and other pests from entering.

When the plumbing is drained, wipe off all fixtures—bath-ub, toilet, sinks, and basins—then pour a cup or so of plumbing ntifreeze (available at hardware stores) into drains to replace the vater in the traps beneath them. This not only prevents damage lue to freezing should water still remain in the trap, but because ntifreeze won't evaporate, it also prevents sewer gases from ris-ng through the plumbing and keeps pests from entering the iouse.

Notify the police, post office, and any delivery services before ou leave, so the house can be monitored immediately and so that nail and goods won't pile up to tip off burglars. If appropriate, ell neighbors of your plans and of how you may be reached. Of ourse you should leave nothing of value in an empty house, but ven so, be sure that all windows are secure. On your way out, lon't forget to lock the doors.

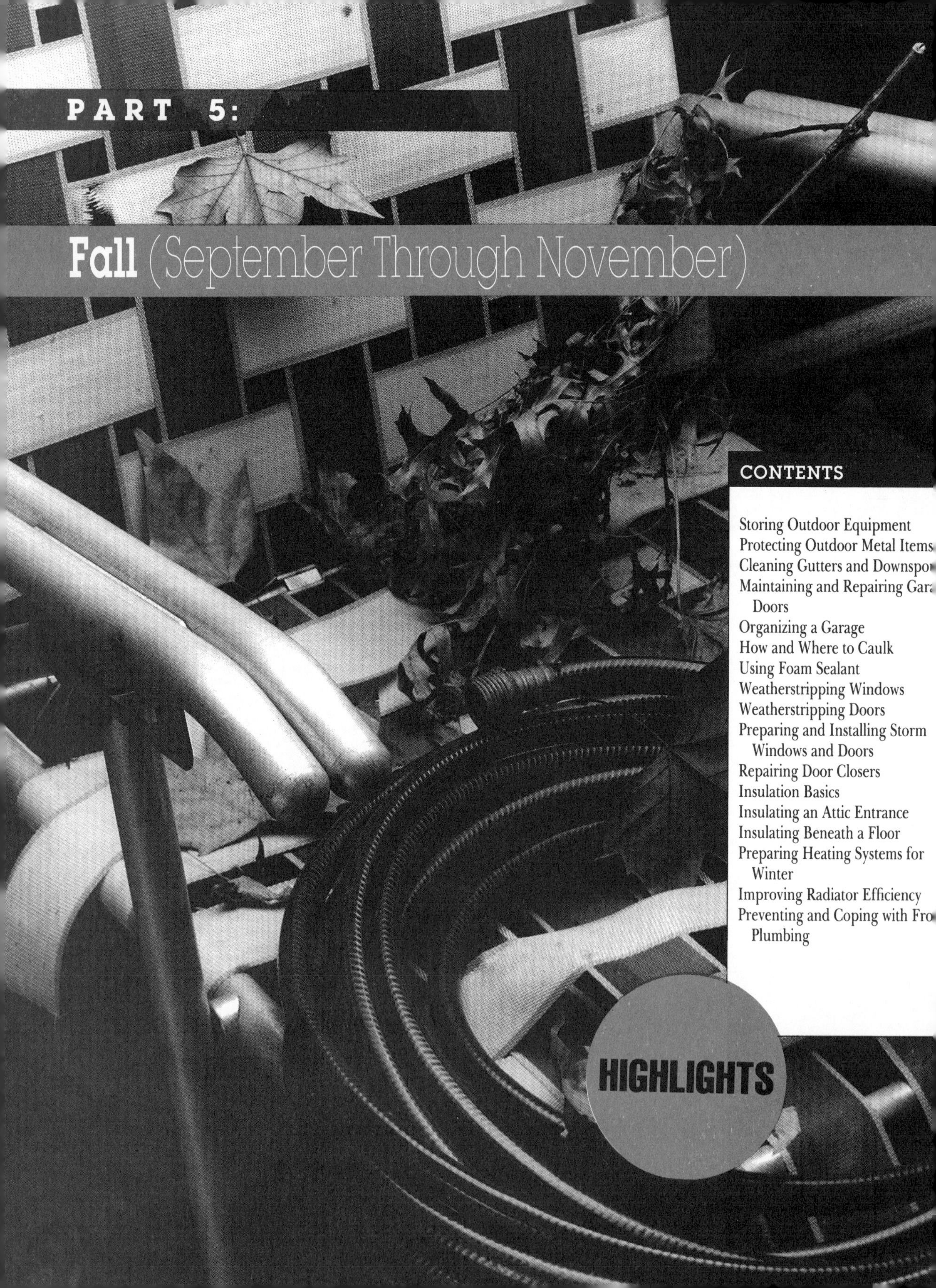

PART 5:

Fall (September Through November)

CONTENTS

HIGHLIGHTS

Storing Outdoor Equipment

Outdoor equipment like patio and picnic furniture, barbecue grills, play items, and tools will last longer and be more quickly available in spring if it is cleaned, repaired, and thoughtfully stored in fall.

Aluminum or chrome lawn furniture should be washed before storing. Rinse it first with hard spray from a garden hose to loosen dirt, then scrub the metal parts and plastic webbing with a scrub brush dipped in household detergent and water. Car-washing solution is also effective. Rinse again with clear water, then allow the items to dry.

Webbing that is torn or frayed can be replaced easily. Kits containing inexpensive replacement webbing for lawn furniture are available at hardware stores. But the plastic webbing that comes with most lawn furniture, and is included in most repair kits, deteriorates in a relatively short period of time when exposed to sunlight.

Webbing of much higher quality, made of nylon formulated to withstand ultraviolet radiation (the agent in sunlight that causes plastic to deteriorate) is available at boating supply and marine hardware stores. Though more expensive, this "ultraviolet-inhibited" webbing lasts years longer and is more comfortable against the skin than plastic.

As a final step, lubricate hinged parts of the furniture by applying two or three drops of any lightweight oil (like 3-in-One) to each joint.

Wash cast-iron or other enameled metal furniture before storing, also. Use the same methods described previously. Car wax affords good protection over clean enameled surfaces but should not be applied where it will accumulate in crevices that are difficult to buff. Wax that cannot be buffed forms an unsightly residue when dry.

Inspect nonaluminum metal furniture carefully for loose paint or rust; if you find any, scrape the areas down to bare metal using coarse emery cloth. Polish away the scratches left by the coarse cloth by rubbing the scraped area with either a finer grade of emery cloth or with fine-grade steel wool until the surface is shiny.

Apply rustproof enamel to the areas by spraying it from an aerosol can rather than by using a brush, which often leaves the repair visible. Be sure to follow the safety and application instructions printed on the label. Two thin coats of enamel dry more quickly and create a smoother surface than one thick coat. If rustproof enamel of the appropriate color is not available, apply rustproof automobile primer first (also from an aerosol can), then cover the primer with ordinary enamel of the desired color.

In some cases even enamel that has been sprayed on will contrast noticeably with the surrounding surface. To camouflage the repair, allow newly painted areas to dry completely, then rub them and the surrounding surface with automotive polishing compound applied according to the manufacturer's directions. This will lessen the gloss of the fresh enamel and remove the faded surface of the surrounding finish, evening out the overall color. Apply a coat of automotive wax afterward to produce a uniform gloss over the entire surface.

Wooden furniture that is to stay outdoors over winter should be washed clean and stored under cover, but not sealed in a way that prevents air circulation. If plastic sheeting is used to cover a picnic table, place small wooden blocks on the table, under the sheeting, to hold the sheeting away from the surface. Weight the corners of the sheet at the bottom, or tape them together, to prevent them from being blown by the wind.

Benches should be stored by sliding them under the table or standing them on their legs on the tabletop. Stacking benches upside down on the top allows moisture to become trapped beneath them.

If wooden outdoor furniture has become blemished or faded, repairs to some kinds can be undertaken before storing. Painted or varnished furniture can be touched up if deterioration is not so widespread that complete refinishing is required. Furniture

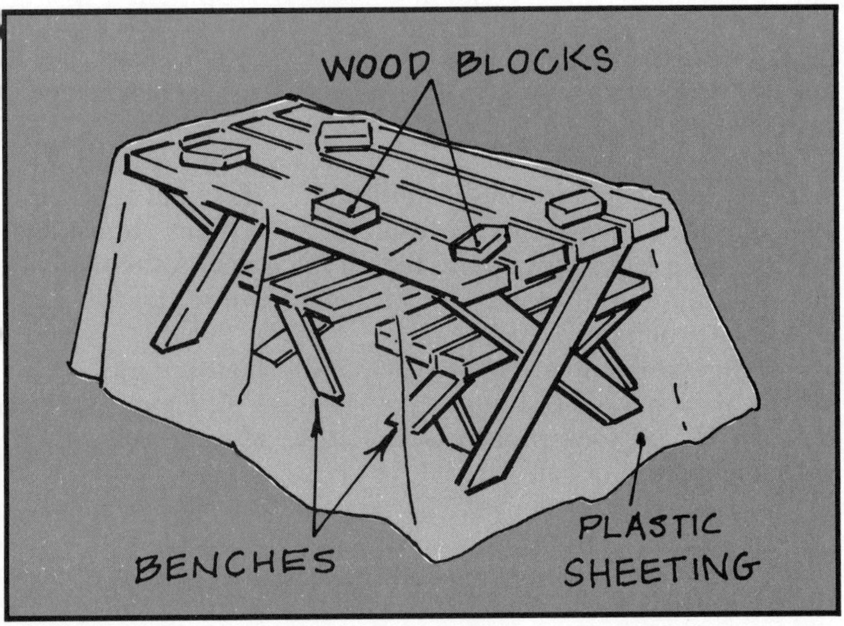

When storing a picnic table beneath plastic sheeting, place small blocks on the tabletop so that air can circulate. Slide benches beneath the table.

inished with stain can be restored by applying new stain. Clear vater-repellent sealer can be applied to furniture whose finish is n good condition.

As for barbecue grills, most will last many years if regularly scrubbed free of ashes with a dry brush and stored away from noisture. Some hardware stores carry heat-resistant enamel es- pecially made for stoves, barbecues, and hibachis. To apply it, the surface of the item must be thoroughly cleaned. Grease can be removed using either ordinary oven cleaner or a less caustic de- greasing spray made especially for outdoor barbecues. This is available at many hardware stores.

Gas-fueled barbecues may be stored outdoors beneath pro- ective fabric or plastic sheeting without disconnecting the gas ank. However, if stored indoors or in a garage, the tank must be disconnected and stored outdoors in a well-ventilated area away from heat, strong sunlight, and unauthorized handling.

Recreational equipment like volleyball nets, croquet sets, and other lawn games should be cleaned and thoroughly dried before storing. Nets should be repaired, if necessary, and carefully folded so they do not become tangled.

Take the opportunity to replace missing or broken items before storing the equipment. By doing so the games will be ready for use in spring and you may also be able to take advantage of fall sales on these items.

Store garden hose indoors or in a garage that offers protection against severe freezing. Drain the hose first and repair it, if necessary (hose repair kits are available at hardware stores), then coil the hose loosely on a hose reel or lay it flat on the floor. Do not hang hose from a nail. This weakens the hose and may cause it to crack when uncoiled.

Other garden items, particularly tools, should be washed free of dirt, then stacked or hung out of the way. Wipe metal surfaces with an oily rag to ward off rust. Lubricate moving parts of tools with a few drops of light oil.

Protecting Outdoor Metal Items

Fall is an ideal time to clean and protect outdoor metal items. Ridding them of rust and corrosion before storage prevents dete-ioration in the winter.

When using cleaning products, follow the manufacturer's in-tructions and safety precautions printed on the container labels. Wear rubber gloves to avoid prolonged skin contact with the roducts, and wash your hands thoroughly after you finish. Un-ss you are using detergent and water, work in a well-ventilated rea to avoid breathing fumes.

Any lightly soiled metal in good condition can be washed with trong household detergent mixed with warm water. Apply the olution with a cloth, sponge, bristled scrub brush, or nylon scour-ng pad. Then rinse with clear water and dry thoroughly using a nt-free cloth or chamois.

Metal that is moderately soiled, or that must be stripped of rease, oil, wax, or other film prior to painting, can be wiped with cloth dipped in mineral spirits.

Metal-cleaning fluid containing mineral spirits or a similar hemical is also available at hardware stores.

Very dirty metal like machinery can be immersed in degreas-ng solution, available at automotive stores. Spray-on degreaser is lso available. Wash the metal with detergent solution to remove he degreaser and grime, then rinse or spray thoroughly with ater, preferably hot.

Alternatively, wash or scrub very dirty metal with kerosene or charcoal-lighting fluid and wash as described. Never use gasoline to clean metals: It might explode.

Tarnished copper, brass, and bronze can be cleaned with a liquid or paste that works by chemical action. These tarnish removers will also eliminate corrosion. Read the label to be sure the cleaner is formulated for the type of metal you wish to clean.

Generally, these products leave a clear film, usually silicone, that temporarily inhibits further tarnishing. If you intend to apply a more durable protective coating like paint or a clear finish, this film must be removed by wiping with paint thinner or mineral spirits.

In all cases, steel wool of a very fine grade (No. 00 or finer) can be used to apply cleaner, remove corrosion, and polish cleaned surfaces. But, to avoid scratches, do not use it on softer metals like aluminum, copper, brass, and bronze. Steel wool will also scratch painted surfaces and those covered with clear finish like lacquer, acrylic finish, or polyurethane.

To remove rust and protect against its return on metal that will be painted, try one of the fairly new preparations called rust

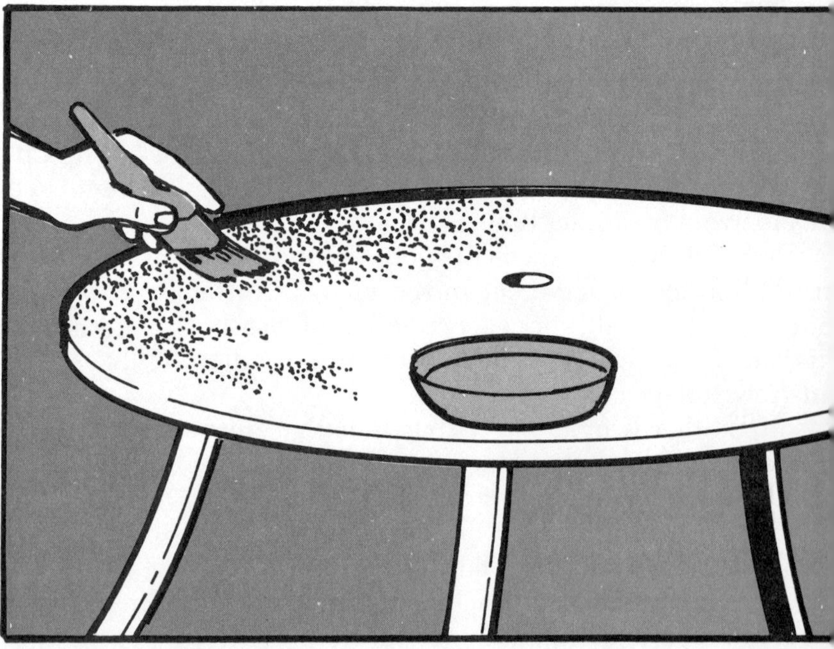

Apply rust converter to stop rust. The converter turns black as it dries and can easily be painted over.

onverters. This will eliminate most of the sanding usually neces-ary when treating rusty metal. In fact, a rust converter actually equires a rusty surface in order to work.

Most hardware stores carry rust converter. Typically, con-erter contains tannic acid or a similar ingredient that combines ith rust to form a black crystalline surface. This protects the etal underneath from further rust and can be painted without dditional preparation. Most converters also contain either a latex ompound or lacquer that adds another protective layer.

Rust converter is available as a liquid or aerosol. To apply it, rst scrape the rusty surface with a wire brush or sandpaper to emove flaking rust and loose paint. Then wash the surface with etergent and water as described, and dry it thoroughly.

Apply the converter in two thin coats. Product formulas dif-er, so follow the manufacturer's instructions about drying time etween coats. Converter is usually white or clear when applied ut becomes black when dry.

When applying liquid converter, either pour it onto the metal r pour as much as you need into a separate container and then pread it with a brush. Do not dip the brush in the original con-ainer after it has touched metal or pour leftover converter back nto the container, or you will contaminate the unused converter.

When the converter is thoroughly dry, usually three to wenty-four hours after application, any oil- or alkyd-based paint an be applied. When selecting paint, read the label carefully to e sure it is compatible with the type of metal being coated.

Specialized paints for metal are available. These include heat-esistant paint for barbecues and stoves, moisture-resistant paint or aluminum gutters, and paint formulated with zinc for rust rotection similar to galvanizing.

As with converter, two or more thin coats of paint produce etter results than one thick one. Instead of paint, a second appli-ation of converter can be made.

To remove rust or corrosion from iron, steel, or aluminum hat is not to be painted, use a chemical jelly containing phos-horic acid. Be sure it is formulated for the metal being treated. o apply it, wash and dry the metal, then spread the jelly liberally ver the surface using a paintbrush.

Allow the jelly to remain on the metal for the time specified n the label, usually no longer than forty-five minutes, then rinse off with water.

Repeat the process as many times as necessary to clean the etal. Buff the dull surface left by the jelly with steel wool or, to void scratches, with an appropriate metal polish.

All unpainted metal surfaces must be coated with oil, automobile wax, metal polish, or hard finish like lacquer, acrylic, or polyurethane to preserve them. This should be done as soon as possible after cleaning because even a few hours is enough time for corrosion to begin.

Cleaning Gutters and Downspouts

Roof gutters protect buildings from serious damage re-
ulting from poor drainage. Cleaning and repairing gutters is best done in spring and fall, but if you can find time to do this job only once a year, fall gutter maintenance is the more important.

When you work on gutters, choose a dry day after the leaves have fallen. Use an extension ladder to reach the gutters, and stand on it below the level of each gutter to work; cleaning gutters by kneeling on the roof invites a fall.

Take care to position the ladder properly before climbing it. The upper end should rest against a firmly anchored portion of he gutter and extend at least 12 inches higher. The foot of the adder should be set away from the base of the house a distance equal to one quarter of the ladder's height.

Carry with you a kit of tools consisting of heavy work gloves to avoid scrapes and scratches), a narrow gardening trowel or a plastic gutter scoop available at some hardware stores, a whisk broom, and a rag or wad of paper toweling.

To carry the tools, use a bucket equipped with a metal hook for hanging. While you are working, place the tools on the edge of the roof in front of you. Hang the bucket from a ladder rung and deposit gutter debris in it.

Start cleaning at a corner near a downspout. First, plug the top of the spout using the rag or paper toweling. Sweep into a pile the contents of the gutter that are within reach and use the rowel or scoop to shovel the material into the bucket. When you are finished, unplug the downspout.

TIP:

Metal ladder hooks for paint buckets are available at hardware stores, or you can make a hook by bending a piece of coathanger wire into an S-shape.

ATTENTION

TIP:

Mesh leaf guards tend to trap leaves and twigs on top of them. A relatively new style of guard is made of smooth aluminum sheet. The front edge curls downward, leaving a gap of about an eighth of an inch from the front edge of the gutter. Water flowing off the roof travels over the curl and into the gutter; leaves and dirt slide off the shield and fall to the ground.

ATTENTION

Move the tools as far in the direction opposite the downspout as you can comfortably reach (about 3 feet for most people) and set them down near the edge of the roof. Then climb down the ladder, carrying the bucket of debris.

Empty the bucket, then move the ladder about 6 feet farther from the downspout and repeat the process. When you climb back up to the gutter, the tools should be within reach.

As labor-saving as it might seem, cleaning gutters by using hard spray from a garden hose often causes more problems than it solves. Dirty water overflowing the gutter can muddy the siding, and debris can become lodged in downspouts. But after you have cleaned the gutters by sweeping them, flush each one with spray from a hose to check how well it drains.

The water should flow smoothly along the gutter and into the downspout. If water accumulates in pools along the gutter's length, its slope may be insufficient.

Gutters should slope downward at least ¼ inch for every 10-foot length. By measuring the vertical distance between the gutter and the horizontal edge of the roof, you can determine the present slope and also calculate the needed slope. To determine if individual gutter sections slope incorrectly, stretch a string from one end of the gutter to the other. The edges of each section should be parallel to the string. If any sections have slipped, inspect the gutter hangers supporting them. Reattaching the sections to any hangers from which they have come loose will probably restore the slope. Replace missing or broken hangers.

Should water fail to drain quickly from a downspout, the spout is probably clogged and must be cleared. To do this, use a plumber's snake or a drain auger. Insert the device into the spout at ground level and force it upward. If the downspout goes into the ground or is connected to more than one gutter, rent a motorized auger. To insert the auger, try to find a section of gutter near ground level that can be removed. The auger can then be directed either up or down. If this is not possible, insert the auger into the downspout opening at ground level.

TIP:

Butyl caulking compound works better to seal aluminum gutter sections. It is quite sticky: To make it easier to apply with a putty knife or gloved finger, dip both in mineral spirits first.

ATTENTION

Installing leaf guards over gutters will help prevent future blockages. Leaf guards are strips of plastic or metal mesh that slide beneath the lowest course of roofing and extend outward, covering the gutter. Water running off the roof can easily flow through the mesh and enter the gutter. Leaves and other debris cannot. Most hardware stores and home centers carry leaf guards. Homemade leaf guards can be made from strips of galvanized wire mesh with holes a quarter of an inch wide.

Leaking joints between gutter sections can be sealed with silicone or vinyl caulking compound. If possible, separate the secions of the joint, apply caulking compound to both surfaces, and hen reassemble. If the sections cannot be separated, clean the surfaces as well as you can. Next, spread caulking compound generously on the inside of the gutter and try to force some into the oint with a putty knife or finger. Smooth the compound so that no ridges can channel water into the leaking area.

Vinyl gutters contain certain seams called expansion joints; hese are left unsealed intentionally to permit the material to expand and contract with changes in temperature. These joints are usually found where straight sections join corner fittings. Do not mistakenly seal expansion joints.

Gutters made of galvanized metal can rust through if not kept clean. One method of repairing rust holes is to scrub the area clean with a wire brush, coat it liberally with asphalt or plastic roofing cement, then press a sheet of heavy-duty aluminum foil over the damaged area. Apply a second layer of cement, then a second sheet of foil. Finish by spreading on a third layer of cement, smoothed with a putty knife.

Wooden gutters should be treated with preservative and repainted about every five years. Be sure the wood is dry, then sand he troughs smooth. Apply a heavy-duty wood preservative containing copper naphthenate and sealer, or a thin coat of roofing cement mixed to brushing consistency with turpentine. Apply a second coat a few days later. Sand and repaint the outside of the gutter with two coats of exterior housepaint.

TIP:

Several new products are available for fixing leaky gutters. For minor repairs there is leak-sealing compound in an aerosol can. Simply clean the rusty area and spray it with the sealer, following the directions on the label.

For more substantial repairs there is metal patching compound, which comes in two parts: a liquid polymer and powdered cement and fillers. The parts are mixed and applied over fiberglass cloth supplied with the kit.

A third product is flexible plastic gutter lining of polyvinyl chloride, the same material used in plastic plumbing pipe. To install it, simply clean the gutter and cement the lining to it with the adhesive supplied. The material comes in long rolls to minimize seams.

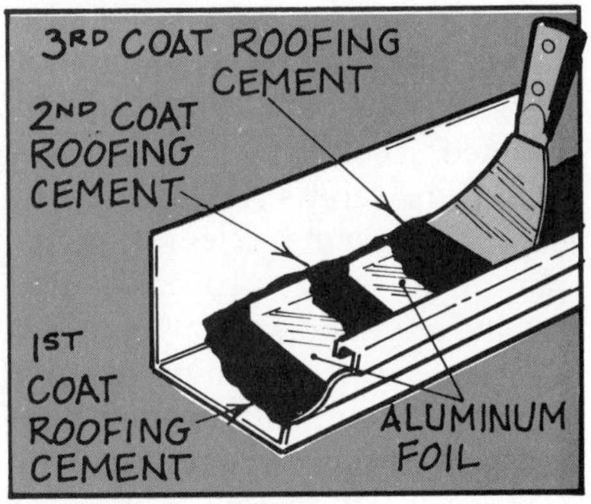

To prevent clogged gutters, install leaf guards.

An effective way to repair rust holes in galvanized gutters is to apply layers of roofing cement and heavy-duty aluminum foil.

Maintaining and Repairing Garage Doors

Happiness is an overhead garage door that slides smoothly up with no more than a tug and descends gently with the same small effort. Because of their many parts, garage doors need periodic maintenance to operate well and safely. Fortunately, the job is usually easy; however, some of the procedures may require two people.

Lubricating the rollers—the small wheels attached to the sides of the door—is the first step. To do this, simply squirt a few drops of lightweight household oil or spray a small amount of silicone lubricant onto their spindles.

Check that the hinges to which the rollers are attached are fastened securely to the door panels. If any hinges are loose, tighten the screws. If the screw holes have become enlarged, replace the present screws with new ones larger in diameter. Be sure that the hinges are properly aligned; the roller spindles should be parallel to the horizontal seams between door panels.

Inspect the condition of the rollers. Metal rollers seldom require attention, but nylon rollers can become damaged. Most hardware stores carry replacement rollers and other parts for garage doors. Replacing a roller usually involves unscrewing its hinge from the doors, then pivoting the roller free from the track.

If the garage door binds, inspect the tracks for misalignment. Where the tracks are vertical, check their alignment with a builder's level. Overhead, measure between them in several places; the distances should be the same.

If adjustments are necessary, loosen the bolts in the slotted rackets that fasten the tracks to the garage wall and ceiling joists. hen tap the tracks with a hammer until they are correctly posi-ioned. Retighten the bolts.

Track sections should also join smoothly end to end, and their dges should form a right angle with the roller spindles. If the rack appears twisted, bend the brackets or install wooden shims eneath them or against the sides of the tracks. Then lubricate he track surfaces with general-purpose automotive grease or pray-on silicone lubricant. If using grease, apply it sparingly or he tracks will become gummy. Spread the grease with a cloth to void injuring your fingers on sharp track sides or metal splinters.

Use the same lubricant, or powdered graphite, on the door andle and lock. If these assemblies do not operate smoothly even fter lubrication, remove them from the door to get to their mov-

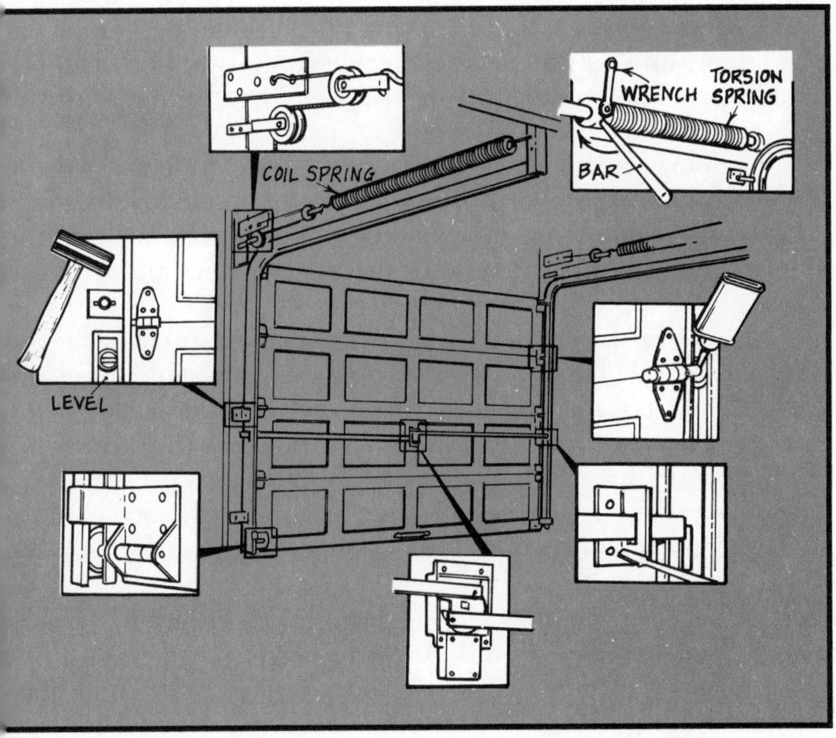

Details clockwise from top left show garage-door parts: coil and torsion springs, roller and hinged bracket, locking bars, lock mechanism, fixture that anchors cable and track, bracket for adjusting track, bracket and pulley at the upper end of the cable.

ing parts. Clean them with a cloth or an old toothbrush dipped in kerosene or charcoal-lighting fluid, then coat the parts with a thin layer of grease.

Misaligned lock bars—the metal rods extending from the door lock to the tracks—can cause door locks and sometimes handles to operate stiffly. Be sure the ends to the bars slide easily in and out of their slots in the tracks when the door lock is operated. If they do not, loosen the screws that fasten the adjustable bar guides at the sides of the door. Then lock the door and reposition the guides by sliding them up or down so that the bars travel smoothly. Retighten the guides.

Check the metal cables that run from the springs above the door to brackets on the door's bottom corners. If a cable is frayed, replace it by first raising the door fully to release all spring tension. Then have a helper hold the door in this position while you unfasten the cable. Do not try to work on a cable that is not completely slack.

On doors with a long coil spring at each side, perpendicular to the door, unhook the damaged cable from its top bracket, unthread it from any pulleys it runs through, then unfasten it from the bracket at the base of the door.

On doors with a single horizontal spring (called a torsion spring) fastened to the top of the doorway, parallel to the door, unfasten the cable from the door first. To do this, unwind the cable from its drum at the end of the axle to which the spring is attached.

The procedure for installing a replacement cable is the reverse of removal. Tighten the brackets or replace them if they are bent or broken. Cables must be the same length in order for the spring tension on both sides of the door to be equal. If the cables are of unequal length, the door may bind. Lubricate the cables and protect them from rust by wiping them with an oiled cloth.

A properly adjusted garage door should remain in place when the bottom is raised 3 feet from the ground. If raised higher, the door should creep upward slowly by itself. If positioned lower, the door should close on its own.

Adjust the springs only if the door does not operate satisfactorily after lubrication and other maintenance. First slacken them by raising and supporting the door. Then rehook the top end of each cable in one of the other holes or hooks in the mounting brackets. Hooking the cable farther from the spring tightens it; hooking the cable closer to the spring loosens it. Both springs should be equally stretched when the door is closed.

Torsion springs develop tremendous power and adjusting them is dangerous. It is best to leave the job to a qualified technician.

Electric garage door openers also require periodic care. Models differ, so consult your service manual. Besides lubricating parts and retightening fasteners, maintenance tasks most often include checking and adjusting the chain or belt tension, checking the settings that govern the opening and closing of the door, and testing the door's safety features.

Organizing a Garage

By the end of summer, most garages desperately need cleaning and reorganizing to put them in shape for winter. Two keys to setting a cluttered garage to rights are getting as many items as possible off the floor and following the advice of the adage, "A place for everything and everything in its place."

Garage walls offer a wealth of storage opportunities. For lightweight items such as garden tools, many varieties of hooks, hangers, racks, and holders are available. These are easy to install and provide the individualized storage necessary to prevent clutter.

Installing pegboard (perforated hardboard) paneling is another possibility. By using the many types of clips, holders, bins, and shelves designed for it, light- to medium-weight items of all kinds can be neatly stored where they are both visible and handy, and additional items can easily be added as they are acquired.

You might also consider making your own storage racks for lightweight tools. Use a length of one-by-three or wider lumber for the rack itself, and pairs of eight- or ten-penny (2½- or 3-inch-long) common nails to hold the items.

Begin by placing the length of lumber on a large, flat work surface like the garage floor. Arrange the items you plan to hang from the rack on top of the board, and mark points on the board for driving nails that will support them. Remove the items, then drive in the nails so that the heads slant upward slightly.

To fasten the rack to the wall, locate the studs first, if they are not exposed. Position the rack as high on the wall as is convenient to allow installing an additional rack below it. Align the rack horizontally using a carpenter's level. Then mark the position of the rack on the studs (or on the wall concealing them), and the positions of the studs on the rack.

Next, take the rack down and place it on top of a piece of scrap wood on the work surface. If you plan to nail the rack to the wall, drive an eight- or ten-penny nail into the board at each of the marked stud positions until the points barely protrude through the underside.

To fasten the rack with screws, drill pilot holes for 10-gauge, 2½-inch-long flathead wood screws all the way through the board. Reposition the rack against the wall and use the holes as guides for drilling pilot holes into the studs. Finish both methods by holding the rack against the wall and installing the fasteners.

When making an additional rack, position the pair of nails so that items hanging from them will fit between those hanging from the rack above.

Sturdy shelves are necessary for storing heavier or large items like lumber, building materials, outdoor equipment, and gardening supplies. Although steel utility shelving and components are

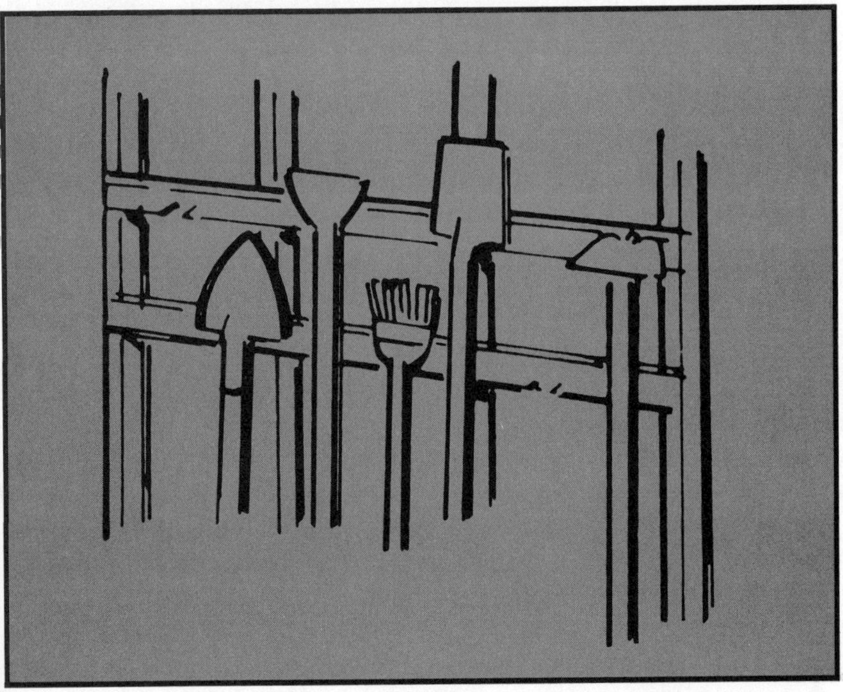

Racks keep lightweight tools handy.

available at home centers and department stores, wooden shelving is easy to make and less expensive.

To make simple wooden shelf brackets, use two pieces of one-by-three lumber—one piece to serve as a horizontal shelf support, the other to serve as a brace for the support, attached at an angle beneath it.

Cut both pieces to the same length (20 inches is the maximum recommended). Then miter the ends of the brace at 45-degree angles so that they slope toward each other.

If the wall studs are exposed, fasten the supports to the sides of the studs at vertical intervals equaling at least the length of a brace, and horizontal intervals of no more than 3 feet. Measure carefully so that shelves placed across the rows of supports will be level. Use two or more seven-penny (2¼-inch-long) nails or 10-gauge, 2-inch-long screws as fasteners.

If the studs are not exposed, find them inside the wall and fasten lengths of two-by-four lumber vertically over those spaced the desired distance apart. Position the two-by-fours so their wide dimension is against the wall. Then fasten the supports to their edges at the intervals described.

Nail or screw one end of each brace to the stud or two-by-four and the other to the underside of the support. To fasten the brace to the support, only a single 3-inch-long nail or screw is needed. However, with either fastener, drill a pilot hole into both pieces first.

Shelves may be wide boards or plywood. Fastening them to the brackets is not usually necessary.

If garage ceiling joists or collar ties are exposed, manageable items that are seldom used can be stored overhead. Lay a sheet of plywood (½-inch-thick or thicker) across the beams to make a platform for them that will be accessible from a stepladder.

If there is sufficient headroom, a second platform can be suspended beneath the beams. To do this, construct U-shaped wooden slings, each consisting of three lengths of one-by-three lumber fastened to create three sides of a square or rectangle. Attach the uprights of each sling to one side of each beam so that the slings are aligned and hang at an equal height. Then lay a piece of plywood across the slings (between the uprights) as a platform.

Valuable items like tools should be kept in locking cabinets. Old kitchen cabinets or gym lockers often suffice. Steel utility cabinets are also available, and, of course, you can make your own cabinets by using plywood.

Hazardous chemicals should be kept in cabinets, too. However, whether purchased or homemade, these cabinets should be designed especially for the purpose and provide both ventilation and security. Limit the amount of hazardous materials, particularly flammables, you accumulate. To find out how to dispose of these in your community, contact the fire department or sanitation authorities. Mount cabinets containing hazardous items high on the wall out of reach of children, but at a level where you can use the cabinets safely.

Store very heavy items, like bags of cement, on boards elevated a few inches off the ground by blocks.

Store seldom-used items on an overhead platform.

How and Where to Caulk

Sealing a home against drafts is important year-round, but it is especially crucial in cool or cold weather. One key to successful draftproofing is applying or renewing caulking compound, the puttylike material used to fill seams between building materials and gaps around items that penetrate exterior walls. Because caulking is most pliable and adheres best when temperatures are above 60 degrees Fahrenheit, early fall is an excellent time to perform this task.

Some places where caulking will do the most good are around stationary parts of window and door frames (weatherstripping should be used to seal the moving parts); where house siding joins at corners or meets the roof eaves and foundation; around wall and roof vents, skylights, and chimneys; around exterior water faucets; and where other plumbing or electric wiring enters the house.

When choosing caulking compound, often simply called caulk, life span and elasticity are most important. As caulk ages, it hardens and cracks, becoming ineffective.

The most durable and elastic caulks are usually the most expensive. But premium products are not necessary for caulking areas that require periodic repainting or repair, or that do not shrink and swell significantly with the seasons.

Probably the best, most economical caulk for general draftproofing is acrylic latex; it flows easily, and cleanup requires only soap and water. There are several grades; most manufacturers

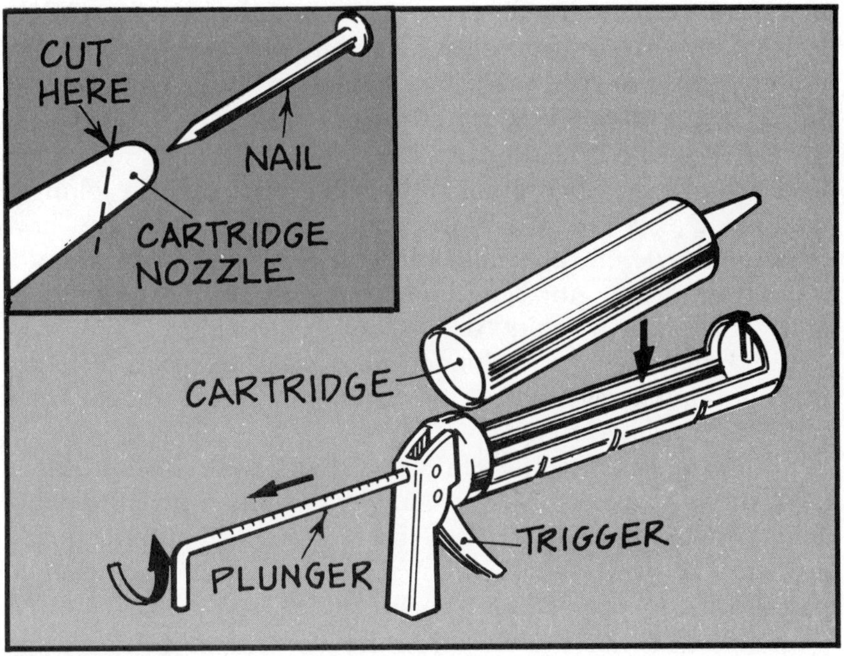

Load a cartridge gun by pulling back the plunger and inserting a cartridge back-end first. Snap the nozzle into the slot at the front end.

Slice the tip of the cartridge nozzle at a 45-degree angle (inset). Insert a long nail to pierce the tube.

estimate that the least expensive and least durable will last five years if covered by a coat of paint. Better grades containing silicone, rated to last ten to twenty years, are often available for not much more.

For caulking masonry and metal surfaces, neoprene or butyl caulk is recommended. Both types are stickier and more adhesive than latex caulks, making them more difficult to apply, and they require solvent (turpentine or mineral spirits) for cleanup. Their rated life span is usually ten to fifteen years. Protective painting is not necessary.

Pure silicone caulk is rated to last a minimum of twenty years. Although solvent must be used for cleanup, applying silicone caulk is easier than applying neoprene or butyl. A drawback of silicone caulk is that paint will not adhere to it. But it is manufactured in several neutral colors as well as clear.

Competing with silicone caulk are so-called high-performance caulks: polysulfide, polyurethane, and others. All are as long-last-

TIP:

Inexpensive caulking guns are fine for applying latex, silicone, and siliconized caulk, but for applying stiff caulk like neoprene or butyl, and for large jobs, a professional gun that delivers more thrust makes squeezing the trigger easier. These guns have a longer trigger than cheaper models and are constructed to reduce flexing.

ATTENTION

ing as silicone and not only accept paint but often cost less. High-performance caulks can be bargains, but when choosing among them it is wise to read the product labels carefully to make sure the life span and painting characteristics suit a project's needs.

Caulk is sold in cardboard tubes called cartridges and is applied using a cartridge gun. To load the gun, pull the plunger back as far as it will go and insert the cartridge, back end first. Press the nozzle on the front of the cartridge firmly into the slot at the front of the gun, then squeeze the trigger several times to tighten the plunger against the back of the cartridge.

With many guns the plunger must be rotated so its teeth are up to pull it back. To advance the plunger after loading, turn it so the teeth face down.

With the cartridge loaded, use a sharp knife to slice off the tip of the nozzle at a 45-degree angle, creating an oval opening about ⅜ inch in diameter. Then insert a long nail into the nozzle to open it. Provided the nail has a head, it can be used later to plug the nozzle, preserving caulk for reuse.

Caulk works best to seal joints that are half an inch or less in depth and width. Deeper cracks should be filled before caulking with wadded fiberglass insulation or other filler. Wider cracks can usually be bridged by making two applications of caulk side by side.

To apply caulk, first make sure the surface is clean, dry (if the instructions on the cartridge specify), and free of old caulk and flaking paint. Position the nozzle against one end of the seam to be filled; the gun should form a 45-degree angle with the seam.

Then push or pull the gun along the seam, squeezing the trigger to force caulking out of the cartridge. Pushing the gun usually forces caulk into the seam more effectively than pulling. Try to produce a smooth, uniform ribbon of caulk that fills and covers the seam. This sometimes requires practice; you must learn to keep the gun moving between trigger strokes, though not always at the same speed.

When you get to the end of the seam, push the nozzle into the caulking to slice it off, then twist the nozzle sharply as you bring it away. Stop compound from oozing from the nozzle by immediately pulling the plunger away from the rear of the cartridge. Wipe off the tip of the nozzle with a cloth or paper towel before starting a new seam.

Caulking need not be smoothed after it has been applied unless the ribbon is extremely distorted. Because caulk shrinks as

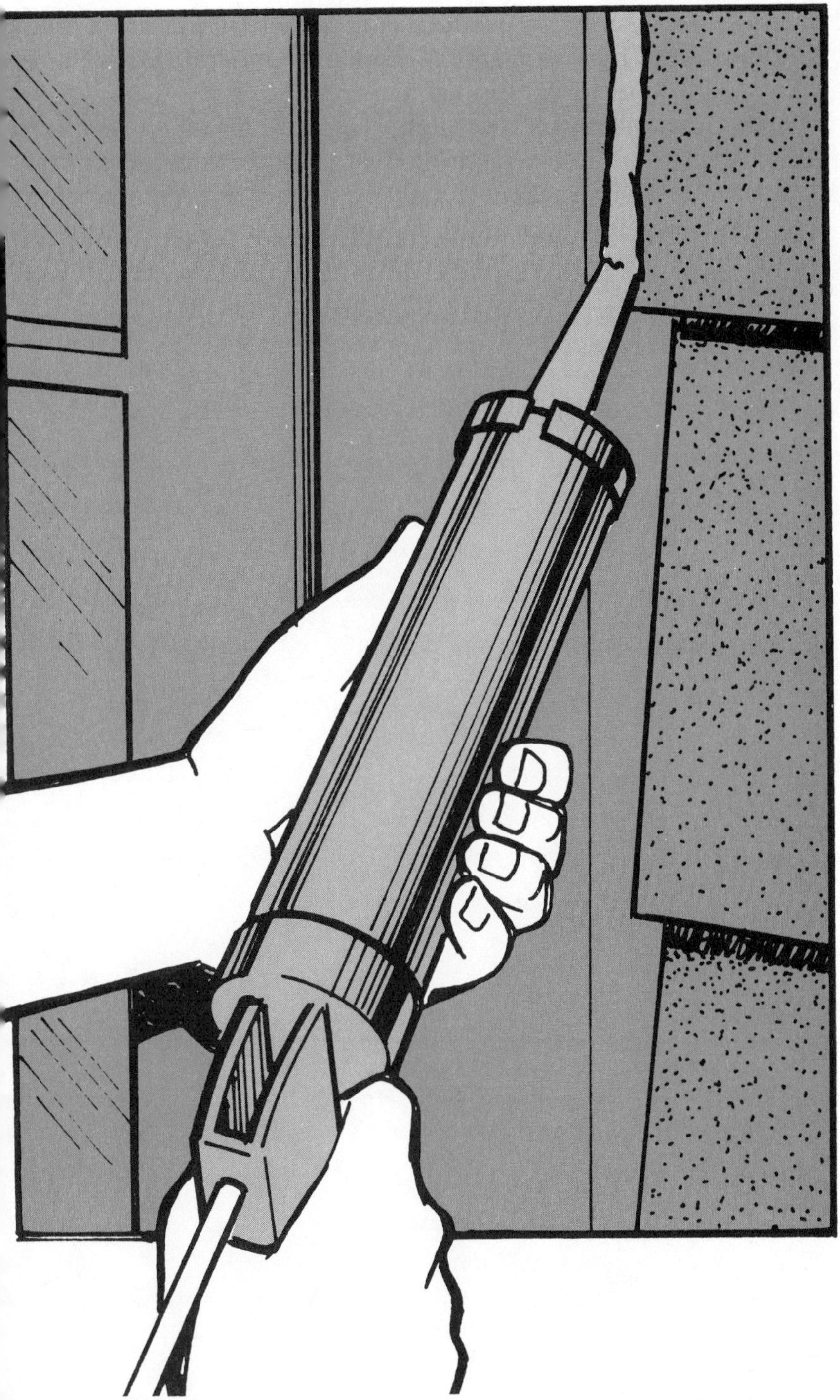

Apply caulk by holding the cartridge gun at an angle and either pushing or pulling the nozzle along the seam as you squeeze the trigger.

TIP:

To plug a caulking cartridge with a nail after it has been opened, insert the nail head first as far as it will go. This will prevent caulk from hardening inside the nozzle. To reopen the cartridge, pull the nail out with pliers.

ATTENTION

it dries, smoothing can produce cracks later. If you must smoot caulk, use the back of a spoon dipped in mineral spirits or, wit latex caulk, your finger dipped in water.

Allow caulk to dry thoroughly, according to the manufactur er's instructions, before painting over it. Otherwise, the paint ma crack as the caulking shrinks. Caulk that does not require paintin is often better left unpainted. Because caulk is more elastic tha paint, caulk's normal shrinkage and expansion will cause the pain to crack.

Using Foam Sealant

Polyurethane foam in pressure cans is a relatively recent product. Advertised primarily as an insulating filler to be used like caulking compound, foam is often better than caulking for filling large gaps because it adheres to almost any material and expands as it flows.

Foam has other uses, too. Applied between loose treads and risers it's an easy cure for squeaky stairs. Used as padding around pipes, foam prevents them from rattling against house framing. Carpenters use foam for delicately wedging window and door frames during installation, as a strong construction adhesive, and as a general crack filler that can be sanded smooth and painted.

Foam even makes an excellent base for automobile body filler, because it adheres well to metal despite constant vibration and flexing.

There is one drawback: Foam is tricky to use. It will bond to skin, clothing, and plastic eyeglasses. During application the can must be held upside down and the flow carefully regulated.

Most foam kits include disposable plastic gloves. They also contain a special nozzle that screws onto the pressurized can and a length of polyethylene tubing to direct foam into awkward nooks and crannies.

You will find it helpful to buy extra gloves (generally they become so sticky they cannot be reused) and a longer length of tubing. The longer tubing will allow you to hold the can properly while directing the foam beneath a large overhang, such as when sealing around an air conditioner or at the top of an exterior wall where siding meets a soffit.

Hold the can upside down and apply foam slowly to judge expansion. Wear disposable rubber gloves.

Depending on the brand, foam expands from 10 to 30 percent as it comes from the can, and expands somewhat more as it cures. Excess foam can be trimmed away later, but to avoid waste and unnecessary work, as well as poor results and the danger of marring neighboring surfaces, you should acquire the knack for applying the foam sparingly while drawing the tube at an appropriate speed along the area to be filled.

Before using the foam, practice dispensing it while holding the can upside down with one hand and manipulating the extension tube along a seam with the other.

Here is how to fill a cavity:

Clean dust and grease from the surfaces the foam will be applied to. It does not matter if the surfaces are damp; slight moisture speeds curing of most foams.

Cover areas where foam may spill or splatter with newspaper or polyethylene sheeting. To protect surfaces that cannot be masked, including skin, apply petroleum jelly.

Shake the can for thirty seconds. Hold the can and tube as shown in the manufacturer's instructions. Release the foam slowly, watching as it emerges through the tube. Regulate the pressure and draw the tube along to fill the cavity 40 to 75 percent full, again according to the manufacturer's instructions. If the cavity is uneven, fill the deepest part first.

Release the nozzle about five seconds before you wish the foam to stop flowing. If you are filling a seam, continue to draw the tube toward the end. When foam stops flowing, pull the tube away quickly.

Do not try to smooth or remove excess foam until it has begun to cure and is no longer sticky. With most brands, this means waiting twenty to forty-five minutes. Then excess foam can be pressed back into the cavity using a dampened finger, an ice cube, or a bevel-edged paint roller (used for corners) dipped in water.

Allow the foam to cure for another eight to twelve hours, then use a razor blade to trim away any excess. The foam can also be sanded and filled with spackling or other filler for a smooth finish.

Because polyurethane disintegrates after prolonged exposure to sunlight, foam applied to exterior locations must be painted or stained.

To store a partly used can of foam, remove the tube and nozzle from the can. Use a pipe cleaner dipped in fingernail polish remover or acetone to clean the nozzle and the can's valve stem. Clean the tube also, or else discard it and use a new one next time.

If the can has no cap, insert toothpicks in the valve stem and into openings in the nozzle and tube. Foam remaining will harden around the toothpicks; when you are ready to use the foam again, pull the toothpicks out and the plugs of hardened foam will come out also.

Uncured foam can be removed from skin, clothing, and other surfaces within five minutes using fingernail polish remover or acetone. If foam hardens on skin, wash with soap and water and apply hand lotion to the area. Foam may peel off after lotion penetrates. If not, continue washing with soapy water and scrub gently. Foam will gradually dislodge. On other materials, once curing has begun foam cannot be removed, even with solvents.

Foam flows and cures best at temperatures between 60 and 90 degrees Fahrenheit. To apply it in colder weather, warm the can at room temperature for several hours.

Cured polyurethane foam is not harmful. (This material is not the same as urea-formaldehyde, an insulating material that was found in the 1970s to emit toxic vapors.) However, do not use foam near excessive heat sources like woodstoves, fireplaces, and stovepipes. Foam will begin to smoke at temperatures above 240 degrees.

Also, avoid storing the can where temperatures may rise above 120 degrees. Foam inside the can may expand, causing the can to explode.

Weatherstripping Windows

Drafty windows rob heat from homes. One of the most ef- fective cures is to seal them with weatherstripping, usually a quick and easy task. In fact, often the most difficult part is choosing the right product from among the array available at hardware stores and home centers.

For double-hung windows, the most effective, durable, and least visible weatherstripping is channel stripping. This is installed inside of the window channels, the grooves in which the windows slide up and down. When the windows are closed, all but a tiny portion of the weatherstripping is hidden from view.

Channel stripping made of metal is the sturdiest variety. It is installed by nailing it along one edge using the small brass nails that are ordinarily provided. Another variety, vinyl channel stripping with adhesive backing, is less expensive and easier to install. However, it may loosen or crack after a few years.

To install either kind of stripping, start by cutting two lengths of material, each equal to the height of the lower window sash plus 1 inch. Raise the lower sash and insert a strip into the window channel on each side, feeding the upper end of the strip into the channel alongside the edge of the raised sash.

Install nails in metal stripping, beginning with the section below the sash. Be sure to sink the nail heads flush with, or slightly below, the surface of the metal. Then close the sash and install nails in the upper inch of stripping protruding above the sash.

TIP:

Window suppliers and some hardware stores carry plastic pulley covers to seal out drafts from sash-weight cavities. Pulley covers are easy to install; screws and gaskets are included.

ATTENTION

Afterward, pry the free edge of the stripping slightly away from the channel so that it will press tightly against the sash when the window is closed.

To install vinyl stripping, pull a small amount of the paper backing away from the adhesive before sliding a strip into place. After positioning the strip, gradually pull the remainder of the backing free while pressing the strip against the channel.

Lower the sash and press the upper portion of the strip against the channel. Then pry the halves of the stripping slightly apart so they will press against the sash.

Next, install strips in the channels of the upper sash by lowering the sash fully and repeating the procedure. If there are pulleys in the sides of the channels, attach stripping above and below them.

With metal strips, install nails in both edges of the upper strips near the ends that lie next to the pulleys. This will prevent the free edges of the upper strips from catching against the top

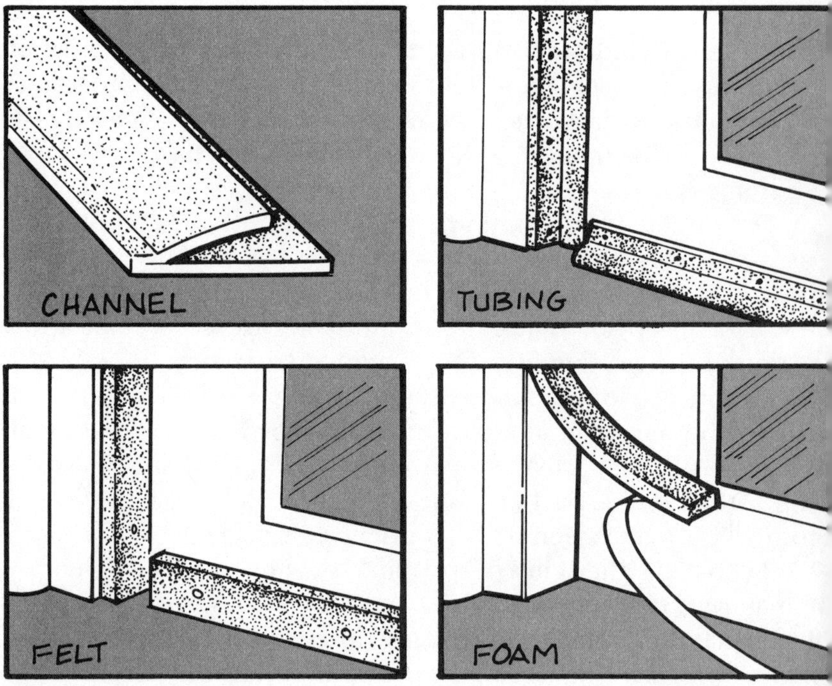

Channel stripping is durable, effective, and nearly invisible when installed. Tubing, felt, and foam are cheaper and more conspicuous, but they provide good short-term results.

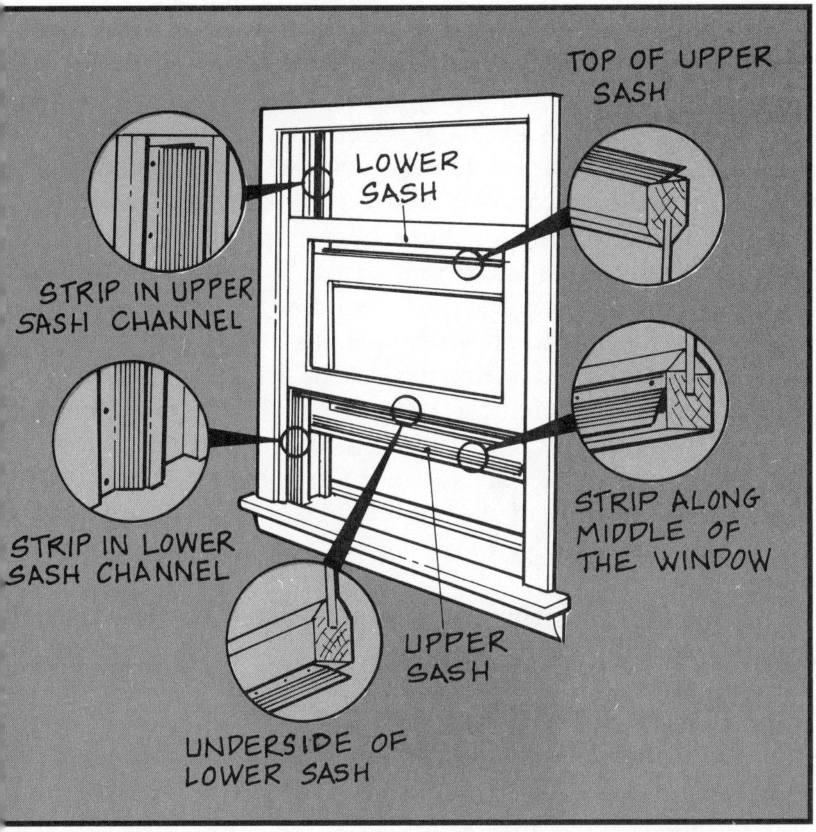

nannel stripping applied to a double-hung window, as en from the inside.

the upper sash when it is raised from a position below the lleys. With vinyl strips, snip the lower corner of each free half f at a sharp angle.

Also apply stripping along the top surface of the upper sash d the underside of the lower sash. The nailing edge or crease ust face indoors.

Finally, apply stripping to seal the gap between the upper d lower sashes where they meet when the window is closed. If u have access to the exterior of the window or can remove the ner sash, mount the stripping against the upper outside edge of e inner sash, with the nailing edge or crease pointing down- rd. In this location, the strip will remain hidden even when the shes are partly open.

If you cannot gain access to this surface, attach the strip ross the lower indoor-facing edge of the upper sash, with the ge or crease pointing upward.

Besides channel stripping, other kinds of weatherstrippi
that are effective include foam-filled or hollow vinyl tubing (som
times called gasketing) and felt or foam strips.

Tubing provides excellent sealing and is more durable th
either felt or foam strips. However, it must be attached to visil
parts of the window and frame, and so installation should be
the outdoor side of the window wherever possible.

To install tubing, cut it into strips. Position each one, exce
the strip across the middle of the window where the sashes me
so that the tube portion lies against both the sash and frame wh
the window is closed. Then fasten the stripping in place usi
staples or tacks. Stretch the stripping slightly as you fasten it
that it does not ripple.

Where the sashes meet, the easiest place to attach tubing
along the underside of the upper sash so that it presses agai
the upper exterior edge of the lower sash. It cannot be put out
sight.

Felt and foam strips are the least durable and least expensi
types of window weatherstripping. Both are simply narrow r
of material that, like the other kinds, must be cut into strips
appropriate length.

Like tubing, both felt and foam weatherstripping must
attached to visible parts of the window. However, because th
lack durability they must be applied on the indoor side.

Felt is attached by using staples or tacks. Foam is usua
adhesive backed and applied as described for vinyl channel str
ping.

No matter what the material, mount the strips as you wou
tubing—but on the inside of the window—so that they seal t
gap between the window frame and the sashes when the wind
is closed. Across the middle of the window, attach the material
the top surface of the inner sash, separated by the window latc

For wooden casement windows, install metal or vinyl chan
stripping. If the window opens toward the exterior of the hou
attach the strips so they flare toward the interior. If the windo
open in, place the weatherstripping to flare toward the outdoo

Metal casement windows usually require special vinyl or ru
ber stripping that is grooved to fit over the inner edges of t
window frame. Some hardware stores, especially those that rep
storm windows, carry stripping for casement windows. Oft
though, you must obtain this special kind of stripping from t
window manufacturer.

Gaps between nonmoving window parts should be seal
with caulking compound. Silicone or siliconized formulas are e

TIP:

Caulking can also be applied to interior window trim where it meets the wall, but care must be taken to do the job neatly. Start by cleaning the outer edges of the trim by washing it with mild detergent, then rinse, dry, and wipe with mineral spirits. Attach strips of masking tape on each side of the seams to protect walls and obtain a straight edge.

Cut the nozzle of a fresh tube of caulking compound off at a 45-degree angle to produce an opening less than a quarter inch in diameter. Apply caulk, then smooth it with a moistened finger to make a slightly concave surface. Gently remove the masking tape by pulling it off at right angles to the surface. For more advice on caulking, see pages 318–322.

ATTENTION

est to apply. Use butyl caulking compound to seal gaps between wood and masonry.

If possible, apply caulking compound around the entire perimeter of the window frame where it meets the exterior siding. Also raise the lower sash and apply caulk where the edge of the sill overlaps the bottom of the window frame and meets the vertical parts of the window frame and trim.

If combination screen and storm windows are installed, caulk these on the outside or inside, sealing the perimeter of the frame. Because aluminum storm window frames expand and contract with temperature changes, these must also be caulked where their sections join. If you can reach only the inside, caulk the section seams at corners. However, if you can reach the outside of the windows, caulk not only the corners but also any vertical seams where frame sections interlock.

Don't use caulk on removable wooden storm windows. Instead, install metal or vinyl channel stripping, positioned to flare toward the outside, so that the strips are compressed when the windows are installed.

Weatherstripping Doors

A **drafty front door can cause as much heat loss as se** eral drafty windows. Although most exterior doors have weathe stripping to seal out drafts, it is often damaged by wear. Replacin damaged weatherstripping or installing new weatherstripping not difficult. There are two parts to the project: sealing the sid and top of the door, and sealing the bottom.

A simple, inexpensive way to seal around the sides and top a door is to attach foam-edged wooden strips to the doorwa These are available at many hardware stores and home center The strips come in long lengths and must be cut to fit with a sa To install them, cut a section equal to the length of the st molding. This is the narrow piece across the top of the door fran against which the door presses when closed.

Place the cut strip on a flat work surface and take three of th small nails usually supplied with the strip. Drive one at each en and one in the middle, but only until the points protrude throug the strip.

Then go outside, close the door, and fit the strip into pla by holding it against the underside of the molding so that th foam touches the door. Press the strip against the door to com press the foam slightly, but not enough to force the door aw from the molding. While holding the strip in this position, dri the nails firmly, but not all the way, into place.

Test the door by opening and closing it a few times. Whe the door closes easily and the weatherstripping is compress along its entire length, drive the nails the rest of the way. The add more nails at approximately 4-inch intervals.

Next, measure the vertical lengths of stop molding on each de of the door frame and cut sections of weatherstripping to fit iem. The tops of these sections must touch the underside of the eatherstripping just installed, and the bottoms must touch the oorsill or threshold.

Install the vertical strips by following the steps just described. /hen you have finished, the foam portion of the weatherstrip-ing should form a continuous seal around the sides and top of ie closed door.

To protect and camouflage the wooden strips, drive the nails elow the surface using a nail set. Then fill the holes with exterior ood putty, sand the filled areas, and paint or stain the strips to iatch the doorway.

More durable kinds of weatherstripping are also available. istead of unprotected foam, one has hollow or foam-filled vinyl ibing, and aluminum strips rather than wood. There are also vo kinds of weatherstripping that will outlast even this: spring ietal and V-stripping. These fit against the sides and top of a oor frame, rather than against the stop molding, and cannot be een when the door is closed.

Spring metal weatherstripping is a thin, flexible strip of ronze or steel. It is attached along one edge with short nails. '-stripping is flexible vinyl folded lengthwise and backed with dhesive. Although less durable than spring metal, V-stripping eals out drafts just as well, and is less expensive and usually easier) install.

Both types of weatherstripping are installed the same way. 'irst, cut a length to fit across the door frame at the top and cut vo lengths to fit along the sides. Then cut the side strips into egments, discarding the material that would otherwise cover the inges and door strike (the metal plate surrounding the latch pening). These items must be left exposed.

Position spring metal strips in the doorway so that the edge) be fastened will be the first edge the door touches as it closes. Vith V-stripping, the crease that divides the strip lengthwise hould face this direction. Adjust both types of strips so that their nattached edge will flatten and lie next to the stop molding when ie door is closed.

Fasten the strips into place by nailing or by pressing the ad-esive-backed portion against the door frame. Then use the blade f a putty knife to pry the unattached edge of the weatherstrip-ing outward, away from the door frame. This will cause it to seal ghtly against the door.

Yet another type of door weatherstripping consists of inter-cking strips of spring metal. One part is attached to the door

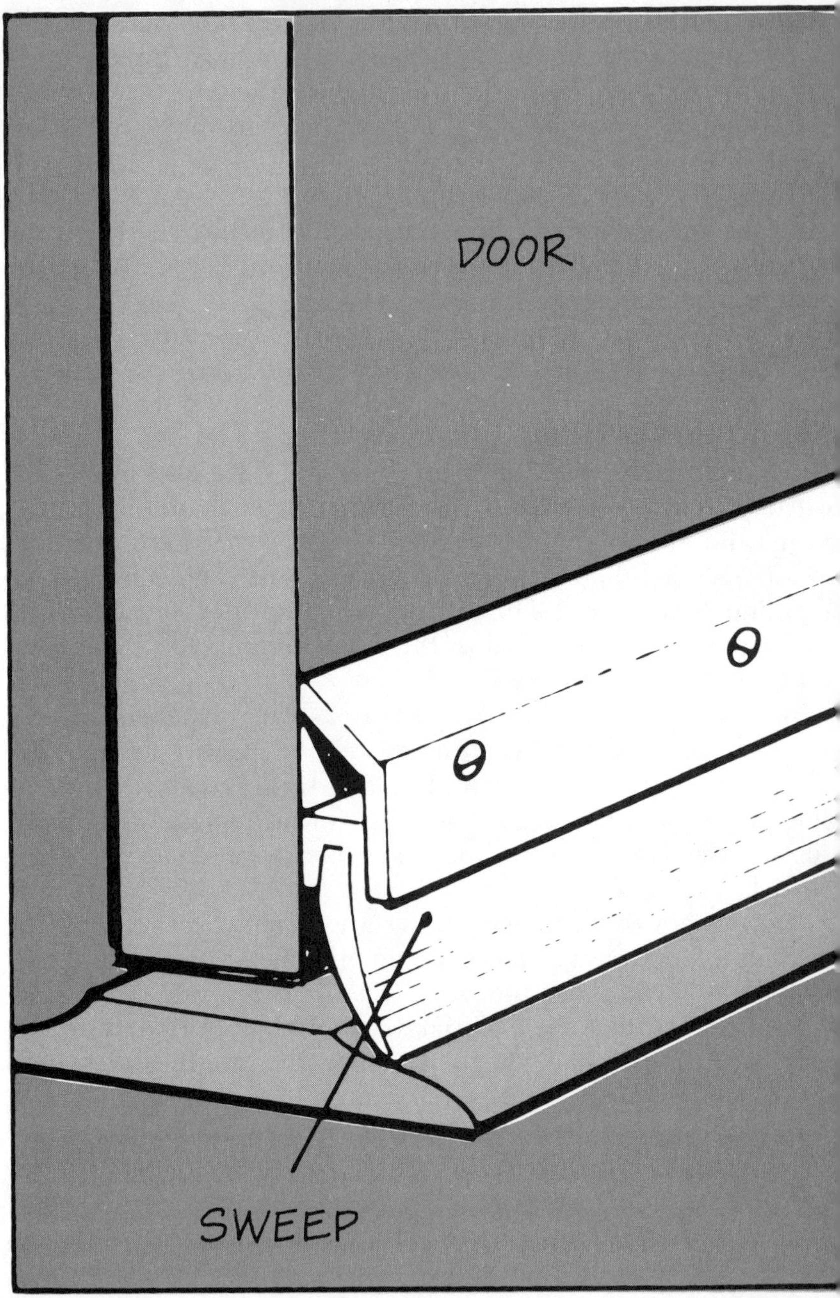

Attach the door sweep to the outside of the door so the bottom edge of the sweep seals against the threshold.

frame and the other to the door, creating an excellent seal. Instal-lation is tricky, however, as it requires careful fitting.

To seal the bottom of a door, install a door sweep, door shoe or weathertight threshold. Installing a door sweep is easy and i scribed below. The door shoe and weathertight threshold usu-y require removing and trimming the door.

If the door opens over a hard-surfaced floor, use a one-piece or sweep. If the floor is carpeted, use a spring-loaded, auto-atic sweep. To attach either kind, position the sweep across the tside edge of the door so that the bottom edge of the sweep als against the threshold but does not prevent the door from ening and closing smoothly.

With a pencil, mark the door along the upper edge of the eep and where the mounting screws must be installed. Drill ot holes into the door—the holes should be slightly smaller an the diameter of the screws—then align the sweep with the arks and fasten it with the screws.

Automatic sweeps usually also require installing a small metal ate or pair of small knobs against the sides of the door frame out an inch from the bottom. These force the sweep, which rings upward automatically when the door is opened, down-ard when the door is closed.

Preparing and Installing Storm Windows and Doors

Most homes feature storm windows and doors as sto dard equipment. Probably the most popular are aluminu framed combination units that include screens as well as gla Because storm windows and doors require little upkeep, m owners pay slight attention to them. But some maintenance advisable, and minor repairs made before cold weather arrives c often prevent major annoyances. If your home lacks storm wi dows or doors, or if you wish to replace existing ones, you c often save money by installing them yourself.

Readying and Maintenance

Rub frames and sashes with fine steel wool once or twic year to rid them of corrosion. Wiping the metal afterward wit cloth dipped in paste wax will protect them further.

Spray window tracks with silicone lubricant to keep sas sliding smoothly. Also, probe the weep holes at the base of w dow frames with a wire to clear them of debris. Weep holes all condensation to escape from the space between the primary wi dows and the storms. Moisture trapped between windows c cause wooden windowsills to decay.

If condensation forms on the inside of storm window sash during winter, add or replace weatherstripping around the p mary sashes. Weatherstripping will prevent warm air in the buil ing from escaping into the space between the windows, whi causes the problem.

If condensation forms on the inside of primary sashes, the roblem is usually with the storms. They may be allowing cold utdoor air to enter between the windows. To solve the problem, rst be sure the storm sashes are properly closed and that they fit ghtly in the window tracks and at the top and bottom of the rame. A common mistake that results in poor fits is confusing the pper and lower storm sashes when closing them. The upper sash the one that fits in the outermost window tracks. The lower sash hould be in the tracks next to it, and the screen should be in the nnermost tracks.

If the storm sashes are properly closed, try renewing or in-talling weatherstripping where their frame meets the frame of he primary window. Caulking is the most effective weatherstrip-ing along this seam, but narrow strips of foam rubber weather-tripping with adhesive backing also can be used. Caulking can be pplied on the outside of the building or to the inside. Foam strips re meant for inside application only.

To cure condensation problems affecting storm doors, check he weatherstripping and thresholds that seal the doorway.

If storm window sashes do not close properly, or if they bind ven when lubricated, the solution is to loosen or remove the rame, reposition it so that the sashes close correctly, then refasten t. This is usually not too difficult provided you have access to the utside of the storm window. You will need a ladder and a few ools, including a screwdriver and probably an electric drill.

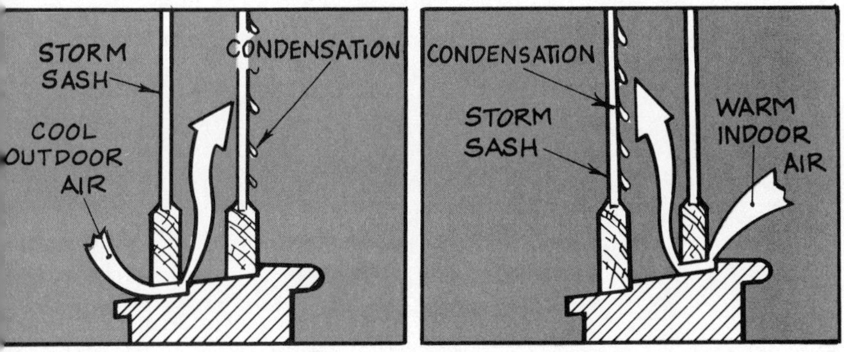

o prevent condensation inside storm sashes, seal rimary windows to keep indoor air from leaking. If ondensation forms on the indoor side of the primary vindows, seal storms to keep out cooler outdoor air.

> **TIP:**
>
> Forcing storm sashes up and down can twist the frames, making a small problem worse. To nip sticking window sashes in the bud, lubricate the tracks with silicone spray or a similar lubricant whenever the problem occurs.
>
> **ATTENTION**

Start by closing both storm sashes if you can. Then go outside and remove the screws holding the storm frame to the primary frame, but leave a single screw in the horizontal piece that spans the top of the storm frame and also a single screw in the piece that spans the bottom.

While someone inside the building operates the sashes, pry gently against the sides of the frame at the top and bottom corners using a putty knife or screwdriver. When the sashes slide smoothly, replace the screws in the frame piece whose positions remain unchanged.

Drill new screw holes into the primary window frame for any pieces whose position did change. To do this, hold each unfastened storm frame piece firmly in its new position and use the existing holes in the piece as drilling guides.

If a new hole in the primary frame will be more than an eighth of an inch away from an original hole, use a drill bit slightly smaller in diameter than the present screws and refasten the frame using those screws.

If the new hole will be less than an eighth of an inch from the original, drilling it will most likely only enlarge the original hole. To avoid this, drill a larger hole and install a larger screw. You probably will have to enlarge the hole in the storm frame also, but with an electric drill and an ordinary—but sharp—hardened-steel bit, this should not be a problem. Operate the drill at slow or medium speed. For aluminum window frames, use aluminum screws with round heads.

After the repositioned storm frame is fastened, apply fresh caulking around the perimeter on the outside of the building. Avoid covering the weep holes.

Installing Storm Windows

If your home does not have combination storm windows, installing them yourself is usually fairly easy. Choose windows that are already prehung; that is, mounted in their frames. These are manufactured to fit nearly all standard window openings and can also be obtained in custom sizes.

To find the size storm window you need, measure the length and width of the primary window frame on the outside. If the frame has blind stops—strips of molding around the perimeter that hold the upper sash in place—select storm windows that can be set into the opening and fastened to them. If not, select windows that overlap the outside trim (called casing) of the primary window.

To install a storm window, first try the fit of the frame by removing the sashes and screen and setting it into the primary window opening. If trimming is necessary to fit the frame to the slope of the windowsill, follow the instructions for trimming that come with the window.

To install the frame permanently, apply caulking to all surfaces that will contact the primary window frame, and press the frame into place. Square it by adjusting the sides until the distance between each pair of diagonal corners is the same.

Next, drill a hole through the top of the storm frame into the primary frame, and a similar hole through the bottom of the frame. (If the storm frame is predrilled, use those holes as guides for drilling into the primary frame.)

Fasten the storm frame to the primary frame by installing the top and bottom screws. Then, while a helper operates the sashes from inside to maintain the frame's alignment, drill holes through the sides of the frame (as well as additional ones in the top and bottom), and install the remaining screws.

Installing Storm Doors

The frames of most storm doors fasten against the edge of the doorway's exterior trim (also called casing). When the storm door is closed, it should be flush with the wide surface of the casing, which is parallel to the surface of the siding.

To determine the width of the frame needed for a storm door, measure the width of the present door opening between the edges of the casing. To determine the height, measure between the top and bottom of the opening, but allow for the sloping upper surface of the threshold. As with storm windows, the bottom ends of a storm door frame must usually be trimmed during installation.

Determine also whether to order a door that is hinged on the right side or the left when viewed from the exterior of the house. For easy passage through the doorway, the hinges should be on the same side as those of the entry door.

To install a storm door, first unpack it carefully from the shipping carton, following the manufacturer's instructions regarding removal of any temporary fasteners. Remove the glass storm pane if it is installed, and also the screen if possible (on some doors the screen is permanently mounted).

Next, test the fit of the door in the opening and, if necessary, trim the frame to accommodate the slope of the threshold, following the instructions that come with the door.

Apply caulking compound to the surfaces of the casing and threshold against which the frame will rest, then position the frame for permanent fastening in the opening.

Have a helper hold the frame while you check its alignment. To confirm that the frame is vertical, hold a builder's level agains it, and also operate the door: If the door swings open or shut b itself, the frame is not vertical. If the door binds, check that th frame pieces meet at right angles by measuring between them a described for adjusting storm windows.

To fasten the frame, begin by installing a single screw at th top. Then install screws along both sides, making sure the fram stays in alignment during the process by operating the door oc casionally.

Repairing Door Closers

Most storm and screen doors are equipped with mechanisms to assure automatic closing and to protect the door from opening too wide or being blown open by wind. Although these door closers seldom break, they need regular lubrication to keep them operating smoothly and occasional adjustment to compensate for internal wear. A common problem caused by both inadequate maintenance and improper installation is that the brackets loosen from the door or door frame.

The most popular door closer is the pneumatic type, consisting of a long, horizontal tube enclosing a piston and rod. Provided the closer is working well, the only maintenance required is wiping the rod with an oily cloth once or twice a year.

If the door swings shut too rapidly or too slowly, however, adjust the closer by rotating the tube. To do this, first open the door a few inches and slide the hold-open washer along the rod until it is against one end of the tube. This prevents the rod from fully entering the tube and the door from closing, and will make reinstallment easier.

Remove the metal pin that links the other end of the tube to the bracket attached to the door. This should be the end opposite the rod and washer. If the rod is attached to the door bracket, instead, the closer is incorrectly installed, which may also be causing the problem.

To remove the pin, tap it upward, using a hammer. Then pull it straight out from the top of the bracket. Some models have no pin; the tube simply unhooks from the bracket.

TIP:

Some door closers are adjusted by turning a screw in the end of the tube opposite the rod. Arrows on the tube indicate which direction to turn the screw. Unhooking the tube from the bracket is not necessary.

ATTENTION

TIP:

To fill screw holes in wooden doors after relocating a closer, either pack them with wood putty or drill them larger using a ¼-inch diameter drill bit and then glue in solid wood plugs cut from dowels. Sand both repairs smooth, then refinish. To repair holes in aluminum doors, fill them with Liquid Solder, a metallic adhesive resembling aluminum in appearance. File the repair flush with the surface, then sand the area with 600-grit silicon carbide paper.

ATTENTION

Instructions on the tube state what direction to rotate it. With most models, if the door closes too rapidly, the tube must be rotated clockwise as viewed from the end opposite the rod. If the door closes too slowly, the tube must be rotated counterclockwise.

Rotate the tube one complete revolution in the appropriate direction. Then reattach the tube to the bracket and test the door. If further adjustment is needed, repeat the process, but rotate the tube only half a revolution each time.

If the closer still does not work satisfactorily, try shifting the position of one or both brackets holding it. Check to see that the rod enters the tube fully when the door is closed. If it does not, and stronger closing is desired, loosen or remove the door bracket, move it toward the hinge side until the rod enters the tube fully, then reattach the bracket. This increases the angle the tube makes with the door.

To achieve the same effect if the rod already fully enters the tube, reposition the bracket attached to the door frame. Refasten the bracket so that its base is at least half an inch away from the door. If less closing power is desired, reposition the brackets to decrease the angle.

Fixing loose brackets may require ingenuity. First try replacing the bracket screws with larger-diameter ones. In wood, longer screws can be tried, but often the thickness of the door is a limiting factor. If the brackets have extra holes more than half an inch away from the present holes, relocate the loose screws or the new ones to the extra holes.

If the surfaces to which the brackets are attached are so damaged that even new screws will not hold, consider relocating the entire closer. Almost any place along the door frame is satisfactory, as long as the necessary angle between the tube and door can be maintained and the washer that holds the door open can be operated easily. When mounting a closer near the top of a door, however, make sure it will not interfere with the doorstop chain. And when mounting the closer near the bottom, be sure it will neither interfere with the threshold of the main door nor be an obstacle.

An alternative to relocating is to repair the original area and reattach the closer. This avoids having to restore the appearance of the damaged area after the closer has been moved.

To patch a damaged door, get a small piece of material similar to that of the door. Cut the strip so that it extends at least 2 inches beyond the damaged area on each side. Drill two or more holes through the strip to accept screws, then hold it in position against the door.

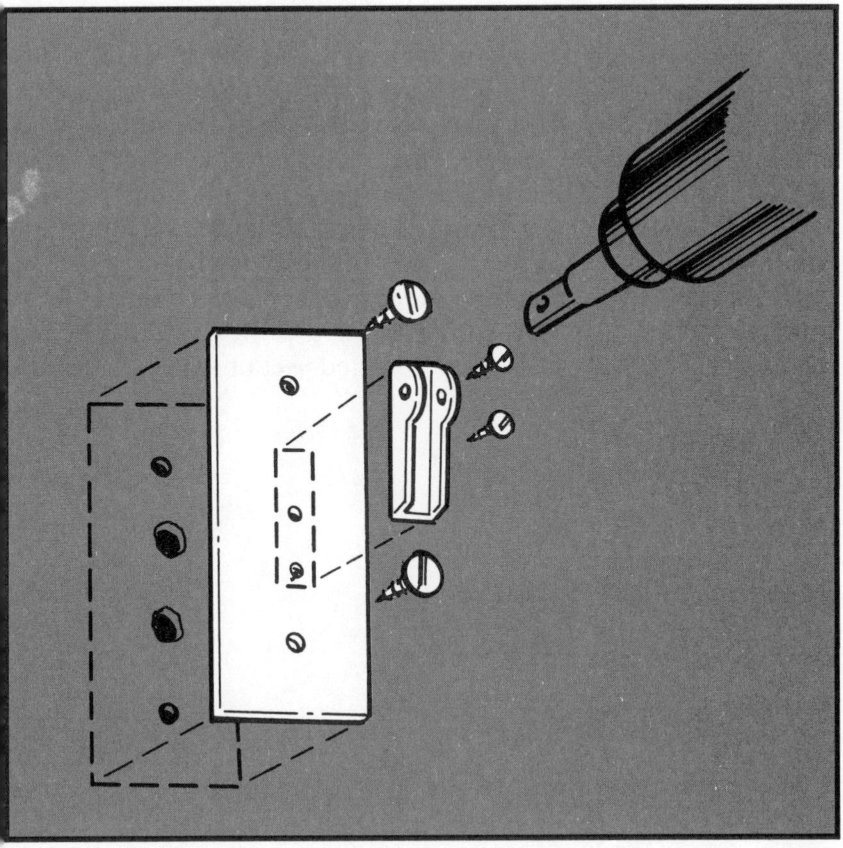

Attaching new material to a door covers damage and permits refastening a loose bracket in its original position.

Using the holes in the strip as a guide, mark the screw locations onto the door with an awl or a nail. Then remove the strip and drill holes for the screws in the door. If the door is wood, use flathead wood screws and drill holes only slightly smaller in diameter than their thickest threaded part. In metal, use panhead screws designed for sheet metal and drill holes just large enough to accept their points. Screws in metal must cut their own holes to fasten tightly.

If the strip is wood, paint it to protect it, then attach it to the door by installing the screws. Drill holes in the strip for the bracket screws, and attach the bracket to the strip directly over its original location.

If the door frame bracket is attached to stop molding (the vertical strip of wood in the door frame that lies next to the outside of the main door when it is closed), replace the molding with a new piece from a lumberyard. Paint it and attach it to the door frame using six-penny (2-inch-long) finishing nails. When nailing, close the main door and place a credit card between it and the molding. This creates a small gap that allows the door to close without binding. Fasten the bracket to the new molding.

Sometimes the door frame bracket is attached to the side of the frame, which is nonremovable. You may be able to repair the damaged area with a strip of new material. Otherwise, relocate the closer or turn the problem over to a professional carpenter, who will probably replace the damaged section with a carefully-fitted patch.

TIP:

Insulation reduces household fuel costs by slowing the passage of heated or cooled indoor air to the outside (and the infiltration of outdoor air to the inside), and contributes to comfort by minimizing drafts and helping to maintain uniform room temperature.

In 1989, the United States Department of Energy increased the recommended minimum amounts for residential insulation. Therefore, if your house was insulated only to meet earlier standards, you may benefit by adding more. You can obtain a free guide to adding more insulation by contacting the Office of Conservation and Renewable Energy Inquiry and Referral Service, P.O. Box 8900, Silver Spring, MD 20907 (tel. 800-523-2929). Ask for the *Department of Energy Fact Sheet,* Publication FS142.

ATTENTION

Insulation Basics

Selecting the right home insulation can be bewildering and can needlessly forestall an otherwise relatively easy installation project. However, the varieties of insulation can be categorized, and by matching what is available within these categories to your situation you can quickly make a suitable choice.

Types of Insulation

The building industry rates insulation capacity by a system called R-values, a measurement of air-flow resistance that gauges how well a material prevents heat from passing through it. The higher the R-value, the more effective the insulation.

Insulation comes in several forms, which differ in composition and insulating capacity. It can be manufactured as loose fill (pellets packaged in bags); in large flexible sheets or spun fiber called blankets; in batts, which are small blankets; and as rigid panels made of plastic foam.

Loose fill insulation is recommended for spreading between attic floor joists and on other horizontal surfaces. Although sometimes advertised as appropriate for filling wall cavities, loose fill settles with time, leaving upper parts of cavities empty.

Blanket insulation is useful for covering exposed frames of walls, ceilings, and floors (or for filling between framing members), and for wrapping heating ducts. Its main advantage is shape: The long, wide strips can often be installed in one piece, reducing the labor involved in cutting and fitting smaller pieces, and also reducing air leakage where separate pieces join. Blanket insulation is particularly useful in old houses that have irregular spaces between studs, rafters, and joists.

Batts are the most common home insulation. They are simply strips of blanket insulation precut to fit between framing members spaced at standard building industry intervals. Most batts are manufactured with a narrow strip of material (a flange) on each side for easy stapling to framing.

Rigid insulation panels are relatively new. Except for some professionally applied foams, they are the only insulation appropriate for exterior use, and are often installed around foundation walls or beneath roof coverings. In new construction rigid insulation is sometimes used in place of plywood as sheathing beneath siding. Indoors, rigid insulation is a good choice for insulating basement or other masonry walls that will be covered with wallboard.

Composition

Loose fill insulation is made of particles of fiberglass, mineral wool (rock wool), vermiculite, perlite, and cellulose, and is easy to pour.

Short-fiber fiberglass is the best insulator, although it is usually more expensive than other loose fills, and is sometimes difficult to find. Long-fiber fiberglass is inexpensive and widely available, though it has only about half the insulating value of short fiber.

Mineral wool is comparable to long-fiber fiberglass as an insulator. It doesn't irritate skin, as fiberglass often does.

Vermiculite (expanded mica) and perlite (beaded glass) are modest insulators and expensive for their abilities, but they are commonly available, and they pour easily into irregular spaces.

Cellulose is the only loose-fill material that is not fireproof; it can be chemically treated, but this makes it corrosive to metals. Cellulose is inexpensive and nearly as effective as short-fiber fiberglass, but it is susceptible to water damage.

Blankets and batts are most commonly made of spun fiberglass or mineral wool. They are nearly equal as insulators; fiberglass is almost always less expensive.

Rigid insulation made of polyurethane and polyisocyanurate are the types most often sold by building suppliers for use as sheathing. More expensive, and for use only as insulation, are extruded polystyrene (called blueboard for its color) and molded polystyrene (called beadboard because it is made by fusing tiny styrene beads together).

All rigid foam insulation is flammable and also will degrade with long exposure to sunlight. It must be covered for durability and separated from the interior of a house by fire-resistant material like gypsum wallboard.

Blueboard is impervious to moisture and may be used outside or in contact with the ground or damp masonry. Beadboard, however, gradually absorbs water and must be used only where it will remain dry.

Vapor Barriers

Another factor to consider when buying insulation is the need for a vapor barrier. Without one, particularly in winter, air from the warm side of an insulated structure can migrate to the cool side, carrying more vapor than it can hold at the lower temperature. The dampness that results as the vapor condenses decreases the effectiveness of the insulation and promotes decay of the framing.

Loose-fill insulation requires a separate vapor barrier, usually a sheet of polyethylene. Before insulating, the sheet is laid down so it will bar the entry of vapor from the warm side of the building, and then the insulation is spread on top.

Blanket and batt insulation are made with a vapor barrier on one surface; it might be asphalt-impregnated paper (kraft paper) or paper coated with aluminum foil. The foil-and-paper facing provides marginally better protection against vapor penetration; otherwise, very little practical difference exists between the two. Both are flammable and must be separated from living spaces by half-inch-thick gypsum wallboard or other code-approved material to satisfy fire-safety regulations in most communities.

Rigid foam panels are manufactured with or without vapor barrier facings. Structural foam panels are usually foil-faced on both sides. Unless one side is specially marked, either side may face toward the interior of the building.

Blueboard, being waterproof, requires no barrier. Beadboard should be separated from warm air by polyethylene sheeting.

Selecting and Installing Fiberglass Insulation

Batts of fiberglass insulation come in standard lengths of 4 and 8 feet. Blankets come in various lengths, packaged in rolls for easy handling. Both are designed to fit the standard spacing between floor and ceiling joists and wall studs; the widths most commonly available are about 15 inches and about 23 inches.

If many batts will require trimming by more than a foot or so, it might be more economical to obtain blankets instead and to

TIP:

Because of its shiny surface, foil-faced insulation is often assumed to be a better choice than the kraft-faced product because of its reflectivity. However, in practice most of the heat reflected by the foil is dispersed by air currents inside the wall, floor, or ceiling cavity, and by conductivity caused by contact between the foil and the inner surface of the wallboard, flooring, or other building material covering it.

TIP:

To prevent condensation problems including ice dams (ridges of ice that form along roof eaves in winter, often producing leaks), make sure that attic insulation extends to the perimeter of the ceiling but not beyond it into the areas above the soffits—the enclosed channels that run beneath the eaves. These must remain open so that air entering them through vents in their lower surfaces can circulate upward beneath the roof before passing to the outside through vents in the gable ends or roof ridge.

Barriers of stiff material that fit between joists to keep insulation away from soffit channels are available at home centers. You can also make your own of heavy cardboard. Fold the ends of the barriers so they fit against the sides of the joists, then attach them to the joists with staples or small nails.

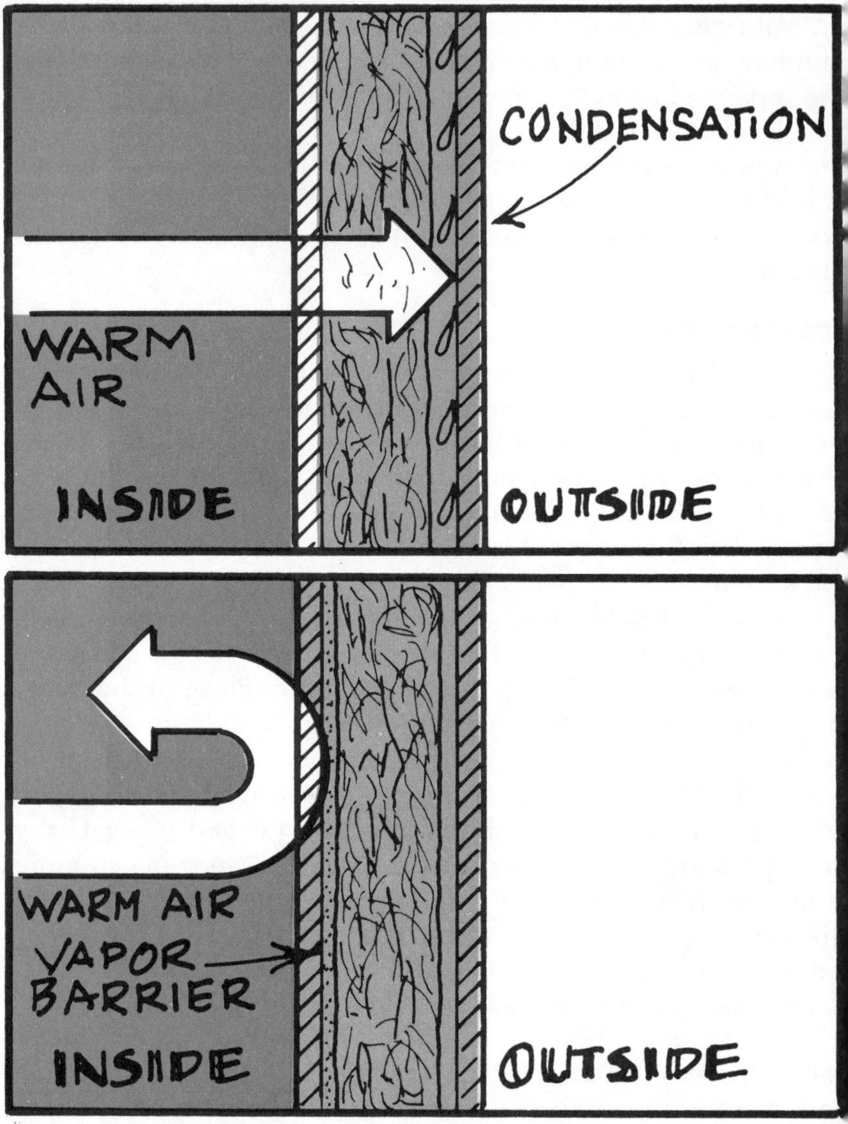

Most insulation needs a vapor barrier, as shown in the second illustration, to block condensation inside walls.

cut strips to the exact size. Always select faced insulation unless you plan to attach a separate vapor barrier or are simply adding new insulation to that already protected against moisture.

The thickness of fiberglass insulation determines its R-value, and many different thicknesses are available. Unless you are adding insulation above an attic ceiling, select the thickness that matches the width of the framing pieces it will lie between. There is no point in adding less insulation than the cavities between framing pieces can accept. But compressing insulation that is thicker than the width of framing pieces diminishes its R-value.

When choosing insulation, consult a local utility company to find out what R-value is recommended in your area.

Many people find handling fiberglass insulation irritating to the skin and respiratory passages. Wearing long trousers and a shirt with long sleeves will help; so will wearing gloves. Showering with plenty of soap as soon as possible after working with insulation will help prevent particles on the skin from working their way into the pores.

To avoid breathing insulation particles, wear a government-approved dust mask available at hardware stores. Also keep windows open or a fan blowing in the room during installation.

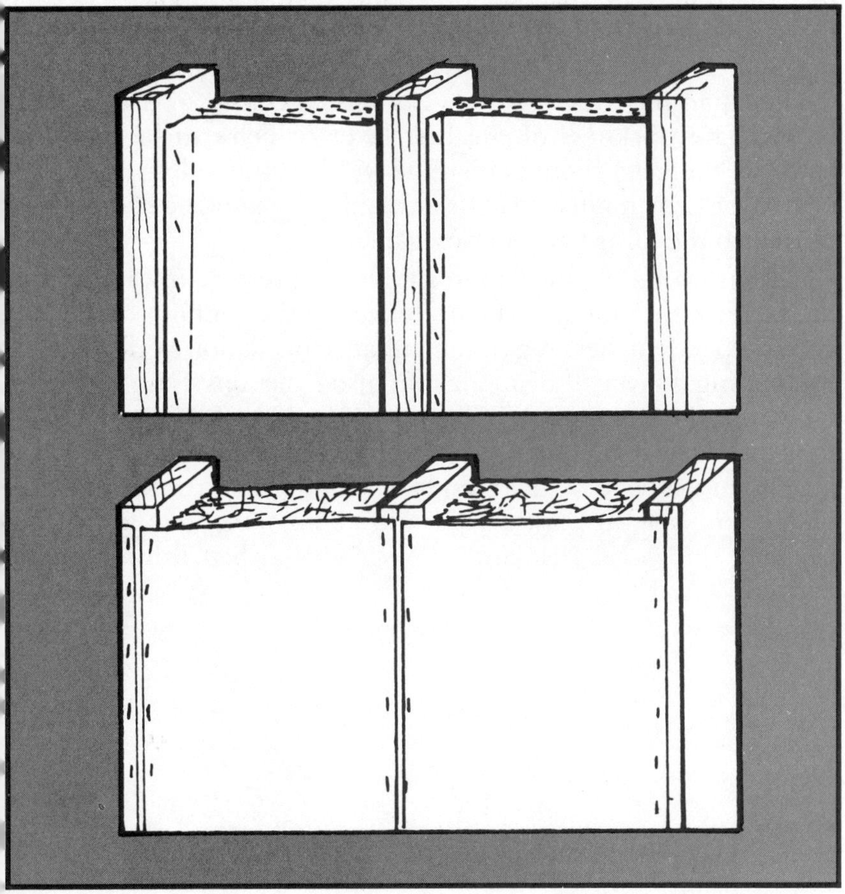

Insulation flanges can be stapled to the sides of studs as in the first illustration, or to their outer edges as in the second. Each method has its advantages.

TIP:

Faced batts installed between rafters and studs in an attic should be oriented so their faced side is visible in order to block moisture rising from the house. However, many fire codes limit the exposure of insulation facing because it is flammable. Before installing attic insulation this way, or if the facing of existing insulation in your attic is exposed, consult a building inspector.

Also for reasons of fire safety, make sure that insulation of any type comes no closer than 3 inches to metal chimneys, stovepipes, and heat-producing fixtures like doorbell transformers and recessed lights. (Lights marked "I.C." are an exception; the initials stand for "insulated ceiling" and designate a fixture that can be safely touched by or covered with insulation.)

TIP:

Foil-faced insulation is a more effective vapor barrier than kraft-faced and is recommended over kraft-faced insulation in areas where moisture is likely to be greatest, for example in bathrooms, laundries, and walls with northern exposure.

ATTENTION

Faced insulation should always be installed with the facing toward the warm side of the building. To install insulation between wall studs, manufacturers usually recommend pressing it gently into place and stapling the flanges of the facing against the sides of the studs. This leaves the outer edges of the studs exposed, making them easier to find when attaching wallboard or paneling. This is the only acceptable method if the wall material is to be glued to studs.

A more effective vapor barrier is achieved by stapling the flanges so that they overlap the outer edges of the studs, covering them. This is also the preferred method if wall material will be nailed or screwed to the studs, because staples holding the insulation will identify the studs' locations.

When adding insulation above ceilings, loose fill can simply be poured into the spaces between joists (after a vapor barrier has been installed), or batts or blankets can be laid down without stapling. For the most effective results, ceiling insulation that is thicker than the width of the joists should consist of two or more layers. The thickness of the first layer (which can be loose fill, batts, or blankets) should equal the width of the ceiling joists. The next layer (which must be batts or blankets) should be laid perpendicular to the joists to cover any gaps.

Beneath floors, insulation should be pressed upward so that the facing either touches the underside of the subfloor or allows a gap of up to 3 inches. A gap can enhance insulation's effectiveness by creating a layer of dead air that also functions as an insulator. However, the gap must be closed at the ends, by folding insulation upward, against the house framing above the foundation. If the insulation needs to be held in place, lengths of wire cut from coat hangers or special plastic rods sold at home centers are placed between the joists. Insulating floors is described fully on pages 355–57.

Insulating an Attic Entrance

In many homes, attic insulation is placed at floor level, spe-cifically between the joists that support the ceilings of the rooms below. This is effective and economical; however, if the attic entrance is not insulated, you can lose substantial amounts of energy in both winter and summer.

There are some easy ways to insulate attic entrances, but before using insulation as a backing for plywood, solid wood, or hardboard, consult your local building inspector to be sure you are complying with fire-safety codes.

If the opening to the attic consists merely of a hatchway covered by a removable piece of plywood or wallboard, you can insulate it simply by attaching fiberglass or rigid foam insulation to the back of the piece and adding a narrow border of adhesive-backed foam weatherstripping around the perimeter of the side facing the living area.

Use the same thickness of insulation as that used in the rest of the attic, or use insulation of equivalent capacity (R-value). Fiberglass insulation with paper or foil facing can be stapled to plywood or glued with construction adhesive to materials that will not accept staples, like wallboard and hardboard.

Rigid foam insulation is easier to apply. Cut two or more pieces of ¾-inch-thick foam to the same dimensions as the hatch cover. If the cover is plywood, use ringed-shank nails with a flat metal washer placed under the head to fasten the insulation to it. If the cover is wallboard or hardboard, glue the insulation instead.

TIP:

For advice on working with large panels of plywood, see pages 41–43.

ATTENTION

Weatherstripping attached to the front of the cover will prevent air from leaking around the edges. Adhesive-backed foam strips are readily available and easy to apply by pressing into place. Usually, the lip of molding around the bottom of the attic opening is wide enough to conceal the strips when the cover is installed.

If the entrance to the attic is a vertical doorway at the foot of a staircase, there are two alternatives. The easiest is to build an insulated hatch cover similar to the kind just described, but large enough to cover the opening in the attic where the stairway enters. Because of the size of the opening, make the cover in two sections that fit side by side.

Begin by cutting the sections out of ½-inch-thick plywood. They should cover the attic opening and overlap the floor or framing around it by about 2 inches on each side.

On top of each section, glue or nail a single layer of ¾-inch-thick rigid foam cut to the same dimensions as the plywood. Then attach a second layer of foam, but stagger these pieces so that they interlock when the cover sections are in place. This will prevent air from passing through the seam between the sections.

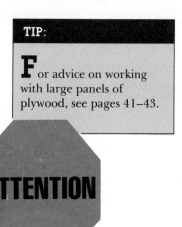

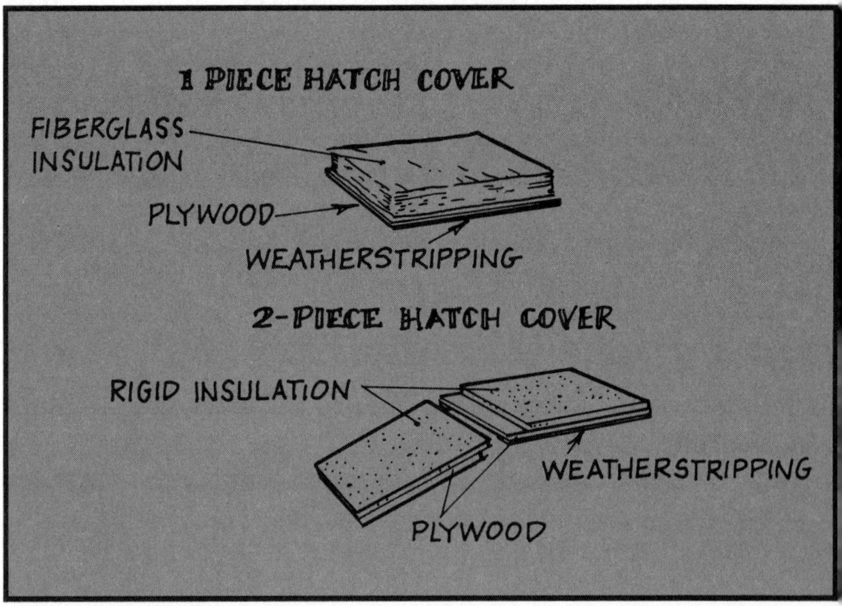

Seal hatchways and staircase openings with insulated covers. The one-piece cover shown here is easy to make.

Overlapping insulation on a two-piece cover seals the seam between sections.

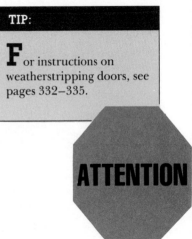

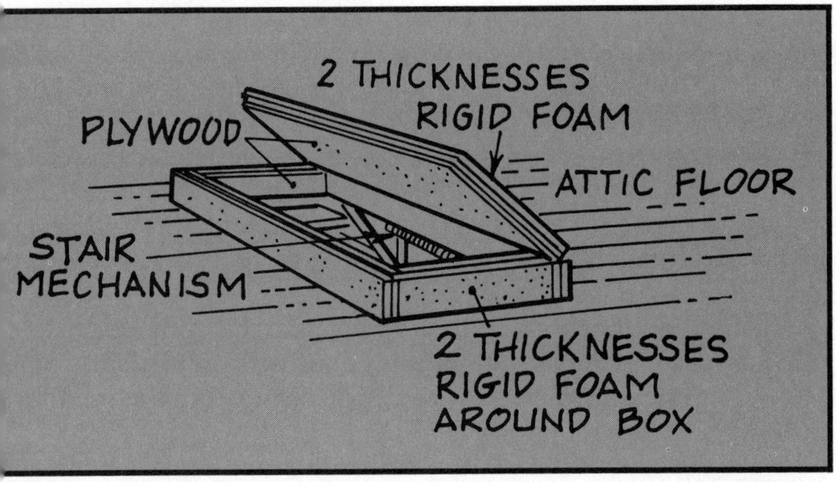

For stairs, fasten an insulated box to the framing inside the opening.

TIP:

For instructions on weatherstripping doors, see pages 332–335.

Cut the piece of insulation for the first section—the section farthest from the head of the stairs—oversize so that one side extends 2 inches beyond the edge of the piece underneath. Cut the insulation for the other section 2 inches shorter than the piece underneath.

Then attach the pieces to the cover sections so that when the sections are placed together the projecting portion of one section overlaps the recess on the other.

Next, fasten adhesive-backed foam weatherstripping to the front of each section, positioning it so that the weatherstripping will be compressed when the sections rest on the attic floor or framing.

When covering the opening with the sections, start with both sections inside the attic. Set the section nearest the head of the stairs into place first. Position the remaining section from underneath as you descend the staircase.

The other alternative is to insulate the walls of the stairwell, the cavity beneath the stairs, and the door.

To insulate the walls, install fiberglass batts if the framing is exposed. Then cover the insulation with wallboard for fire safety. If the interior of the stairwell is finished, holes can usually be drilled in the walls at the top and bottom and loose-fill insulation can be blown into them.

Generally, this is a job for a professional insulator. After filling, the holes are patched and the walls refinished.

To insulate beneath the stairs, either remove the top tread from the staircase and fill the cavity by pouring in loose-fill insulation or drill holes in the material beneath the stairs and have insulation blown in.

To insulate the door, attach two layers of rigid foam to the back, using nails with washers under the heads, and attach weatherstripping to the doorway, as for any entry door. Adhesive-backed vinyl V-stripping is a durable, inexpensive type that is easy to apply.

If rigid foam cannot be used to insulate the door because of code regulations, replace the present door with an insulated one. Prehung models that include a door frame feature built-in weatherstripping.

Folding stairs installed in an attic entrance can be insulated by building a plywood box around the opening, projecting into the attic, and covering it with a two-piece insulated lid like the one described or with a one-piece lid fastened to an upper edge of the box with hinges.

Measure from inside the opening to the height that the stairs project into the attic when folded. Then make the box by cutting four pieces of ½-inch-thick plywood an inch or so wider than this dimension to fit around the perimeter inside the door opening.

Attach the pieces of the box by nailing them to the framing that forms the opening. Next, fasten insulation around the outside of the box and then install the top.

Insulating Beneath a Floor

In winter, an unheated basement or crawl space can act like a block of ice beneath the rooms above. Although insulating the attic and above-ground perimeter walls of a house and installing weatherstripping are crucial steps for conserving energy and reducing costs, insulating above an unheated basement will reduce costs even further and eliminate uncomfortable cold floors, too.

If the basement or crawl space has a dirt or gravel floor, this must be covered first with moistureproof material. Otherwise, rising water vapor will saturate most insulation in the ceiling. This will ruin the effectiveness of the insulation and, worse, hasten decay in the wooden framing to which it is attached.

To cover a basement or crawl space floor, use 6-mil-thick polyethylene plastic sheeting, often called vapor barrier. The material is relatively inexpensive. Rolled strips about 3 feet wide are easiest to handle, but single large sheets may be more economical and save installation time.

Lay strips one at a time. Fasten the end of a roll to the wall about 4 inches above the floor with duct tape or mastic adhesive. Asphalt roofing cement is also satisfactory. Then place a two-by-four or a pair of bricks on top of the plastic to hold it against the corner where the wall and floor meet. Unroll the strip and fasten it to the opposite wall, positioning another two-by-four or pair of bricks on top of the plastic there as well.

When laying the first and last strips, one long edge of each must be turned upward and taped or cemented to attach the material to the side walls of the opening, and two-by-fours or

TIP:

Beneath floors it is important that all bays between joists be filled with insulation and that insulation surrounding bridging (cross braces), pipes, and wiring in bays be cut to accommodate these items, not compressed beneath them. To fit insulation around bridging, cut the strip in two at the bridging, then make lengthwise slits in each piece to create tabs. Fit one tab of each section beneath the bridging, the other above it.

ATTENTION

bricks placed along the fold. The remaining strips covering th floor should overlap by about 6 inches. Taping or weighting thes seams is optional.

The unheated space must also be equipped with vents t allow moisture that does accumulate to escape to the outside. Mos basements and crawl spaces have vents or operable windows in stalled in the walls during construction. These should be left ope even in winter.

If the space is unvented it is imperative that vents be adde to prevent the decay of floor framing and the onset of othe moisture problems, whether or not insulation is added.

The most effective, yet economical, insulation for basemen or crawl space ceilings is usually ordinary fiberglass. Six-inch-thic material, which has a thermal value of R-19, provides a high de gree of insulation and is the thickest standard size that will fit th cavities between floor joists. (Joists are the boards that span th space between the foundation walls and support the floorin above.)

Unless the joists are uniformly spaced to create cavities 14½ inches wide—a standard dimension in contemporary construc tion, but rare in older homes—it is more economical to obtai insulation in blanket form rather than batts, which are made to fi the standard-size cavities. Both kraft-paper-faced and foil-face insulation are acceptable. Avoid unfaced insulation.

Measure the length and width of each cavity, then use a utilit knife to cut strips of the correct size from the blanket. The easies way to cut insulation is with the fluffy side up.

Place the area of the cut on a flat work surface such as a piec of plywood. Then use a long straightedge or board to compres the insulation and act as a cutting guide.

Install the insulation so that the facing, which acts as a vapo barrier, is toward the warm side of the area, that is, directly be neath the flooring of the room above. Where joist cavities are o standard width (14½ inches), commercially manufactured flexibl wire or fiberglass rods, called insulation supports, are the bes solution for fastening. These are available where insulation is sold

To install the supports, first press part of a strip of insulatio into a cavity between two joists. Do not compress the material this lessens its effectiveness. The facing should either make bar contact with the underside of the flooring or else should create a air space below it (closed at the ends) of up to 3 inches.

Then, at intervals of about 16 inches, install a support b pressing it upward against the exposed side of the insulation t span the cavity.

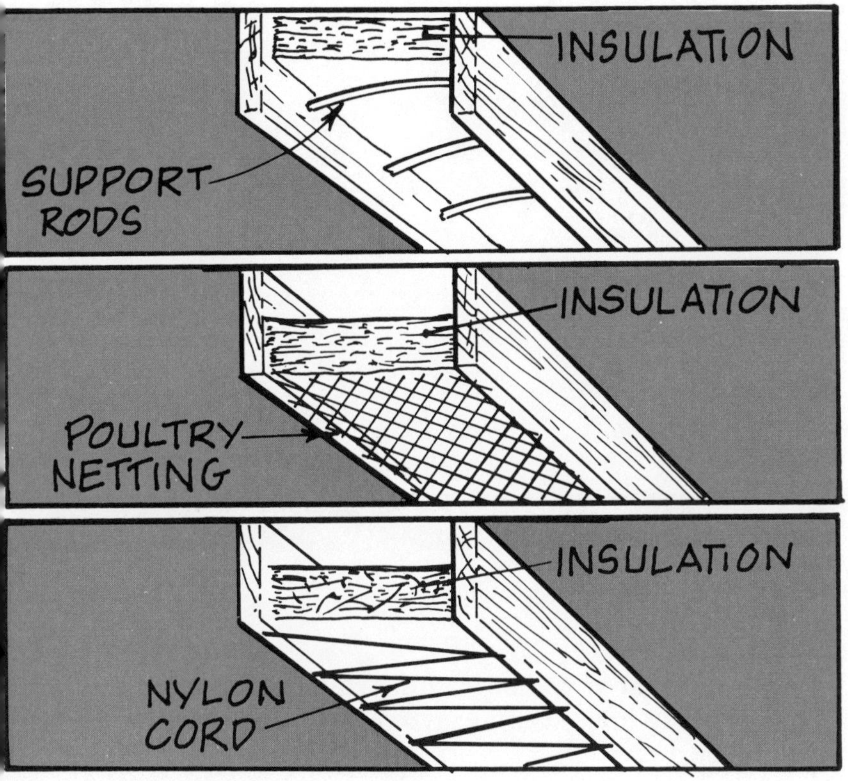

Because insulation must be installed with the vapor barrier facing the underside of the floor, attaching it presents problems. Flexible fiberglass or wire support rods are usually the best solution.

Two other methods of attaching insulation are by using poultry netting and by lacing with nylon cord.

The supports measure longer than the distance between the joists. Pushing upward bends them slightly, allowing them to fit and at the same time applying pressure to the ends so that the supports remain in place. Do not press the supports so tightly against the insulation that the material above them is compressed.

You can make your own insulation supports by cutting lengths of coathanger wire to the correct size. Another method of securing insulation is to span the cavities between joists with strips of poultry netting (chicken wire), using staples to attach it to the joists' lower edges after the insulation is installed.

Still another method is to drive large-headed roofing nails along the lower edges of the joists, then crisscross the space beneath the insulation with nylon cord, wrapping it around the nails.

Preparing Heating Systems for Winter

The arrival of cooler weather and shorter days brings th need to ready home heating systems, woodstoves, and fireplac for use.

For safety reasons and because of the complexity of mo home heating equipment, a qualified professional heating tech nician should inspect and service it annually. A professional chim ney sweep should check woodstoves and fireplaces.

Qualified heating system service is usually available from o or gas suppliers. Or look on the furnace for the name of th company that installed it. Licensing of heating industry techni cians varies between communities and there is no standard o qualification. For help in finding qualified service, call your loca consumer affairs department and learn what licensing arrange ments are enforced in your area. Then question prospective heat ing service companies. Ask them for proof of liability and worker compensation insurance, how long they have been in business what professional organizations they belong to, and for the name of customers you can contact as references.

A thorough inspection and servicing of an oil furnace shoul include checking for air leaks; cleaning and checking the filte system, combustion-air blower, and burner motor; examining th firing system (burner nozzle and ignition electrodes); and adjust ing the draft regulator on the stack (the pipe leading from th furnace to the chimney). It should also include cleaning the chim ney base where the stack enters it and inspecting safety device ɩurner disconnect switch, primary safety switch, and stack con-ol switch).

You can also ask for instrument testing in addition to stan-ard visual checking of the flame size and color for maximum ɔmbustion efficiency. Instrument tests should include gauging noke density and carbon dioxide content, and taking the tem-erature of combustion exhaust inside the stack. A thorough tech-ician will also inspect the fuel oil storage tank(s) and supply line.

For a gas furnace, far less servicing is required. Included ɩould be vacuuming the inside of the furnace, cleaning and ad-ısting the burners, and checking the pilot light or ignition sys-

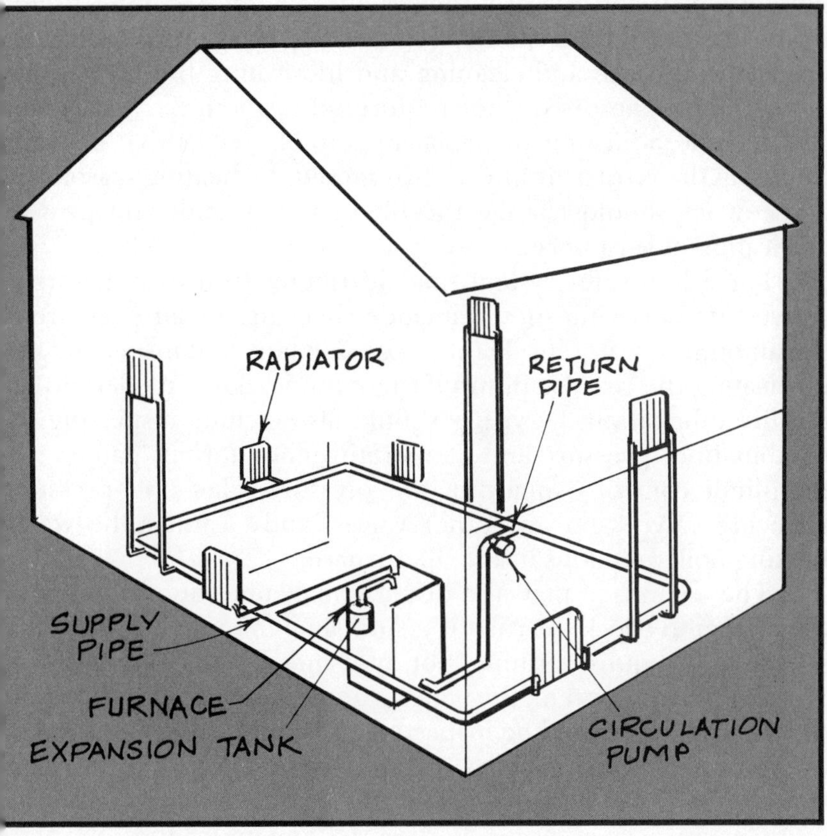

ousehold heating systems are sometimes complex. In a ypical system supplying hot-water heat, water warmed by ırnace travels through the plumbing to radiators or onvectors where heat is given up; cooled water then avels back to the furnace. A circulator pump supplies ressure; the expansion tank allows water to expand and ontract with temperature changes.

TIP:

About every five years, air ducts should be inspected and cleaned if necessary by a professional duct-cleaning company. For more about duct cleaning, see page 362.

ATTENTION

tem, burner flame controls, thermocouple (a safety device), gas pressure regulator, and valves and plumbing supplying the furnace. The technician should also check the draft hood connection and inspect the base of the chimney for soot and debris, although none should be present.

As with an oil-fired furnace, you can request instrument testing for combustion efficiency. The tests are usually the same except that measuring carbon monoxide in flue gases normally replaces gauging smoke density (gas furnaces should produce no smoke).

Annual heating system service should include inspection and maintenance of the heat-distribution system. For a forced-hot-air system, which consists of a blower and air ducts leading to and from registers, service should include cleaning the heat exchanger inside the furnace and cleaning and lubricating the blower and motor. Some motors do not require lubrication. Service should also include adjusting or replacing the blower's drive belt and changing the return air filter. Throughout the heating season, the homeowner should change the filter every month and provide lubrication at least once.

For a hot-water system that distributes heat to radiators or convectors, servicing should include checking the air pressure or the amount of water inside the expansion tank and inspecting and lubricating the circular pump if there is one. Some models do not require lubrication. Servicing should also include inspecting the combination pressure-and-temperature-monitoring gauge, the high-limit control (Aquastat), the pressure-relief and pressure-reducing valves and any other valves, and cleaning the water-heating boiler sections inside the furnace.

The technician may also drain a small amount of water from the system to check for rust. If a sufficient amount is present, the system may require flushing, but this is not needed annually.

For a steam system, the boiler gauges showing water level and steam pressure should be inspected, as should the low-water cutoff valve and pressure-relief or safety valve. As with a hot-water system, the boiler sections inside the furnace should be cleaned and a small amount of water may be drained to check rust content. This check should also be done monthly by homeowners.

Radiators and convectors often must be freed of trapped air after being idle for several months, and sometimes also require adjusting so that heat is dispersed evenly throughout the house. Because these jobs can be done by the homeowner, they are not usually part of routine professional service.

Woodstoves and fireplaces should be cleaned and checked for ·acks or deteriorated masonry before use. All controls, especially ıe damper in the stovepipe or at the base of the chimney, should ınction correctly. Most important is that the stovepipe or chim-ey be inspected, cleaned, and repaired if necessary. It is best to ave this done in early spring, before accumulated deposits arden and make cleaning more difficult. Nevertheless, if the ovepipe or chimney has not been cleaned since last season, have done now. Most qualified chimney sweeps are members of ıther the National Chimney Sweep Guild or the Wood Heating ducation and Research Foundation.

Improving Radiator Efficiency

For safety, efficiency, and economy, your furnace should b professionally inspected and serviced before the start of each hea ing season. Just as important for efficiency and economy is a annual inspection and tune-up of the heating system's delive points: ducts and registers in hot-air systems; radiators and co vectors in steam and hot-water systems. Usually, an amateur ca do this easily.

If your house is heated by forced hot air, the ducts should b professionally vacuumed about every five years and after any e tensive remodeling that involves demolition. Have this done by professional duct-cleaning company. Keeping ducts and registe free of dirt increases the amount of heat they can deliver and als reduces the amount of dust entering the air when the system operating.

You can help keep ducts clean by vacuuming the registe throughout the year as part of normal housecleaning. Als change the blower filter at monthly intervals during the heatin season if the filter is a glass-fiber type, or wash it if it is aluminu or plastic. The filter is inside the furnace, near the blower.

With steam or hot-water systems, careful—but not difficult- maintenance is required for the radiators or convectors, whic both do the same thing. (Convectors are tubes surrounded by th metal fins; they are usually enclosed in a baseboard housing.)

Dust and vacuum radiators and convectors before use eac year. During the heating season, they should be cleaned eve month for greatest efficiency.

You can increase the heat a radiator or convector sends to-
vard the center of a room by taping a sheet of aluminum foil to he wall behind it. The foil should be the same width and height s the appliance.

For most efficient operation, radiators or convectors should ot be covered except by ventilated covers that are part of their lesign. Covers must have openings at the bottom to admit cool ir and at or near the top to distribute warm air.

Metallic paint on a radiator reduces its ability to give off heat y as much as 18 percent. To restore the full effectiveness of a adiator painted with metallic paint, repaint it with any light-col- red, matte-finish paint. Existing paint can stay on the radiator, ut for the new paint to adhere, surfaces must be clean and the adiator cool when it is applied.

Convectors are seldom painted because they are usually en- losed in a housing. But they should be inspected during cleaning, nd any bent fins should be carefully straightened so that none ouch each other. Straighten fins with a putty knife or wide-jawed lamping pliers.

TIP:

The best method for cleaning air ducts involves removing the dirt by vacuuming and the use of small metal balls called skippers that swirl around inside the ducts, breaking deposits loose. (Some companies promote using an encapsulant to seal dirt to the duct lining; this can cause health problems when the encapsulant eventually wears away.) After cleaning, ducts can be treated with sealers or disinfectants.

leeding

In months when radiators and convectors are not used, air ometimes enters them. This causes them to heat poorly by pre- enting hot water or steam from filling them completely.

The procedure for removing trapped air is called bleeding. o bleed a hot-water radiator, first turn on the furnace and let it each normal operating temperature. The circulator (a pump ounted near the furnace that forces water through the system) nust be running too. Next, turn on the radiator by opening the upply valve at the base to admit hot water.

Near the top, on the end opposite the supply valve, find the mall bleeder valve, which must be opened to let trapped air out. lany bleeder valves are slotted and can be opened and closed sing an ordinary screwdriver. Others call for a special socket rench, sold at hardware and heating supply stores.

Hold a teacup, coffee mug, or pan with a handle under the leeder valve and unscrew the valve counterclockwise. Air should scape, followed by a stream of hot water under pressure.

Catch the water in the container while closing the valve tight. Vithin a few moments, the radiator should heat along its entire ngth. If it does not, repeat the process. If no air escapes or if ater does not flow freely, the supply valve or interior of the adiator may be blocked. Call for professional service.

To release air from a radiator, open the vent valve until water flows.

If a steam radiator does not heat fully, tilting it so it slopes toward the supply valve may cure the problem. If the supply valve leaks, replace the packing material beneath the packing nut.

Some hot-water convectors must be bled individually, as de scribed. But with others, the process usually involves opening single valve in the plumbing that returns water to the furnac from the heating system. This bleeds all the convectors at once.

Steam radiators (convectors are rare) have automatic vent that do not require manual bleeding. If a radiator fails to hea fully, elevate the end farthest from the supply valve by puttin blocks about an inch thick under the legs at that end. If this doe not cure the problem, or if steam escapes from the vent durin operation, the vent may be clogged or defective.

To service a malfunctioning steam vent, shut off the radiatc by turning the supply valve clockwise. Let the unit cool, the remove the vent by unscrewing it.

Shake the vent vigorously to loosen any rust inside. Try t blow air through the threaded end. If you are successful, reinsta the vent and open the supply valve. The radiator or convectc should operate normally.

If you cannot blow air through the vent, or if steam escape from it, try cleaning the vent by soaking it overnight in pair remover if it seems to have been painted over, or by boiling about twenty minutes in distilled vinegar if mineral deposits hav blocked the opening. If these remedies fail, buy a new vent. (Ven should be replaced every three or four years in any case.)

eaking Supply Valve

Another frequent problem with hot-water and steam radia- ors and convectors is leakage around the supply valve. Usually he problem is worn-out packing; this is sealant resembling string, ocated beneath a large nut called the packing nut on the valve tem just below the knob.

As a remedy, first try tightening the packing nut with a vrench or pliers. If this does not work or if the valve then becomes oo difficult to turn, replace the packing.

To do this, close the supply valve and remove the knob by oosening the screw in the top. Using one wrench to hold the base of the valve steady, use a second wrench to loosen and remove the acking nut from the valve stem. Unwind the old packing, then vrap new packing (available at hardware stores) clockwise around he base of the valve stem and tighten the nut down over it.

Test the repair by opening the supply valve. Minor seepage nay occur for up to an hour; if it continues, the valve may be lefective and require replacing, another job for a professional.

Ioises

Steam radiators and their plumbing often develop pounding oises. Though these can be annoying and difficult to trace, in lmost all cases the cause is water trapped somewhere in the sys- em.

In a steam-heat plumbing layout, most often a single loop of ipe leads upward at an angle from the boiler, continues through- ut the house to the highest point, and then returns to the boiler. ndividual extension pipes joined to the main loop at various lo- ations supply the radiators.

Steam travels under its own pressure from the boiler into the adiators. As it cools there, it condenses into water. Gravity then auses the water to trickle back to the boiler in a stream running long the bottom of the pipe against the current of the steam.

Unless both the plumbing and the radiators are sufficiently loped, this two-way flow of steam and water cannot take place.

Settling of the house, remodeling, or other structural changes an alter the slant of both radiators and plumbing. When water ollects in an insufficiently sloped area, its presence blocks the low of steam through it. The hammering or banging noises that esult are actually the sounds of trapped water being slammed gainst the sides of the piping by pressurized steam attempting to force its way past. If noise comes from a radiator, elevate the end farthest from the supply valve (using blocks as described above), so that the radiator slopes toward the valve. If noise is elsewhere, settling, remodeling, or broken plumbing fasteners may have caused a run of pipe to slip. You may be able to locate misaligned pipes yourself, using a builder's level. However, if the plumbing is hidden, consult a licensed plumbing and heating contractor. To cure most noises in a hot-water radiator or convector, be sure that the supply valve is fully open when the device is on and fully closed when it is off.

Preventing and Coping with Frozen Plumbing

When water freezes and expands inside pipes, it can cause major damage requiring expensive repairs. Frequently, the pressure causes the pipes to burst or, at the least, to leak at the seams. And, because pipes usually freeze when and where coping with them is most difficult, preventing the problem is as important, if not more so, than knowing what to do if it occurs.

The household pipes that are most vulnerable to freezing are those that run through unheated crawl spaces, attics, and uninsulated or poorly sealed exterior walls. Outdoor faucets and fixtures in unheated outbuildings and plumbing in vacation homes are similarly at risk.

The surest way to prevent pipes from freezing is to drain them before cold weather arrives and keep them empty all winter. Owners of vacation homes should drain the entire plumbing system each fall; this is also worth considering when leaving any house for two weeks or more in cold months, in case a protracted power failure disables the furnace and temperatures inside the house drop below freezing.

Draining the entire plumbing system is, of course, impossible in homes that are inhabited year-round, but you may be able to drain and close some vulnerable parts of the system, particularly pipes supplying water to outdoor faucets.

To drain these, first close the shutoff valves on the pipes supplying them. The valves are located indoors, usually in the basement, about 3 feet from the outside wall.

TIP:

If you use an outdoor faucet at times during the winter, consider installing a frost-proof type in place of an ordinary one. Properly called a frost-proof sill cock, it looks like an ordinary outdoor faucet attached to a 3-foot length of plumbing pipe. However, the valve controlling the water is at the far end (it replaces the shutoff valve), connected to the faucet handle by an internal linkage. Because the valve is indoors when the faucet is installed, it cannot freeze; nor is water trapped in the part of the pipe that passes to the outside.

ATTENTION

Next, open the faucets, letting any water in the pipes run ou and leave them open until the water supply is turned on again i the spring. That way, any water remaining in the pipes can ex pand if it freezes without creating damaging pressure.

Pipes that cannot be drained and that run through unheate or poorly heated areas must be protected. Where they are acces sible, metal pipes can be wrapped with electrical heating cabl which is available at hardware stores. Follow the manufacturer' instructions. Most cable is thermostatically controlled and need no monitoring. Heat is supplied by plugging the cable into a ordinary wall socket. For plastic pipe as well as metal, a new typ of heating cable is available that is installed inside the pipes them selves. This cable, too, is thermostatically controlled and operate on ordinary household current.

After attaching either type of cable, wrap the pipes with ir sulation to preserve the heat generated by the cable. Insulatio designed especially for plumbing is widely available. The easie

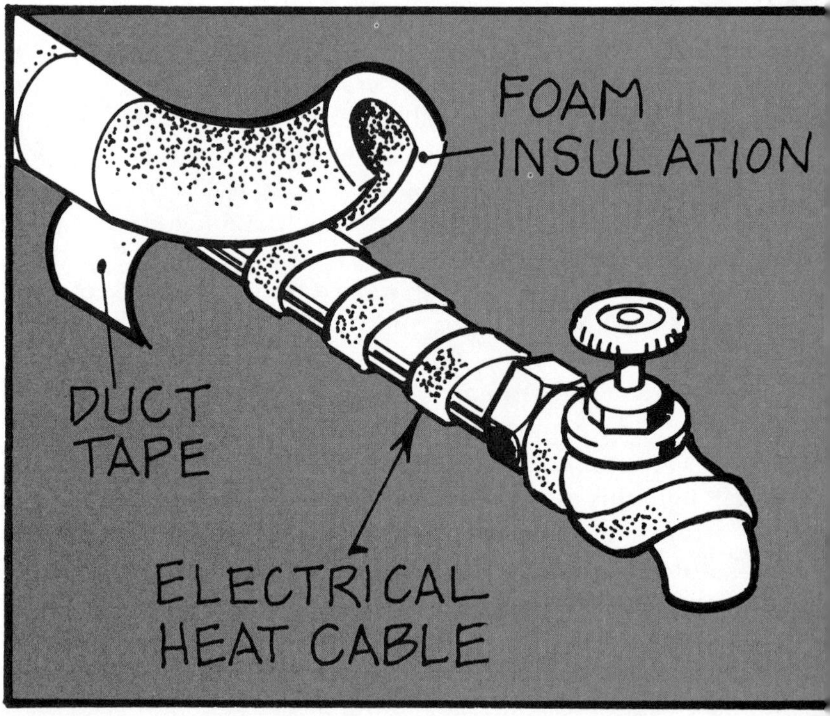

To protect an exposed pipe, wrap it with an electrical heating cable. Cover it with plumbing insulation and then plug the cable into a wall socket.

ind to use consists of foam sleeves that are slit lengthwise. After lipping these over the pipes, cover the slits with durable utility ape, like aluminized duct tape. This insulation alone may be all hat is necessary to protect pipes exposed to minimal heating.

Pipes that are inaccessible because they are enclosed in walls ;enerally need only slight protection because the wall affords suf-icient shelter. Start by scrupulously sealing openings in unheated pasements and attics that allow air to pass through the wall cavity ontaining the pipe. This prevents cold drafts from penetrating he cavity and allows the air trapped inside to function as insula-ion. Use either caulking compound or polyurethane foam as a ealant.

At the expense of creating air movement and losing some ndoor heat, you can also cut a small opening in part of the wall hat is in a heated part of the building and install a louvered vent lesigned for hot-air heating systems. These are available at heat-ng supply stores. Opening the vent allows air from inside the nouse to warm the pipe. If more heat is desired, place a portable pace heater in front of the vent and aim the heat into the cavity.

Whenever a heavy freeze is expected, leave faucets that are connected to vulnerable pipes open slightly so that water trickles continuously from them. Moving water is less likely to freeze than vater that is still, and the trickle is visible proof that all is well.

If a pipe does freeze, locate the blockage by ascertaining vhich faucets work and which do not, starting with the faucet 'arthest along the pipe from the supply entrance (where the water neter is located). Leave all faucets connected to the frozen pipe open so that pressure created by the ice will be lessened and so hat water can escape when the ice is thawed. Then use a heat amp or hair dryer to warm the frozen section or, if the pipe is naccessible, the area of construction enclosing it.

If the problems of a freeze are compounded by a power out-age, it is best simply to delay action. Do not pour hot tap water on 'rozen plumbing or, even worse, try to thaw pipes with a propane orch. The hot water usually freezes on the outside of the pipe and the torch can cause frozen pipes to explode if the heat pro-duces steam. And striking the pipes to try to break up the ice could cause the pipe to crack.

PART 6:

Winter (December Through February)

CONTENTS

HIGHLIGHTS

TIP:

If you cannot restart your furnace or you suspect a dangerous situation, you will have to call the heating company. It is a good idea to know the phone number ahead of time, not to wait until the furnace breaks down. Often the company that installed the furnace or last serviced it will leave a label on the furnace itself. If none is present, look in the Yellow Pages under "heating equipment" to find a company that will service your furnace. For problems with a gas furnace, call the utility company.

ATTENTION

Restarting a Furnace

When a furnace unexpectedly stops working or fails to tart, there are several safe, simple procedures you can try before alling for professional service or, if you live in an apartment, the uilding superintendent. Such breakdowns are rarely dangerous, ven in furnaces that burn explosive natural gas. Naturally, how-ver, do not hesitate to call for service if you feel uncertain about ow to proceed or if you suspect danger.

The first thing to check is the thermostat, which governs the utomatic operation of the furnace. Usually, it is located in the nain living area. If the dial or other control is set to a lower emperature than that showing on the thermostat's thermometer, dvance the control 5 to 10 degrees higher than the thermometer eading. If the thermostat has a timer, check that its settings are orrect. If the thermostat has batteries, replace them with new nes.

Making these adjustments should restart the furnace. If they lon't, and if the furnace is an oil burner, next inspect the emer-gency switch that governs power to the furnace. This is usually nounted on a wall at the top of a stairway leading to a basement urnace or just inside the doorway of the furnace room.

Most emergency switches have red cover plates that are learly labeled, but in other respects they resemble ordinary wall witches and can be switched off inadvertently. Returning the witch to its "on" position should permit the furnace to run nor-nally.

TIP:

Low-voltage thermostats, the kind having a mercury-bulb switch visible when the cover is removed, can often be bypassed to start the furnace by a technique called jumpering. Turn off the power to the furnace at the service panel and the emergency switch (see page 371). Remove the thermostat cover and locate the low-voltage terminals marked "R" and "W" on the base connected to red and white wires from the wall. Fasten a jumpering wire—a short length of electrical wire with alligator clips at the ends, available at electronic supply stores—to both terminals. This bypasses the thermostat switch. Restore power to the furnace, first at the service panel then at the emergency switch. The furnace should start. Turn the furnace off at the emergency switch when the room becomes warm. Repair or replace the thermostat as soon as possible.

ATTENTION

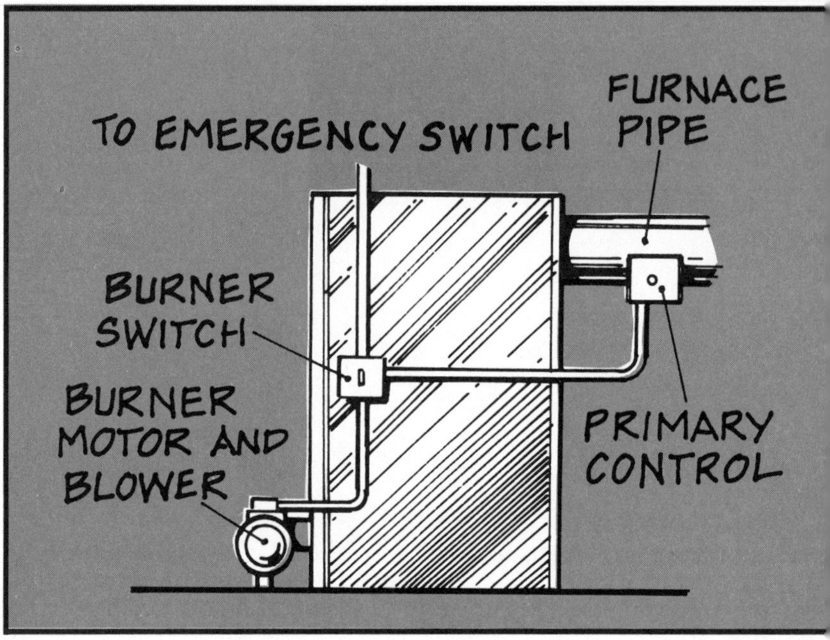

To restart an oil furnace, make sure the burner switch is on, then press the primary control button once.

If the furnace still will not start, go to the service panel o fuse box and check whether the circuit breakers or fuses control ling the furnace have tripped or blown.

Tripped circuit breakers are easy to spot and reset. However identifying the condition of cartridge fuses used for furnaces i not. If you have reason to suspect the fuses—for instance, if they are more than five years old—replace them at this stage and see if the furnace restarts. Otherwise, carry out the remaining proce dures; if they fail, replace the fuses as a last resort before calling for service.

Except in the case of fuses that fail because of age, a trippe circuit breaker or blown fuse governing a furnace indicates a problem that should be checked by an electrician or heating ser vice technician.

Make sure there is oil in the fuel storage tank, otherwise the furnace will not function. To get an accurate reading from the gauge, tap it with your finger to loosen any stuck parts.

Go to the furnace and find the burner switch, which is con nected to a metal-sheathed electric cable on or near the furnace The burner switch resembles the emergency switch—both contro the same circuit—and make sure the switch is turned on.

Also find the primary control unit, alternatively called the gnition safety relay. This is a metal box mounted either on the urnace pipe leading to the chimney or on the furnace above he burner. After waiting thirty minutes if the furnace is hot, et the thermostat in the living area to activate the furnace, then ress the button on the primary control.

The furnace should start. If it does not, press the button a econd time. If this attempt fails, move the burner switch to the off" position and call for service.

Some gas furnaces feature electrical spark ignition that must e serviced by a professional. Older gas furnaces are ignited by a ontinuously burning pilot flame. To restart these, first check

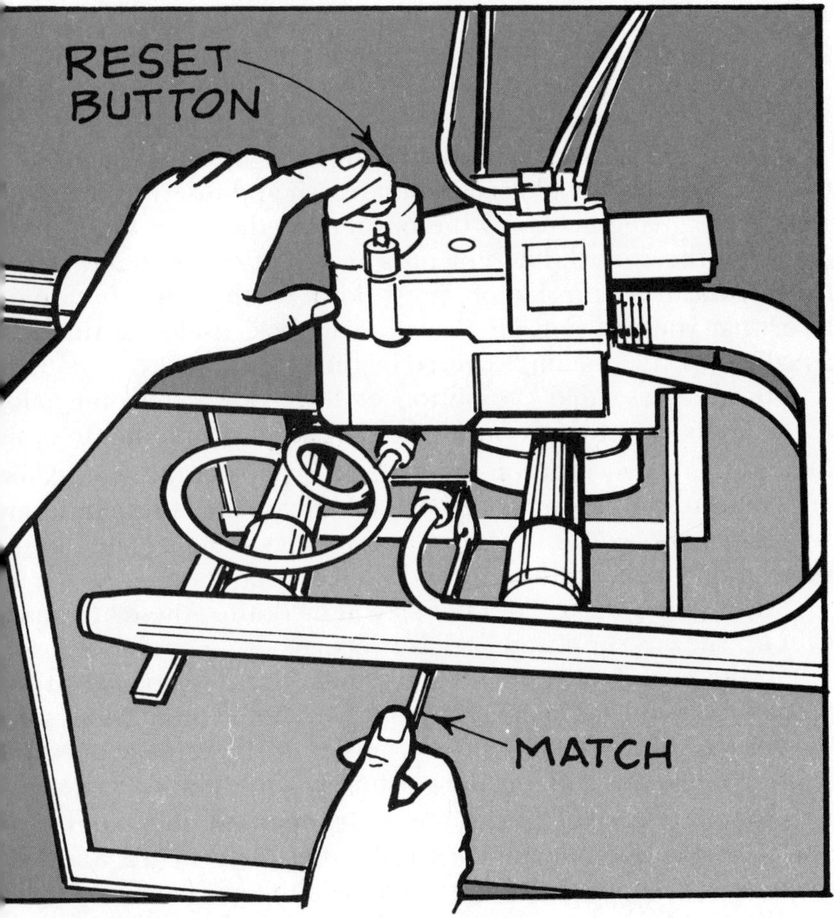

To relight the pilot flame on most gas furnaces, depress he dial, button, or lever on the reset device for one ninute after igniting the burner with a match.

TIP:

If a wrench or pliers is needed to turn off the main gas supply, keep such a tool within reach of the valve for emergency use.

ATTENTION

whether the pilot flame has gone out. To view the flame you mu usually remove an access panel on the furnace.

If the flame is out, follow the instructions for relighting printed on the furnace or pilot assembly. Generally, the proce dure involves first turning off the gas supply. On many furnace this is done by turning a control knob on the pilot assembly in th "off" position.

On older furnaces without a control knob, this is done b closing both the main inlet valve and the pilot inlet valve, whic are found on the gas inlet pipe near the furnace. The pilot inle valve is the smaller of the two. Turning the valve handles so tha they are perpendicular to the pipes on which they are installe shuts off the gas.

Wait at least five minutes for accumulated gas to dissipate During this time, turn the thermostat governing the furnace to it lowest setting; next, turn on the gas supply to the pilot burne either by moving the control knob to the "pilot" setting or b reopening the pilot inlet valve on the gas inlet pipe.

Now light a match and hold it in front of the pilot burner Often you must use a long wooden match and insert it far into small hole giving access to the burner. At the same time, pres down on the control knob or on a reset button beside it. If th furnace has no control knob, press down on the single button o lever that you will find on a small metal box inside the furnace usually near the opening covered by the access panel.

In all cases, hold the button or lever down until the pilo flame lights, and then continue holding it for a full minute or a long as the instructions on the furnace specify. If the pilot flam goes out during this time or when you release the button or lever repeat the procedure up to two more times, holding the butto or lever down about thirty seconds longer each time.

If the pilot flame does not stay lighted after these attempts shut off the gas supply and call for service.

If the pilot flame remains lit, turn the control knob to "on" o reopen the main gas inlet valve. You then should be able to restar the furnace by advancing the thermostat. If the furnace does no light immediately, shut off the gas supply and call for service.

Should you smell gas at any time, open all doors and win dows. Do not operate any electrical outlets or switches. Shut of the main gas supply valve, located beside the gas meter, by turn ing the handle so it is perpendicular to the pipe on which it is installed. If the odor does not dissipate, evacuate the building and call the utility company from a nearby telephone.

Curing a Smoky Fireplace

Nothing spoils the warmth and cheer of a cozy indoor fire more than a smoky fireplace. The problem can be caused by a variety of conditions, some of which are simple to cure, some less so. Fortunately, fireplace masons typically are both knowledgeable and conservative. To avoid constructing a smoky fireplace, they generally rely on tried-and-true designs that, if anything, sacrifice heating efficiency for qualities essential for containing smoke and channeling it up the chimney.

Before lighting a fire in a fireplace that smokes, try the following procedures.

First, make sure the damper is open completely. The damper is a hinged metal plate attached inside the fireplace at the top, where it joins the chimney. Its purpose is to regulate the amount of air passing up the flue. When starting a fire, the maximum amount of air is necessary.

Most dampers are controlled by a notched lever that you can feel by reaching up into the fireplace. To open the damper, push the lever upward, either with your hand or with the tip of a fireplace poker. Later, to control the size of the blaze and conserve fuel, you can lower the damper a few notches using the poker. The correct way to regulate a fire after it is well lit is to lower the damper until the fireplace begins to smoke, then raise it a notch at a time until smoking stops.

Naturally, you must also make sure that the chimney is clean and unobstructed. To check for obstructions, try looking upward into the chimney from below when the damper is open. Use a

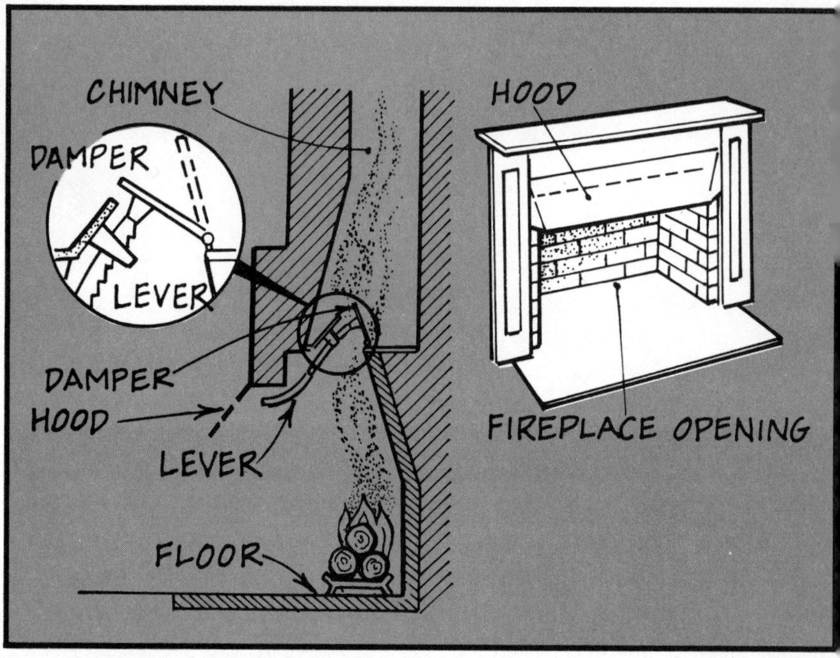

Three ways to prevent a smoky fireplace: open the damper further, build the fire far back in the fireplace, and raise the fuel by placing it on andirons or a grate.

Installing a fireplace hood lowers the height of the fireplace opening to contain rising smoke.

flashlight and wear goggles or safety glasses. Otherwise, go up on the roof and peer down into the chimney.

Chimneys should be inspected and cleaned at least once a year. If yours has not been serviced within this period, have the job performed by a qualified chimney sweep. After an initial cleaning, you may decide to perform further regular maintenance yourself. (See the chapter "Inspecting and Cleaning Chimneys and Fireplaces").

Lay the fire on andirons or a raised grate so that all logs and kindling are arranged as far toward the rear of the fireplace as possible. No fuel should project forward beyond the inside edge of the chimney breast, the overhanging lip of masonry that forms the upper edge of the fireplace opening.

Raising the fuel off the fireplace floor allows plenty of air to enter the fire from underneath, enhancing combustion. Also, raising the fuel has the effect of reducing the height of the firebox, the area of the fireplace where burning takes place. Often, this is enough to cure smoking caused by a firebox that is too high or one that requires a strong updraft to operate properly.

Before lighting the fire, ignite a few sheets of rolled-up newspaper and allow them to burn completely. This warms the air in the firebox and initiates an updraft. Then light the fire by igniting kindling near the base.

If smoking occurs after these measures have been taken, try opening a nearby window a few inches. This will increase the amount of air entering the fire and should strengthen the updraft.

If smoking persists, consider reducing the firebox height still further. Obtain a panel of sheet metal about 15 inches wide and as long as the width of the fireplace opening. A scrap of wide aluminum siding will do, or attach aluminum foil to one side of a piece of plywood.

Hold the panel against the chimney breast at a point even with its lower edge. While the fire is burning, gradually slide the panel downward over the fireplace opening until the smoke is contained. Mark the panel to indicate how far it extends.

Replace the panel with a permanently installed fireplace hood or deflector of this size. These are available through fireplace and woodstove suppliers. Alternatively, consider obtaining folding glass doors that fit across the fireplace opening. When closed, they seal the fireplace but continue to admit air for combustion through vents. Heat is reflected into the room through the glass.

Smoking also can be the result of outdoor conditions. Puffs of smoke entering a room from beneath the chimney breast are evidence of downdrafts, cold air spilling down the chimney despite the heated air rising. These can occur during windy weather and, if occasional, may be ignored.

However, if downdrafts are frequent, first make sure that no foliage overhangs the chimney or interferes with air flowing around it. If any does, prune it back at least 10 feet from the chimney. To function properly, a chimney should be the highest object within a 10-foot radius and should project at least 3 feet above a flat roof and 2 feet above the peak of a pitched roof.

Consult a fireplace mason before taking steps to lengthen a chimney. A common lengthening method is to attach a metal or masonry chimney cap above the flue opening. The cap not only increases the height of the chimney but also alters air currents over the opening.

Sometimes, particularly in tightly sealed houses, the smell of stale smoke fills a room hours after a fire has gone out. In some cases the cause simply may be cold air descending naturally into the chimney, but at other times it may be also the result of heating equipment or exhaust fans expelling air from the house. This can create a slight vacuum that actually draws air indoors through the chimney. In both cases the smell is the odor of soot lining the flue.

To remedy the problem, first make sure that heating equipment has its own air supply connected directly to the outdoors. If it does not, consult a heating engineer. If the air supply is adequate, an easy solution is to install a chimney-top damper, operated by a chain extending into the fireplace. The damper can be closed from indoors after a fire is extinguished, and will prevent outdoor air from entering the flue.

Household Fire Safety

Making your home safe from fire requires eliminating fire hazards, installing an adequate system of smoke detectors, and learning how to respond in case a fire does start. The leading causes of home fires—kitchen accidents, faulty household wiring, heating equipment and appliances, improperly stored flammable liquids, and thoughtless smoking habits—are all preventable, often easily, quickly, and inexpensively. The key is to act immediately. The sooner you take steps to safeguard your home from fire, the less you risk your own life and the lives of family members and other occupants.

Tour your home to search out fire hazards. In the kitchen, check to see that cooking surfaces are free of grease buildup and that curtains, napkins, pot holders, and aprons are kept well away from burners and heat. If fire extinguishers are installed, be sure they are the correct type, are fully charged, and that you know how to use them. Do not store newspapers or paper bags near the stove. Check that major appliances such as the refrigerator and dishwasher are in working order and keep them in top condition by cleaning them regularly and having them periodically maintained by a qualified service technician. Keep small appliances clean and functioning properly, and always unplug them when not in use.

Have household wiring, the furnace, fireplaces, and chimneys professionally inspected by qualified technicians or fire officials. Worn-out or overloaded wiring is particularly dangerous because

APARTMENT OWNERS:

Municipal regulations regarding the number and placement of smoke detectors and other fire-safety equipment like sprinkler systems, alarms, and fire extinguishers are quite specific. Follow their requirements to the letter; if parts of a building not under your jurisdiction do not seem adequately protected, notify the fire department or local code-enforcement office, listed in the telephone book.

HINT

fires can start unnoticed behind walls and smolder for long periods before bursting forth. If your home was built between 1965 and 1973, have it checked for the presence of aluminum wiring. This type can overheat or loosen—also causing a fire—if mistakenly connected to outlets and switches not specifically designed for use with aluminum.

Pay particular attention to the use of extension cords. Never use extensions as permanent wiring. Instead, install additional wall outlets or have them installed by a licensed electrician. Also, avoid connecting more than one heat-producing appliance such as a curling iron, hair dryer, or electric heater to the same extension cord. When using an extension cord with a heavy-duty appliance or with power tools, be sure the cord is rated to accommodate increased electrical loads. Ordinary household extension cords are not sufficient.

Check space heaters for frayed or damaged wiring, and make sure their tip-over safety switches work. Keep heaters at least 3 feet away from anything combustible, including drapes, tablecloths, and upholstered and solid wood furniture.

In rooms with fireplaces, make sure fire screens fit closely around the full perimeter of the fireplace to prevent sparks from flying out. Even so, never store newspapers, kindling, or firewood near the fireplace opening. Never leave a fire unattended.

Relocate your home workshop if it is near a pilot light. Fumes and sawdust from project materials can ignite or explode in the presence of an open flame. No matter where you set up shop, flammable liquids should not be kept indoors. Store them instead in ventilated, locking safety cabinets, preferably installed in a separate shed away from the building. Rags and paper containing flammable substances should be disposed of promptly after use. Because local policies differ, call the fire department to learn recommended disposal procedures for your community.

Smoke detectors are crucial. According to the National Fire Protection Association, having working smoke detectors reduces by half your chances of dying in a home fire. Ideally, each room and hallway in your house should have at least one detector. As a minimum, there should be a smoke detector between each bedroom and the rest of the house and one at the head of each stairway. Other important locations include utility rooms, the basement, the attic, and closets containing heating equipment.

Installing detectors is merely a matter of attaching them to a wall or ceiling with screws. Detectors should be mounted as high in a room as possible. If attached to a ceiling, detectors should be at least 6 inches from the nearest wall. Detectors mounted on walls should be between 6 and 12 inches below the ceiling. Do not

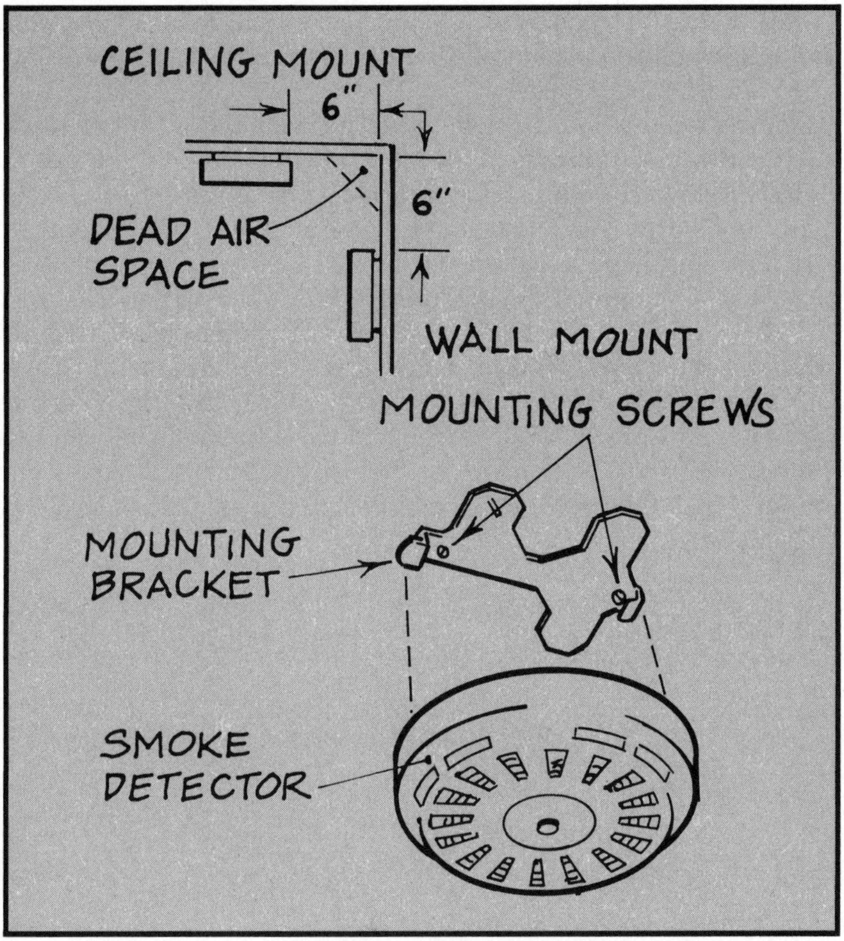

Installing smoke detectors on walls or ceilings is easy, but be sure to place them at least 6 inches from corners.

install detectors where temperatures routinely fall below 40 degrees or rise above 100 degrees Fahrenheit, nor where normal kitchen smoke or automobile exhaust can set them off. Test smoke detectors once a week. Never apply paint over them.

If a fire does occur—even a small one—everyone should evacuate the house immediately and meet outside at a predetermined location. Call the fire department from a neighbor's phone. Do not attempt to put out a fire with an extinguisher unless you are experienced with using one and are positive the extinguisher on hand is correctly rated for the type of fire you must use it on.

Most important in assuring safety in case of a fire is developing and practicing a family escape plan. To develop a plan, go through each room in the house and determine at least two ways to leave it in an emergency. Then make a large sketch of your home's overall floor plan and mark these exits clearly on it. Post the plan where it is clearly visible.

Practice evacuating the house often, even if it means climbing out windows or tramping across flower beds. To safely exit upper-story windows, install fire ladders, available at hardware and department stores. Flexible ladders can be anchored permanently to the floor and kept ready for use in a storage box beneath a window. Leave the top of the box unattached for easy removal.

In a real fire, darkness, confusion, toxic gases, and smoke obscure vision and prevent clear thinking. Occupants must rely on training to escape. During drills, practice crawling on hands and knees to exits to avoid smoke and heat. Instruct children that they cannot hide from a fire by entering a closet or by crawling under a bed. Once outside, remember never to return to a burning building.

Curing Indoor Condensation

Chronic mildew on walls and ceilings, peeling paint that exposes bare material underneath (not just earlier coats of finish), sweating windowpanes, and crumbling plaster; all of these frequently are signs of indoor condensation. Most often this condensation—water in household air changing from vapor to liquid—occurs in winter. But it can crop up anytime.

Damage can result if the condition is prolonged. Remedies exist—some simple and some not—but the subject is complex and many building engineers disagree on certain strategies. To better understand the problem, this is how condensation develops:

As air becomes warmer, its ability to absorb moisture (in the form of vapor) increases. The amount of moisture actually contained in a mass of air, compared with the amount it is capable of containing at that temperature, is called the relative humidity. At 100 percent relative humidity, an air mass can hold no more water vapor.

When air cools, its ability to contain water decreases. Eventually, cooling air reaches a temperature at which it is overloaded with moisture, and so must give some up. The temperature at which this occurs is called the dew point.

The dew point of an air mass varies according to the air's relative humidity. The more moisture the air contains, the higher the dew point temperature.

When the dew point is reached, causing the relative humidity of the air mass to become 100 percent, water vapor in the air condenses to liquid. Because it is then heavier than air, it is lef behind as dampness. This process ceases when rising tempera tures or reduced moisture content cause the relative humidity o the air mass to fall below 100 percent.

In winter, heated air inside a home can, and usually does contain much greater amounts of moisture than the cooler ai outside. This indoor moisture migrates toward its drier counter part.

In days before homes were well sealed and insulated, mois indoor air passed quickly outdoors through cracks in windov frames and doorjambs and other openings.

Much heat was carried, and lost, with it. But this proces prevented condensation because the temperature of the indoo air stayed above the dew point until it encountered the outsid air.

In most homes today, because of energy-efficient construc tion methods, far less heat escapes with moist air, and so its dew point often occurs within wall or ceiling insulation, or on interio surfaces.

The cure is basically twofold: Indoor moisture levels shoul be reduced, and what moisture remains should be prevented fron entering walls and ceilings. Moisture levels can be reduced b installing adequate fans and ventilators in excessively damp area like bathrooms, laundry rooms, and kitchens to expel moist ai from the building. Supplement these with portable electric de humidifiers.

Do not vent clothes dryers indoors to capitalize on the fre heat they provide. The vented air is moist from the wet clothin inside the dryer and will condense indoors if not conducted ou of the building.

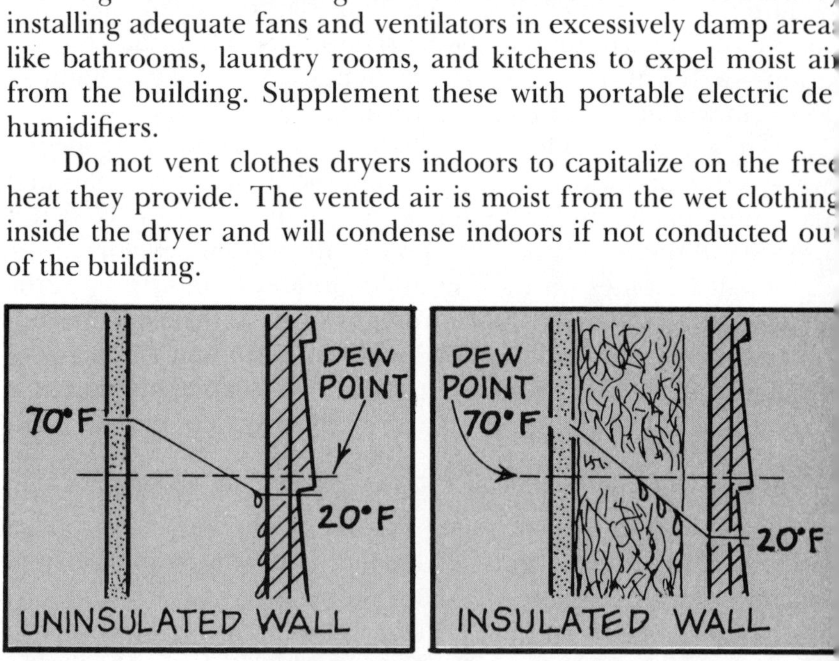

Moisture forms sooner inside an insulated wall from which little heat escapes. This can lead to moisture problems that are not encountered in an uninsulated wall.

A range hood above the stove will capture cooking vapors; on the stove, steaming pots should be covered with lids until the water inside cools. Houseplants, which give off moisture, should be kept to a minimum.

If you have a basement or crawl space with a dirt floor, prevent the moisture in it from rising into walls and living spaces by laying 6-mil-thick polyethylene sheeting over the floor and several inches up the walls. The sheeting, commonly called vapor barrier, is available at home centers and building supply stores. Overlap all seams when spreading the vapor barrier and anchor it by weighting it along the edges with bricks or boards.

Foundation walls should have louvers or windows that open. Leave them open year-round for ventilation, regardless of the energy loss. (Insulate the basement ceiling if the floor above becomes cold.) If there are no vents, some must be installed.

Vapor barriers are also crucial in halting the migration of existing moisture, which might condense inside walls, rot the construction, and dampen the insulation, diminishing its effectiveness.

In new construction and extensive renovation, attaching polyethylene sheeting across walls and ceilings just under wallboard has become standard practice and is quite effective.

However, if walls are already finished and no renovation is planned, a workable vapor barrier can be achieved after surfaces are dry and condensation is eliminated. Do this by applying vinyl wallpaper or two coats of oil-based (alkyd) paint to perimeter walls and ceilings that separate living spaces from an unheated attic or the roof.

Vapor barrier paint, specially formulated for the purpose, is also available from paint stores and home centers. If paint is already peeling, walls must be dried and cleaned and peeling paint removed.

Also seal openings around pipes, vents, television antenna connections, electrical wires, doors, and windows. Use caulking compound, foam sealant (available in spray cans), or weatherstripping. Gasket kits are available at hardware stores for sealing behind electric switch plates and wall receptacles, problem areas that are often overlooked by builders.

If you want to monitor household moisture levels, use a hygrometer. Inexpensive ones are available from scientific supply stores and some mail-order retailers. Relative humidity readings should average below 30 percent during winter months. However, even if they are higher, problems are unlikely to develop unless outdoor temperatures also average below freezing.

Radon Testing and Solutions

Radon is an odorless, tasteless, invisible, radioactive gas formed by the natural breakdown of uranium in soil and rock. It is found nearly everywhere and has always been present. Because it is a gas, radon tends not to stay in one place but to migrate, following paths of least resistance through the ground, and eventually rising into the atmosphere.

Outdoors, radon escaping from the earth is immediately diluted by air and poses little danger. However, radon rising into a home by way of the basement or foundation can become trapped and concentrated. When breathed over a long period of time, radon in concentrated proportions has been associated with an increased risk of lung cancer.

Not all homes are endangered by radon. Even in areas where high overall levels of the gas have been detected, some homes show little evidence of infiltration. On the other hand, some homes in areas where overall radon levels are low have been found to contain very high levels. The only way to tell if you and your family are at risk is to test for radon in your home. You can do this yourself, easily and inexpensively. And if corrective action is necessary, there are many steps you can take to remedy the problem before calling in professionals.

Begin by making an initial screening test. By contacting your state health or radiation-control department or regional office of the Environmental Protection Agency (EPA) you can usually obtain a list of reputable test kit manufacturers from whom to select an initial testing device costing as little as ten dollars.

Most devices consist of a small canister containing charcoal. When you receive it, place it in the lowest livable area of the home—usually the basement. Following the instructions, open the canister and allow the charcoal to absorb air for the time specified, usually three days to a week. Keep the windows and doors to the area closed as much as possible for at least twelve hours before opening the canister and for the duration of the test. When the time is up, close the canister and mail it to the designated laboratory for analysis.

The lab results will indicate whether more testing should be done. If so, the use of a more accurate testing device, called an alpha track detector, is usually recommended. To perform the test, several detectors are placed throughout the house. These are left uncovered for a longer period of time than a charcoal canister, usually from one to three months but sometimes for as long as a year. Then they too are returned to the lab.

Your risk from exposure to radon depends on the amount of the gas entering your home and the length of time it remains. Lowering radon levels, then, is a twofold process of sealing out as much radon as possible and improving ventilation to prevent radon that does enter the home from lingering.

TIP:

In 1991, the EPA "action level," above which steps to reduce radon levels are recommended, was 4 picocuries per liter of air (pCi/l). This is not a risk-free level; outdoor concentrations of radon in air average about .05 pCi/l. The EPA considers lowering radon counts to below 4 pCi/l impossible for some homes and financially impractical for others. Radon levels in water are considered a problem only in supplies drawn from private wells. If you have a well, call the EPA to learn the current standard for radon in water.

ATTENTION

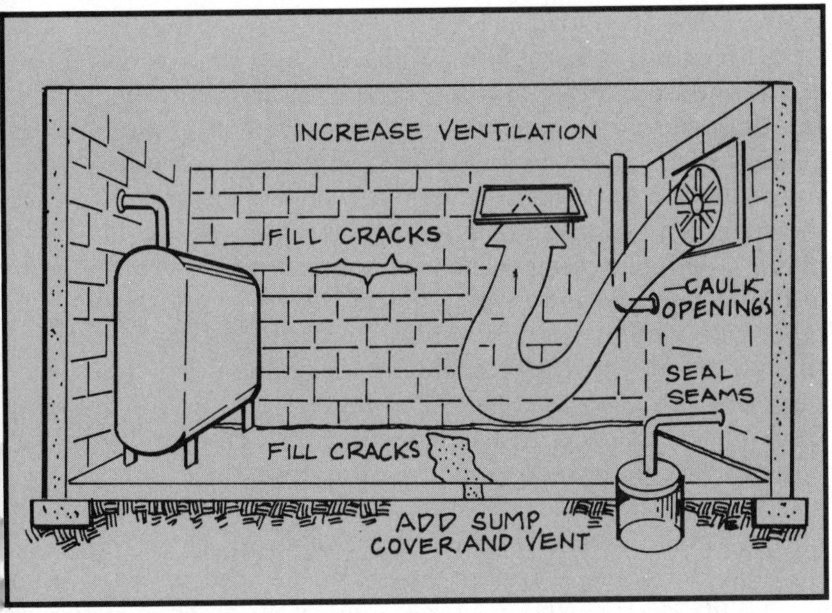

Sealing openings and providing constant ventilation generally are the most effective ways to keep radon levels to a minimum.

> **TIP:**
>
> To find a qualified radon mitigation or testing contractor, contact an office of the EPA or your state health department. Mitigation contractors should have successfully passed tests qualifying them for listing with the EPA's Radon Contractor Proficiency Program (RCPP) and should be able to produce a photo identification card issued by the EPA. Testing companies should qualify for listing with the EPA's Radon Measurement Proficiency Program (RMPP). Each state also has regulations regarding the licensing of radon-control contractors.

ATTENTION

The simplest and least expensive approach—and often the only one needed—is to seal the basement floor and walls with easily obtained materials and ventilate the area with ordinary fresh-air fans. Flowable silicone sealant is recommended for filling cracks, seams, and small holes in floors. Use nonflowable silicone caulking compound for making the same repairs to walls. Another suitable sealant for floors and walls is polyurethane foam, available in pressure cans. Seal around pipes that pass through the foundation, and if possible plug the holes in the top row of hollow concrete block foundations if they are not completely covered by the house framing. For plugging, use mortar or polyurethane foam.

Cover the repairs with a brush-on epoxy sealant. While the epoxy is still tacky, add nonshrinking cement grout and bonding mix. Afterward, or if no repairs are necessary, porous concrete or block walls and concrete floors should be sealed by coating them with epoxy sealing compound. If the surfaces are relatively nonporous, waterproof latex paint can be used instead.

If the basement floor is dirt or gravel, or has areas of either material, these must be covered with poured concrete, then sealed and coated as described. Crawl space floors generally cannot be covered—there's not enough room. Instead, attach polyethylene sheeting beneath the floor of the house and ventilate the crawl space as described further on.

Drains and sump openings present a special problem. If they are not needed, fill them with gravel and cap them with cement. If a drain absolutely must be used, cap it with a removable piece of sheet metal or tile and uncover it only when necessary. With a sump, make a permanent cover out of light sheet metal and seal the edges with caulking compound where it meets the floor. Use plastic (PVC) plumbing to make an exhaust pipe for the sump by inserting one end into a hole cut in the cover and leading the other end outdoors. Attach a small fan to the end of the pipe and run it frequently to draw escaping radon out of the sump. In some cases you may need to add another pipe to bring air into the sump from outside, in order to avoid creating a partial vacuum that will actually draw more radon into the sump from the ground.

To ventilate, concentrate on the area closest to the ground. Getting rid of radon in the basement or crawl space means it can't rise into the house. In most cases, all you need to do is install heavy-duty electric window fans in some of the basement windows and leave the remaining windows open so that radon-laden air can be forced out. The fans should be capable of moving 240 cubic feet of air per minute and enough fans should be installed to achieve two complete changes of air per hour. Be sure to install fans so they draw air from outside into the basement, not the other way around. In a crawl space, install fans by enlarging some of the existing vents. Wiring to crawl space fans must be rated for outdoor use. For best results, keep fans in a basement or crawl space running constantly.

Run a follow-up test with alpha track detectors after completing these procedures. Chances are, you will have cleared up the problem. However, if radon levels are still high, consider professional repairs. Having already sealed your house yourself, you'll save a great deal on the cost.

Repairing Squeaky Stairs

Squeaky, wobbly stairs are more than just a nuisance. They can become hazardous if trouble spots are allowed to worsen. Some stair problems are easy to fix. But because of the complexity of stair construction, severe problems are often best left to an experienced carpenter.

Squeaks are caused by loose or broken stair parts rubbing together. If you can pinpoint the squeak, applying powdered graphite or silicone lubricant to the spot may silence it. Both are available at hardware stores. But lubrication will not remedy the underlying problem.

To find the source of squeaking, remove any carpeting or other covering from the stairs. (You have to do this in any event, even to apply a lubricant.) Then step slowly on each stair. When you step on one that squeaks, rock back and forth on it until you are sure which part is moving.

Inspecting stairs at night or early in the morning is often best, because at these times background noise is slight and squeaks are easier to trace. It often helps to have someone rock on the tread while you examine the stairs. Shining a light on the joints will help you detect even slight movement.

When a squeaking spot is found, try to repair it from the underside of the staircase. The repair will be stronger, and because it will be hidden, it will be easier to make. If the staircase has several squeaks or is severely damaged, removing wallboard or other paneling to gain access to the underside is usually worthwhile.

Underneath the stairs, look first at the sides of the treads and isers. The treads are the horizontal boards you stand on; the isers are the vertical boards that link them. Check to see if both est in grooves cut in the stringers, which are the long, slanting oards that rise from the lower floor to the upper. If they do, vedges usually hold the parts in place, and tightening them will ften cure the squeaks.

To tighten the wedges, simply strike them with a hammer. On some stairs, both the vertical wedges that press against the acks of the risers and the horizontal wedges that press against he undersides of the treads are accessible. On others, the hori- ontal wedges overlap the bottoms of the vertical ones. With this rrangement, the wedges pressing against the risers can be tight-

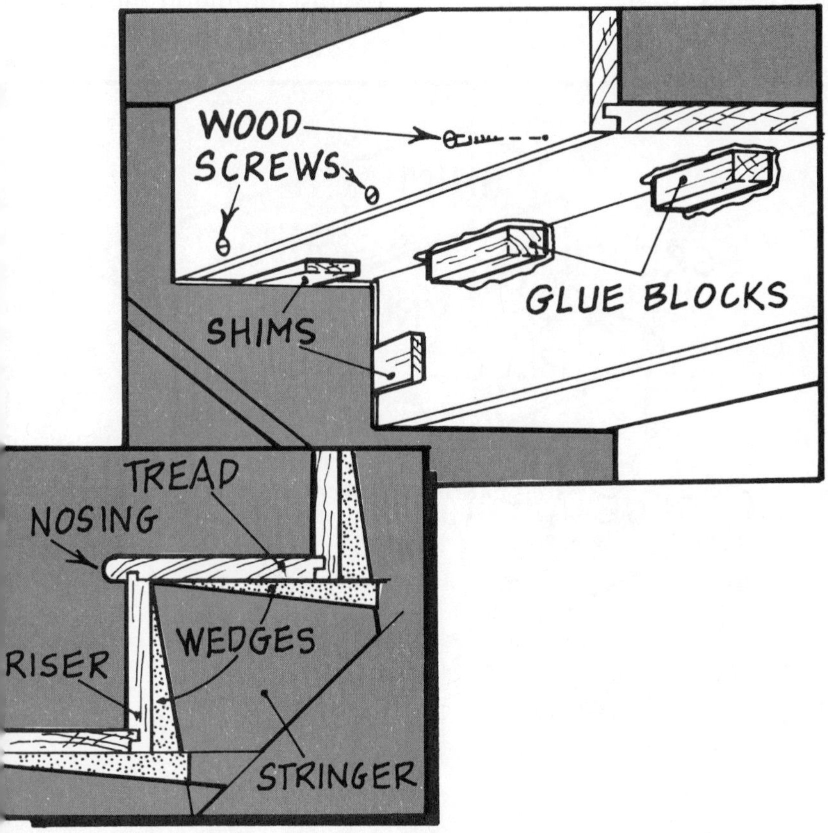

Repairs made beneath stairs are usually strongest and east visible. Blocks, screws, and wedges driven into grooves in stringers can stop squeaks.

TIP:

To supplement glue blocks, force silicone adhesive caulking compound into any gaps between the tread and the riser. In the event that the stair parts move even with glue blocks installed, the adhesive will keep them from touching, causing a squeak.

ATTENTION

ened only after first removing the horizontal wedges beneath them.

If tightening the wedges seems to work, use the stairs for a week or two before reinstalling any wallboard or paneling that ha been removed. If the squeaks return, one or more of the wedge has loosened. Find the loose wedges and coat each with a thin application of all-purpose wood glue. Then reinstall them.

Many risers and treads rest on notches cut in the tops of the stringers. Driving shims (thin wooden wedges) into the seams be tween the stair parts and the stringers will usually cure looseness The best shims to use are wooden shingle scraps. These are avail able in packages at lumberyards and from some home centers.

You will also find wooden blocks fastened where the treads and risers meet at right angles. If any blocks are loose, knock them off completely with a hammer, then sand them clean and reglue them. To fasten a freshly glued block, rub it back and forth where you want it until it stays in place. Avoid standing on the stair for

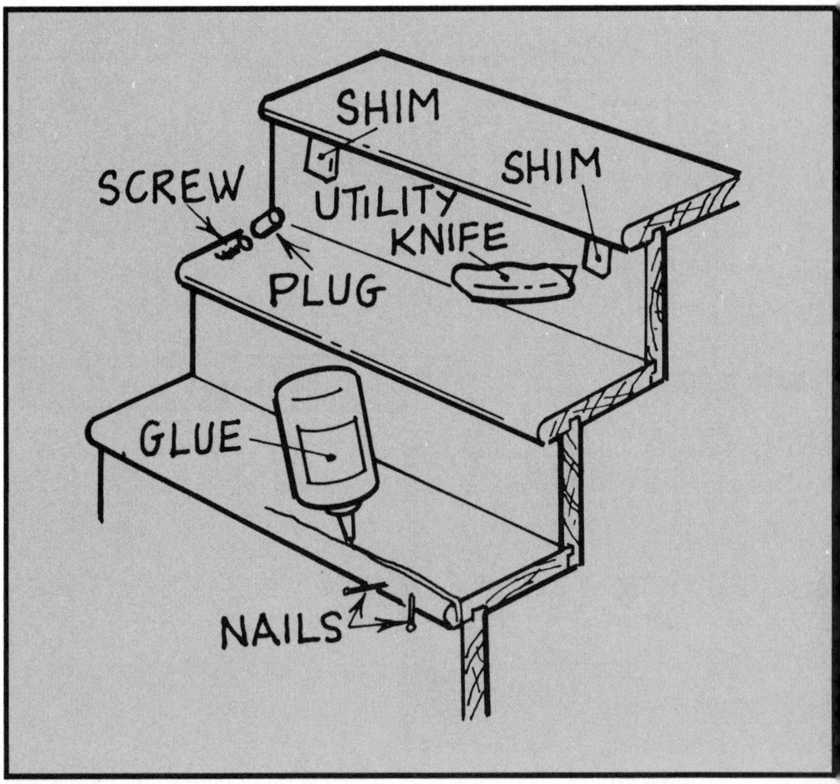

Shims (trimmed flush after installation), nails or screws, and glue can be used to repair stairs from above.

about twelve hours, until the glue dries. You can also supplement the blocks beneath the stairs or add blocks beneath stair joints that have none.

If the base of a riser rubs against the rear edge of a tread below, install screws through the riser and into the tread to bind the pieces. Use screws 2 inches long or longer. Drill holes for them first to avoid splitting the wood.

If you cannot make repairs from underneath the stairs, you will have to install wedges and metal fasteners from above. Here are some hints to help conceal the work:

When installing wedges, use long ones to avoid marring finished surfaces. Apply glue to the tip of the wedge, drive it into place between loose parts with a hammer, then use a sharp utility knife to trim away the excess wood flush with the seam.

When installing screws, predrill holes using a profile bit that matches the size of the screws. Profile bits widen the entrance to the screw hole so that the head of the screw can be installed below the surface and the hole filled with putty or a wooden plug. Profile bits, putty, and plugs are available at hardware stores.

Nails can be used if you have enough room to swing a hammer. Although they do not bind parts together as strongly as screws, they are easier to hide. Spiral-shank or ring-shank nails at least 1½ inches long have the greatest holding strength.

When using nails, drive a pair angled toward each other into the squeaky spot. Drill holes first using an ordinary straight drill bit that is slightly smaller in diameter than the nails. Sink the nail heads below the surface using a nail set, then fill the depressions with wood putty.

A problem that may begin as a squeak is a crack in the nosing, the part of the tread that projects beyond the front of the riser. Cracked nosings are unsightly and unsafe. Replacing the tread—a major task—is usually required if the nosing breaks off.

To repair a cracked nosing, work glue into the crack using a playing card as an applicator. Wiggle the cracked portion gently as you apply glue, and squeeze the crack together until an even line of excess glue is produced along the seam. Then drill holes and drive nails at angles into the edge of the nosing to hold the split together. Wipe away excess glue with a damp cloth.

Repairing Banisters

Banisters, or staircase posts and railings, are as much safety feature as they are a decorative element. This combinatio makes repairing loose or broken banisters important, but als somewhat complicated because fasteners are usually hidden.

If a banister wobbles, check first for loose newel posts. Thes are the large vertical posts at the top and bottom of the staircase

Solid newel posts are usually bolted to a joist underneath th floor. To tighten a bottom post, search in the basement beneat the stairs for its location. You should see the base of the pos protruding vertically through the subfloor and extending acros the joist, forming a right angle with it. Use a large adjustabl wrench or an automotive socket wrench to tighten the bolts tha fasten the post to the joist.

Lag bolts are most often used. These are actually large screw that penetrate the joist but do not pass completely through it. I because of wear to the wood surrounding the bolts, lag bolts car not be tightened, either drill new holes and install additional la bolts elsewhere along the base of the post, or remove the bolt drill completely through the post and joist (using the preser holes as guides), and install carriage bolts with washers and nut in place of the lag bolts.

On landings and upper floors, bolts for newel posts may b accessible by removing wooden plugs found along one side of th post, near floor level. If plugs are not visible, you may have t

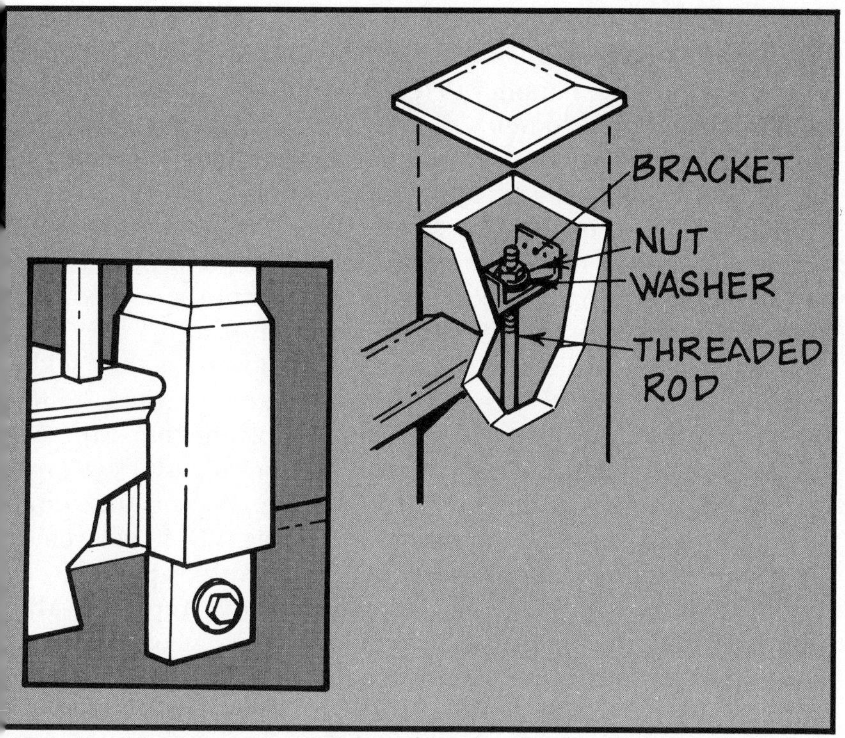

'ix a wobbly banister by tightening the newel post bolt(s), ısually accessible by going into the basement, beneath he staircase.

f a hollow newel post wobbles, the culprit is probably a oose interior bracket. Tightening the fasteners inside the ›ost should solve the problem.

'emove ceiling material beneath the stairs or a section of the flooring surrounding the post to expose the bolts.

In older homes, newel posts are often hollow and rest on top ›f the subfloor instead of passing through it. Inside the post is a ıorizontal bracket through which is threaded a long, vertical steel ›od that bolts the post firmly to the floor.

To get at the bracket and rod, remove the top of the post by apping it with a mallet. Tighten the nut on the end of the rod 'ith a wrench. Also inspect the bracket and tighten any fasteners hat attach it to the post.

If the newel posts are tight but the banister still wobbles, heck the handrail. Most rails are constructed of sections joined y bolts running through the center. Underneath the rail are ıoles (sometimes plugged) that allow tightening the bolts by using hammer and nail set or screwdriver to turn star-shaped nuts.

To tighten a nut, place the tip of the nail set or screwdrive against one of the points or lugs of the nut. Strike the other en of the tool with the hammer to turn the nut—clockwise to tighten counterclockwise to loosen.

Spindles that are loose or damaged are usually more difficul to fix than wobbly newel posts and handrails. To tighten loos spindles, drive thin, glue-coated wooden wedges into the sean where the spindle meets the underside of the handrail. They wi not be noticed there. After the glue dries, trim the wedges care fully with a sharp utility knife to hide them further.

Damaged spindles usually must be removed, as they seldor can be repaired neatly while in place. Reglue cracked spindle with wood glue. To clamp the seam after applying glue, wipe awa excess glue, then wrap the glued area tightly with adhesive tape.

After the glue is dry, remove the tape. Wiping the spindl with mineral spirits or penetrating oil such as WD-40 will remov sticky tape residue without damaging clear finish or paint.

If damage is more severe, spindles must be replaced. Man staircases built during the past twenty-five years incorporate stan dard spindles and other banister parts that can be obtained a lumberyards or building supply stores. Older or custom-bui spindles usually must be duplicated from scratch by an exper enced cabinetmaker.

To remove a spindle, inspect the base to determine how it i installed. If necessary, pry away molding or blocking covering th seam. Then twist the spindle, or tap it with a mallet, to free th ends from their sockets in the staircase and handrail.

Watch for nails or other fasteners in the ends. If possibl remove these; otherwise, work the spindle parts free gradually s that the fasteners also come out without causing further damage

Some spindles appear square at their base but are actuall held in place by a dowel extending into a hole in the stair trea beneath the spindle. To remove this type, try twisting it to brea the glue (if necessary) and then raising it vertically, forcing upward into the socket in the handrail, until the end of the dow clears the surface of the stair.

Pull the spindle downward at an angle to remove it from th handrail. If you cannot remove the spindle this way, saw it in tw and remove each piece separately.

To reinstall spindles, first clean any dried glue from the sock ets using a strip of sandpaper wrapped around a dowel. The spread glue on the ends of the spindles and follow the remova procedures in reverse.

Replacement spindles with doweled bases may require trim ming to fit. To do this, first measure from the top of the hole i ıe underside of the handrail to the surface of the stair tread ontaining the hole for the dowel.

With a saw, trim the upper end of the spindle so that the istance between the tip and the bottom of the squared-off poron of the base equals 3/8 inch less than this distance. Then trim ıe dowel beneath the squared-off portion to create a 1/4-inch-long ub.

Test the fit of the trimmed spindle. If the tip tapers too ıarply to permit forcing it upward into the socket in the handrail, ınd it near the top to decrease its circumference.

When the spindle can be fitted into place, apply glue to both nds and reinstall it. Clamping glued spindles is unnecessary.

Remedies for Door Problems

Hinged doors that rub or bind often require only minor repairs. However, to avoid worsening a problem or creating new ones, it is important to determine the cause of symptoms first and to work carefully when remedying them.

To analyze most door problems, open and close the door while standing on the side where the hinges are visible. Note any places where contact between the door and the frame occur.

If the latch edge of the door (the edge with the knob) has recently begun to rub the frame near the top or bottom corner, check for loose hinges. To do this, open the door fully to gain access to the screws, and try tightening them with a large screwdriver (the longer it is, the greater its turning force). Even a fraction of a turn can make a difference.

To avoid ruining the screw slots, use a screwdriver with a tip as wide as the length of the slots. If the screws are covered with paint, dab them with a cotton swab dipped in paint remover. Before trying to turn the screws, let the remover work for five to ten minutes, then scrape the slots clean with the tip of the screwdriver or a straightened paper clip.

If the holes have become enlarged and the screws cannot be tightened, remove and replace them with screws of the next larger diameter. If the hinges will not accept larger screws, or if the wood is cracked, plug the holes with short lengths of wooden dowel (available at hardware stores), and then drill new holes.

To plug the holes, first remove the door and hinges. To remove the door, tap the hinge pins up and out of the hinges using a hammer and a flat-blade pry bar or a large screwdriver. Remove the lower pin first to prevent the door from toppling.

'o plug enlarged screw holes, fill them by gluing in short engths of wooden dowel. Drill holes in the dowels to einstall the hinge screws. If a hinge is mortised too deep n the frame, add a thin cardboard shim behind the hinge vhen refastening it.

To remove the hinge leaves, take out the screws and tap or push the leaves sideways to avoid chipping the notches (called nortises) in which they are installed.

Using a ¼-inch-diameter bit, drill into the holes about a quarer of an inch beyond the length of the old screws. Saw lengths of ¼-inch-diameter dowel to fit, then glue them in the holes using vhite or yellow wood glue. Work glue into any cracks around the noles as well.

TIP:

Old paint on doors may contain lead, which is harmful if ingested. After removing paint, collect all residue in a bag and deposit it in the trash.

When the glue is dry, place the hinge leaf in its original position and drill carefully centered pilot holes into the ends of the dowels. Then install the original screws or replacements. The diameter of the pilot holes should equal the thickness of the screw shaft, excluding the threads.

If the hinges are not loose and the problem has been persistent, the hinge diagonally opposite the rubbing corner may be mortised more deeply into the frame than the other hinge. The remedy is to insert a homemade cardboard shim behind the deeper hinge. Use the thinnest cardboard you can find. If it is insufficient, more shims can be added.

Make a shim by cutting cardboard to the same shape and size as the hinge leaf fastened to the door frame. To install the shim, first slide a wedge beneath the door to support it, then remove the screws holding the hinge leaf to the frame. Carefully slide the leaf out of its mortise, fit the shim in place, and refasten the leaf.

If a door rubs along the top or binds when closed, the cause is usually an accumulation of paint along the door edges or stop molding (the strip against which the door presses when shut). Removing the paint should cure the problem, usually without removing the door. Apply paint remover with a brush—carefully to avoid a mess—to either the door edges or the corner where the stop molding meets the frame. If you are applying remover at the top of the door or frame, stand on a stepladder so it won't drip on you.

After letting the remover work, scrape the areas down to bare wood with a narrow putty knife or small hook scraper. Test the door. If it no longer rubs, a thin coat of fresh paint should be applied to cover the bare wood.

If rubbing persists or occurs elsewhere, the cause is probably warping, faulty construction, or settling of the building. Open the door and hold a long builder's level or straightedge against the section of the frame where the rubbing occurs. If the ends of the level or straightedge do not lie flat, find the bulge that causes them to rock and mark it with a pencil.

Minor bulges can be sanded flat by using first coarse, then finer, sandpaper wrapped around a block, or by careful use of a belt sander. Do not sand paint that may contain lead; the dust can be hazardous. (If any paint on the door was applied before 1977, assume that it contains lead.) The best cure for a bowed frame—and the recommended alternative to sanding a frame coated with paint that may contain lead—is replacement, usually a job for a professional.

If the door frame is not warped, inspect the door. Test it with the straightedge and mark any bulges. To restore the fit, remove he door from the frame and narrow or shorten it with a sharp ıand plane.

When narrowing a door, even if the bulge is on the latch ·dge, planing is best done on the hinge edge to avoid removing ınd replacing the latch hardware. Set the door down on folded owels to protect the latch edge. One way to brace the door while 'ou work is to wedge one end into a corner where two walls meet.

Remove the hinges and apply paint remover to the edge of he door with a paintbrush. After letting the remover work and craping away the loosened paint, plane very thin shavings along he entire edge of the door, always moving the plane in the direcion of the wood grain. (To determine the direction of the grain, lane a few strokes in the direction that feels smoothest. If the lane slides with little effort and produces smooth, curly shavings, 'ou are probably planing in the correct direction. Planing against he grain is more difficult and usually produces coarse shavings ınd splinters or chips in the surface.)

To shorten a door, lay it flat on sawhorses. Shave along the op edge, holding the plane on its side. To avoid chipping the orners, work from the ends toward the middle.

Stop planing when the ends of the straightedge no longer ock. If the door has been shortened, rehang it to test the fit. If he door has been narrowed, check the fit by setting the door in he doorway and trying to slide a nickel between the long edges nd the frame. When this is possible, deepen the hinge mortises vith a chisel to compensate for planing. Then reattach the hinges nd rehang the door.

If neither the door nor the frame are warped yet the door vill not latch, check the alignment of the latch and the strike plate n the frame. If misalignment is less than an eighth of an inch, try emoving the plate, placing it in a vise, and enlarging the latch pening by filing it.

If misalignment is more severe, the plate can be repositioned ower or higher on the door frame by elongating the notch in vhich it fits. Use a chisel to do this.

However, if the problem seems to be that the door does not lose far enough for the latch to enter the strike plate opening, he remedy is to reposition the stop molding farther toward the utside of the door frame. This permits the door to swing farther nto the frame.

After removing the stop molding by careful prying, close the loor so that it latches. Then refasten the molding around the loor, just far enough from it so you can slide a credit card beween the molding and the door's outside surface.

Repairing and Replacing Door Locks

Door lock problems, or having to replace a lock for securit reasons, do not always mean that the entire doorknob and latc assembly must be removed or replaced. Often, it is sufficient t remove only the lock cylinder, the part containing the keyhole The cylinder can then be taken to a locksmith for repair, replace ment, or changing the key.

Provided the lock has a removable cylinder (most quality made locks for entry doors do), removing and reinstalling th cylinder is usually an easy job requiring few tools. In fact, if fas teners cannot be removed with ordinary tools, a licensed lock smith will be needed. When reinstalling a cylinder, make sure th key enters with its serrated edge up. Here are instructions fo removing and replacing the cylinders of four popular types o locks.

Key-in-knob. This has a keyhole in the exterior doorknob. O many models, the knob must be removed before the cylinder ca be removed. Inspect the base of the knob carefully. If you find tiny hole in the collar—the part surrounding the spindle—th knob can usually be removed in this way: First, insert the key i the slot, turn it a quarter turn clockwise and hold it in that posi tion. Next, insert the point of an awl, ice pick, or small nail int the hole and press it to disengage the catch on the spindle tha secures the knob. If the knob has two holes, part of the catch wi be visible beneath the correct one. Beneath the other will be onl a smooth surface.

While pressing the tip of the tool, pull on the knob. It should slide a fraction of an inch. Then remove the tool and slide the knob completely off the spindle. Pull or pry the halves of the knob apart to free the cylinder, which can then be removed after withdrawing the key.

The cylinder can be reinstalled by following the procedure approximately in reverse. Insert the key into the cylinder. Slide the knob onto the spindle up to the knob catch. Turn the key a quarter turn clockwise. Depress the knob catch with a pointed tool and push the knob completely onto the spindle.

Key-in-knob locks that do not have holes in the exterior knob, or for which the key has been lost, can usually be taken apart by removing two long screws from the plate attached to the interior side of the door. If the screws are not visible, they may be beneath a decorative escutcheon, called a rose, covering the plate. This can be slid off the spindle after first removing the interior doorknob by the method described or by depressing a small wire clip at the base of the knob. Inexpensive key-in-knob locks often do not have replacement cylinders.

Mortise. This has its mechanism enclosed in a rectangular metal case recessed into the edge of the door. The cylinder is installed through the outside of the door and fits into a threaded hole in the side of the case. It is held in place by a long setscrew installed perpendicular to it, through the edge of the door.

To remove the cylinder, open the door and remove the narrow faceplate that surrounds the latch and other protruding parts. Two screws usually fasten the plate. Beneath it you should find the head of the setscrew, aligned horizontally with the cylinder, just below its center. Loosen the setscrew about six turns but do not remove it.

Insert the key in the lock and use it to turn the cylinder counterclockwise. To simplify reinstallation, count the number of turns required to remove the cylinder (usually about six). If the cylinder sticks, keep loosening the setscrew and loosen the screws in the edge of the door that hold the case at the top and bottom.

A cylinder that is hard to unscrew can sometimes be turned by gripping it with channel-locking pliers, the type used to make plumbing repairs. Wrap the jaws of the pliers with electrical or adhesive tape first to prevent them from marring the finished surface of the cylinder. This method cannot be used if the cylinder is surrounded on the outside of the door by a rotating metal collar, called a bezel.

To reinstall the cylinder after it has been repaired or replaced, simply screw it back into the lock case the same number of turns or until the latch and dead bolt operate smoothly. Then retighten the setscrew and any other screws that were loosened. Reinstall the faceplate.

Rim. This is an auxiliary latch that attaches to the surface of the door near its edge. The bolt is on the interior side of the door and may be vertical or horizontal. To remove the cylinder, first remove the screws that fasten the lock case to the inside of the door. Lifting away the case should expose a metal retaining plate, also fastened to the door.

If the plate is loose, try tightening the screws holding it. This may solve the lock problem. Otherwise, remove the screws passing through the plate into the cylinder and free it by pushing the cylinder out of the door on the exterior side. To reinstall the cylinder, follow the procedure in reverse.

Dead bolt. This is a horizontal bolt installed in the edge of the door. Mechanically, it is similar in many ways to a key-in-knob lock. However, removing the cylinder follows virtually the same procedure as for a rim lock.

Unscrew the thumb-turn assembly on the door's interior side. On models without a retaining plate beneath the assembly, this may be all that is necessary; just push the cylinder out of the door on the outside. On models with a retaining plate, remove the screws passing through it into the cylinder. Removing additional screws in the end of the cylinder will usually unfasten any ar-

A key-in-knob lock (left). To remove the lock cylinder on most models, both doorknobs must be removed first.

A mortise lock (right). To remove the cylinder, loosen the long setscrew located beneath the face plate.

A rim lock. The cylinder is accessible after removing the ock case mounted on the inside of the door.

A deadbolt lock. To remove the lock cylinder, first remove he thumb-turn assembly on the inside of the door.

nored housing surrounding the keyhole. To reinstall the cylinler, follow the procedure in reverse.

Repairing and Replacing a Key-in-knob Lockset

Key-in-knob door locks are by far the most popular variety. Not only are they relatively inexpensive, they are also easy to nstall. However, the price of such economy and simplicity is often he need to replace the entire lockset—doorknobs, latch bolt, and ock—when problems occur like knobs that stick and latches that do not operate smoothly despite being correctly aligned.

If the doorknobs wobble, it may mean only that threaded parts—screws, bolts, or the spindle connecting both knobs—are loose and require tightening. To do this, look first for screw heads on the plate on the interior side of the door. If you find any, tightening them may solve the problem. If no screw heads are visible, remove the doorknob and try rotating the rose beneath it.

If the rose is threaded, rotating it clockwise may tighten it against the door and cure the wobble. If it only spins, try simply sliding it off the spindle. If that does not work, look for a slot in the edge or a clip resembling a staple. If there is a slot, insert the blade of a screwdriver or fingernail file into it and twist or pry. If there is a clip, press on it while prying between the edge of the rose and the door.

The right technique should cause the rose to pop free of a plate that is either threaded onto the spindle or fastened to the door with screws. Tighten the plate by screwing it farther onto the spindle or by tightening the screws. Replace the rose, then the doorknob.

If the spindle slides back and forth, adjust it while the inside doorknob and rose are removed. First, gauge the distance the shaft moves when pushed or pulled, then remove the plate. Rotate the rose on the outside clockwise—in most cases that rose is threaded—until the shaft moves the required distance. Replace the plate. (If you cannot rotate the rose on the outside of the door you may have to remove it, together with the doorknob. Beneath that rose also should be an adjustable plate.)

Most locksets can be entirely removed by first detaching the inside doorknob, rose and plate, and then pulling on the exterior doorknob to withdraw the remaining assembly, including the spindle. To remove the latch, remove the screws fastening it to the edge of the door and pull or pry it free.

Replace the old lockset with one the same size. Most are adjustable, but when shopping for a new lockset, take the measurements of the door thickness, diameter of the hole bored through the door, the distance (called the backset) from the center of the hole to the edge of the door, and the diameter of the hole bored into the edge of the door for the latch.

To install the new lockset, follow the instructions supplied by the manufacturer. If the lockset is the same size as the one you removed, no new holes need be drilled. Install the latch first, and if necessary a new strike plate in the door frame. Then fit the lockset into the door from the outside—be sure the keyhole is correctly positioned—and adjust the length of the spindle to suit the door thickness. Install the plate and rose (if there is one) and remaining doorknob. Then test the door.

Repairing Sliding Doors

Sliding doors are often a better choice than swinging doors for closets, cramped doorways, or as patio entrances. But minor adjustment is frequently required to keep sliding doors operating smoothly.

There are several styles of sliding doors. The kind with two panels that slide past each other are called bypass doors. These are most often used to span wide closet doorways.

Bypass doors are suspended from the top by brackets. Rollers, usually made of nylon, attached to the brackets glide in metal tracks fastened to the top of the door frame. At floor level, shallow U-shaped guides prevent the doors from swinging in and out at right angles to the track.

If bypass doors jam, derail, or fail to close tightly, first make sure the brackets with the rollers attached are securely fastened. Try wiggling them if they are accessible. If a bracket is loose, tighten the screws that hold it to the door.

If you cannot reach the brackets or determine whether they are loose by wiggling them, remove the doors. To do this, first remove the guides fastened to the floor. Unscrew them and set them aside. If any are bent or broken, replacements can be obtained at home centers or other stores that sell sliding doors. Sometimes bent metal guides can be straightened with pliers.

Have a helper grasp the outer door along one of its long edges while you grasp the other edge. Working together, tilt the door so that the bottom rises away from the inner door. At the same time, push upward. This will free the brackets from the track. Set the door against a nearby wall. Remove the other door the same way.

With some bypass doors, the brackets can be freed from the track only at certain spots. If you cannot remove a bypass door by the method described, examine the track for openings in the sides of the channels. Slide the door along the track until the rollers on the brackets line up with these openings, then try again.

With the brackets easily accessible it is no problem to tighten them. If the screw holes have become enlarged, replace the screws with the next longer or thicker size.

If the brackets are slotted to allow adjusting their position on the door, try to refasten the brackets in their original position. You can usually determine this from wear marks on the bracket. Otherwise, turn the screws until they are almost tight and finish tightening them after rehanging the door. Properly installed, the brackets should allow the bottom edge of the door to hang 3/8 to 1 inch above the floor.

Rollers often become cut or dented from derailing. If any are badly damaged, consider replacing them by obtaining new brackets containing them. Also inspect the tracks by sliding your fingers lightly across their edges, but be careful in case any sharp burrs obstruct the channels.

Burrs can often be smoothed away with a file. In some cases you may have to remove the door track to do so. If the track is bent or the sides of the channels are dented, replacing the track is usually the best solution.

When you are ready to rehang the doors, wipe the tracks clean using a paper towel or cloth, then spray them with dry silicone lubricant. Do not lubricate tracks or rollers with oil or grease; dust will accumulate and the parts will become gummy.

To replace bypass doors, simply reverse the removal procedure. Doors should hang level when installed. Reattach the floor guides, positioning them so that the doors slide smoothly without rubbing against each other.

Sliding doors made of panels that fold are called bifold or accordion doors. These are also suspended from an overhead track, but one that contains only a single channel. Although some doors hang from roller brackets enclosed in the channel, most are attached by short, flanged spindles that slide in the channel, rather than roll.

To reinstall spindles that have slipped out of a channel, look for an opening in one of the channel sides, usually near an end. Fold the door until the disengaged spindles align with this opening, then slip them back in one at a time.

To cure most problems with bypass doors, tighten or adjust the screws holding the brackets to the doors.

At the sides of a doorway, bifold and accordion doors are fastened at the top and bottom by fixed metal pins. A bracket in the track and one mounted where the side of the doorway meets the floor holds each pin in place. For the door to slide smoothly, the pins must be aligned vertically. When binding occurs, usually it is because the brackets have slipped out of alignment.

If you can gain access to the single screw in each bracket that locks it in position, you can usually realign the brackets without removing the doors.

First loosen the brackets slightly, unless they are already loose, and use a ruler or plumb bob to position the door vertically close to the side of the door frame. Then have an assistant hold the door in place while you retighten the bracket screws.

If you must remove a door to make adjustments, first slide the spindles out of the track. Then lift the door vertically at the edge where the pins are attached and tilt the bottom away from the bracket attached at floor level. To reinstall the door, follow the procedure in reverse.

Repairing Squeaky Floors

A squeaking wood floor is annoying, but seldom more than an inconvenience. Repairs are usually easy, even for the inexperienced.

Finding the cause of a squeak is often the hardest part. It helps to know that most floors are constructed in two layers. The top layer—the visible flooring—is called the finish floor.

Although the seams between finish floorboards suggest that the pieces are square-edged, they are actually interlocking. Each floorboard is fashioned with a groove along one long edge and a projecting flange—called a tongue—along the other. The floor is laid so that the tongue of one board fits into the groove of its neighbor.

Nails are driven at an angle through the floorboards, along the tongue edge. When the boards are fitted together, the nail heads are hidden by the upper portion of the groove.

Beneath the finish floor is the subfloor. Usually, this layer consists of thick plywood or particleboard, but in older houses the subfloor is often a layer of lesser-quality floorboards resembling the finish flooring. Above a basement or crawl space, a layer of felt building paper is often sandwiched between the finish floor and subfloor to inhibit moisture rising from below. Some older houses do not have subflooring. Instead, the finish floorboards are extra-thick.

The subflooring (or the single-layer finish flooring) is fastened with nails to the joists that support the floor.

When you hear a squeak, it is almost always due to floorboards, subflooring, or joists that have loosened. Walking on the spot causes wood to rub against wood or against nails that have pulled free.

The root of the problem is often warping. But other common culprits are improper or insufficient nailing, and failing to allow slight gaps between the floorboards or between subflooring panels during their installation. The gaps provide room for boards or panels to expand when humidity levels increase. Another cause can be loose or insufficient bracing of the joists, so that they flex when the floor above is stepped on.

To find a squeaking spot, have someone walk slowly over the floor while you listen with your ear close to the floorboards. When the exact spot is pinpointed, mark it with a piece of chalk or tape. You can temporarily silence squeaks by lubricating floorboards where they rub, using powdered graphite lubricant or silicone spray designed for lubricating window tracks. Talcum powder also works.

But for a lasting solution, loose floor parts must be refastened. If the ends of two floorboards are rubbing, this can be done from above by driving eight-penny (2½-inch-long) spiral-shank flooring nails into each board. Install two nails on each side of the seam where the squeak occurs. Angle the points of the nails in each board toward each other, making sure that they pass through the subflooring and enter the joist below. If no joist is present, permanent refastening can only be done from underneath the floor, as described further on.

If the floorboards are hardwood, drill a pilot hole for each nail, slightly less than the nail's diameter and about three quarters of its length, before installing it. Otherwise you risk splitting the board or bending the nail. To avoid marring the wood by striking it with the hammer, drive the nails only to within an eighth of an inch of the surface, then use a nail set to drive them the rest of the way so that the heads are buried approximately an eighth of an inch below the surface. Cover the nail heads with colored wood putty or filler.

Repairs made from underneath the floor will be invisible and are often stronger. To locate a squeaking spot from below, have someone above tap the floor with a hammer or bounce on the spot while you watch for movement underneath with a flashlight. An easy method of refastening loose floorboards from below is to insert wooden shims (thin wedges) between the tops of the joists and the subflooring. The best shims to use are cedar shingle scraps, available from lumberyards.

TIP:

Patented metal brackets for eliminating squeaks can be used instead of shims and additional joist sections. The brackets, which are available at home centers, consist of a Z-shaped steel strap that fits over the joist, a square steel plate that is fastened with screws to the underside of the subfloor, and a long bolt that joins both pieces. Tightening the bolt draws the joist and subfloor together, silencing the squeak. One bracket will stabilize about 4 square feet of flooring.

ATTENTION

To install a shim, apply ordinary wood glue to both sides and tap it into the gap using a hammer. Drive the shim only until it is snug. Driving it too firmly may lift the floorboards and cause a squeak to develop elsewhere. Let the glue dry overnight before walking on the spot.

If a gap between the underside of flooring and a joist is more than a foot long, or if the finish flooring appears to have sunk in that spot, the joist may be warped. Restoring support to the flooring is usually possible by attaching a length of two-by-six lumber against the side of the warped joist so that the upper edge of the new piece presses against the flooring where the gap occurs.

To do this, cut the two-by-six about a foot longer at each end than the length of the gap. Apply construction adhesive to the top edge of the lumber and to the underside of the flooring. Then have a helper hold the piece against the warped joist while pressing the piece upward against the flooring.

Fasten the piece by first driving several ten-penny (3-inch-long) common nails at a slight upward angle through the two boards to firmly seat the new piece against the underside of the flooring. Then install several $2\frac{3}{4}$-inch flathead wood screws, staggered at approximately 6-inch intervals through the piece into the joist.

A severely warped or undersized joist may require this treatment along its full length (a technique called sistering), or a sup-

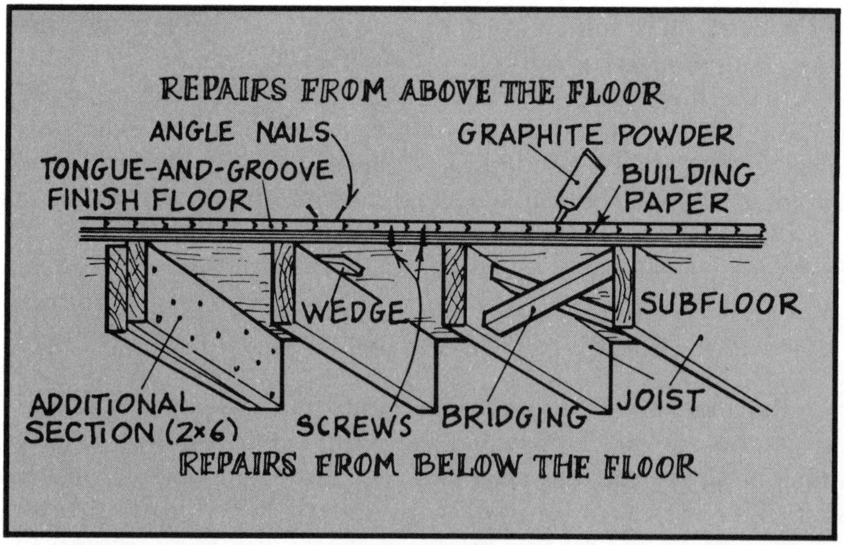

To cure squeaks temporarily, use powdered graphite or a similar lubricant. For permanent repairs, install wedges, screws, nails, additional joist sections, or bracing.

plementary post or adjustable column may be installed beneath the joist to provide vertical support.

If no gaps are visible from underneath the floor yet squeaks persist, often the finish flooring has come loose from the subfloor. Nailing through the floorboards and into the joists from above, as described, sometimes remedies the problem. However, if you can accurately determine the combined thickness of the finish floor and subfloor, screws that measure approximately a quarter of an inch shorter than this can be driven upward from below to fasten the flooring layers more securely.

If parts of the floor seem springy when walked on, inspect the X-shaped bracing, called bridging, between the joists. To test bridging, pull hard on each piece. If any wooden bridging is loose, hammer it more tightly or install new nails. Metal bridging strips usually have no nails. To tighten them, simply hammer against their lower ends. If renailing wooden bridging is difficult (it usually is, due to limited space for swinging a hammer between joists), install new metal bridging nearby instead.

Replacing Floorboards

Damaged wooden floorboards can be repaired by replacing them, but such repairs are almost always visible. A less obtrusive and often more practical solution is to replace only the damaged sections, using patches made from new or similar floorboards. The job requires modest carpentry skills but usually is within the range of most amateurs.

The best time to patch floorboards is in winter when low humidity levels widen existing gaps between boards, making sections easier to remove and install. If the flooring is exposed and covered with clear finish, careful tinting of the patches or refinishing of the entire floor may be necessary to hide the repair. This is not necessary if the floor is painted or covered by carpeting or other material.

Do not start the job until you are sure you can obtain replacement floorboards that duplicate the ones to be repaired. Sources to check are lumberyards, flooring suppliers, and salvage dealers. You will probably need to take a sample of the flooring with you to make a suitable match. If you can find a spare scrap, so much the better. If not, remove a sample from the damaged area or from an obscure area like a closet floor, following the instructions below carefully.

The first step in patching floorboards is to mark the area of each to be removed, using a carpenter's square or a drafting triangle. Draw a line perpendicular to the sides of the board and at least an inch beyond the area to be replaced. If sections of several adjoining boards must be patched, stagger the lines so that the cut ends will be at least 6 inches apart. This will make the repair less visible. If no subfloor is present, sections must be cut so that their ends lie over the centers of the framing joists supporting them.

There are two ways of handling the next step, depending on whether you feel more comfortable with a chisel or with an electric drill. If you choose the chisel, use a sharp, 1-inch-wide butt chisel and a hammer to make vertical cuts through the floorboards on the marked lines.

The second method, with a drill, will save time, particularly when working with thick flooring. Drill a row of large holes across each end of the damaged section; the outer edges of the holes should touch the marked lines.

Use a spade bit and, if you like, a vertical drilling guide. Afterward, square the ends of the drilled board with a chisel, removing the wood around the holes. When using this method, be careful not to damage the subflooring or joists.

Whether chiseling through the entire board or merely removing the wood left after drilling, you should next hold the chisel so its beveled side faces the section of flooring to be removed. Strike the chisel with the hammer so the blade penetrates about a quarter of an inch of wood. Then move the chisel so the edge of the blade is parallel to the marked line and about half an inch away. Hold the tool at a 45-degree angle with the beveled side of the blade up and strike the chisel to remove a wedge-shaped chunk of waste. Be careful not to drive the chisel past the vertical cut. Most floorboards are three quarters of an inch thick, so this procedure will have to be repeated several times.

Finally, chisel two lengthwise cuts along each section of the damaged floorboard so that the wood can be removed in three strips. With a flat pry bar, lift the middle strip first, then free the strip containing the grooved side of the floorboard and then the one containing the tongued side.

Work from the center of each strip toward the ends. When you are finished, remove any protruding nails or, using a nail set, drive them below the surface of the subfloor or joists.

To remove any other damaged boards, repeat the procedures outlined above, chiseling or drilling the ends. It is usually possible to pry out these boards without splitting them.

Saw lengths of replacement floorboards to fit the spaces exactly. If hand-sawing, use a miter box to make sure the ends of the patches are square. Also cut a piece of flooring about 6 inches long to use as a hammering block.

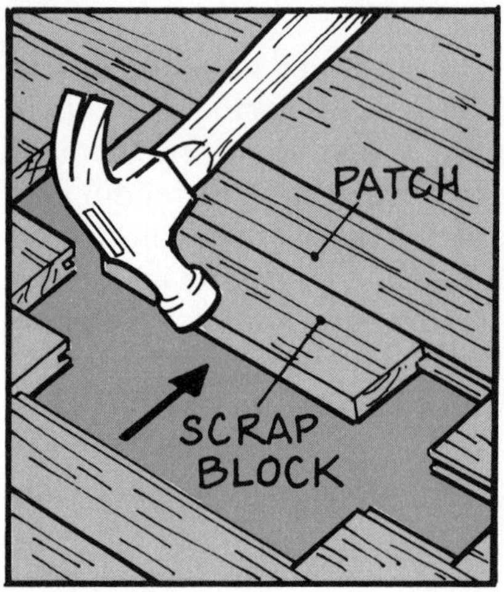

Fit the grooved side of each patch over the tongue of the adjoining floorboard and hammer it gently into place using a scrap block made from spare flooring.

To fit a patch that cannot be slid into place, chisel away the lower part of the groove, then tap the board home.

To install the first patch, place it so that its grooved side fits over the tongue of the existing floorboard next to it. Slide the grooved side of the hammering block over the tongue of the patch and gently tap the patch into place by striking the block with a hammer.

Use washers, cardboard, or coins as spacers between the patch and the sides of the adjacent board to create a gap the same width as those between other floorboards. Then fasten the patch to the subflooring or joist with 2½-inch-long cement-coated finishing nails or spiral-shank flooring nails. Remove the spacers when this step is completed.

Drilling pilot holes for the nails is recommended to prevent splitting but is not always necessary. Use a bit whose diameter is slightly smaller than that of the nail.

Starting in the middle of the board, space the nails along the length of the tongued side at 8- to 10-inch intervals. If the patch is less than a foot long, four nails, two at each end as described below, will hold it. Install the nails along the upper corner of the tongue, and aim them in toward the center of the board at about a 45-degree angle so they pass through the board before entering the subfloor or joist. Use a nail set to drive the heads of the nails below the surface.

For a patch consisting of a single board or for the last board n a larger patch, carefully remove the bottom part of the groove vith a chisel. Leave the top part of the groove so there is no unslightly gap visible from above. Then tap the pieces into place rom above.

To fasten such pieces and to prevent them from warping, lrill pairs of pilot holes at a 45-degree angle half an inch from the ends and edges. Follow this same procedure for short patches and or the ends of the undamaged floorboards that were cut when naking the patch. Install nails, sink their heads, and then fill all he nail holes with wood putty tinted to match the color of the loor.

Carpet Care

Rugs and carpets need regular care: frequent light cleaning to remove dirt before it becomes embedded, attention to the pile, and deep cleaning about once a year. Although hand-knotted, fragile, and antique rugs require special handling, ordinary tufted rugs and carpets made of synthetics or wool can be cared for with the following techniques:

For routine cleaning, vacuum rugs and carpets weekly or more often, using a home vacuum cleaner with a carpet attachment. Vacuuming against the pile direction removes the most dirt and also raises the nap, maintaining its springiness.

To preserve pile beneath furniture, either set the furniture legs on carpet casters—plastic pedestals that rest on spines—or move the furniture or the rug about an inch each week so the legs do not always compress the same fibers.

To restore crushed pile, raise it by scraping against the direction of the nap with a ruler or credit card; then hold a steam iron set on medium about 3 inches above the pile to dampen and swell the fibers. Allow the area to dry completely before replacing furniture.

To prevent stains, clean up spills as soon as they happen. Keep a container of general-purpose foam or powdered carpet cleaner (available at supermarkets) on hand for the purpose.

To clean up most spills, first gently remove as much of the spilled material as possible without rubbing any into the pile. Fluids can be absorbed by placing a paper towel over them; thicker substances can be scooped up with a pair of spatulas or putty knives.

Next, apply the cleaner according to the manufacturer's instructions. Usually this involves spraying or sprinkling cleaner over the spill, waiting for it to absorb the remaining substance, and then vacuuming up the residue.

If this is not effective, or if staining occurs, there are specific remedies to try. Begin by testing dry-cleaning fluid or spot-removing solution sold at carpet stores (this is also good to keep on hand) on an inconspicuous area of the rug. If it does not remove dye from the fibers, use it on the stain.

If another remedy is needed, ask the carpet store manager for advice. Some carpet stores offer free charts containing formulas and methods for removing all manner of stains and substances.

Minor burns can be removed by sanding away the charred ends of pile fibers with 220-grit sandpaper wrapped around a finger or a stick. Afterward, wash the area with a solution of water and either dish detergent or detergent for woolen clothing until the burn marks disappear; rinse by sponging with clear water.

Small areas of damaged or missing pile can be rewoven: Thread a curved upholstery needle with pile yarn the same size and color as that damaged, then insert the needle under a strand of the backing material into which the pile is woven. (If the pile is

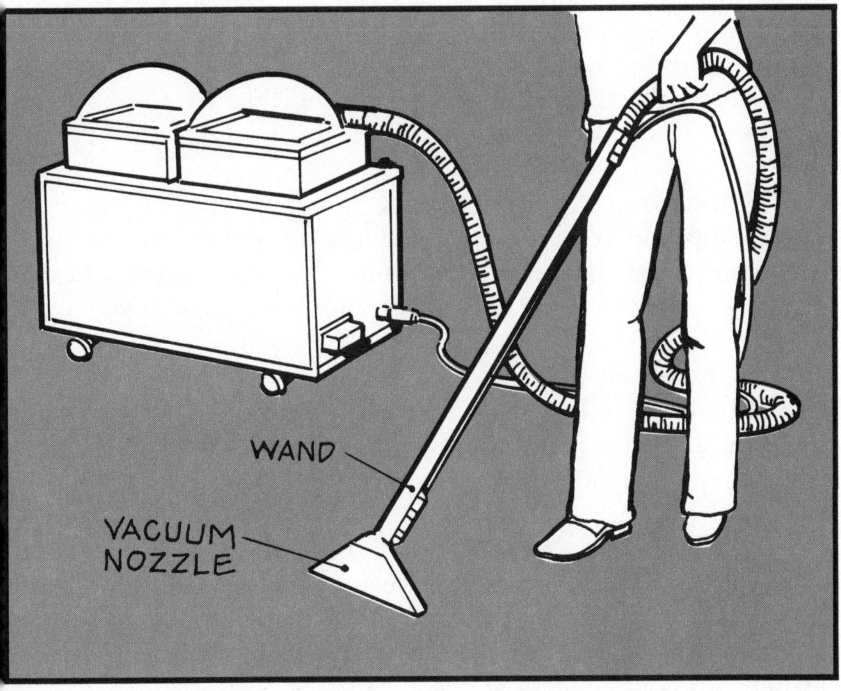

To deep-clean a large rug or carpet, use a rented cleaner.

damaged but not missing, remove it before this step.)

Pull the needle up, then pass it under the strand again to form a loop in the yarn.

Continue until the damaged area is filled in. Match the loops to the size and spacing of those surrounding it. For cut-pile, make the loops slightly higher, then clip them to the correct height later using sharp scissors.

Deeply cleaning a small rug can be done outdoors. Vacuum the rug indoors first, and test it for colorfastness by soaking a corner with warm water and wiping it with a white paper towel. If no color rubs off, the rug is colorfast. (If color does rub off, have the rug cleaned professionally, or dry clean it yourself indoors with solvent-impregnated cleaning powder and a rented powder-brushing machine.)

Assuming the rug is colorfast, lay it facedown on a hard surface like a driveway. Spray the backing with hard spray from a garden hose to wet it thoroughly and loosen embedded dirt.

Scrub the backing with a bristle brush dipped in mild carpet detergent, available at carpet stores. Begin in the center and scrub in wide, circular strokes. After covering 2 or 3 square feet, rinse the scrubbed area by spraying it. Change the detergent when the suds turn gray or when sediment collects in the bucket.

If the rug is fringed, use a combing motion to brush the strands with detergent until they are clean. A stronger solution of detergent can be used.

After washing, rinse the rug a second time by spraying it in the center and working the suds toward the edges, ahead of the spray.

Continue rinsing until no more suds appear. Then turn the rug face up and repeat the procedures. However, when rinsing the second time, have a helper pull a squeegee across the rug from the center to the edges to remove as much soapy water as possible.

Dry the rug by hanging it, or by spreading it face up on a dry lawn. Brush the pile to raise the nap. Do not expose a rug to strong sunlight for more than two days, otherwise the dyes may fade. Move a spread-out rug occasionally to avoid damaging the lawn.

To deeply clean a large rug or carpet indoors, rent a so-called steam cleaner. These do not really use steam; instead they use hot tap water. Besides being available from carpet stores and rental centers, steam cleaners are often available from supermarkets, dry cleaners, and department stores.

To use the cleaner, fill the dispensing tank with hot water and cleaning solution (usually supplied) according to the manufacturer's instructions. Fill the receiving tank with only enough water to cover the bottom, and add defoaming solution (also usually supplied) in the amount specified.

Attach the pressure and vacuum hoses leading from the sweeper, or wand, to the tank unit. Plug in the cleaner, then wait a moment for the pump to fill. Never turn on the cleaner unless there is liquid in the dispensing tank.

Start cleaning in a corner, on the opposite side of the room from the door. Hold the wand's vacuum nozzle on the floor so its opening is perpendicular to the carpet's surface.

Squeeze the trigger, releasing cleaning solution from the pressure hose, as you pull the wand toward you at a slow, steady rate, but not so slow that the carpet is saturated. After pulling the wand about 3 feet, release the trigger and push the wand forward over the same path to vacuum the solution from the carpet.

Repeat the process, then make several forward and backward strokes at slightly different angles, without dispensing cleaning solution.

When liquid no longer empties into the receiving tank from the vacuum hose, move the wand to an adjacent area of carpet.

Continue until the carpet is cleaned, then sweep the still-damp pile with a broom to raise the nap.

Caring for Hand-knotted Rugs

Fine hand-knotted rugs are often works of art, yet many owners use them every day. Handmade antique and silk rugs, whic are both precious and fragile, should be used daily only with grea caution and should be cared for professionally. However, mos fine hand-knotted wool rugs, those less than fifty years old, ca withstand normal household use, and as long as they are in goo condition, they can be cleaned and cared for by amateurs.

Routine cleaning to remove surface dirt and dust should b done daily by sweeping with a hand broom or with a mechanical not electric, carpet sweeper. Experts do not recommend the fre quent use of a vacuum cleaner because its powerful suction ma loosen the knots that hold the rug's yarns in place.

If you do decide to vacuum, use an ordinary carpet attach ment, not a motorized carpet cleaner with rotary brushes. Th recommended frequency: about once every week over high-traffi areas like stairs and hallways and about once every two to fou weeks over the entire carpet.

Be particularly careful not to vacuum over the fringed bor ders of a hand-knotted rug. The fringes can be sucked into th vacuum, destroying them and causing damage to the war threads—the rug's foundation—which may then require profes sional repair.

Rotate rugs every six months (more frequently in high-traffi areas) by turning them 180 degrees. At this time, no matte whether you routinely vacuum or sweep your rugs, flip them ove and vacuum them on the back, using the vacuum's motorized carpet attachment, if you have one. This will remove dirt that has found its way to the base of the pile. Because this settled dirt acts as an abrasive each time the fibers of the rug move, it causes wear and damage more than almost any other form of negligence.

Rugs of manageable size can be beaten by hand to remove embedded dirt, using an old-fashioned cane or wicker rug beater. If the rug is easily transported, hang it outdoors on a clothesline and gently beat it from the back. If that is not possible, flip the rug pile down on the floor, then lift up one section and beat it. Remove the dirt that falls to the floor from one section before moving on to the next.

Rugs should be washed every two years or so, even those that are swept or vacuumed regularly. To test whether or not a rug is due for washing, turn a corner of the rug pile side down and tap the back with your finger. If grit, especially broken wool fibers, spills from the rug, washing is necessary.

All rugs made by hand should be washed by hand. Most owners likely will choose to have this done by professionals: Be sure to select only reputable experts who specialize in cleaning the type of rugs you own. But if you choose, you can wash undamaged wool rugs at home.

If the rug is small enough, place it on a table or countertop for comfort. Otherwise, any hard, dry surface, including a floor, will do. Beat the rug thoroughly to remove all loose grit and fiber. This is extremely important, because if this step is ignored, mud will form during cleaning—and when that mud is dry, it can damage rugs fibers severely.

After beating the rug, test for colorfastness. Mix half a cup of mild, nondetergent rug shampoo, the type that, once dry, can be removed by sweeping or vacuuming. Dilute to the proportions recommended by the manufacturer. Mild shampoo used for dogs and other animals can also be used.

Apply the solution with a natural-fiber brush—a fine horse-grooming or animal-care brush available at pet stores is recommended. Start with a small inconspicuous area, preferably one with an intricate pattern. Gently massage the solution into the rug using short, overlapping strokes and taking care not to soak the material.

After about a dozen strokes, wipe the area with a clean white cotton cloth. If any coloring comes off, the dye is not colorfast and the rug should be professionally washed.

If no coloring appears on the cloth, proceed with the washing. Spread the rug pile-side up on the work surface. Dip the brush into the solution, shake off the excess, then scrub small areas of the rug at a time in succession, using the same gentle, overlapping strokes employed for testing. Again, be careful not to soak the fibers.

Proceed in rows across the rug, applying a uniform amount of solution and keeping the number and strength of brush strokes constant. Brush each section first against the direction of the pile, then reverse the process, brushing in the direction of the pile. Do not try to brush the fringe. Handle the rug carefully: When damp it will be heavier than normal.

When finished, carry the rug, rolled or flat (never folded), to a hard, nonabsorbent surface for drying, preferably outdoors exposed to direct sunlight. However, do not expose the rug to direct sunlight for more than two days. If no outdoor location is available, spread the rug indoors on a floor covered with thick newspapers in a sunny or heated room equipped with a fan to circulate air. Allow the rug to dry completely. Once a day (or more often if necessary), roll up the rug and replace the newspapers underneath as they become damp.

After the rug is dry, sweep or gently vacuum away the powdery shampoo residue. Finish by using a clean broom to brush the rug in the direction of the pile.

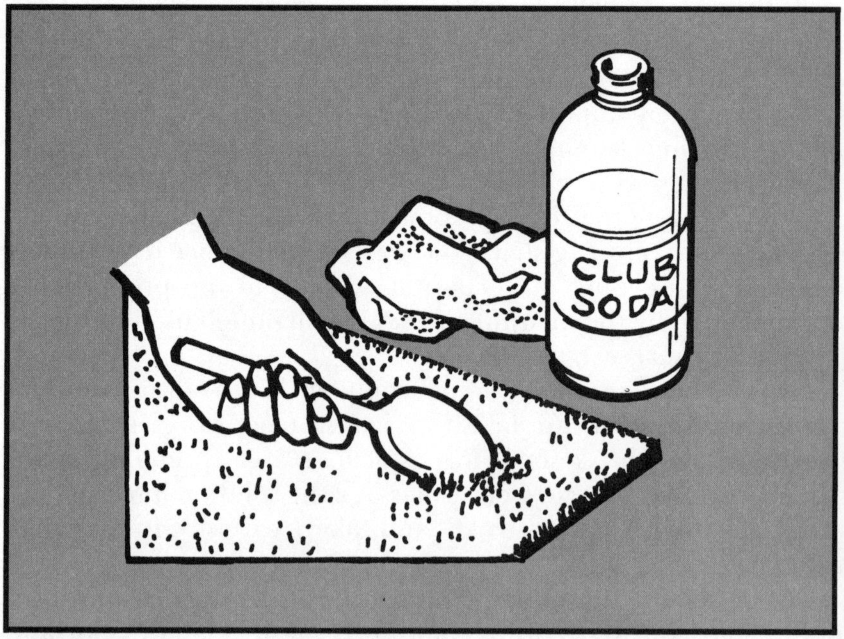

For most spills, scoop up the material with a spoon, rinsing with small amounts of club soda or water until the scooped-up liquid is clear.

Most spills can be removed from wool rugs if quick action is ken. If water soaks the pile, lift the rug and blot up the water by essing pads of wadded paper towels against the spot on both des. Then dry, using warm, not hot, air from a blow-dryer. Rub e nap of the dried pile with your fingers to restore its texture.

With all other spills, use a spoon to scoop up as much of the illed material as possible. Then, except for greasy or waxy spills, rine, blood, or eggs (protein stains), add a tablespoon or so of ld water or club soda to the spot and continue scooping, adding ater from time to time until the water comes clear.

One tablespoon of a mild soap, like that used for fine washles and woolens, mixed with a pint of lukewarm water can be plied instead. After that, rinse with clear water, following the chnique just outlined.

For greasy and waxy spills, after scooping up as much mateal as possible, place two or three thicknesses of brown paper ver the spot and gently press the area with a warm iron to absorb e soil into the paper. Then spot-clean with the mild soap soluon and rinse, as described above.

In the case of urine, apply a mixture of 2 tablespoons white istilled) vinegar and a pint of water, then rinse and blot as deribed. To remove protein stains, apply a solution of half a cup f salt dissolved in a quart of water. If necessary, apply the soap ixture afterward.

Repairing Blemished Wood Surfaces

Furniture finish blemished by scratches or stains can often b repaired relatively easily, provided the damage does not penetrat to the wood beneath. Success lies in using the gentlest method possible in making the necessary repairs.

Surfaces that have become dull, darkened, or sticky may onl require cleaning to restore their original luster. Apply a high quality liquid furniture cleaner specifically formulated to remov dirt and accumulated wax from finished wood surfaces. Severa brands are usually available at hardware stores and home centers where you can also find the other preparations mentioned below

When using furniture cleaner, apply it with a soft cloth. Af terward, cleaned pieces should be wiped with lemon oil to restor natural oils removed by the cleaner, and one or two coats of past wax should be applied to provide protection to the finish.

A furniture cleaner may also erase very light scratches, cloud patches, and white or light-colored stains (dark stains usually in dicate penetration of the wood). The cleaner does this by dissolv ing a tiny layer of the surface finish, which wiping with the clot then redistributes. The process is called reamalgamation. Whe stronger solvents are used, reamalgamation is also effective i repairing more extreme blemishes.

Reamalgamation works best on shellac and lacquer finishes It works less well on varnishes and not at all on modern finishe like polyurethane, epoxy, and polyester. Testing the finish wil reveal the solvent appropriate for reamalgamating it; this will als identify the finish as one requiring different treatment. Test firs for shellac, a common finish on older furniture and one quit susceptible to damage.

Dip a cotton swab in denatured alcohol and rub it over a mall, obscure area of the piece. If the finish dissolves, it is shellac. f nothing happens or if the finish becomes white or hazy, wipe he spot clean and repeat the process using a clean swab dipped n lacquer thinner. If the finish dissolves this time, it is lacquer.

If neither solvent dissolves the finish when used alone, try ixing the two in equal parts. If the finish then dissolves, it is a ixture of shellac and lacquer.

Finishes that only soften, no matter which of the two solvents re used, are probably varnishes. Finishes that show no change an also be varnishes—some types are strongly resistant to solvents—but if the piece is relatively new or has been refinished ecently, it may also be polyurethane or another synthetic.

When the finish has been identified as one that can be reamalgamated, clean it with furniture cleaner, as described above. hen dampen a gauze or cheesecloth pad about 2 inches square ith the appropriate solvent. Wipe the cloth very gently over the ratched or stained area, stroking in line with the scratches first, hen parallel with the grain of the wood. Do not overdo the procedure. Stop as soon as the damaged area is filled.

Allow the repair to dry overnight. If the area appears lighter han the surrounding area, apply a very thin layer of shellac ixed with an equal part of denatured alcohol to the spot, and llow it to dry. Use a small artist's paintbrush. Follow this procedure even if the finish on the piece is lacquer or varnish.

If the color is still too light, pour a small amount of thinned hellac into a jar and darken it with a drop or two of penetrating tain, available in many colors. Choose a shade that is slightly arker than the existing finish. Brush a drop of the new mixture ver the mended spot, and allow it to dry.

Continue to darken the mixture with stain, and test it on the pot until the right shade is achieved. Then apply a thin layer over he entire lightened area. Allow it to dry, then apply a coat of aste wax over the repair to protect and blend in the shellac.

Large areas—even entire pieces—can be rejuvenated by reamalgamation, but practice is required to achieve good results. The rocedure is the same as for small jobs, except that a larger pad is sed and no shellac is applied afterward.

To repair scratches in solvent-resistant varnish or synthetic nishes, fill them by rubbing with an appropriately colored wax tick. Unless you are experienced, avoid using repair sticks made f colored shellac, which are more commonly available. Although uch sticks are the choice of most professional refinishers, they ust be melted and the resulting liquid is difficult to control.

TIP:

Repairs to polyurethane finish can sometimes be made using products formulated for recoating polyurethaned wood floors. These are available from flooring companies. Test the product first on an inconspicuous spot.

ATTENTION

White rings left by drinking glasses can be rubbed away using a fine abrasive like table salt or rottenstone.

Penetrating oil finishes—linseed oil, tung oil, or combina tions of both, with or without an added stain—do not show dam age from scratches. If such a finish needs to be renewed, simpl add another coat. If you don't know what oil was used originall you can use either linseed or tung oil or a combination, appropr ately stained. Adding up to 50 percent mineral spirits or turpen tine will aid penetration.

Stains that do not respond to reamalgamation—white ring left by drinking glasses, for example—can usually be removed b rubbing them with fine abrasives, no matter what the finish. Sta by rubbing with a cloth dabbed in silver polish containing whiting an abrasive made from chalk, or by sprinkling table salt on th stain and rubbing it with a cloth dipped in salad oil. Using vinega or lemon juice instead of oil increases abrasiveness and may als lighten the stain. If lightening is desired and vinegar or lemo juice does not work, try rubbing with ammonia alone.

The coarsest abrasive to try is rottenstone, a form of slat Sprinkle some on the stain and rub it with a cloth dipped in sala oil or water. Rub in tiny circles until the stain is gone, then wit the grain until no scratches are visible when the surface is viewe at eye level in strong light. Rubbing, especially with rottenston dulls finish. So as a final step, apply a coat of paste wax.

Repairing Sticking Drawers

Cabinet drawers that stick or bind are high on the list of fe's little irritations. But the trouble is generally curable—once it as been identified.

When the problem is seasonal, it is often better to do nothing, ince the cure can cause more problems than it solves. Drawers hat stick only during summer and return to normal in the fall sually do so because of high humidity, which causes the wooden arts to swell and rub against one another. Once the humidity ubsides, so does the swelling. So if you plane away the excess in he summer, you will be left with a wobbly drawer in winter.

But if the stickiness persists throughout the year, repairs are n order. Usually the cause can be found in the sliding mechaisms or surfaces—the runners at the base of the drawer or the uides in the drawer cavity that provide tracking.

There are basically two kinds of drawers: those whose runers (the bottom surfaces of the drawer) slide on guides that are art of the cabinet frame, and those that are suspended from the abinet sides by metal or wooden tracks.

First, find out exactly where the drawer is sticking. Check the liding surfaces or mechanisms for obstructions, warping, and ear. If the drawer has runners or wooden tracks on the sides, emove it entirely. If the drawer is mounted on metal tracks, pull out as far as it will go.

To check the wooden runners or tracks, slide your fingers ently over them. Watch out for splinters. If the runners feel ough but are reasonably flat, smooth them by rubbing lightly with fine-grit sandpaper held in a sanding block or wrapped around a flat-sided piece of wood. Then lubricate them by rubbing a bar of soap or a candle on them, or by spraying them with silicone lubricant.

If any runners or wooden tracks are worn or broken, they should be repaired. But to gauge their condition accurately, first make sure the drawer guides are in good working order.

With the drawer pulled out, check and lubricate the guides and clean them with an ice pick or nail wherever debris has collected. Use a hammer and a nail set to drive protruding nail heads below the surface. If a guide is loose, try to refasten it in its original position, using either woodworking glue or small nails. Differences in color, old nail holes, and glue residue usually make it fairly easy to tell where it should go.

Align the guides so that they are parallel. Large drawers sometimes have a central guide beneath them. Be sure it is parallel to the guides at each side of the cabinet.

Drawers supported this way usually also have a plastic clip called a track holder, attached to the lower edge of the back of the drawer. It fits over the central guide and keeps the drawer on course. Be sure that the track holder fits squarely over the drawer guide beneath it and that the fasteners are tight.

To restore worn guides, insert thumbtacks along the concave abraded portion to compensate for the wear and even out the surface, or install small right-angled nylon brackets known as drawer glides. Placed at intervals along the guides, these support the drawer fully on both sides. Lubricate the guides.

Reinstall the drawer in the cabinet. If it still sticks, turn your attention to the runners again. Remove the drawer and rub chalk along the bottom edges of the runners. Then push the drawer in and out a few times.

If the runners are warped—the most probable cause of the sticking—the chalk will have been rubbed away from the problem areas. First try sanding the runners with medium-grit sandpaper wrapped around a block. Every twenty-five strokes or so, test your progress by laying the narrow edge of a ruler on the runner and looking for gaps.

In the case of severe warping, clamp the drawer in a vise and use a sharp block plane to remove the high spots. Always plane in the direction of the wood grain to avoid chipping the surface.

If a drawer wobbles or won't slide in a straight line, the runners or the guides may be worn rather than warped. Holding a ruler against the surface of the runner or guide and checking for gaps is the best way to test for wear.

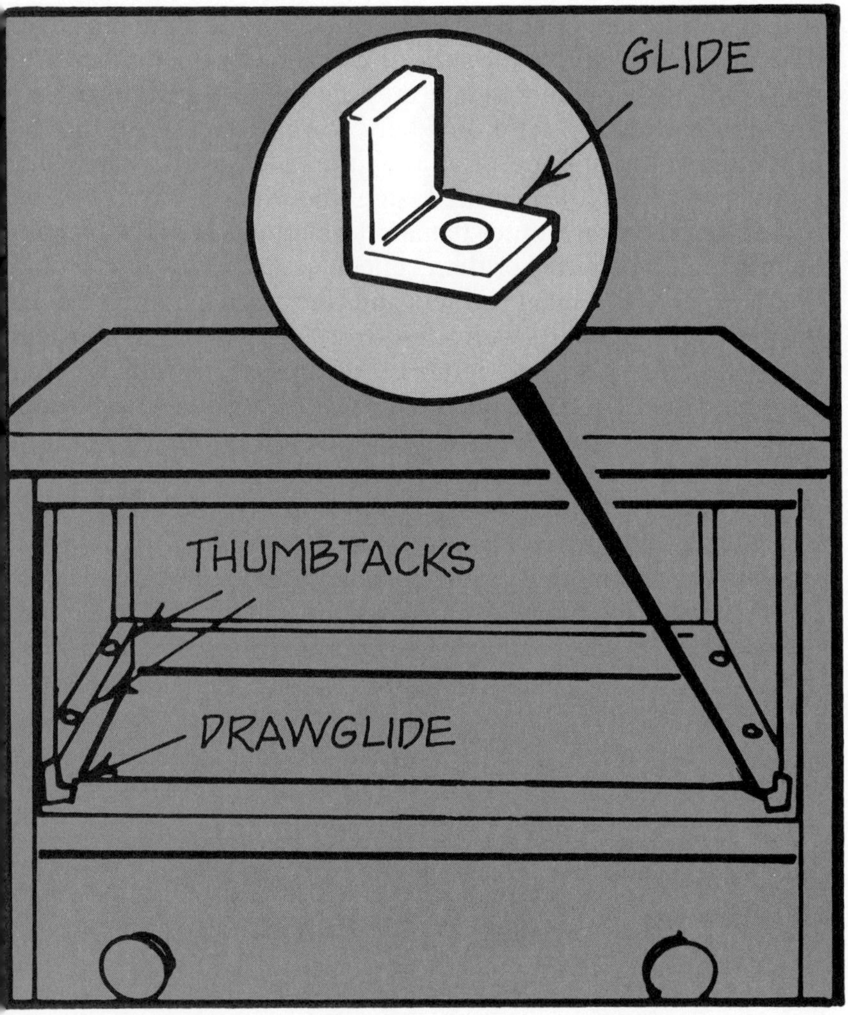

To restore a worn drawer guide, use thumbtacks on the worn portion or attach nylon glides on both sides.

To raise the worn edge of a runner so it is level with the rest of the surface, try using the thumbtack technique suggested for worn guides. Push them into the edge at the low points, and if necessary, adjust the height by placing paper or thin cardboard shims beneath them. You can also use nylon stem bumpers, available at cabinet supply stores, but to insert these you must drill holes in the runner.

If a runner is severely worn, plane or sand it flat and level, then rebuild it to its original dimensions by attaching strips of wood veneer to the planed surface. Use hardwood veneer called edge banding, which comes in a roll and is usually backed with heat-sensitive adhesive.

Place the veneer adhesive-side down on the runner's edge s that any excess width overhangs the outside of the drawer. The press it on with a moderately heated clothes iron. Afterward, tur the drawer over and set it on a hard work surface. Using the sid of the drawer as a guide, trim away the excess with a razor-shar utility knife. Sand the trimmed edge smooth.

Plane a broken runner flat and level, then rebuild it by gluin on a strip of wood thicker than veneer.

Drawers with metal runners and tracks can generally be fixe by lubricating the parts with a few drops of lightweight househol oil. If this doesn't work, remove the drawer, tighten any loos fasteners, then clean the parts with a cloth or cotton swab dippe in kerosene or cigarette lighter fluid. Lubricate the parts with o before reinstalling the drawer. If parts are bent or damaged, or sticking wheels cannot be freed, replace the mechanism.

A note of caution: Ordinary furniture can be fixed by mo amateurs with modest woodworking skills, but fine cabine should always be taken to a professional cabinetmaker or furn ture-repair specialist if the job involves anything more than clea ing and lubricating the drawer runners.

Cleaning Marble

Marble is durable, but its finish can be soiled and stained over time, and its surface dulled. Periodic maintenance will keep marble looking its best, and prompt action will remove most stains.

Marble used in homes falls into two broad categories: honed and polished. Honed marble has a satin finish that resists scratches better than polished marble and is less slippery when wet. It is used primarily for flooring, even though, because of its relative roughness, it is easily soiled.

To clean honed marble, wash it as often as desired, using marble-cleaning solution available from marble supply companies or the following method: First, wet the surface with clear, hot water. Then sprinkle on a mildly abrasive alkaline household detergent containing bleach. Never wash marble with soap of any kind. The grease it contains will penetrate the pores of the marble and darken it.

Scrub the surface with a stiff-bristled brush or, on large floors, with a rented power scrubber. Use overlapping circular strokes.

Allow the cleanser foam to remain on the surface for several minutes while the bleach works. Afterward, rinse the surface thoroughly with plenty of clear water and wipe it dry with towels or other absorbent material.

To protect honed marble, clear sealer containing silicone can be applied to a cleaned surface after it is completely dry. Sealer is available at stone supply companies and at some home centers.

Polished marble is glossy and smoother than the honed typε Its most frequent uses are for wall veneer, fireplace trim, furnitur tops, and similar decorative items.

Polished marble requires gentler treatment than honed mar ble to avoid scratches. To wash polished marble, first wet th surface with clear hot water. Then apply a mild detergent lik dishwashing liquid that contains no abrasives. The detergen should be about pH 7 (never lower) and must not contain aro matic additives. (These, which are used to give detergent a pleas ant scent, are usually acids that can etch the surface of th marble.) When washing small areas, apply the detergent straigh from the bottle. For larger areas, mix the detergent with water i a bucket, following the manufacturer's instructions. Marble-clean ing solutions from a marble supply company can also be used.

Next, scrub with a soft cloth. Work in small, overlappin circular motions. If the surface being cleaned is vertical, start a the bottom and work upward to avoid streaking. After washing rinse the surface thoroughly with clear water and a second clot or a sponge. Change the rinse water frequently. Dry the surfac with a soft, absorbent cloth or chamois.

To protect and enhance the finish of polished marble, appl wax. Use a nonyellowing paste wax, beeswax, or a wax produc formulated for use with marble. Be sure the surface is clean an thoroughly dry beforehand.

Most stains can be removed from honed and polished marbl by applying pastes made by mixing various cleaning compound For stains caused merely by heavy accumulation of dirt or grim mix whiting—a mildly abrasive powder available at paint stores– or plaster of paris with either household chlorine bleach or percent hydrogen peroxide solution (available at drugstores) t the consistency of cake frosting. Use approximately a pound c whiting or plaster to cover a square foot of marble. Do not us vegetable material like corn starch or a substitute for whiting o plaster; it may cause stains.

Wet the stained surface and surrounding area with the sam liquid used to make the paste. Spread the paste over the stain in layer approximately half an inch thick, then cover the paste wit a large piece of plastic wrap. Use masking tape or duct tape t seal the wrap to the marble around all four sides. This will preve the paste from drying.

Allow the paste to remain on the marble for forty-eig hours. Then remove it by scraping with a wooden spatula or pla tic scraper. Paste that sticks to the marble can be loosened b wetting it with water.

Rinse the area thoroughly with clear water. If the stain is still isible, repeat the procedure; otherwise, wipe the area dry with a oft cloth or chamois.

Stains caused by metallic or organic substances, oil, grease, or at require different treatment and may be difficult to remove if ot attended to promptly.

Rust-colored metallic stains, caused by wet iron or steel in rolonged contact with marble, sometimes can be removed simply y rubbing with a coarse cloth like burlap. More effective is to pply a thick coating of rust-removal jelly containing phosphoric cid (available at hardware stores), following the manufacturer's nstructions. On honed marble, the stained area can be scrubbed vith scouring powder between applications.

To remove green metallic stains caused by copper and ronze, mix a paste of whiting or plaster and equal parts of house-old ammonia and either sal ammonica (aluminum chloride, vailable at some pharmacies) or table salt. Cover the paste with lastic wrap to keep it moist and leave the poultice in place for orty-eight hours. Repeat if necessary.

Organic stains—these are often pinkish—are caused by sub-tances like coffee, tea, fruit juices, tobacco, and water or residue

'o remove stains from marble, wet the surface, spread aste containing cleaning agent thickly over the stain, hen cover with a large piece of plastic wrap taped on all ides. After 48 hours, scrape off the paste.

from fresh flowers. To remove these, apply a paste made of whit ing or plaster mixed with 20 percent hydrogen peroxide solutio (hair bleach). Cover the paste with plastic wrap and leave it fo forty-eight hours. If a second treatment is necessary, add house hold ammonia to the paste—ten drops of ammonia to one cup o paste—just before covering it.

To remove stains caused by oil, grease, or fat, apply a past made of whiting or plaster mixed with acetone or mineral spirits Cover with plastic wrap and let it sit for forty-eight hours. Repea if necessary.

Wear and some stain-removal methods can dull polishe marble. To restore its glossiness, repolish the surface by rubbin it with tin oxide powder, also called putty powder (available fro marble supply companies and some art supply stores that stoc sculpture materials). Alternatively, aluminum oxide powder fron the same sources can also be used.

Wet the cleaned marble, then sprinkle the powder lightl over the surface. Rub vigorously in overlapping circular motion with a cloth pad or use an electric buffer. When the gloss returns rinse the surface thoroughly with clear water and wipe dry.

Repairing Veneer

Veneer is usually a thin layer of attractive wood that is glued to the surface of thicker, less attractive wood to enhance its appearance. Traditionally, veneer has been associated with fine, highly decorated, expensive furniture. However, nowadays it is used more widely as a relatively inexpensive covering for moderately priced, undistinguished woodwork made of plywood or particleboard.

Because most veneer ranges in thickness from one twenty-eighth of an inch to as little as one forty-second of an inch, damaging veneered surfaces is easy. Luckily, making repairs often can be easy, too.

One common problem is the lifting of veneer along the edge of a piece of furniture, such as at the corner of a tabletop or the side of a cabinet. This can result from wear, deterioration of glue, or, if the piece has been refinished, from excess sanding. It is important to repair lifted veneer as soon as it is noticed, or else moisture seeping into the crack can loosen more glue, or the lifted veneer can be accidentally torn away.

To repair lifted veneer, first insert the end of a fingernail file, emery board, or the tip of a paper clip into the crack and scrape out as much deteriorated glue as possible. Be careful not to raise the loose veneer too high. If the area is large enough, try blowing the powdery glue dust out of the crack after scraping using a plastic soda straw. This can be done by flattening one end of the straw and inserting it into the crack.

Reglue the veneer by spreading ordinary woodworking glue into the crack with a toothpick or an artist's palette knife. Hardware stores also carry glue-filled syringes made for this purpose. Press the veneer down and release it several times to spread the glue. Then wipe away any excess with a damp cloth.

TIP:

Veneer on furniture built before World War II is usually bonded with animal-hide glue. This softens easily when dampened or exposed to heat (usually such accidental softening is the cause of the damage), and mending can sometimes be done by carefully applying moisture and heat with a clothes iron. Before attempting the repair, test the composition of the finish by rubbing a cotton swab dipped in denatured alcohol over a small, obscure area of the veneer. If the alcohol dissolves the finish or turns it cloudy, the finish is probably shellac, which will be damaged by moisture or heat. Therefore, it will be necessary to refinish the piece after the repair is made. To perform the repair, lay a damp cloth towel over the area and heat it with the iron set on low. Check the veneer often to avoid scorching it. When the glue beneath the veneer softens, remove the iron and towel. Immediately press the veneer flat with a rolling pin, then apply pressure with clamps or a weight. Leave the spot alone for twelve hours while the glue dries.

ATTENTION

Next, clamp the veneer until the glue hardens. Use one or more small C-clamps or spring clamps, which resemble clasp-type clothespins. Place plastic wrap on top of the veneer to avoid marring the veneer surface, then sandwich the repair between small scraps of wood. Attach the clamps so that the jaws press against the scraps.

Another problem is blistering; that is, when a small section of veneer not close to an edge lifts up. This has several causes, the most common being deterioration of glue from age or its contact with heat (such as putting a cup of hot coffee on the veneer).

To repair a veneer blister, first make a slit across it using a very sharp, preferably new, single-edge razor blade. When making the slit, follow the direction of the wood grain so that the seam will be less visible after the repair is made. Then, while pressing one portion of the blister down flat, use one of the applicators mentioned previously to force glue beneath the raised portion.

Press the portion of the veneer down and release it several times to spread the glue, then repeat the process with the remaining portion. Finish by covering the repair with a sheet of plastic wrap, then weight it down with at least 20 pounds of material, such as books or bricks. It is usually best not to try to remove deteriorated glue prior to regluing; doing so can mar the edges of the slit and create an unsightly repair.

Cracks, too, sometimes occur in veneer. These are usually caused by wood shrinkage and show up most often on antiques that have relatively thick veneers that are not as flexible as thinner, modern veneer.

Fine veneered furniture that has developed cracks can be taken to a restorer, who likely will fill the cracks with melted shellac, carefully tinted to match the surrounding wood. Amateurs can fill cracks in lesser-quality pieces using light- or dark-colored wood putty made for use as crack filler. Such putty is available at hardware stores. If an obscure portion of unfinished veneer can be scraped to produce sawdust (do not use sandpaper, otherwise the dust will contain particles of abrasive), excellent putty the same color as the veneer can be made by mixing the dust with a small amount of white woodworkers' glue.

Chipped veneer that requires patching is the most difficult damage to repair. A professional will often perform the task using a veneer punch. The punch cuts from the chipped surface an irregularly shaped area large enough to include the defect. Then the punch is used again to cut an identically shaped patch from a piece of replacement veneer. The patch is then glued into the area from which the defect was removed.

Unfortunately, veneer punches are expensive and seldom worth the investment for most amateurs. However, to obtain nearly the same results, use the following method:

First, obtain a piece of replacement veneer from a woodworker's supply store and carefully stain it to match the surface requiring repair. Using a straightedge and a sharp utility knife, cut a diamond-shaped patch from the replacement veneer that will be large enough to fit over the defect. The long dimension of the patch should be parallel to the direction of the wood grain.

Next, place the patch over the area containing the defect and orient it to match the grain direction of that surface. Using the knife blade for accuracy, trace the outline of the patch onto the surface.

Set the patch aside and use a razor-sharp chisel to cut through the damaged veneer. Follow the traced outline but always keep the chisel on the waste side. When you are finished, gently pry up the wood within the outline and scrape away the dried glue.

The patch should either fit exactly or be a little larger than the damaged spot. If necessary, trim it with a straightedge and a fresh utility knife blade. When it fits, glue it into place and clamp or weigh it down as previously described. Applying finish should hide the seams of the patch all but completely.

TIP:

Precise clamping is necessary for perfect veneer repairs. For best results, practice clamping veneer before applying glue, and have all supplies within reach when needed.

ATTENTION

To repair chipped or missing veneer, trace the outline of a patch onto the damaged surface. Remove the veneer containing the defect, then glue the patch into place.

Uncluttering a Clothes Closet

There is a universally recognized remedy for clothes closet clutter: Close the closet door! This solution is simple, quick, and effective, and thus wildly popular. But what happens when the inevitable occurs, and because of growing clutter the door no longer closes?

Conventional clothes closets—those spanned by a single rod for hangers with a single shelf above—waste space. Not only do the design and placement of the fixtures fail to provide sufficient surface area for storing items, they ignore the need for compartments, which are essential in combating clutter.

You can gain more room—often much more—and end clutter by reorganizing the contents of an existing closet and installing numerous storage compartments. Fixtures designed for this purpose may be purchased ready-made from stores specializing in closet accessories and from many department stores and home centers. If you are handy with tools, you can make your own.

Whether you decide to buy or build your way to a roomier closet, the first step is to reorganize its present contents. Begin by resorting all the items into two groups: those that are used within the room where the closet is, and those that are not. Decide whether any items used elsewhere genuinely need to be stored in the closet, and move them closer to their area of use if possible.

Of the remaining items, determine frankly whether any can be discarded or given away. For many people, parting with possessions long held—however unneeded—is difficult, especially if

In a typical clothes closet, the single rod and shelf promote clutter and hamper effective use of space.

Remodeling a closet so shelves are at the top eliminates stooping and simplifies installation of multiple clothing rods.

An easy way to make efficient use of space is to arrange clothes by length, then fill in the space above and below with freestanding shelves or other storage containers.

the items are in good condition. One way to decide whether or not to keep something is to think whether anyone has used it in the last ten months. If so, keep it. If not, get rid of it or at least store it elsewhere.

When the only items left are those you think must remain, you are ready to redesign the closet layout and obtain the necessary fixtures.

First, temporarily rehang all the clothes. Arrange them so that the longest hang at one end of the rod and the shortest at the other. Then stand several feet away and examine the area beneath the clothes. This and the area above the clothes constitute the closet's additional storage space.

The simplest way to use this space is to fill it with freestanding shelves, some to fit beneath the clothing and others to fit between the upper shelf and the closet's ceiling. Modular shelves for closets can be bought and suitably arranged, or you can make shelving yourself from ¾-inch-thick plywood.

TIP:

If the positions of studs inside closet walls do not permit fastening shelves directly to them, or if purchased units have metal corner brackets that do not align with studs, attach long strips of one-by-three-inch lumber to the wall by screwing these to the studs. Then attach the units to the strips. Two strips are needed for each unit: an upper one for fastening and a lower one to hold the bottom of the unit out from the wall so it hangs vertically. Even if the strips extend beyond the sides of the shelves they won't be noticed behind clothing.

ATTENTION

Convenient distances between shelves are 6, 9, and 12 inches. Nine inches tends to be the most useful, but variety helps. Shelving that is installed below shoulder height may be as deep as the closet itself (usually 22 to 24 inches). However, overhead shelves should not exceed 20 inches (less if the closet doorway does not extend to the ceiling); otherwise reaching into them will be difficult. All shelves should be less than 32 inches wide to prevent sagging.

Clothing that is seldom used or is out of season may be grouped in hanging storage bags. You will gain additional hanging space for short items of clothing by screwing another rod beneath the main rod or suspending it from the rod above with lightweight chain. Suspended rods, which are essential if the closet is not partitioned vertically, are available from closet accessory stores. You can also easily fashion a rod from a length of broomstick or pipe and suspend it with chains and S-shaped metal hooks from a hardware store.

Shelves at the top of the closet eliminate stooping. They, and clothes hung in multiple rows, are the keys to designing the most sophisticated and efficient closet layouts.

To provide a variety of spaces for long and short clothes, segment the closet with short hanging rods of different sizes, and add drawers and shelves above. First, plan the layout on graph paper. Begin by drawing a rectangle to scale consisting of lines representing the closet sides, top, and floor. Next, group the clothing by length, and hang it from the rod.

Measure the width of each group and the distance from the bottom of the longest item in it to the floor. To that distance, add the distance from the top of the closet down to any shelving above the clothes rod. Measuring to scale on the drawing, come down this total distance from the line representing the top of the closet. Draw horizontal lines across the rectangle, as long as the width of each group of clothes. These lines will be stepped, indicating the bottom of the clothing.

Turn the sketch upside down. Now the space beneath the clothing appears at the top, and the stepped line represents the heights at which short rods should be hung. The clothing should all hang evenly from the bottom.

To construct a closet from this layout, remove the existing upper shelf and install modular or custom-built shelf units whose sides partition the closet vertically. Use the widths of the clothing groups as a guide to the placement of the vertical partitions and the height of each group to determine the number of shelves above it. Using screws 2½ inches long, fasten the units securely to the wall studs. To find these inside the wall, use an electronic stud sensor, available at hardware stores.

Then attach sections of hanger rods (also corresponding to the widths of the clothing groups) to the partitions at the height that allows the longest item in each group to hang clear of the floor. Metal cleats for mounting rod sections are sold at hardware stores.

In addition, or as an alternative to shelves, you can install drawers, wire baskets, sliding trays, and other custom features between partitions. All these are available in closet accessory stores.

Installing Shelves and Cabinets

Adjustable wall shelves, the kind featuring metal standards that are slotted to hold brackets sold with them, are versatile, easy to obtain, and relatively inexpensive. Wall cabinets, too, are readily available in many different styles and price ranges. Both shelves and cabinets are reasonably easy to install, but there are a few pitfalls.

Shelves

When selecting shelving, visit a hardware store, home center, or lumberyard that stocks a complete line of standards and brackets. These are made in varying sizes. Compare the unit price of long standards with that of shorter ones. You may find, for example, that a single 6-foot-long standard costs less than two 3-foot lengths. If you already own a hacksaw, you can cut the longer piece into two shorter ones and save money.

Brackets, too, come in light- and heavy-duty thicknesses, as well as in several lengths to accommodate shelves of different widths.

Prefinished shelves, which are usually made of particleboard covered with veneer, are often available with the standards and brackets in 8-, 10-, and 12-inch widths. Consider whether these meet your needs or whether you will save by obtaining solid lumber, plywood, or other material and making the shelves yourself.

The usual thickness for wooden shelving is three quarters of an inch; for plywood and manufactured wood like particleboard,

⅝ inch is sufficient. Lumberyards will usually cut lumber and sheet materials to specified sizes for a small fee per cut.

To determine how many standards to buy, consider the load the shelves must support. For heavy items like books and large plants you will need to space standards closer together than for lighter loads. The recommended span between standards is no more than 24 inches for heavy-duty shelves and no more than 32 inches for light-duty shelves. Provided the load on a shelf is evenly distributed to prevent tipping, the ends of a shelf can extend unsupported about 6 inches for heavy loads and 9 inches for light loads.

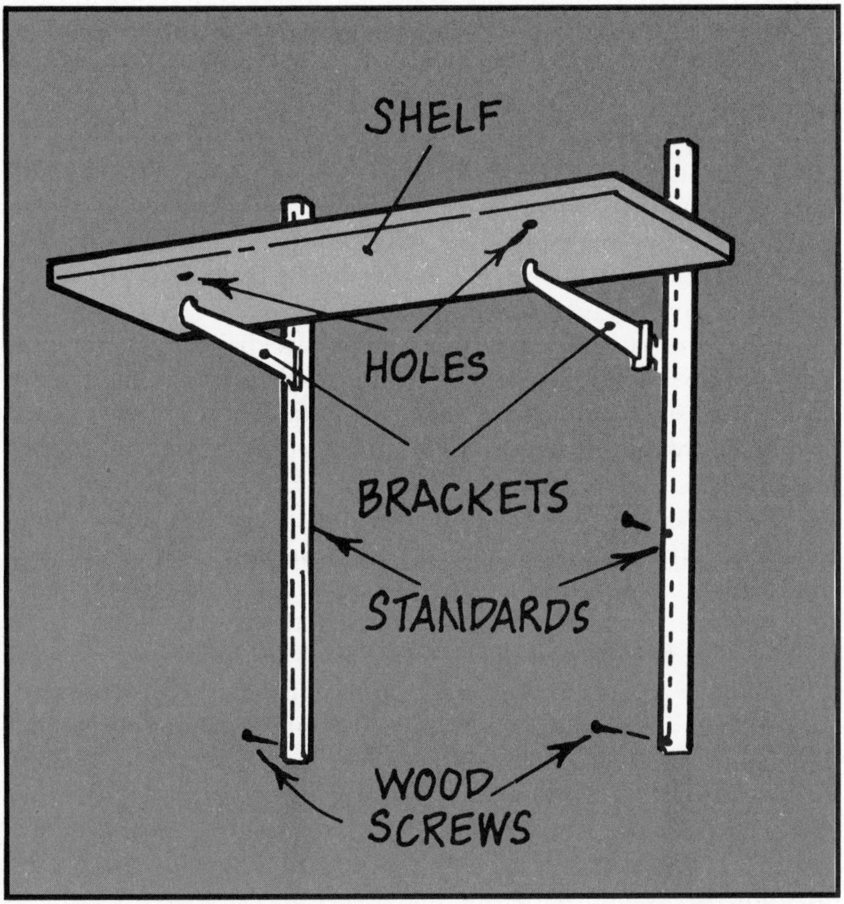

Careful measuring is needed to align shelf standards. On wide shelves, drill holes underneath to accommodate ends of brackets.

TIP:

Several new varieties of hollow-wall fasteners have been introduced that vie with expansion anchors and conventional toggle bolts for strength and surpass them in convenience. Among these are Grip-It screw anchors manufactured by Black and Decker (these consist of a self-tapping screw anchor that can be installed without drilling), Wall-Grabb'r expansion fasteners manufactured by Grabco (these are installed by hammering and cause only minor wall damage if they must be removed, making patching easier), and Toggler toggle bolts manufactured by Mechanical Plastics Corporation. Unlike conventional toggle bolts, these permit removing the bolt from the wall after the toggle is in place.

ATTENTION

When attaching the standards to the wall, choose fasteners that suit the wall's construction. If it is conventionally built of either wallboard, paneling, or lath and plaster covering vertical wood studs, use roundhead wood screws to attach standards, provided they can be positioned so that the screws will enter the studs.

Fastening the standards to the studs is the strongest method of attaching shelves to framed walls. Studs are usually located at 16-inch intervals, but to find those that aren't, look for holes left by previous shelves, cabinets, or hanging pictures, or use a magnetic or electronic stud sensor, available at hardware stores. The electronic devices work best but are more expensive. Instructions are included with both types.

Another way to find studs is to drill test holes for them in the wall. If possible, drill the holes at floor level after removing the baseboard molding; that way, the holes can be easily hidden by reinstalling the molding. Where this is not possible, drill the test holes just above the baseboard. Later, to conceal them, fill the holes with spackling compound and touch them up with paint.

The resistance of the drill will usually tell you whether the bit has penetrated a stud or has merely punched through the wallboard or plaster covering the cavity between studs. To be sure, probe the hole with a wire. If the wire meets resistance, you know the hole enters a stud.

Where standards must be placed between studs, use hollow wall fasteners. There are several varieties. Expansion anchors are easiest to install and strong enough for moderately heavy loads supported by more than the minimum recommended number of standards.

These consist of a metal sleeve that is inserted into a hole drilled into the wall. A matching bolt is then installed and tightened firmly, compressing the sleeve against the rear of the wall. The bolt can then be removed, passed through a hole in the standard, and reinserted into the sleeve.

Stronger than expansion anchors and also better-suited to plaster walls are toggle bolts. These have hinged metal wings that fold against the bolt to allow the fastener to be inserted in the hole drilled for it. Once inside the wall, the wings unfold, providing clamping pressure against the rear of the wall when the bolt is tightened. When installing toggle bolts, the bolt must be passed through the standard before the wings are attached. Once inserted, toggle bolts cannot be removed without losing the wings inside the wall.

For masonry walls use masonry bolts. Like expansion anchors, these have a sleeve and matching bolt that can be removed after the assembly is inserted in a hole drilled into the wall.

After choosing the shelving components and fasteners, follow these steps to install them:

First, measure from either the floor or ceiling to determine the top of the first standard. Mark the spot with a sharp pencil, then hold the standard in position directly beneath the mark. If the standard is a type with shaped slots, make sure it is right side up.

Insert the pencil point or a nail through the top screw hole in the standard and make a mark indicating the center of the hole. Remove the standard and drill a hole for a fastener, centered on the mark.

Install the fastener and the standard loosely. To mark the positions of remaining fastener holes, either use a level to make sure the standard hangs vertically or raise the bottom end of the standard and release it, allowing the standard to swing like a pendulum. When it stops swinging, gravity will have aligned the standard so it is vertical. Press the standard carefully against the wall and mark the holes.

Next, install the remaining fasteners and tighten them gradually, as a group, to fasten the standard to the wall.

To determine where to place the remaining standards, measure horizontally from the top of the standard you have just put up. If possible, use a level; otherwise, make a mark at the appropriate interval and then measure down from the ceiling the same distance that is above the attached standard.

Install the remaining standards. Be sure they are all right side up. To attach the brackets, slip them into the slots in the standards and then use a hammer to tap them downward until they are firmly seated. Then lay the shelves across the brackets.

Shelves can be up to approximately an inch and a half wider than the length of brackets supporting them. To ensure that these shelves lie flat, set them in place and mark the positions of the tips of the brackets on the undersides. Then remove the shelves and drill holes about a quarter of an inch in diameter and a quarter of an inch deep at these spots. Reinstall the shelves so that the tips of the brackets fit into the holes.

Wall Cabinets

Hanging an individual wall cabinet is in many ways similar to hanging an adjustable shelf. But hanging a group of adjacent cabinets, called a run, can be tricky.

In both cases, the first step is to mark the position of the cabinet(s) on the wall. To be secure, at least two of the fasteners that attach a cabinet must penetrate studs. Methods for finding studs are described earlier. However, when installing cabinets, drill test holes for locating studs where cabinets will cover them, rather than at floor level.

Mark the stud locations by drawing vertical lines on the wall. To aid positioning, the lines must be long enough to extend beyond the top and bottom of a cabinet. Afterward, use a carpenter's level to draw a horizontal line on the wall indicating the bottom edge of an individual cabinet to be installed, or of each cabinet in a run.

If you are installing a run of cabinets beginning at a corner, you need make no further marks. For an individual cabinet, draw lines indicating the cabinet's sides. For a run that does not start at a corner, indicate the exposed side of each end cabinet.

Next, temporarily install a horizontal board on the wall to support the cabinets. Use one-by-three lumber at least as long as the width of one cabinet. If you are installing a run of cabinets whose lower edges are at the same height, the support can be as long as the run's total width. Align the support so that its upper edge is even with the horizontal line on the wall. Fasten the support through the wall and into the studs using screws, so that it can be easily removed later.

Now you are ready to hang an individual cabinet or a corner cabinet starting a run. Begin by lifting it into position and resting its bottom edge on the support. While a helper steadies the cabinet, stand on a stepladder and hold a level vertically against the cabinet in several places. Be sure that the cabinet is pressed against the wall at both the top and bottom.

If the level shows that the cabinet tilts outward at the top, insert wooden shims behind the cabinet at the bottom. The shims must be long enough so that they can be held in place by the fasteners used to attach the cabinet to the wall. If the cabinet tilts outward at the bottom, insert shims behind it at the top. Also set the level horizontally on top of the cabinet to check whether it tilts to one side. However, if the support is attached accurately, the cabinet should be horizontal.

With the helper still steadying the cabinet, drill holes for screws and, where necessary, hollow wall fasteners through the mounting rails at the top and bottom of the cabinet. Be sure the holes pass through any shims. Cabinets up to 30 inches high and 24 inches wide need at least four fasteners (two at the top and two at the bottom). Larger cabinets need additional fasteners spaced horizontally at 16-inch intervals and vertically at 10-inch intervals.

Screws should be No. 8-gauge roundhead wood screws with flat washers and must be long enough to penetrate wall studs at least 1 inch. Hollow wall fasteners should be equally sturdy. The strongest type are toggle bolts, described earlier.

Install the fasteners, beginning with those at the top. When you are finished, remove the support. Unless you are installing a run of cabinets (the procedure is described below), fill the screw holes with spackling and cover them with paint. Trim any exposed shims flush with the outside of the cabinet and cover the gap

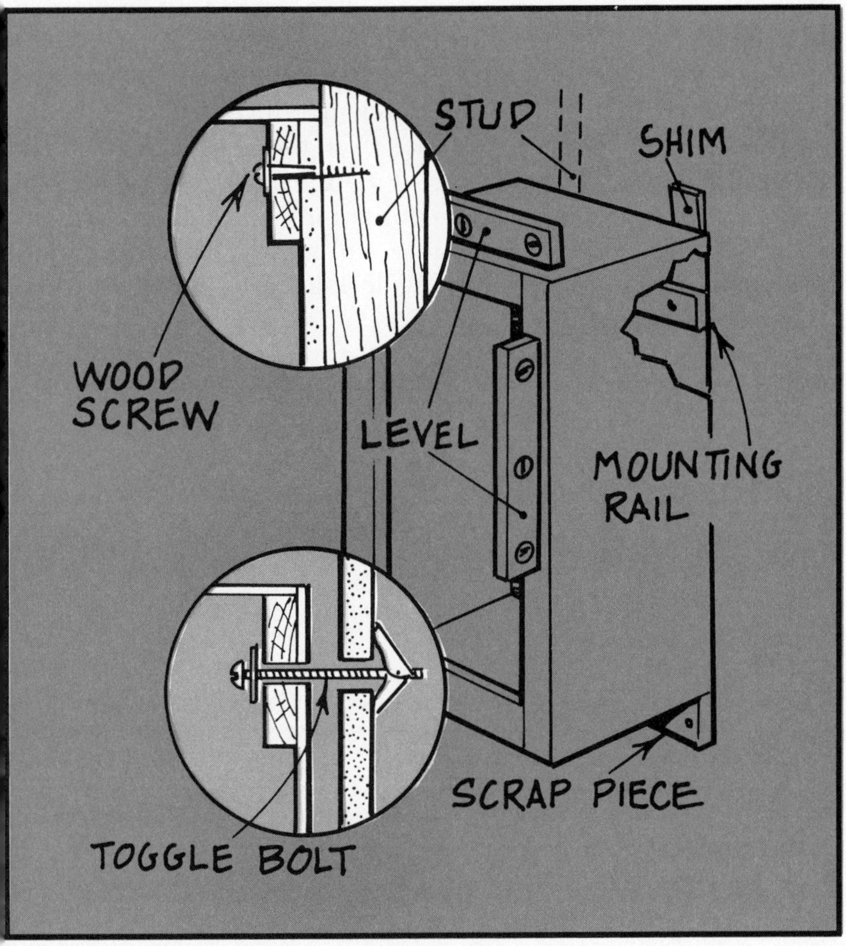

When hanging a wall cabinet, rest it on scrap lumber temporarily fastened to the wall at the correct height. Attach the cabinet to wall studs with roundhead screws; where there are no studs, use toggle bolts or other sturdy hollow-wall fasteners. Check surfaces with a level; make adjustments by installing shims behind the cabinet.

between the wall and the back of the cabinet with molding. Erase or wash off visible pencil lines.

If you are installing a run of cabinets, the best-looking results with the least overall effort are usually achieved by joining all the cabinets, except corner cabinets, before hanging them.

To do this, clamp the cabinets side by side using C-clamps. Be sure the front edges of the cabinets are flush and that any gaps between them close fully.

Install screws to fasten the front frames of the cabinets together. Use drywall screws if you can drive them with an electric drill or screwdriver. Otherwise, drill and counterbore pilot holes and install No. 6-gauge flathead wood screws. Install at least two screws per pair of cabinets (one screw about 3 inches from the bottom, the other the same distance from the top). Next, remove the clamps.

Hang the run of cabinets by positioning and shimming them as a unit and fastening them to the wall individually. More than one helper may be necessary. Divide long runs into groups of three or four cabinets each.

Appendices

CONTENTS

HIGHLIGHTS

Selecting Nails

Hardware and building supply stores carry a bewilder ing variety of nails, as anyone who has ever shopped for them ca testify. The reason is the diversity of building materials; nearly al require nails with specific properties.

Nails generally are driven through a thin piece of materia into a thicker one. As a rule of thumb, the correct length of a na is three times the thickness of the thinner piece. However, nail for fastening very thin material such as asphalt shingles or hard board paneling should be long enough to penetrate the thicke material about three quarters of an inch.

Where a nail chosen by the rule of thumb would penetrat the thicker piece completely—as when nailing two pieces togethe that are of equal thickness—two or more nails each about on quarter of an inch less in length than the thickness of both piece combined are usually sufficient.

The rule of thumb applies primarily to nails with smoot shanks (sides). Shorter nails can be used whose shanks are coate to enhance friction or are threaded or shaped in some other way Longer nails must be used when fastening into materials with littl holding ability of their own.

When selecting nails for construction projects, check buildin code requirements for your community; these generally are quit specific. For other uses, consult selection charts, usually availabl at stores that sell nails. The charts, together with the description given here of the different types of nails and their properties should enable you to make effective selections.

Most nails are made of steel or aluminum. Most smooth shanked steel nails are available bright (unprotected against rust or galvanized (zinc-coated) for use where moisture is present.

Conventional nails are classified according to the penny systen —a number followed by the abbreviation "d." The number i believed to have referred originally to the nail's price per hundre (the "d," a traditional British abbreviation for "penny," perhap derives from the denarius, a Roman coin). Today, the number i a measure of length that also incorporates overall size and weight

The larger the penny size, the longer, thicker, and heavie the nail. In sizes up to 10d, the length of a nail can be determine by dividing the penny size by four, then adding half an inch. Fo example, a 6d nail is 2 inches long. The penny size of finishing nails includes the thickness of the nail head; that of common nails (another type) does not.

Common nails are the most familiar type. They feature thick, flat nail heads, are larger in diameter than other types, and are smooth-shanked. Use common nails for all rough and heavy construction.

Box nails look like common nails but are smaller in diameter. As a result, they have less of a tendency to split boards when driven near the ends. They are designed for constructing boxes and crates but are suitable wherever boards must be nailed close to their ends or edges.

Cement-coated box nails are often call sinkers. Because the resinous coating provides increased holding strength, they are made an eighth to a quarter of an inch shorter than bright box nails having the same penny size. The friction created by driving sinkers causes the cement to melt. This quickly resets when the nail stops moving; consequently, sinkers must be installed rapidly

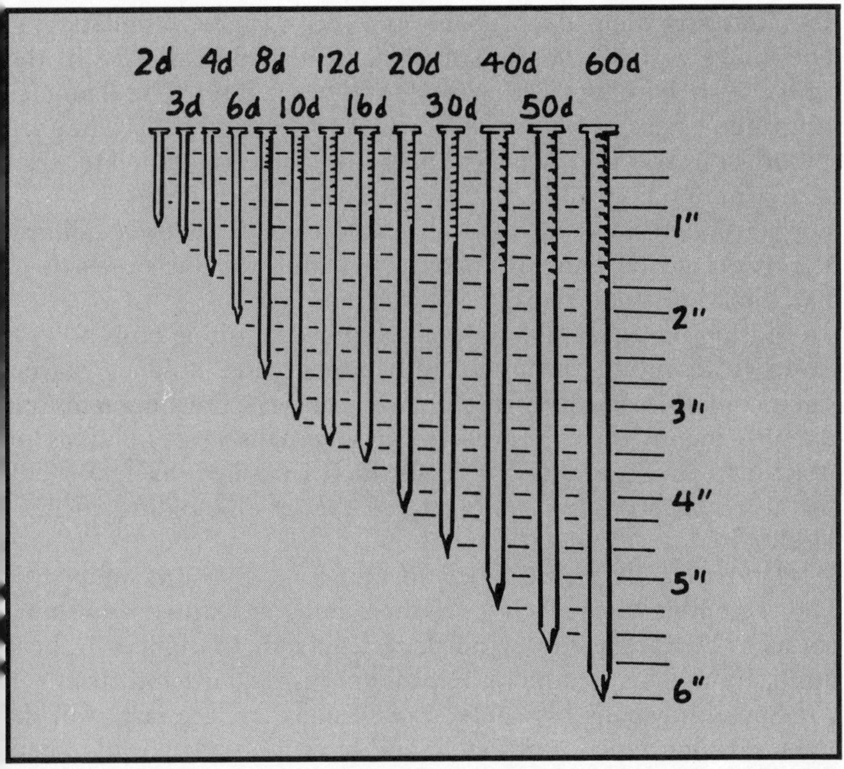

Chart shows the relationship between penny sizes and actual length of conventional nails with heads.

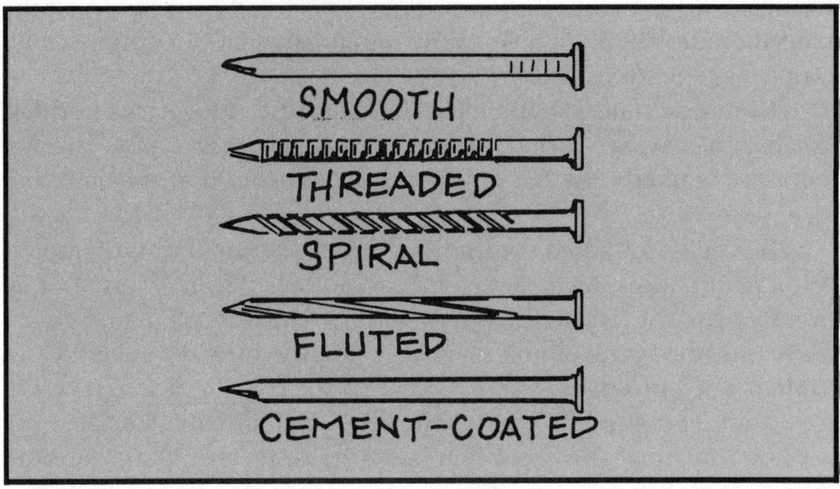

Nails come in a variety of shanks. Each has advantages.

with only a few hammer blows, because once the resin hardens the nail will be difficult to drive farther and will likely bend.

Finishing nails are probably the second most familiar type. They have a small, nearly spherical head with a dimple in the center for driving below the surface with a nail set. The diameter of finishing nails is the smallest of all conventional nails. They are smooth-shanked and typically used for cabinetry, paneling, trim—anywhere nail heads must be concealed.

Hardened finishing nails, threaded to increase their holding power, are called paneling nails. They are available in colors to match manufactured hardboard wall paneling.

Casing nails resemble smooth-shanked finishing nails but are larger in diameter, stronger, and have greater holding power. Their conical heads differ slightly from those of finishing nails but are also meant to be concealed. Casing nails are intended for attaching window and door trims (which are called casings). They are also suitable for fastening large pieces of molding such as baseboard.

Drywall nails are designed for attaching gypsum wallboard. They resemble box nails but are threaded and feature very sharp points. They are made of hardened steel that is blued by heat sterilization. This treatment helps them resist stains and rust.

Sheathing nails resemble drywall nails but are larger in diameter, unhardened, untreated, and have a broader head. Their purpose is to attach insulated wall sheathing or other soft paneling that has little inherent holding ability.

Siding nails resemble box nails but are usually threaded like drywall nails or have a spiral-shaped shank. They are meant for ttaching wood siding and shingles and also hold well in particle-oard and other types of manufactured wood.

Flooring nails most closely resemble casing nails, with ıreaded or spiral shanks and sturdier heads. The spiral-shank ariety have the greatest holding power. As their name implies, ooring nails are designed for fastening hardwood floorboards.

Roofing nails have very broad heads and sometimes threaded r spiral shanks. They are heavily galvanized and are intended for ecuring roof shingles or other roofing material.

Masonry nails have a large-diameter fluted or spiral shank nd are made of hardened carbon steel. They are meant to be riven by sledge or ball peen hammer into concrete.

Selecting and Using Wood Screws and Bolts

U**se screws or bolts in wood when greater holding power** ıan that provided by nails is necessary, or when pieces may need) be disassembled later. You must use screws when access is avail-ble to only one side of the pieces being fastened; if both sides are ccessible, bolts may be used instead, and are usually stronger. crews are also appropriate when hammering may cause damage, s when installing fasteners in a plaster wall.

crews

Ordinary wood screws are made of steel, either stainless or lated, or of aluminum, brass, or bronze. All these resist rust and orrosion. Steel screws are strongest. Stainless steel screws offer ıe greatest resistance to rust and corrosion but often are twice as ostly as plated steel. Aluminum screws are lightweight, relatively ıexpensive, and the best choice when fastening aluminum to ood outdoors. If screws and the materials they fasten are made f different metals, moisture can cause both to corrode.

Brass and bronze screws resist corrosion better than plated eel and aluminum, and where their screw heads will be visible ıeir color may be more attractive. Their cost is comparable to ıat of stainless steel screws.

Wood screws have heads that are either flat, round, or oval, ith either a single slot, for use with an ordinary screwdriver, or a ross-shaped slot that requires a Phillips screwdriver.

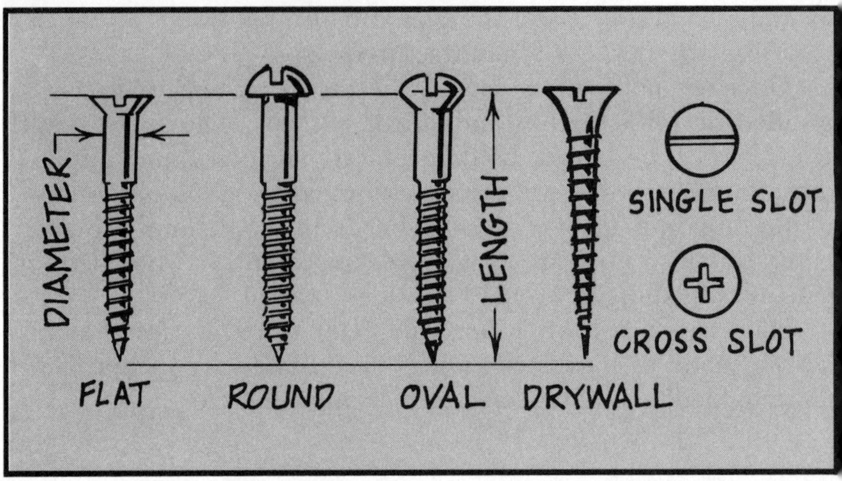

Most wood screws have flat, round, or oval heads with single or cross-shaped slots. Screw length includes only the portion of the screw designed to enter the wood. Diameter is measured on the shank. Drywall screws are popular because they do not require pilot holes when driven with power tools.

Flathead screws are installed so the head is flush with or below the surface of the wood. Generally, they are not intended for frequent removal and are often permanently covered with filler or a wooden plug.

Roundhead screws are meant to protrude from the surface to make removal easy. They are also used with materials too thin to allow sinking screw heads flush.

Oval-head screws, meant for easy removal, are more attractive than roundhead screws, but part of the head must be sunk into the wood.

The style of the slot usually makes little difference. Driving very large screws is easier if they have single slots. When a slip of the screwdriver can mar a finished surface, as with furniture, using screws with cross-shaped slots is less risky.

Screw sizes are defined in two ways: the diameter, given as a gauge number; and the designated length in inches, which tells how much of the screw will go into the wood. Hardware stores typically carry screws with gauge numbers ranging from 2 (about 3/32 inch) to 18 (about 9/32 inch). When choosing screws, length is usually the most important factor; it includes the part of the head that lies below the surface when the screw is installed.

A screw's length generally should be three times the thickness f the thinner piece through which it is to pass. (Screws should ways be installed through the thinner piece into the thicker one the pieces are of different thicknesses). All of the threaded ortion should penetrate the thicker piece. Screws to be installed the end of a board parallel with the grain should be four and a alf times the thickness of the piece being fastened.

No practical rule of thumb exists for choosing the correct iameter. As a guide, use 6- to 8-gauge screws when the thinner iece of wood is up to half an inch thick; 8- to 10-gauge screws hen the thinner piece is a half to three quarters of an inch thick;)- to 12-gauge screws when the thinner piece is three quarters to ı inch thick; and 12-gauge screws and larger when the thinner iece is more than an inch thick.

Estimate a diameter that the wood can accommodate without litting. For screws installed in the edge or end grain of a board, e diameter should be less than half the thickness of the wood.

To prevent the wood from splitting when installing wood rews, a pilot hole must be drilled. Although pilot holes must be curately positioned, they need not be precisely measured for ost home repairs.

When installing a screw in softwood like ordinary construc- on lumber, drill a hole three quarters of the screw's designated ngth. Use a drill bit of the same diameter or slightly smaller idth than the solid core of the screw's threaded part (called the ot).

Then, if the screw has a flat or oval head, use a countersink- g bit to drill a larger cone-shaped hole at the surface deep ough to recess the screw head. With a roundhead screw this ep is unnecessary.

To install a screw in hardwood, drill the first segment of the lot hole equal to the full designated length of the screw. Then, gardless of the type of screw head, enlarge the hole in the thin- r piece using a bit the same diameter as the screw's shank (the ıthreaded upper portion). Finish by enlarging the second hole th the countersinking bit if the screw is flat or oval-headed.

A pilot bit makes it possible to drill two- or three-stage pilot oles in a single step. Several styles are available at hardware ores; better designs are adjustable in length, but a separate bit is eded for each gauge of screw being installed.

When installing a screw, use a screwdriver that fits the slot actly. Lubricate long screws entering hardwood with soap or ax.

For many household chores, drywall screws, made for attaching wallboard, have all but replaced traditional wood screws among owners of power screwdrivers. Drywall screws are inexpensive, rust-resistant, and, when power-driven, do not require a pilot hole, even to sink the screw head flush with the surface.

Bolts

Bolts (except lag bolts, described below) are threaded fasteners with flat ends. Most are meant to be used with washers and nuts, making them removable. Bolt sizes are given in diameter and length (always measured from the base of the head to the end), sometimes accompanied by number of threads per inch. For example, a ½″ × 6″ × 13 bolt has a ½-inch diameter, a 6-inch length, and the threads at the end measure thirteen per inch.

In the United States, nuts and bolts are classified by the American Standard for Unified Threads. Most bolt threads are either coarse (UNC) or fine (UNF). Most imported nuts and bolts have metric sizes and thread dimensions that are not interchangeable with American sizes.

Bolts and nuts stocked by most hardware stores usually have coarse threads. Because these are deeper than fine threads, attaching nuts is easier. But coarse threads are also looser, causing nuts to fit less tightly, and are not as strong, because the threads cut more deeply into the shank. For situations where maximum strength is needed for a given diameter, ask for bolts with fine threads.

The following are the most common types of bolts:

Lag bolts. These are actually large screws featuring unslotted square or hexagonal heads and pointed ends. They are for use where extra strength is needed but where access is limited to only one of the surfaces being fastened.

Machine bolts. These are perhaps the most familiar type; they have square or diagonal heads and flat ends. Machine bolts are used when disassembly of parts is frequent.

Carriage bolts. These have round heads with a square or hexagonal projection underneath that bites into the wood when the nut is tightened, keeping the bolt from turning. In some situations, the round head may be more attractive than a square or hexagonal shape.

Stove bolts. These have slotted heads that are flat, round, or oval like screw heads. A variety featuring round but flattened heads that rise less prominently above the surface are called oven bolts. Both stove bolts and oven bolts are tightened with a screwdriver and a wrench used simultaneously.

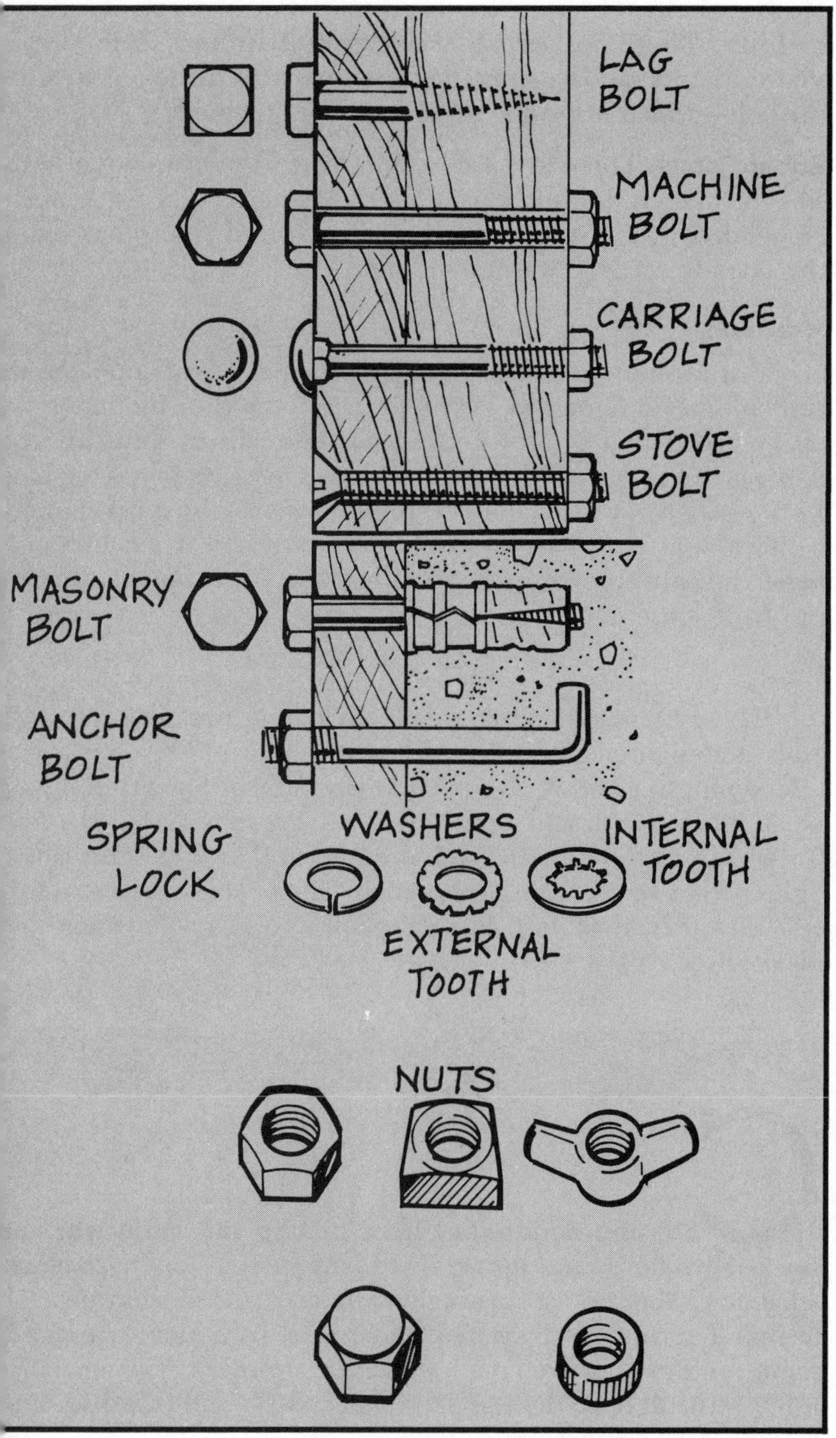

olts generally have flat ends and are designed for use
rith washers and nuts.

Masonry bolts. These are used to fasten wood or metal to concret or brick. There are several styles, but all feature some kind c sleeve that expands against the masonry to provide a grip whe the bolt—which fits inside the sleeve—is tightened.

Anchor bolts. These are used primarily to fasten wooden hous sills to concrete foundations. One end is bent at an angle and i embedded in the concrete when it is poured; the other end i threaded to accept a washer and nut.

Washers

Flat washers—smooth disks, usually metal, with a hole in th center—are designed to distribute the force of a tightened nu over a broad area, thus protecting wood directly underneath fro damage. They can also be used as spacers in case a bolt is too lon Lock washers—which come in several designs, the most commo being a split ring—serve a different purpose: When tightene beneath a nut, they force tension back against it, preventing th nut from loosening.

Nuts

These are used to fasten bolts by being threaded onto the ends and tightened firmly against the back of the joint or a intervening washer. Nuts come in many shapes for different pu poses, but their thread sizes must always match that of the bol for which they are intended. Wing nuts and knurled nuts can b tightened by hand, without a wrench. Cap or acorn nuts cover th end of a bolt, making it less dangerous to rub against and als more attractive.

Abrasive Papers

C**hoosing sandpaper from among the many varieti** stocked by hardware stores and home centers often perplex amateurs, and not surprisingly. Modern coated abrasives, th technical term for sandpaper and related products, contain n sand; some are not even made of paper. However, making choic is not difficult once the way sandpaper works and the differenc between varieties are understood.

Sandpaper consists of sharp-edged (abrasive) particl bonded to a backing material, usually paper or cloth. The partic lges act like tiny chisels. Each shaves a minute quantity of mate-al from the surface against which it is rubbed.

Naturally, coarse particles, which are relatively large, remove ore material with each cut than finer particles. This means that nding with coarse-grade sandpaper is quicker than with fine. owever, the scratches made by coarse particles also are large. hus the surface they produce is rougher.

The key to achieving both fast results and a smooth surface to use several grades of sandpaper. By rubbing with successive ades, each having finer particles than the one before, large, eep scratches produced by quick-cutting coarse particles can be ficiently reduced to small, shallow ones that are imperceptible. surface that is smooth is not scratch-free: The scratches remain-g are simply too small to be felt or seen.

To make choosing possible, all sandpaper is graded according particle size, called grit number. Theoretically, this categorizes rasive particles according to the number of openings per inch a screen through which they can pass. The most widely used stem of grit numbers ranges from 12 (coarsest) to 600 (finest). n older system, still sometimes used on flint-coated and garnet-ated sandpaper (described further on) uses numbers and mul-le zeros. These range from 4 (coarsest) to 10/0 (finest).

Grit numbers are usually printed on the sandpaper package d on the backs of sheets. A description of the particle size, lpful in correlating different grading systems, usually accom-nies the grit number. For most sanding jobs, simply choosing ndpaper on the basis of its word description will enable you to tain the proper succession of sandpaper grades.

Following are the most commonly available grades of sand-per:

tra coarse (24 to 36 grit). Approximate for removing thick paint other heavy finish and heavy rust.

arse (40 to 60 grit). For removing large amounts of wood or etal from unfinished stock.

edium (80 to 100 grit). For removing small amounts of wood, ht rust, and preparing wall and ceiling surfaces for painting.

ne (120 to 180 grit). For final sanding of bare wood beneath paint d removing slight imperfections.

tra Fine (220 to 360 grit). For sanding between coats of finish or r producing an exceptionally smooth surface on unfinished rdwood.

Although particle size is the most important factor to compare when selecting sandpaper, you should also consider the material from which the particles are made.

Sandpaper coated with flint particles is an old-fashioned variety. Flint dulls quickly. However, because flint-coated sandpaper is inexpensive compared to other types, it is economical to use for removing paint or other sticky substances. These clog the paper by filling the spaces between the particles, and often ruin it as rapidly as the particles become dull.

Garnet-coated sandpaper is another old-timer. Garnet is sharper than flint because it is harder, but its particles nevertheless dull more readily than the synthetic abrasives that have replaced it. Still, garnet paper is less expensive than newer types and is a good choice for short sanding chores and hand sanding unfinished wood.

The workhorse of modern sandpapers is aluminum oxide. This material is sharper, and therefore faster cutting, than either flint or garnet and resists dulling longer. It can be used to sand any material and is available with either paper backing or cloth.

Paper backing is fine for general sanding by hand; but for use with a power sander choose cloth, because it is both stronger and more flexible. Aluminum oxide paper is also available with a waterproof backing that allows moistening it for wet sanding, a technique used both in auto body repair and furniture manufacture to produce the smoothest surfaces.

Topping the list is silicone carbide paper. It is sharper, harder, and more durable than the previously mentioned abrasives, and is also more expensive. Silicone carbide paper is particularly suited for sanding metal, although like aluminum oxide paper, it can be used on any material. It, too, is available with paper, cloth, or waterproof backing.

One other type of sandpaper deserves mention: emery cloth. This early developed synthetic abrasive was once considered the finest material for smoothing metal. However, it is dull, slow cutting, and quick to wear out.

Do not use emery cloth for polishing electrical components such as contact points. Rubbed-off particles, if not removed completely, can conduct electricity and cause a short circuit. For sanding electrical items, use any of the other abrasive papers mentioned.

A final point to consider when choosing sandpaper is whether it is closed coat or open coat. With closed-coat sandpaper, particles are closely spaced. Because there are more particles per given area, cutting is quicker. However, because of this close spacing, the paper is more easily clogged.

With open-coat paper, particles are spaced farther apart. Cutting is slower but clogging is less. Closed-coat paper is suitable for most sanding jobs and produces a smoother surface. But open-coat paper is best for sanding soft material such as plastic and for removing finishes.

Choosing Adhesives

Most adhesives or glues for home repair are strong and easy to use, but choosing the right kind can be confusing. When making a selection, consider primarily the glue's ingredients, listed on the label, rather than any recommended applications. Although many glues specify that they will bond materials like wood, metal, and plastic, differences between them—like whether the finished joint is rigid or flexible, waterproof, or whether clamping is required—make some glues more appropriate for certain tasks than others.

Four kinds of glue are usually enough to have on hand: aliphatic resin, cyanoacrylate, epoxy, and polyvinyl acetate. These and other popular varieties are described below. Virtually all glues are available at hardware stores. Those that aren't can usually be obtained from suppliers of materials requiring them.

Aliphatic resin glue. This is also called yellow woodworking glue and carpenter's glue. It is the choice of most professionals for gluing wood, and can also be used on other porous surfaces like leather, felt, and cork. It is strong, and pieces being glued can be positioned in plenty of time (about fifteen minutes) before the glue becomes sticky.

Aliphatic resin glue is moderately water-resistant but is not a good choice for outdoor items. Pieces being glued must fit closely (the glue will not fill gaps) and be clamped together for about half an hour. Full curing takes about twenty-four hours. Excess glue that has not hardened can be removed with water.

Ordinary aliphatic resin glue dries a light cream color. A dark-colored variety is available for gluing dark woods. Both can be sanded and painted, but like most glue, neither absorbs stain.

Contact Cement. This is usually used for gluing sheet materials like plastic laminate countertops. No clamping is required; pieces coated with cement bond instantly. (This can also be a drawback, because pieces cannot be slid together or adjusted for a better fit.)

Water-based contact cement that contains no solvents is safer to use than solvent-based cement, which is both flammable and a health hazard. When using either type, carefully follow all precautions listed on the container.

Construction Adhesive. This is a synthetic rubber that comes in a cartridge and is applied with a caulking gun. Among its uses are attaching sheets of wallboard or other paneling to house framing. The bond it produces is flexible, which allows glued building materials to shrink and swell due to humidity changes. Construction adhesive contains solvents, and thus is flammable and dangerous to breathe. Follow the manufacturer's instructions when using it.

Cyanoacrylate. Glues of this type are the so-called super glues. They bond in seconds, without the use of clamps, to almost any material. (Allow twenty-four hours for curing.)

Although expensive, they are meant to be used in very small amounts (typically one drop per square inch) and only for small repairs. Of the two kinds available, liquid and gel, the former works best on nonporous surfaces like glass, the latter on porous surfaces like china. Pieces being glued must fit closely; the adhesive will not fill gaps. Both dry clear.

Be careful not to get cyanoacrylate glue where you do not want it; the glue will bond to skin. To remove dried glue, use acetone or a product containing it such as nail polish remover.

Epoxy. This glue produces an extremely strong, long-lasting bond that is also waterproof. Epoxy can be used on porous and nonporous materials, and, unlike most other glues, is excellent for filling gaps. Although clamping or applying hand pressure is required, quick-setting epoxy is available that needs pressure for only about five minutes. Depending on the variety, epoxy glues require from thirty minutes to three days to cure. All dry cream color and can be painted. Sanding is difficult.

Epoxy is tricky to use because it must be mixed from two ingredients, a resin and a hardener, both sold together. Too much resin slows drying; too much hardener weakens the glue.

Epoxy for minor repairs comes in mated tubes or plastic syringes. For large jobs like building outdoor furniture, both ingredients are available in cans. Epoxy is flammable, irritating to skin and harmful to breathe. When using it, obey the instructions printed on the label.

Hide Glue. This old-fashioned glue is desirable for some jobs precisely because of qualities often considered drawbacks: It takes up to an hour to become sticky and produces a relatively weak bond that is easily dissolved with hot water.

Hide glue is excellent for use on large surfaces that can be lamped, like veneer tabletops, and for furniture that may require epair later. It also fills gaps. Liquid hide glue is easier to use than hat sold as flakes because no mixing is required. The glue dries n amber color and can be sanded and painted.

lousehold Cement. This is all-purpose clear adhesive sold in a ube. It is inexpensive, but slower to dry and less strong than yanoacrylate (which has all but replaced it) and requires clamp-ng. Solvent-based household cement, which is harmful to reathe, becomes sticky in about a minute. The safer, silicone-ased variety, which contains no solvents, becomes sticky in about en minutes. Both require twenty-four hours for complete curing.

lastic Resin. There are two types: urea formaldehyde and resor-inol formaldehyde. Both are for gluing wood and require clamp-ng; the former is sold as a powder to be mixed with water, the atter as a powder to be mixed with liquid resin accompanying it.

The urea-formaldehyde glue is highly water-resistant and ries a light tan color. The resorcinol glue is waterproof (its chief ses are in marine construction and building outdoor furniture) nd dries dark red. Both types can be painted, but sanding is ifficult.

Plastic resin glue is toxic. Use it carefully, according to the nanufacturer's instructions.

olyvinyl Acetate. This is also called white glue and PVA glue. It as virtually the same properties as aliphatic resin glue, but is less trong. It can be used on wood (an advantage it has over aliphatic esin glue is that it dries nearly clear) but is better suited for gluing ighter-weight porous materials like paper, cardboard, cloth, and eather.

Buying Lumber

B**uying lumber at a lumberyard can be confusing. You** eed to know the terms to use to ask for what you want, and how ımber is sized, graded, and priced. You should also know how to lentify defective lumber.

erms

Any piece of lumber less than 2 inches thick and 8 inches vide is called a strip; any piece less than 2 inches thick but more than 8 inches wide is called a board. Pieces of any width that ar more than 2 inches thick but less than 5 inches thick are calle dimension lumber. Any piece whose smallest dimension (thicl ness or width) is at least 4 inches is called a timber.

Yards typically stock only standard-sized lumber used fc house construction. That which comes from evergreen trees– pine, fir, and spruce, for example—is classed as softwood; lumbe from deciduous trees like oak, maple, and walnut is classed a hardwood.

Sizes

Lumber dimensions are always given starting with the thicl ness in inches, followed by the width in inches, and last by th length, usually in feet.

The thickness and width by which lumber is designated ar nominal dimensions—those to which pieces are cut at the mil Nominal dimensions do not account for shrinkage later durin drying or any trimming necessary to smooth them for sale.

With softwood, lumber having a nominal thickness of 1 inc actually measures about a quarter of an inch less; that with nominal thickness of 2 inches or more actually measures abou half an inch less.

Softwood with a nominal width of 2 inches through 5 inche has an actual width about half an inch less; that with a nomin width greater than 5 inches has an actual width about three qua ters of an inch less.

For example, if you ask at a lumberyard for a one-by-fou strip (a standard softwood size), the piece you get will measu only about three quarters of an inch thick and about 3½ inche wide; a two-by-eight board will measure about 1½ inches thic and about 7¼ inches wide. (The exact actual dimensions may va up to an eighth of an inch from these figures.)

Nominal thicknesses for hardwood are usually expressed i quarters of an inch even if the dimension is greater than an incl For example, hardwood lumber designated 4/4, which is pro nounced "four quarter," is nominally 1 inch thick.

Nominal thicknesses of hardwood differ from actual thicl nesses by about $\frac{3}{16}$ inch for smoothed lumber up to 1¾ inche thick, and by about a quarter of an inch for smoothed lumber th is thicker. (Hardwood is sometimes available smoothed only o one side; its actual thickness is closer to the nominal dimension.)

Differences between nominal and actual widths can vary a much as three quarters of an inch for pieces wider than 4 inche so when ordering, specify the actual width you need.

Lengths for lumber are always actual. If you ask for a 10-foot-long board, that is what you will receive. Softwood lumber usually comes in lengths ranging in 2-foot increments from 8 to 16 feet. Hardwood lengths generally range in 1-foot increments from 4 to 16 feet.

Grades

Lumber is graded according to quality and appearance. Softwood grades are based on the use of pieces intact or after minimal trimming; hardwood grades have developed mainly from the number and size of cuttings that can be made from rough boards for use in furniture parts, flooring, and similar products. Most softwoods are classed Select or Common. The grades of Select lumber are: B and Better (or 1 and 2 Clear), which allows only pieces free of any but minor blemishes; C Select, which allows some minor blemishes, including small knots; and D Select, which allows imperfections on one side that can be covered by paint, and larger less easily disguised imperfections on the other.

The grades of Common lumber are: Number 1 (or Select Merchantable), which allows minor blemishes and tight knots less than 2 inches in diameter (all defects must be away from the board's edges); Number 2 (or Construction), which allows tight knots and blemishes up to 3 inches in diameter (none may be near edges); Number 3 (or Standard), which allows pieces to have either several coarse or loose knots accompanied by other major blemishes, or a single large defect surrounded by good wood; Number 4 (or Utility), which allows pieces to contain more knots and blemishes than Number 3, and even some holes; and Number 5 (or Economy), which is the lowest grade of usable lumber.

For trim, molding, and finish woodwork, one of the Select grades is usually the best choice. For most other home repairs, Common Number 2 grade is usually sufficient.

Lumber for structural use—rafters and joists, for example—carries additional grading. Before buying any, ask a local building inspector for the grades specified by building codes in your area.

Hardwoods are graded primarily by the percentage of unblemished wood in a board. The finest grade is FAS (or Firsts and Seconds); boards of this grade must usually be at least 6 inches wide and 8 feet long, and more than 81 percent of the surface must be free of defects.

The next grade is Select. Boards of this category must be at least 4 inches wide and 6 feet long, and have one side comparable to FAS.

The remaining grades are: Number 1 Common, which admits lumber narrower and shorter than Select that is at least 66 percent unblemished; Number 2 Common, for which boards must be at least 50 percent unblemished; Number 3A Common, for which boards must be at least 33 percent unblemished; and Number 3B Common, for which boards must be at least 25 percent unblemished.

Pricing

Molding, dowels, and some dimension lumber like studs are often sold by length, called linear or running feet. Most other lumber is usually sold by nominal volume, called board feet. One board foot equals an abstract volume 1 foot long by 1 foot wide by 1 inch thick. An easy way to find the number of board feet in a piece of lumber is to multiply its nominal thickness in inches by its nominal width in inches and then multiply this number by the board's length in feet; then divide the product of all three numbers by twelve. For example, a two-by-four board 12 feet long contains 8 board feet.

Normally, you won't order lumber in units of board feet, because the dimensions of the pieces you want are usually a more important consideration. But by comparing the board-foot prices of different grades of lumber you can determine which is most economical; often you can save money by buying a large quantity of lesser-grade lumber and using only the best portions.

Defects

Most lumberyards will let you select pieces individually if you ask to do so, especially if you are buying relatively small amounts. Besides knots—those places where branches formed in the tree's trunk—lumber may have other defects like cracks, chips, and pockets of sap, all of which have specific names depending on their location and cause. In general, isolated defects do not diminish the overall strength of a board; and because lumber is graded on the basis of its defects, you should expect to see them in quantities consistent with the quality of lumber you are inspecting. Most defects can be filled and painted; however, knots and complex grain patterns can be difficult to plane or sand smooth.

Warped lumber, which is lumber that is bent in any direction, twisted, or cupped across its width, should be avoided. Although cupped lumber can sometimes be planed to flatten it (of course, this diminishes its final thickness), lumber warped in other ways is generally unmanageable.

Identifying lumber that has already warped is easy: Simply sight along the length of boards, holding one end at eye level.

Sight first along the top, then turn the board and sight along one edge.

Be aware that much lumber for sale in lumberyards is not completely dry and may warp as it dries further. Often you can tell by a difference in weight that one board contains more moisture than another; always select the board that is lighter. Also, inspect the segments of the growth rings visible at each end of the board. Segments that are uniform in thickness, evenly spaced, and close together usually indicate wood that is more stable than that with erratically spaced segments of different thicknesses.

Boards whose ring segments are at or near right angles to the wide surfaces will have far less tendency to warp—and particularly to cup—than those whose ring segments slant diagonally or are curved. (You can tell the direction in which a board will cup by noting the direction that the segments curve: Because greater shrinkage always occurs on the side of the board that was closest to the outside of the tree, cupping will always occur on the convex side of the curved segments.)

Storage

Even if the lumber you obtain is straight, it can warp if not stored correctly. Boards should be stacked horizontally on blocks that raise the first piece about 2 inches off the ground and support it about every 2 feet. Subsequent boards should be separated from those beneath them by strips at least three quarters of an inch thick, also at 2-foot intervals.

Short pieces of lumber can be stacked vertically or at a very steep angle. Lumber stored outdoors should be covered to protect it from moisture but left unsealed to allow plenty of ventilation.

Plywood and Other Manufactured Wood

Of the varieties of manufactured wood paneling used in home construction and repair, plywood is certainly the most popular. It is also the most difficult to select. Made by gluing thin layers (called plies) of wood together like a sandwich, so that the the grain of each ply lies perpendicular to the one below it, plywood comes in many types and degrees of quality.

The most commonly used plywood is called veneer-core. It consists of softwood plies, usually Douglas fir or Southern yellow pine, although a variety of other woods from standardized species groups are also used. Another type of plywood is called solid-core. Used chiefly for cabinetmaking, it consists of plies surrounding either solid wood strips or a sheet of particleboard (another manufactured wood paneling discussed later).

A third type of plywood, also liked by cabinetmakers, is called hardwood plywood. Manufactured in veneer-core and solid-core styles, one or both outer plies are of fine hardwood such as birch, oak, or Philippine mahogany, with more exotic species also available.

All plywood consists of an uneven number of plies, with the grain of the front (called the face) and back plies running parallel to the panel's long dimension.

With softwood plywood, the two outer plies are each graded A through D according to American Plywood Association standards of quality and appearance. A grading stamp on each piece of softwood plywood prominently displays these letters. The grade of the face side is always listed first.

Plywood graded A-A consists of top-grade face and back panels, each free of blemishes and sanded smooth. It is appropriate for use where clear finish is to be applied and where both sides of the panel will be visible.

However, where only one side of the plywood will be exposed or if one or both surfaces are to be painted, a more economical choice is plywood with just one top-quality side, A-B or A-C, or an even lesser grade such as B-B, B-C, B-D, C-C, or C-D. Lesser-grade plies contain checks (splits), knotholes, and patches. The greater the number and size of the defects, the lower the grade.

Hardwood plywood is graded according to the quality of its outer plies by the Hardwood Plywood Manufacturers Association

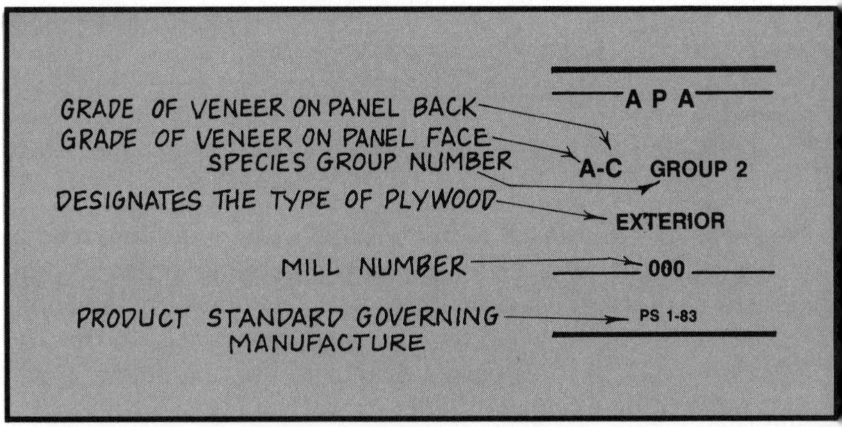

Typical grading stamp found on plywood describes its quality and lists other specifics of its manufacture.

and American National Standards Institute. Premium quality is graded A and good quality B or 1; lesser qualities are graded with numbers 2 through 4. Hardwood plywood may be stamped along an edge or have a label attached.

The moisture resistance of plywood is indicated by its exposure rating, which is included on the stamp. With softwood plywood, a rating of Exterior declares panels able to withstand continuous exposure to moisture and extreme weather conditions.

The rating Exposure 1 indicates panels are moisture-resistant, but should be protected from continuous direct exposure to outdoor conditions. (Exposure 1 plywood is usually used for construction sheathing that is covered with roofing or siding material.)

Exposure 2 and Interior ratings are given to panels that must be kept dry.

Hardwood plywood uses a different rating vocabulary—Technical, Type I, Type II, and Type III in descending order of moisture resistance—and also includes Marine grade, in which water resistance is only a single factor.

Easier to choose among manufactured wood panels are particleboard, waferboard, oriented strand board, and hardboard. Particleboard is made from sawdust and tiny wood particles bonded with resin. The material is heavy and relatively brittle, but is extremely stable and excellent for use as countertop and floor underlayment, as well as partitions in built-in cabinets.

Particleboard is usually stamped with a three-symbol code such as 1-A-1. The first symbol indicates whether the board is made with urea-formaldehyde glue (Type 1) or phenolic resin glue (Type 2).

Type 2 particleboard is resistant to water and high temperatures (Type 1 is not), so is often the best choice for use in kitchens and bathrooms. Both types dull cutting tools quickly.

The second symbol—A, B, or C—indicates the density of the particleboard (high, medium, or low, respectively). High-density particleboard is the heaviest; it is more rigid and can span greater distances without sagging than medium- or low-density board. The third symbol—(1 or 2)—is a strength classification. Class 2 can support greater loads and hold fasteners more tightly than Class 1.

Similar to medium-density particleboard is a product called medium-density fiberboard (M.D.F.). Because it is made from wood particles that have been broken down into even smaller wood fibers, smoother edges result when the material is cut, and the product is also easier to paint. However, such fine dust is produced when working with M.D.F. that wearing a dust mask is recommended.

Waferboard, also called flakeboard, is made like particleboard but consists of large wood fragments bonded in a random arrangement to form panels whose surface has a mosaic appearance. Used chiefly as an inexpensive substitute for lesser-grade plywood, waferboard is similar to Exposure 1 plywood in water resistance; also, it holds nails and other fasteners more strongly than either particleboard or plywood.

Oriented strand board, called OSB for short, is a more carefully manufactured waferboard, stronger overall than the ordinary variety. The wood fragments used in OSB are separated according to size, then laid down in layers resembling plywood plies, with the grain direction of the majority of fragments in each layer running perpendicular to the layers above and below. Phenolic resin glue is used, making the product water-resistant but not waterproof.

Hardboard, sometimes called fiberboard, is made from processed wood and other fibers bonded with lignin, a wood by-product. Available only in thin panels up to 3/8 inch thick, hardboard is graded S1S (one side smooth and the other rough) or S2S (both sides smooth). Tempered and Service-tempered grades of hardboard both are stronger and more moisture-resistant than hardboard graded Standard or Service.

Paints and Other Finishes

Here is a guide that will help you decide what kind of primer and paint or other finish to apply to various household surfaces. The recommendations are general; follow the instructions on the manufacturer's label.

EXTERIOR SURFACES	RECOMMENDED PRIMER	RECOMMENDED PAINT OR FINISH
MASONRY		
Brick	Alkali-resistant; masonry surface conditioner; cement-based paint.	Alkyd or latex housepaint (acrylic-latex preferred); cement-based paint; water-repellent sealer.

EXTERIOR SURFACES	RECOMMENDED PRIMER	RECOMMENDED PAINT OR FINISH
Cement and cinder block	Same as above.	Same as above.
Concrete	Same as above.	Same as above.
Stucco	Same as above.	Same as above.
METAL		
Aluminum	Metal primer.	Alkyd or latex housepaint (acrylic-latex preferred); aluminum paint; metal enamel.
Brass, bronze, or copper	Same as above.	Same as above; also metal polish, lacquer, acrylic, or polyurethane.
Bright iron or steel	Same as above; also cement-based paint, or primer containing zinc.	Same as above; zinc primers also may be coated with bituminous roof coating.
Galvanized steel	Same as above (allow galvanized steel to weather six months before painting).	Alkyd or latex housepaint (acrylic-latex preferred); metal enamel; bituminous roof coating.
PLASTIC		
Vinyl	Latex.	Acrylic latex housepaint.
WOOD		
Clapboards	Alkyd or latex; stain-sealing primer-sealer where necessary.	Alkyd or latex housepaint.
Natural wood siding, shingles, trim	Water-repellent sealer.	Exterior clean finish; stain; water-repellent sealer.
Plywood	Alkyd or latex; stain-sealing primer-sealer where necessary.	Alkyd or latex housepaint.
Porch and deck flooring	Alkyd or latex porch and deck primer.	Alkyd two-part epoxy or polyurethane porch and deck paint; acrylic latex porch and deck paint.

EXTERIOR SURFACES	RECOMMENDED PRIMER	RECOMMENDED PAINT OR FINISH
Pressure-treated lumber	Water-repellent sealer; Alkyd or latex regular or porch and deck primer. (Allow pressure-treated wood to weather two months before painting.)	None required, but will accept alkyd or latex housepaint or porch and deck paint.
Roof shingles	Water-repellent sealer.	None.
Windows and painted trim	Alkyd or latex; stain-sealing primer-sealer where necessary.	Alkyd or latex trim enamel.

INTERIOR SURFACES	RECOMMENDED PRIMER	RECOMMENDED PAINT OR FINISH
FLOORS		
Asphalt tile	None.	Wax.
Ceramic tile	None.	Tile sealer containing silicone.
Concrete	Water-repellent sealer.	Wax.
Linoleum	None.	Shellac; wax.
Vinyl	None.	Liquid vinyl floor finish.
Wood	Clear wood sealer; tinted filler-sealer; alkyd or latex floor primer.	Clear floor finish; alkyd or latex floor paint.
WALLS AND CEILINGS		
Acoustical tile	Alkyd or latex.	Alkyd or latex flat wall paint.
Brick	Alkali-resistant; masonry surface conditioner; cement-based paint; water-repellent sealer.	Alkyd or latex house or wall paint (acrylic-latex preferred); cement-based paint; no paint required over sealer.
Concrete	Same as above.	Same as above.
Plaster	Alkyd or latex; stain-sealing primer-sealer where necessary.	Alkyd or latex flat wall paint; semigloss recommended in kitchens and bathrooms.
Wallboard	Same as above.	Same as above.
Wood paneling	Clear wood sealer; tinted filler-sealer; alkyd or latex.	Clear wood finish; alkyd or latex flat wall paint.

EXTERIOR SURFACES	RECOMMENDED PRIMER	RECOMMENDED PAINT OR FINISH
Wood trim	Same as above.	Clear wood finish; alkyd or latex semigloss wall or trim paint.
MISCELLANEOUS		
Exposed heating ducts	Alkyd or latex.	Light-colored alkyd or latex flat or wall paint (tan or beige recommended).
Radiators and convector covers	Same as above.	Same as above.

Household Electric Wire

Technically, electric wire is a single strand or group of twisted strands used as an individual conductor. Cable is two or more wires enclosed in the same sheathing. Each wire in a cable (sometimes with the exception of the grounding wire) is separately insulated to keep it from touching the others, which would cause a short circuit.

Local electrical codes specify the type and size of wiring (that is, wires and cable) to be used for all situations. Before beginning any electrical project or purchasing any materials, consult a local building or electrical inspector, or a reputable local supplier of electrical equipment.

Types

Wires for household appliances and applications, and wires that make up cables for residential wiring, are usually one of three types, based on their insulation: Type T (the most common), is wire encased in minimum-grade thermoplastic insulation; Type TW is wire with heavier thermoplastic insulation resistant to water and some corrosive materials; and Type THW is wire with even heavier thermoplastic insulation that resists high temperatures as well as moisture and corrosion.

In older homes, wire with rubber-and-fabric insulation is often found instead. The types are usually R, RW, or RWH, which correspond to the Type T wires already described.

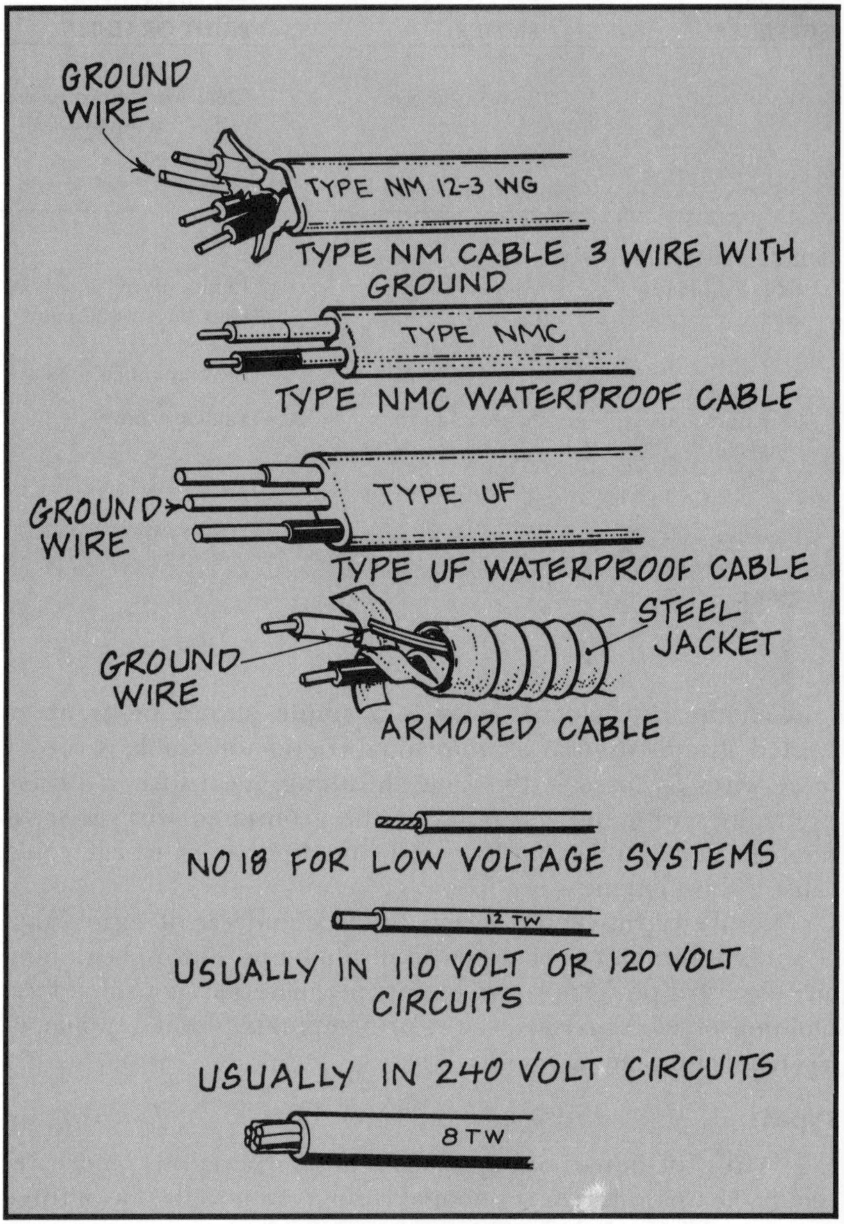

Common types of household electrical cable (top). Common sizes of household wire (bottom).

There are several other types of wire used less commonly. Except for very thin sizes, all wire is printed along its length with its type and size (sizes are explained on page 478) and with other information, including the maximum voltage that can safely pass through it and the mark of a testing agency such as Underwriters' Laboratories, Inc. (UL), or the name of the manufacturer.

Most household wiring involves cables. The most commonly used is nonmetallic sheathed cable, often called Romex (a popular brand name). Indoors, Type NM cable is preferred for all dry locations. It consists of two or more Type T or TW wires and a bare copper grounding wire. Brown paper or jute wrapping fills the spaces between wires (this material absorbs what little moisture may be encountered and keeps it away from the wires); the cable's sheathing is flexible plastic.

In basements, laundry rooms, and other areas where dampness is present, Type NMC cable is preferred. This contains wires similar to those in Type NM cable, but they are embedded in the plastic sheathing, rather than merely enclosed. This eliminates the need for paper or jute, which can rot if it becomes permanently moist. Sometimes the insulated wires are also wrapped in fiberglass to shield them further.

Codes often allow Type NMC cable to be used outdoors above ground, but for most outdoor applications and wherever cable must be buried in the earth, Type UF cable is more often specified. This is similar to Type NMC but offers even more protection.

Like wire, all nonmetallic sheathed cable is stamped with important information at regular intervals along its length. Included is the cable type and also the number and size of the wires inside. For example, cable stamped "12/2 G TYPE NM" indicates Type NM cable containing two size 12 wires and one grounding wire.

Older houses may have metal-armored cable called BX (also a brand name) instead of Romex. It contains two or more insulated wires and either a bare copper grounding wire or a flexible metal strip, called a bonding strip. The wires are wrapped in heavy paper to protect them from abrasion against the metal housing.

BX cable can be used only in dry locations. Some codes continue to specify its use in walls and other areas where many nails may be driven.

Pipe, called conduit, can also be used as sheathing around wires. Conduit differs from water pipe in that the inside surface is smoother, allowing wires to be pulled through it easily and without damage. The most common conduits for residential use are EMT (electrical metal tubing), made of thin-walled galvanized steel or of aluminum, and PVC (polyvinyl chloride), which is plastic. Both can be used indoors and outdoors above ground. For burial, codes generally specify rigid conduit made of thick-walled galvanized steel.

Unlike cable, conduit and the wires it is to enclose are purchased separately. During installation of the conduit, the wires are threaded inside.

Sizes

Wire sizes are given as American Wire Gauge (AWG) numbers ranging (for household use) from 4/0 (or 0000) to 18. Smaller numbers designate thicker wires; these have greater capacity for carrying electricity than thinner wires.

Generally, if you are installing a new circuit you should use cable containing 12-gauge copper wire. This is recommended by most codes and is thick enough to carry 20 amps safely; thus, it can be protected by a 20-amp circuit breaker and used to supply kitchen and bathroom appliances in addition to ordinary lighting and other low-wattage fixtures.

If your house is not new, you will probably find that it contains cable with 14-gauge wire. This was once standard for lighting and ordinary circuits, and is still permitted by codes in some areas; but 14-gauge wire is too thin to safely accommodate more than 15 amps, which now is considered inadequate. There is no danger in extending a circuit containing 14-gauge wire by using 12-gauge, provided the correct circuit breaker (usually 15 amps) for the 14-gauge wire is retained.

Wire for high-wattage appliances like air conditioners, water heaters, ranges, oil burners, and heavy-duty workshop equipment varies according to the amount of electricity the item requires. For high-wattage items operating on 120-volt circuits, 10-gauge wire is often sufficient; items operating on 240-volt circuits generally require 8-gauge or 6-gauge wire.

Note that the information concerning wire sizes, safe amperage loads, and typical uses is general and based on copper wire. If for some reason you must use aluminum wire—which is discouraged (see the section on aluminum wiring further on)—generally you must use the next size larger than that recommended for copper. For example, a 20-amp circuit with aluminum wire requires 10-gauge wire, rather than 12-gauge.

Also note that the longer a circuit extends the more voltage is lost in overcoming the wire's resistance to the flow of electricity. Wire for a very long circuit (over 35 feet for a 20-amp circuit using 12-gauge wire) must be larger than that recommended above to provide sufficient voltage to appliances and fixtures located near the end. For specifics, consult one of the authorities mentioned earlier.

Color

The color of insulation covering wires usually indicates their function in a cable or when attached to a fixture or appliance. This helps prevent errors when connecting wires. Black, red, and blue are the colors reserved for hot wires—those that carry current away from the service panel. White is the color reserved for neutral wires—those that carry current back to the panel. Green and green with yellow are the colors reserved for grounding wires; these carry current only if a malfunction in the wiring occurs.

When buying wire for new projects, always follow the color code above. When adding new wire, keep its colors consistent with existing wire. Never rely on the color of an existing wire when identifying it; use a circuit tester to determine whether it carries current.

Aluminum Wiring

Because it has been linked to increased residential fires, aluminum wiring is no longer recommended. Codes in many areas ban its use in new construction, but some codes still permit both all-aluminum wire and aluminum wire that is copper-clad.

If you are planning any new wiring, use all-copper wire even though it is more expensive. It is safer, more convenient, and in the long run a better investment than aluminum.

Residential Water Pipe

Following is a guide to the varieties and characteristics of water pipe commonly used in residential plumbing systems. All pipe is designed and sold by nominal diameter. When purchasing pipe, ask the supplier for specifics of sizing; bring a sample of existing pipe you wish to match.

PIPE	USES	AVAILABLE FORM
COPPER		
Type K	Rigid and soft.	Thickest wall; suitable for underground and interior water supply.
Type L	Rigid and soft.	Medium wall; suitable for interior water supply.

PIPE	USES	AVAILABLE FORM
Type M	Rigid.	Thin wall; recommended only for nonpressure use above ground but allowed as light-duty water-supply pipe by some codes.
PLASTIC		
ABS 40-grade (acrylonitrile-butadiene-styrene)	Rigid (black).	DWV.
CPVC (chlorinated polyvinyl chloride)	Rigid (beige).	Cold- and hot-water supply.
PB		
(polybutylene)	Flexible (black).	Cold- and hot-water supply.
PVC 40-grade and pressure grade (polyvinyl chloride)	Rigid (white, beige).	DWV (40-grade); cold-water supply (pressure grade).
STEEL		
Galvanized	Rigid; requires threading.	Cold- and hot-water supply.
CAST IRON		
Service grade; extra-heavy grade	Rigid.	DWV; especially underground beneath driveways and near tree roots.

Masonry Products

The basic ingredients of masonry products are Portland cement, hydrated lime (calcium hydroxide), sand, and gravel. Portland cement is a manufactured product consisting of limestone, chalk, clay, and other natural products fired in a kiln, pulverized, and bagged. The usual bag weighs 94 pounds and contains 1 cubic foot of material.

Blending Portland cement and lime produces a dry mixture called masonry cement or mortar cement. This, too, is sold in bags containing 1 cubic foot. However, one bag of masonry cement weighs only 70 pounds. Masonry cement is seldom used by itself; it is generally mixed with sand as described below.

Mixing sand with masonry cement produces mortar, which is used for bricklaying and repointing. Bags of mortar mix containing sand and masonry cement are easier to use and more economical for small projects than purchasing the ingredients separately and mixing them yourself. Bags of mortar mix usually weigh 80 pounds and contain $\frac{2}{3}$ cubic foot of material, enough to lay about fifty bricks or repoint about one hundred.

Portland cement mixed with sand is properly termed grout, but is more often simply called cement. It is used for patching cracks, as a bedding for flagstone or slate, as a topping over existing concrete, and as stucco. Like mortar mix, it is available in 80-pound bags containing $\frac{2}{3}$ cubic foot. This is enough to cover about 8 square feet by a depth of 1 inch.

Portland cement mixed with sand and gravel is concrete. This is often mixed from separate ingredients because it is usually needed in large quantities and also because the size of the gravel may vary depending on the project. (For a slab, the average diameter of the gravel should be between one fourth and one third of the slab's thickness.)

However, concrete mix is available in bags, and like mortar and sand mix is usually the best choice for small projects. The gravel contained in most concrete mix is suitable for pouring slabs at least 2 inches thick. It can also be used for pouring footings, setting fence posts, and for a similar applications. A bag of concrete mix generally weighs 80 pounds and contains $\frac{3}{5}$ cubic foot, enough to cover $3\frac{1}{2}$ square feet by a depth of 2 inches.

Mixing

Mixing masonry products is not an exact science. When using the bagged ingredients mentioned above, follow the manufacturer's instructions. Always add the liquid (usually water) to the dry mix; if you do it the other way around, blending the ingredients and obtaining the right consistency will be more difficult.

For mixing batches of material using separate ingredients, consult a knowledgeable supplier and read books beforehand on masonry for amateurs, available in bookstores and libraries. Variables affecting the proportions of ingredients include the use for which the masonry is intended, the environmental conditions it must withstand, the moisture content of the sand added during mixing, and the size of any gravel. Often, you must also take into account atmospheric conditions (temperature and humidity) at the time of mixing.

Decimal and Metric Equivalents of Common Fractions

FRACTION	DECIMAL	MILLIMETER
1/64	.015625	.3969
1/32	.03125	.7938
3/64	.046875	1.1906
1/16	.0625	1.5875
5/64	.078125	1.9844
3/32	.09375	2.3813
7/64	.109375	2.7781
1/8	.125	3.1750
9/64	.140625	3.5719
5/32	.15625	3.9688
11/64	.171875	4.3656
3/16	.1875	4.7625
13/64	.203125	5.1594
7/32	.21875	5.5563
15/64	.23475	5.9531
1/4	.25	6.3500
17/64	.26525	6.7469
9/32	.28125	7.1438
19/64	.29675	7.5406
5/16	.3125	7.9375
21/64	.328125	8.3344
11/32	.34375	8.7313
23/64	.359375	9.1281
3/8	.375	9.5250
25/64	.390625	9.9219
13/32	.40625	10.3188
27/64	.421875	10.7156
7/16	.4375	11.1125
29/64	.453125	11.5094
15/32	.46875	11.9063
31/64	.484375	12.3031
1/2	.5	12.7000
33/64	.515625	13.0969
17/32	.53125	13.4938
35/64	.546875	13.8906
9/16	.5625	14.2875
37/64	.578125	14.6844

19/32	.59375	15.0813
39/64	.609375	15.4781
5/8	.625	15.8750
41/64	.640625	16.2719
21/32	.65625	16.6688
43/64	.671875	17.0656
11/16	.6875	17.4625
45/64	.703125	17.8594
23/32	.71875	18.2563
47/64	.734375	18.6531
3/4	.75	19.0500
49/64	.75625	19.4469
25/32	.78125	19.8438
51/64	.796875	20.2406
13/16	.8125	20.6375
53/64	.828125	21.0344
27/32	.84375	21.4313
55/64	.859375	21.8281
7/8	.875	22.2250
57/64	.890625	22.6219
29/32	.90625	23.0188
59/64	.921875	23.4156
15/16	.9375	23.8125
61/64	.953125	24.2094
31/32	.96875	24.6063
63/64	.984375	25.0031
1	1.	25.4001

Converting U.S. Measure and Metric Measure

	SYMBOL	WHEN YOU KNOW:	MULTIPLY BY:	TO FIND:
LENGTH				
	in	inches	25.4	millimeters
	in	inches	2.54	centimeters
	in	inches	0.0254	meters
	ft	feet	0.3048	meters
	yd	yards	0.9144	meters
	mi	miles	1.609	kilometers
	mm	millimeters	0.039	inches
	cm	centimeters	0.393	inches
	m	meters	39.37	inches
	m	meters	3.281	feet

	m	meters	1.094	yards
	km	kilometers	0.621	miles
AREA				
	in^2	square inches	6.452	square centimeters
	ft^2	square feet	0.929	square meters
	yd^2	square yards	0.836	square meters
	mi^2	square miles	2.59	square kilometers
	cm^2	square centimeters	0.155	square inches
	m^2	square meters	10.764	square feet
	m^2	square meters	1.196	square yards
	km^2	square kilometers	0.386	square miles
VOLUME				
	in^3	cubic inches	16.387	cubic centimeters
	ft^3	cubic feet	0.028	cubic meters
	yd^3	cubic yards	0.764	cubic meters
	cm^3	cubic centimeters	0.061	cubic inches
	m^3	cubic meters	35.314	cubic feet
	m^3	cubic meters	1.308	cubic yards
WEIGHT				
	oz	ounces	28.35	grams
	lb	pounds	0.453	kilograms
	t	tons	0.907	metric tons
	g	grams	0.035	ounces
	kg	kilograms	2.2	pounds
	mt	metric tons	2204.62	pounds
	mt	metric tons	1.002	tons
CAPACITY (liquid)				
	tsp	teaspoons	5.0	milliliters
	tbsp	tablespoons	15.0	milliliters
	fl oz	fluid ounces	29.574	milliliters
	c	cups	0.237	liters
	pt	pints	0.473	liters
	qt	quarts	0.946	liters
	gal	gallons	3.785	liters
	ml	milliliters	0.034	fluid ounces
	l	liters	4.227	cups
	l	liters	2.113	pints
	l	liters	1.057	quarts
	l	liters	0.264	gallons

TEMPERATURE

To convert from degrees Fahrenheit (°F) to degrees Celsius (°C), first subtract 32, then multiply by 5/9.

To convert from degrees Celsius to degrees Fahrenheit, multiply by 9/5, then add 32.

Index

Note: Page numbers in italics refer to illustrations and tables.